ROSA BARBA

STUART COMER
SHANAY JHAVERI
ÉLISABETH LEBOVICI
JULIE AULT

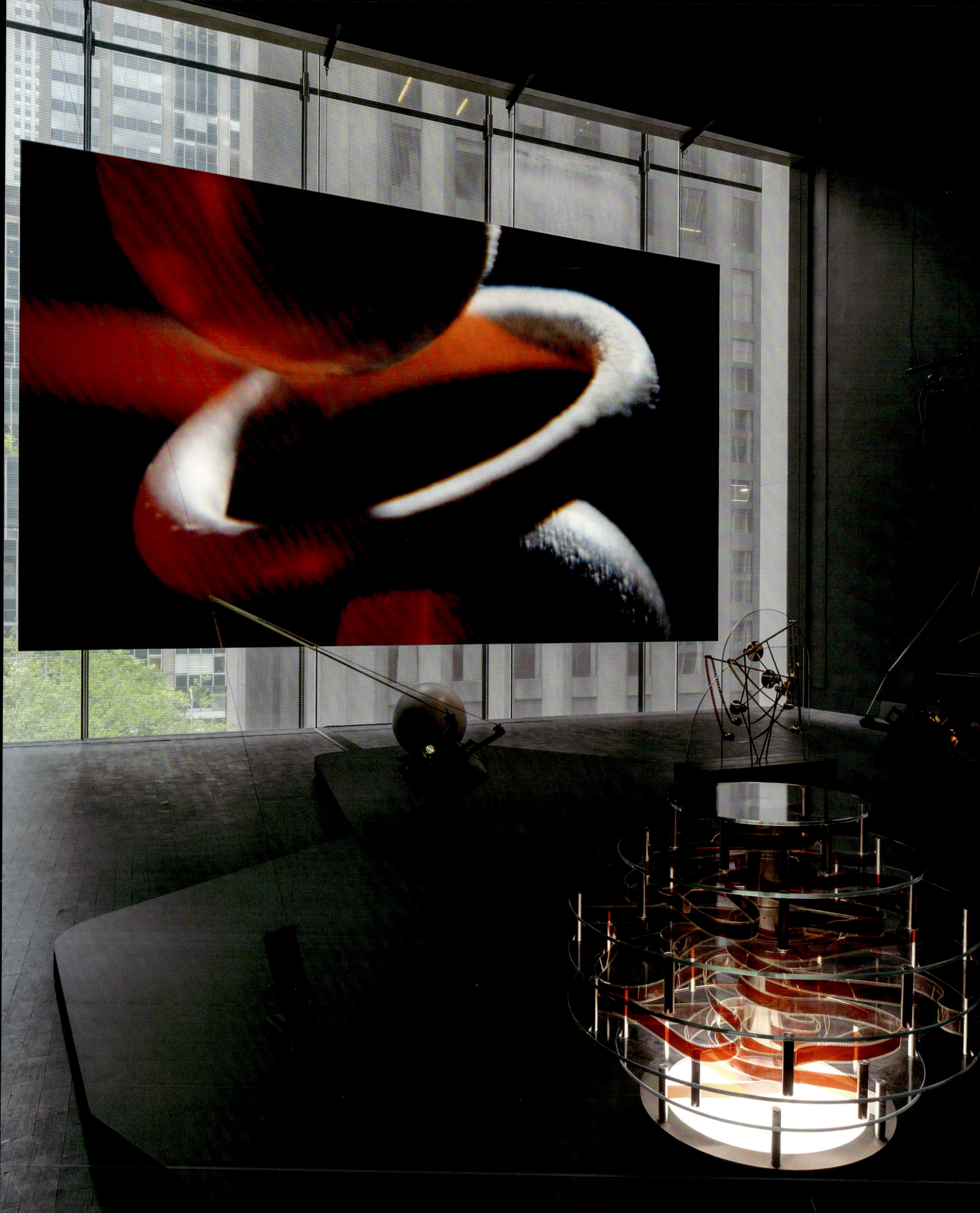

background,
CHARGE, 2025
35MM FILM, COLOUR, SOUND
25 MIN. 33 SEC.

foreground, from left,
CONDUCTOR, 2014
SILICONE MEMBRANE,
SPEAKER, SOUND
Ø 60 CM

WIREPIECE, 2022
16MM FILM PROJECTOR,
16MM FILM, LENS, DRUM
STRING, BRIDGE SADDLE
PIECE, PICKUP MICHROPHONE,
PRE-AMP, PLINTH

AS FIXED IN FLUX, 2025
STEEL, ALUMINIUM, GLASS,
MOTORS, 35MM FILM
115 X 108 X 39 CM

OFF SPLINTERED TIME, 2021
GLASS, MOTOR, LED LIGHT,
35MM FILM
80 X 80 X 70 CM

WIREPIECE, DOUBLE STOPS,
2025
16MM PROJECTOR, 16MM
FILM, LENS, DRUM STRINGS,
BRIDGE SADDLE PIECES,
PICKUP MICHROPHONES, PRE-
AMPS, PLINTH

INSTALLATION VIEW AT THE
MUSEUM OF MODERN ART,
NEW YORK, 2025

CONTENTS

INTERVIEW 005 Stuart Comer in conversation with Rosa Barba. SURVEY 051 Shanay Jhaveri, *Interrogating the Qualities of Space*; Élisabeth Lebovici, *Time Zones* (73). FOCUS 101 Julie Ault, *Rosa Barba's Nocturnal Light*. ARTIST'S CHOICE 121 Robert Creeley, *The Revelation*, 1953 (122); Robert Creeley, *There Is*, 1964 (122); John Temple, *Meditation on a Landscape*, 1965 (125); Charles Olson, *Poem 143: The Festival Aspect*, 1965 (126); Robert Duncan, *Chords*, 1965 (129); Susan Howe, *Untitled (from Tom Tit Tot)*, 2013 (130). ARTIST'S WRITINGS 133 *Inventory of Cinematic Spaces: A Fictional Library* (excerpt), 2022 (134). CHRONOLOGY 145 Bibliography (157).

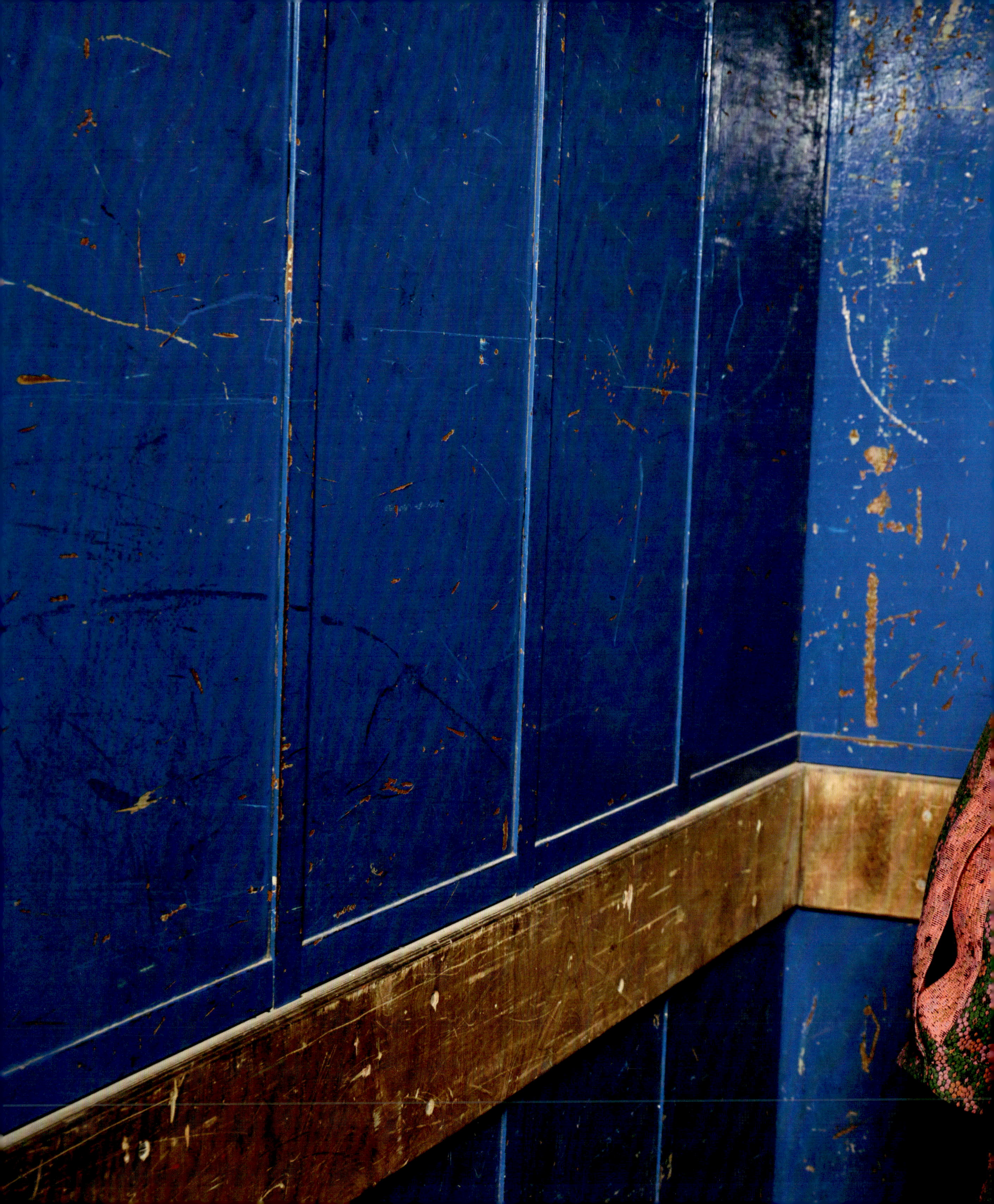

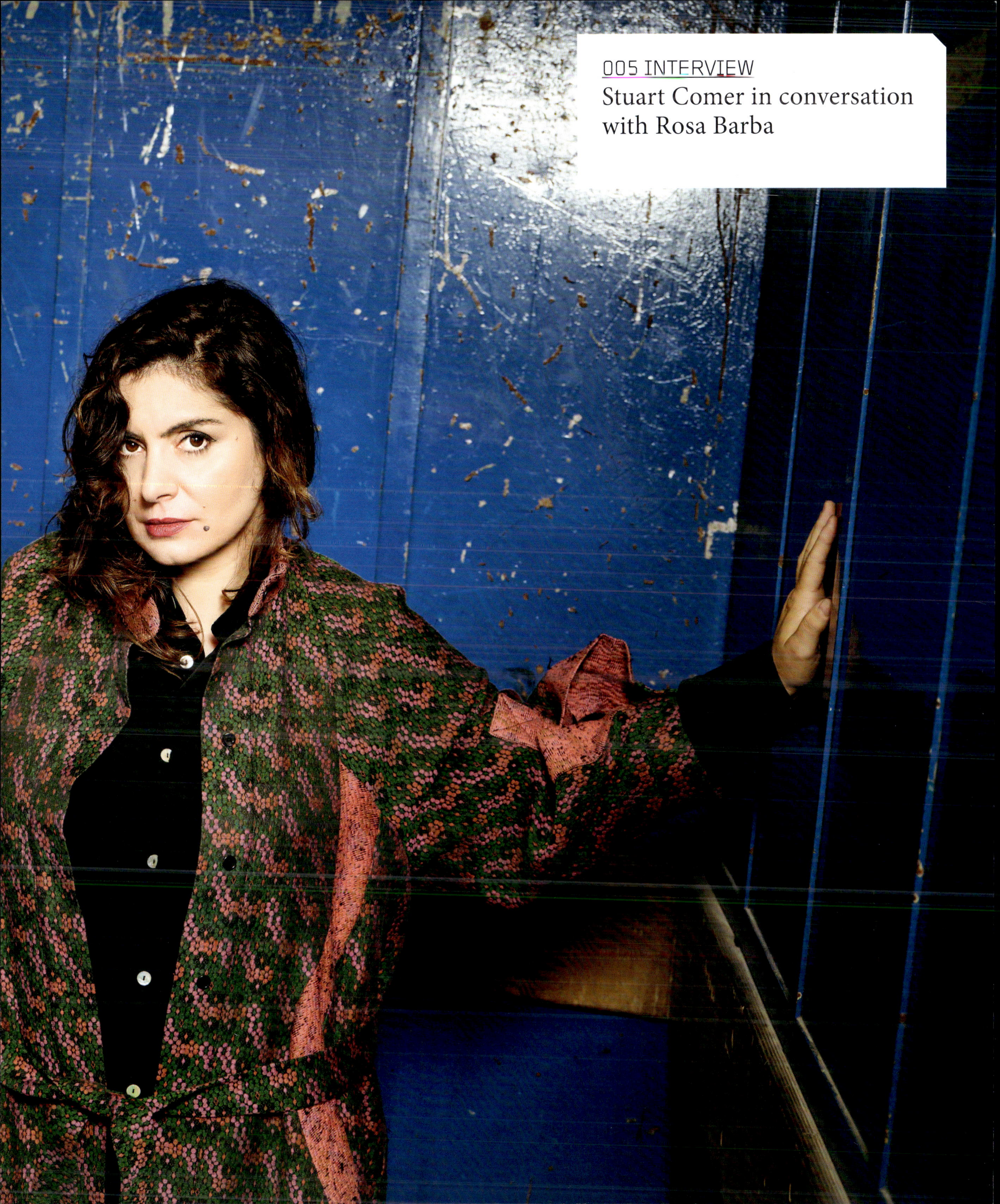

005 INTERVIEW

Stuart Comer in conversation with Rosa Barba

previous pages,
ROSA BARBA, BERLIN, 2025

background,
CHARGE, 2025
35MM FILM, COLOUR, SOUND
25 MIN. 33 SEC.

foreground,
WIREPIECE, DOUBLE STOPS, 2025
16MM PROJECTOR, 16MM FILM, LENS, DRUM STRINGS, BRIDGE SADDLE PIECES, PICKUP MICHROPHONES, PREAMPS, PLINTH

INSTALLATION VIEW AT THE MUSEUM OF MODERN ART, NEW YORK, 2025

STUART COMER: *Rosa, we begin this interview watching a vivid, early summer sun raking across Berlin as it slowly sets. It seems an appropriate way to enter into this conversation and into your work, which stakes its fundamental questions around both the material and immaterial operations of cinema: light, the apparatus, the space around, and the space in between. What first drew you to work with film as a medium – particularly at a moment when the looming obsolescence of celluloid forced a reconsideration of both the promise of cinema and its past?*

ROSA BARBA: Since I started to experiment with my camera – initially a photographic still camera, and since the early 1990s a 16mm film camera – I've come to understand it as a drawing instrument. I use it as a handheld camera, close to my body; the weight of the camera, along with the subjects filmed through my lens, determine the length of the sequence. I work within the limitations my film camera provides – through three- to ten-minute film takes.

This also amplifies the camera's performative aspect. Everything needs to be compressed in terms of decision-making and observation to accommodate this limited time. It reorients my subjects – the landscape or people – so that they appear to stand on a stage, delineated by the camera's lens. There's no repetition or erasure within these specific moments, and the camera itself extends into a conceptual practice that also recasts the viewer's own staging.

Also, the imprint through light was – and still is – very fascinating to me. The images undergo a transformation where the light draws them back to the material and is then projected onto and beyond a screen.

COMER: *Having started with still photography, what led you to the moving image?*

BARBA: A still photography camera was my first instrument, which I carried closely with me from the age of fourteen. It helped me to understand the world around me through chosen perspectives. Developing the analogue materials in the darkroom at school, or often at home in the bathroom, was another meditative experience of seeing those specific investigations becoming visible in front of me in a durational appearance.

A few years later, I was given a Super 8mm camera by a neighbour, and I started to eagerly experiment with moving images. I realized that I was able to slow down the footage to distill the essence of the still image (this could even happen through speeding up as well) and to make visible what was happening between the frames.

At nineteen, I was then able to start using a 16mm camera, which allowed me to work on my first longer film – *Panzano* (2000) – where I confronted different layers in my narration, through documentation, fiction and performance. This film initiated many methodologies and established tools that I would continue to use for later films. I used the camera as a drawing instrument that follows and dialogues with the erratic decisions and expressions of the non-actors who play the film's protagonists. The non-actors came to the stage with their desires, which were expressed during these collective performances. *Panzano* also uses sound recordings that include the accidental sounds that occurred while constantly recording the whole set. The fire crackling in the fireplace turned into an ongoing 'hum' for the whole film.

COMER: *You emerged during a time when large-scale and multiple-screen video installations had become a prominent form in the art world. This format sought in part to create a more mobile and active spectator, to shift the viewer's attention away from a single screen or a single point of focus and activate the gallery spatially in a manner that was arguably more difficult*

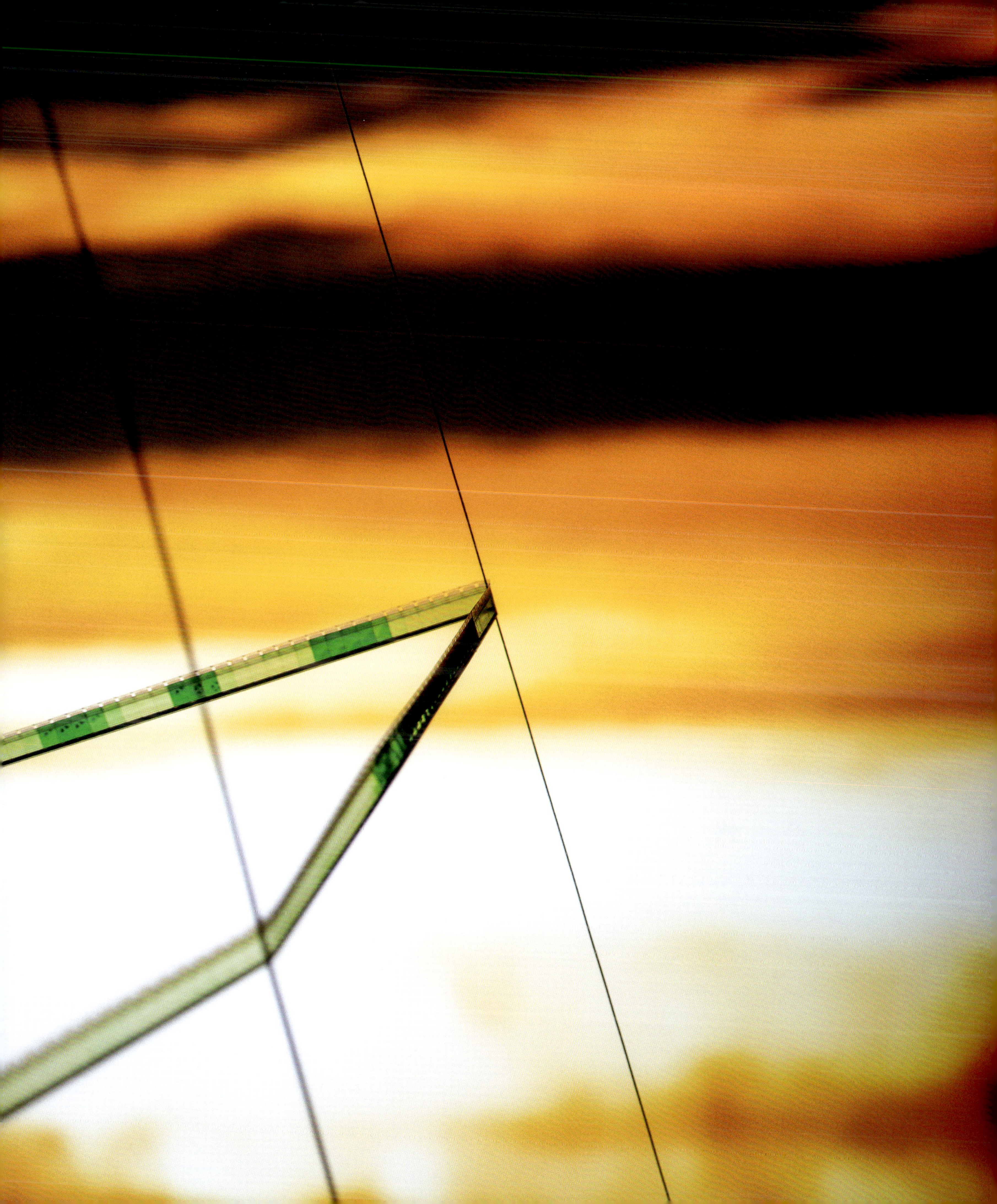

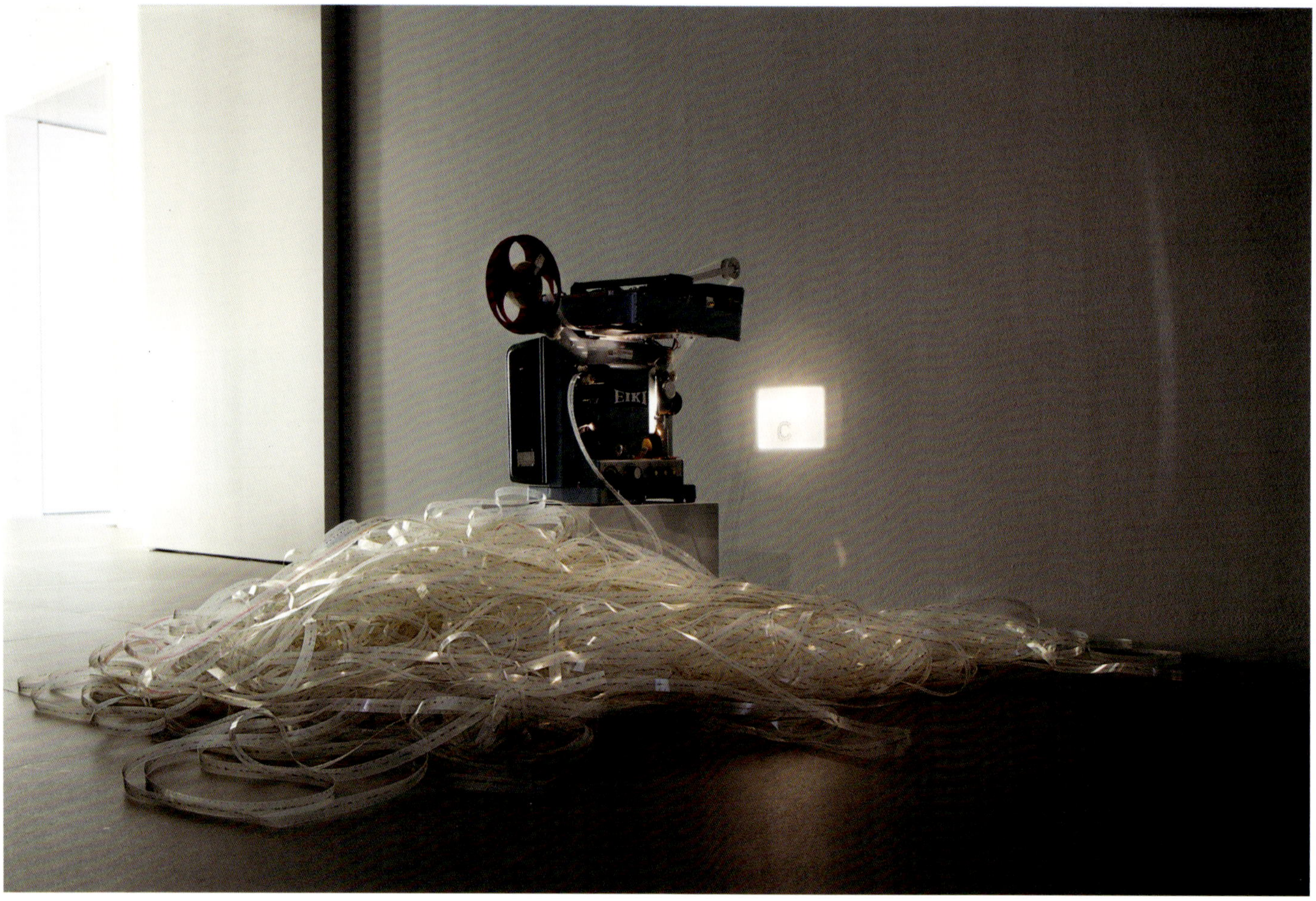

left,
SPACELENGTH THOUGHT, 2012
16MM FILM, PROJECTOR,
TYPEWRITER

INSTALLATION VIEW AT
KUNSTHAUS ZURICH, 2012

opposite,
PANZANO (WITH ULRIKE
MOLSEN), 2000
16MM FILM, COLOUR,
MAGNETIC SOUND,
22 MIN.

to achieve in the conventional proscenium arrangement of the cinema. Your work is often immersive, but the projector and the apparatus are more present – you foreground them as something for the viewer to negotiate as much as the projected image. Space and cinema are sculptural in your work, and so is the apparatus. What kind of conditions or politics does this generate for the spectator?

BARBA: My objective is to create a spatialization of temporal conditions, situating the viewers (in and outside of the film) in a state of suspended time. This isn't a narrative time, but an extended one that overspills in between works. It's exactly there, in the space between fragments, that the narrative is constructed, and time moves on another created layer. I try to make evident an unresolved tension between narrative and its imagination as it evolves.

The notion of space as architecture relates to the community that shares those spaces, geographically and mentally. As mentioned before, an important dimension of my work is the context of staging and performance, revolving around the question of how a performative setting can be created where fact and fiction can be intertwined. I've been questioning the industry of cinema with respect to various forms of staging, such as gesture, genre, information and documentation, and I started to take those individual ingredients out of their conventional contexts by reshaping and representing them anew. I did this by giving them an agency, autonomy. It's an experiment with and an expansion of time-based forms into sculptural objects or speculations; that is, into spaces that are self-organized. It's an ever-changing, ever-evolving, shifting process. The frames are created to reveal a volume. The cinematic space becomes all space.

Holding the camera by hand and therefore turning the body into a medium – which leads the movement like a curved line toward the capturing by the camera – is a journey that includes the idiosyncrasy of my own position in the specific moment, activating

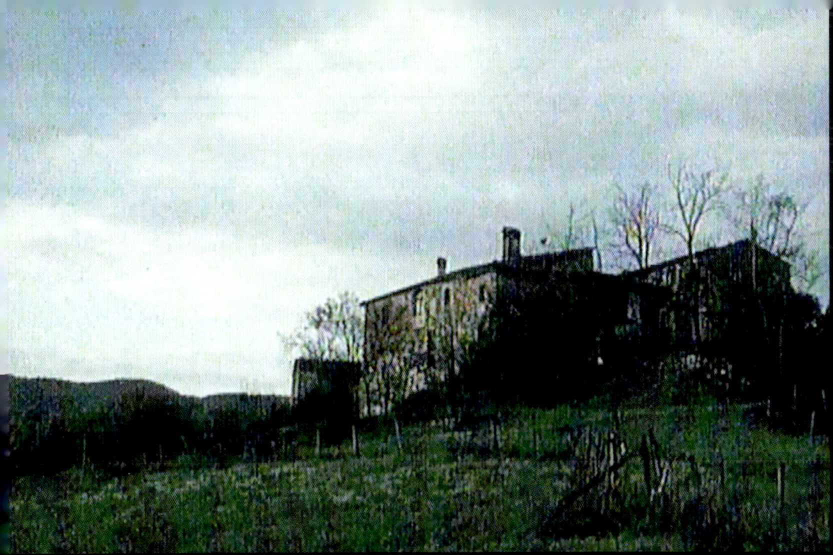
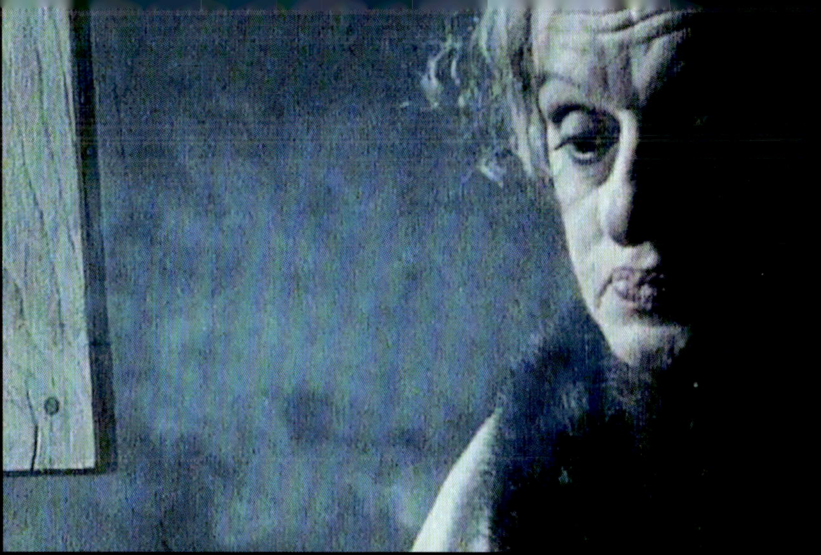
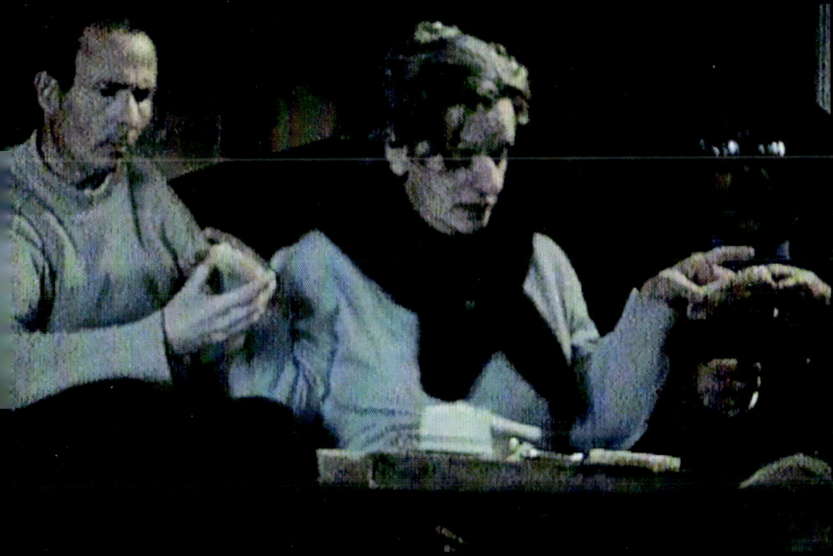
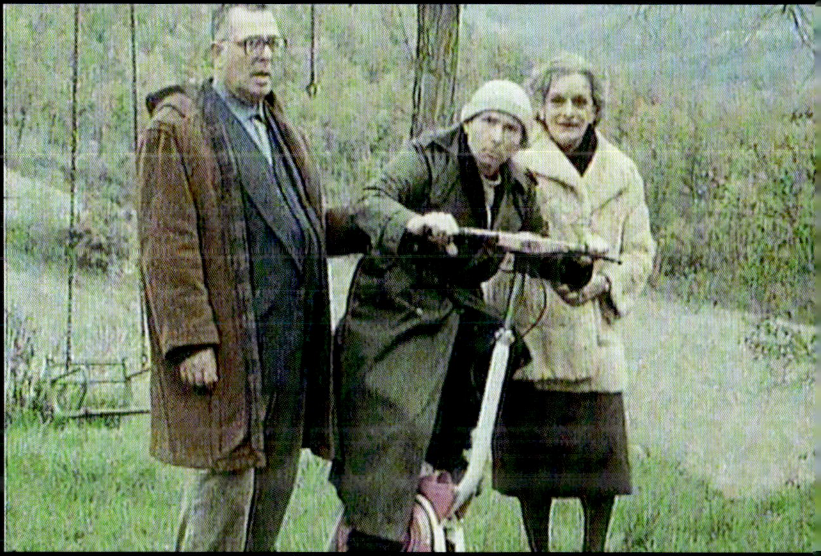
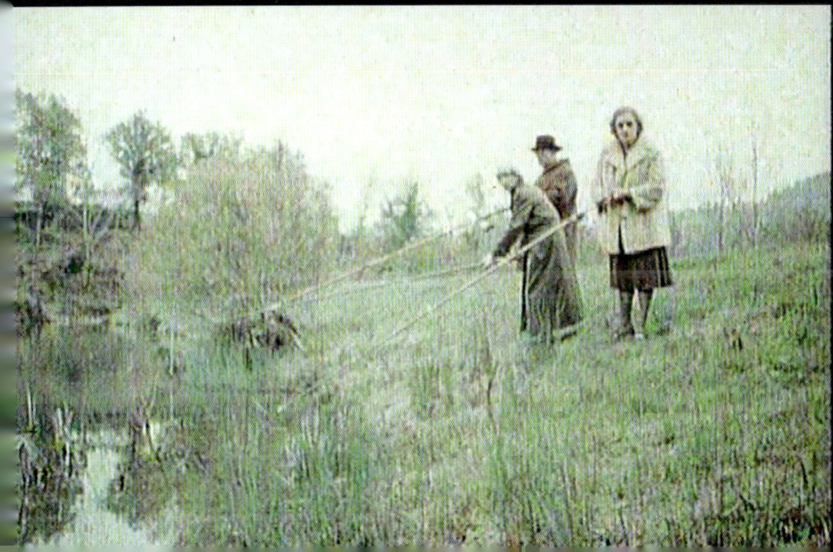
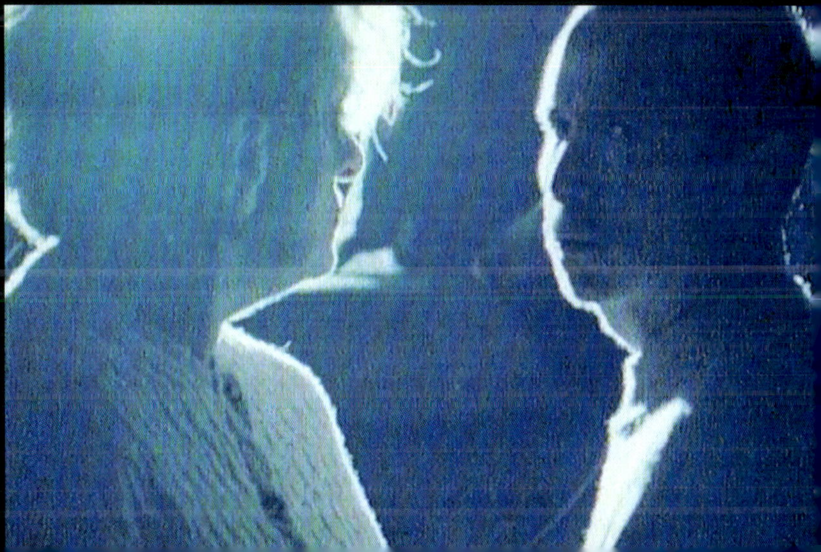

and including the subconscious as a mechanism in order to reach the space beyond what's immediately being filmed.

It's an uncertain space, since it exists with no anchors, as none are created through this perceptive approach, and it manifests itself as a temporal condition articulated in space –temporal because the movement can never be repeated in the same way.

COMER: *How does the interplay between light, material and projection shift the relationship between information and abstraction in your work?*

BARBA: Fields of information and non-information. This oscillation activates the perceiver, changes gears, and transports us to another layer of consciousness.

I understand projected light as a sculptural medium. We cut from white light what we don't see. I view this interplay of light and material more as a distillation of form than as a structural analysis of its component parts that filmmakers of the late 1960s or 1970s might have been investigating. My work is informed by social and cultural research; the representation of the subjects is more akin to the construction of peculiar monuments than to the pleasure or celebration of the material in my sculptures, installations and publications. I work with the confrontation of different layers in my narration, each of them using its own medium within the range of cinematic possibilities.

The role of the viewer and reader in the space becomes as performative as the material. In the sculpture *Spacelength Thought* (2012), for example, a typewriter sits above a film projector typing a monologue onto blank 16mm film, which is projected letter by letter. The viewer witnesses the production in real time and can anticipate the printing and reading. They can wander in time and be part of the production, which is changing over time in the present space, fragile and unpredictable, since the machine could possibly stop and even break down.

And this was another aspect I explored: how to release machines from their functionality and make them do other things. They can be used as one component of many to orchestrate a body of experience through working with the 'autonomy of the material' and with space in a very physical and almost tangible way.

The movement conducted by the body and mind, which has a limited duration due to the weight of the film camera, enters into dialogue with the flickering light of the camera. Lots of images get lost in the in-between of the black frames, which follow every imprint of an image frame. It's this oscillating stage of appearing and disappearing images that causes the image to float into another layer of consciousness. This stage involves the removing of information in order to sharpen and abstract the object we're observing, which we're trying to represent in a different 'light' and at the same time abstract with perspective, vibration, and the idiosyncrasies of the person holding the camera, while simultaneously incorporating the non-information space through the flickering mode. The vibrating sequence, composed of subsequent information and non-information, is the device that no longer represents a situation or object.

COMER: *Despite its engagement with the presumed obsolescence of film, your work isn't nostalgic. If anything, it suggests that the spaces and structures we create to carry memory and culture are always fragile, but that fragility can be constructive. Cinema and the museum are never separate in your work; they're symbiotic.*

BARBA: I began this process of deliberate fragmentation in my work nearly two decades ago, during my art studies, through working with specific aspects of the projected image. This fragmentation later became more condensed into observable phenomena in my sculptural approach, with a strong use of the language of loops as a continual transposition of material into an image and back again. Alongside the use of the fragment, the strategy of repetition has always helped me to formulate an idea. Fragmentation and play are an active process for me, which opposes the idea of nostalgia.

PERPETUAL RESPONSE TO SOUND AND LIGHT (AT THE LOCKER PLANT), 2013
SPOTLIGHT, SOUND

INSTALLATION VIEW AT LOCKER PLANT, CHINATI FOUNDATION, MARFA, TEXAS, 2013

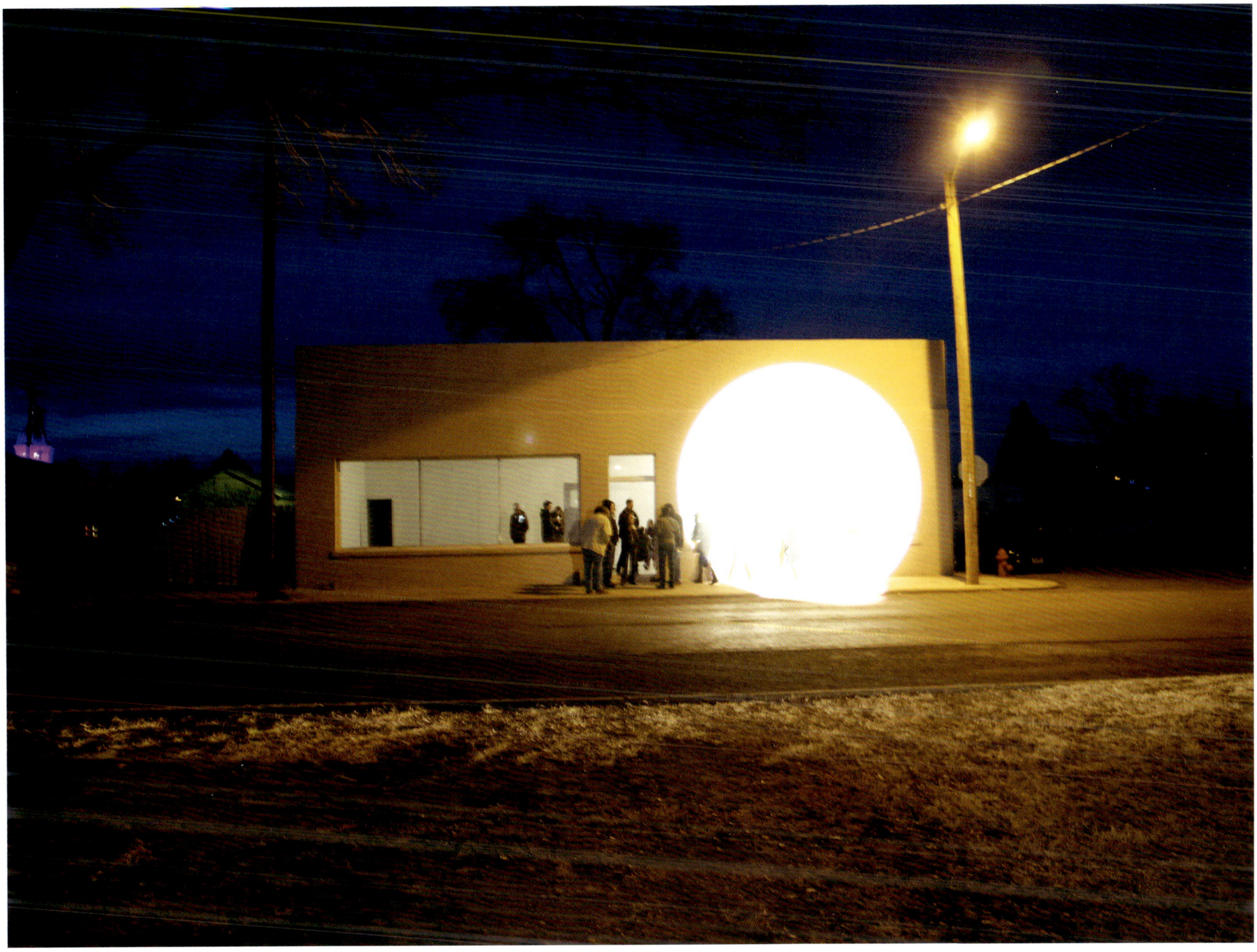

I aim to describe or fill a space that we can't grasp with language. While a conceptual grounding may be essential to outline or mark this space, everything else happens in between, or beyond, this framework. It's the constant questioning and reconfiguring of the elements of cinema that produces the space beyond. It's a fragility found in the oscillation between the experience of the present and that of memory. The encounter with this temporally present stage shapes and produces both the work and the spaces where it's shown. I perceive cinema and the museum as an encounter of elements.

COMER: *Regarding the performative dimension of your work, but also some of its formal and technical aspects, how much of this has to do with your background in sound and music?*

BARBA: Early on, I practised modern dance (Graham technique mostly) and music (flute, guitar and later cello), which informed and shaped my understanding of filmmaking and thinking of exhibitions in terms of rhythm and spatial explorations. Also, how sound can be a source that activates or directs another action was an early method in my works. I also removed the image of film, leaving only the optical soundtrack as information in some of my early pieces.

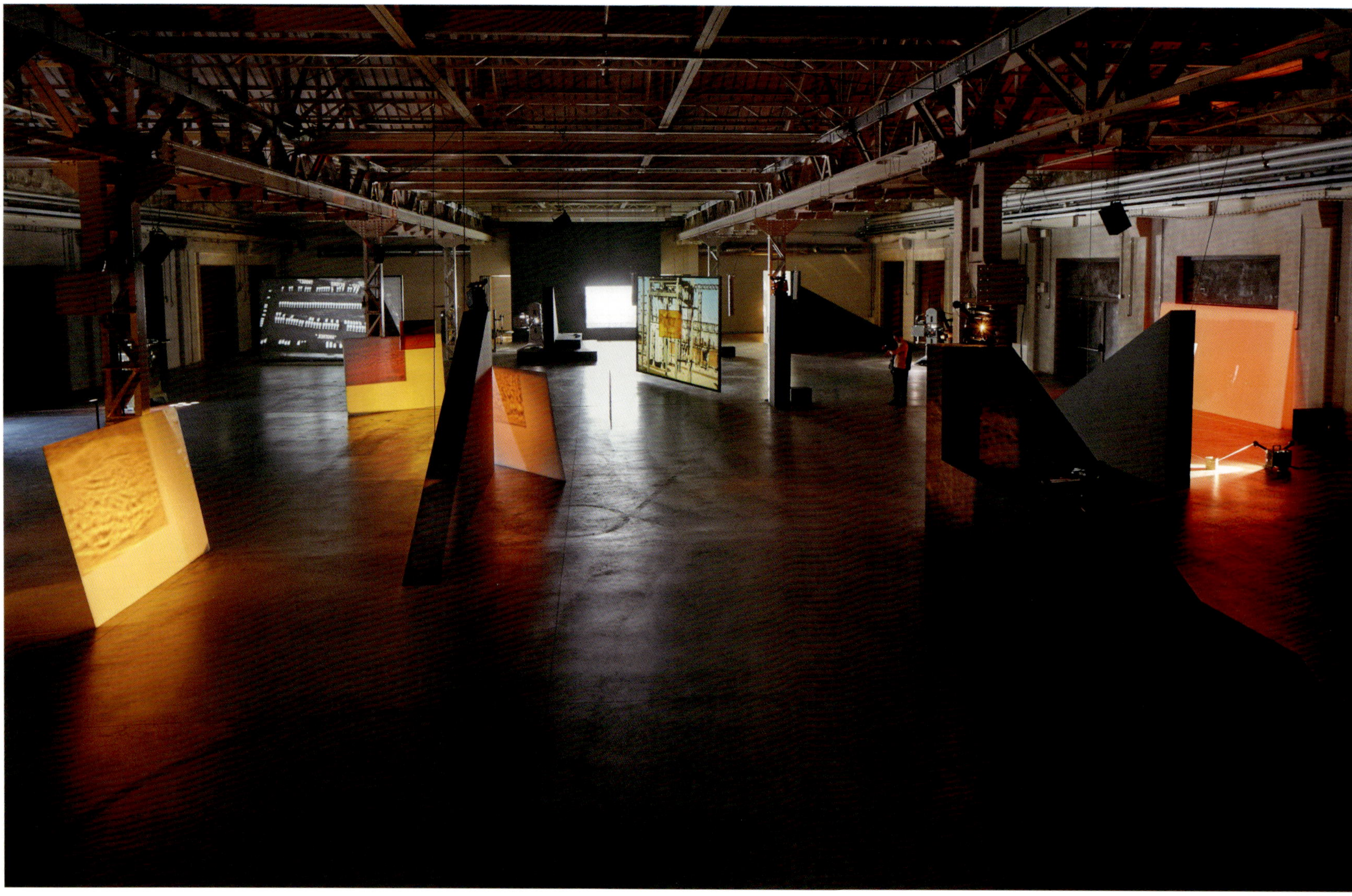

In *Perpetual Response to Sound and Light* (2013), the light-sound piece I produced for the Locker Plant in Marfa, I was directing a spotlight into the building, synched with the passing of freight trains in front of my temporary studio. The spotlight was fed by the rhythms of the trains and therefore literally pumped the light into the building through the large studio window. The whole building seemed to float like a light sculpture when a train passed.

It was beautiful, at that time, to be in conversation with Zoe Leonard, who created a camera obscura installation a few metres further down the street at the Chinati Foundation's Ice Plant building. We both brought light into these respective spaces, activating them in different ways. I'm interested in creating a performative setting where fact and fiction can be intertwined – starting from the methodology of filmmaking and then also installing works in a manner that highlights the technical apparatus.

One 'musical' instrument is the camera that I carry, with my whole body leading the movement. The weight of the camera, its mechanical sounds, and my awareness of time as the films runs through the gate are leading factors in my production process. It's the uncanny vibration transmitted through the body that directs the camera movement in order to create a captured space that extends into a drawing by combining these different sources, which play together.

COMER: *I'm curious about the relationship between a work like* Western Round Table *(2007) and your subsequent focus on landscape. Your earlier works often construct a system without conventional images – you've called* Western Round Table *an 'enigmatic*

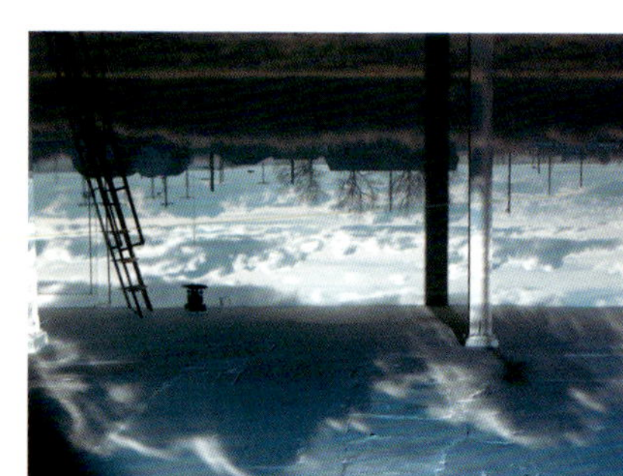

ZOE LEONARD
100 NORTH NEVILL STREET, 2013
INSTALLATION VIEW AT CHINATI FOUNDATION, MARFA, TEXAS, 2013

opposite,
HEAR, THERE, WHERE THE ECHOES ARE, 2016–21
16MM PROJECTORS, 35MM PROJECTOR, GLASS FILTERS, SCREEN, SOUND, PERFORMATIVE ELEMENT

A HOME FOR A UNIQUE INDIVIDUAL, 2013
2 X 35MM FILM, OPTICAL SOUND
14 MIN

FROM SOURCE TO POEM, 2016
35MM FILM, COLOUR, OPTICAL SOUND
12 MIN

BOUNDARIES OF CONSUMPTION, 2012
16MM FILM, MODIFIED PROJECTOR, FILM CANS, 2 METAL SPHERES

INSTALLATION VIEW AT PIRELLI HANGARBICOCCA, MILAN, 2017

below, from left,
THE EMPIRICAL EFFECT, 2010
16MM FILM TRANSFERRED TO DIGITAL, COLOUR, SOUND, 22 MIN

A HOME FOR A UNIQUE INDIVIDUAL, 2013
2 X 35MM FILM, OPTICAL SOUND
14 MIN

FROM SOURCE TO POEM, 2016
35MM FILM, COLOUR, OPTICAL SOUND
12 MIN

INSTALLATION VIEW AT PIRELLI HANGARBICOCCA, MILAN, 2017

document'; it's a speculative exercise. Later works seek to determine a new cinematic language to capture the landscape and different topographies. How has the space between the projectors in Western Round Table *determined your understanding of the spatial politics in later works?*

BARBA: I began my investigation of inscriptions and social transformations manifested in the landscape between 2006 and 2010 with a series of works like *They Shine* (2007), *Waiting Grounds* (2007), *Western Round Table* and *The Long Road* (2010). I shot my first film in the American desert in 2006 when I'd spent several months in Los Angeles and its vicinity. I was fascinated by the inscriptions one could find preserved in the desert – the landscape as a document. I understood this as a screen and started to record the inscriptions with my 16mm camera.

They Shine is filmed in 35mm and concentrates some eleven hours of filming into four minutes. It shows the image of a solar thermal power plant in the Mojave Desert. The desert offered ideal conditions for the plant: a vast stretch of flat land that almost always receives direct rays from the sun. *They Shine* is four minutes of accelerated time, allowing us to observe the full movement of the reflectors over a single day as they follow the sun's course. The mirrors move in unison, resulting in a perfectly synchronized choreography. We see no workers leaving the factory. We're thus confronted with the model most suited to cognitive capitalism: a factory activated remotely, by machines without bodies.

In *The Long Road*, we see a whole language, a kind of alphabet, that soon we won't be able to decipher anymore. This language is an image engineered into the earth, which will

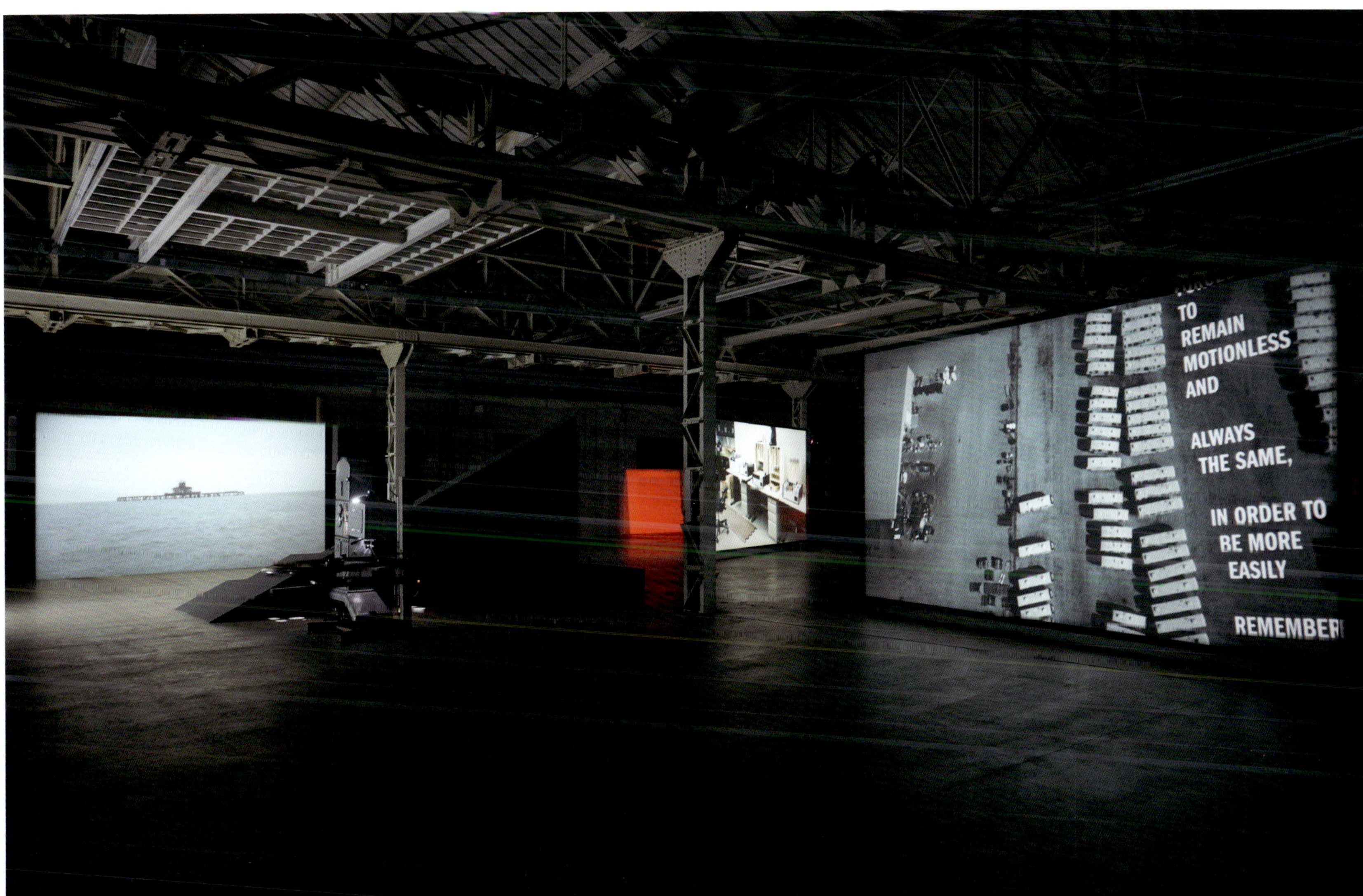

THE EMPIRICAL EFFECT, 2010
16MM FILM TRANSFERRED
TO DIGITAL, COLOUR, SOUND,
22 MIN.

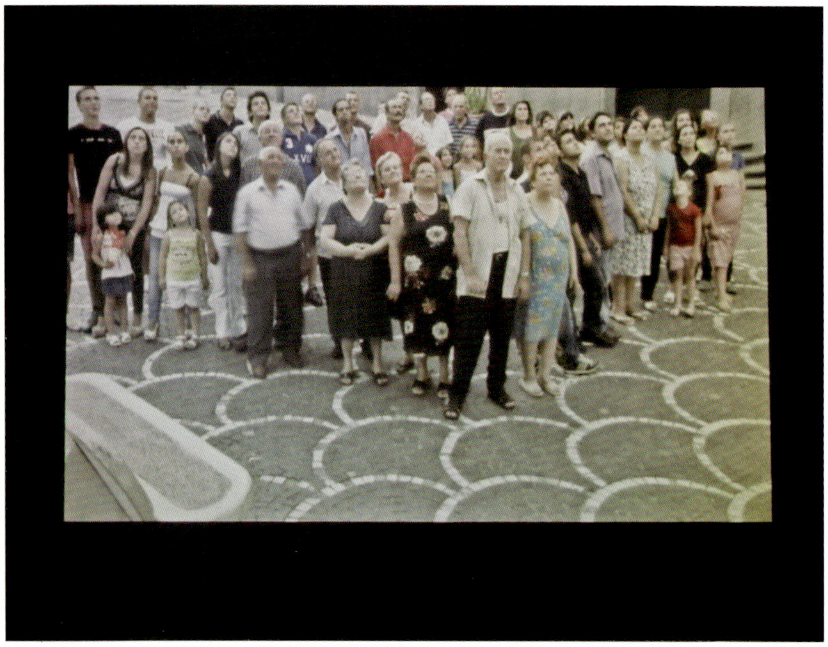

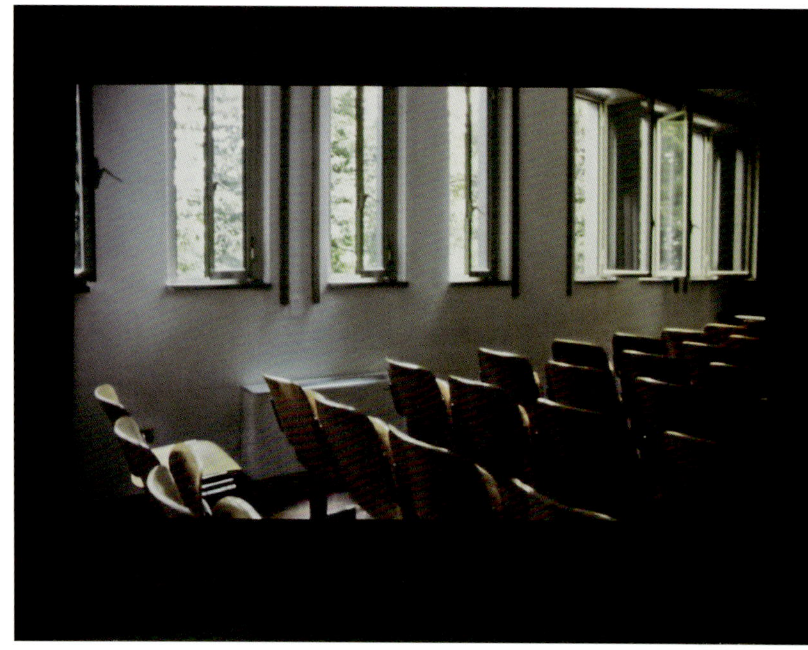

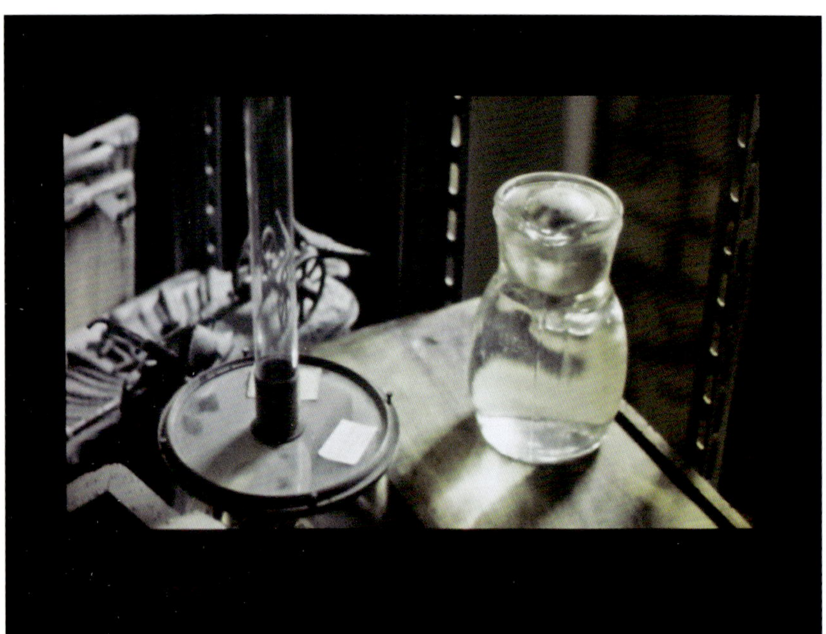

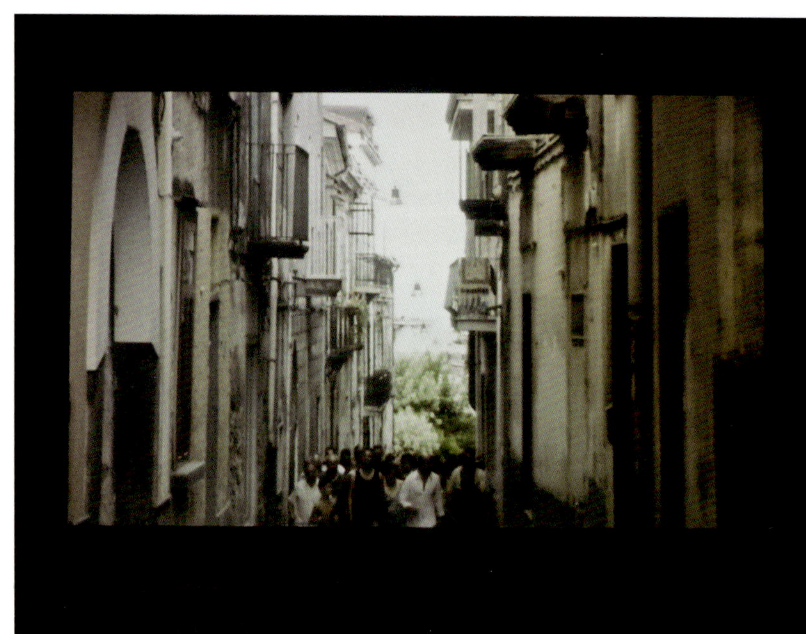

FROM SOURCE TO POEM, 2016
35MM FILM, COLOUR, OPTICAL SOUND
12 MIN.

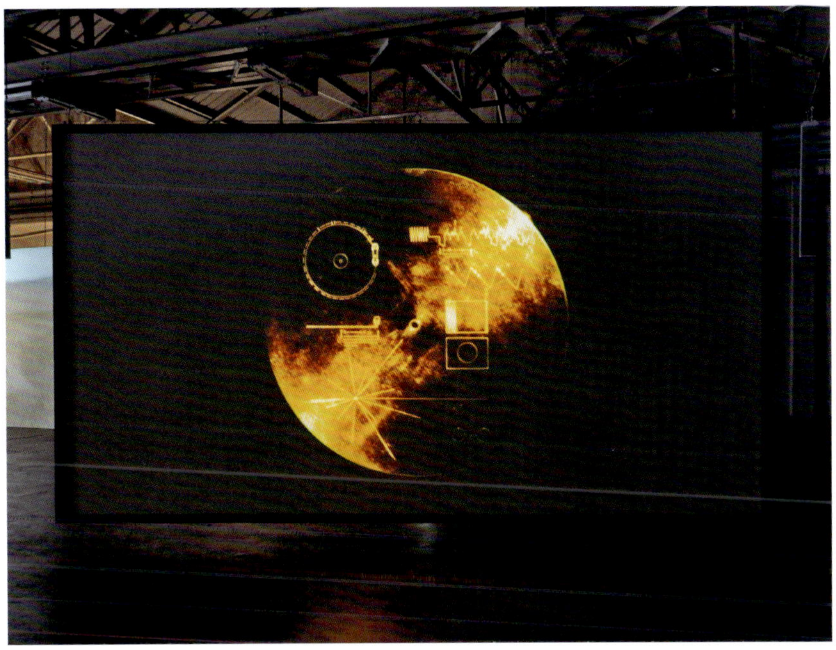

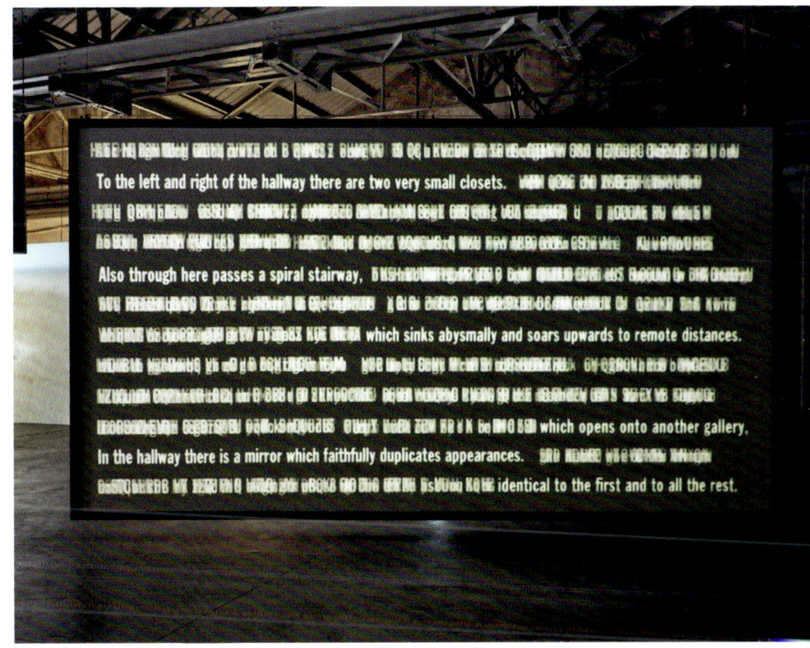

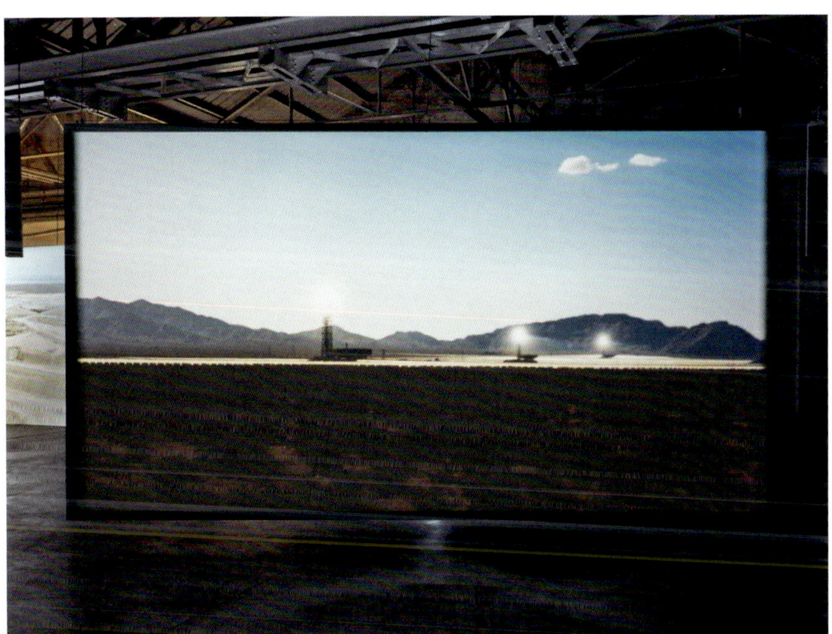

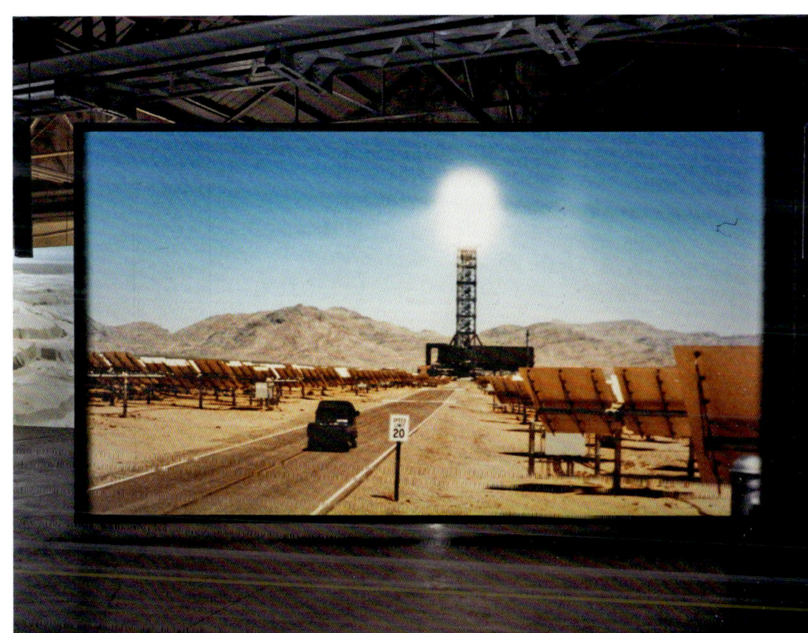

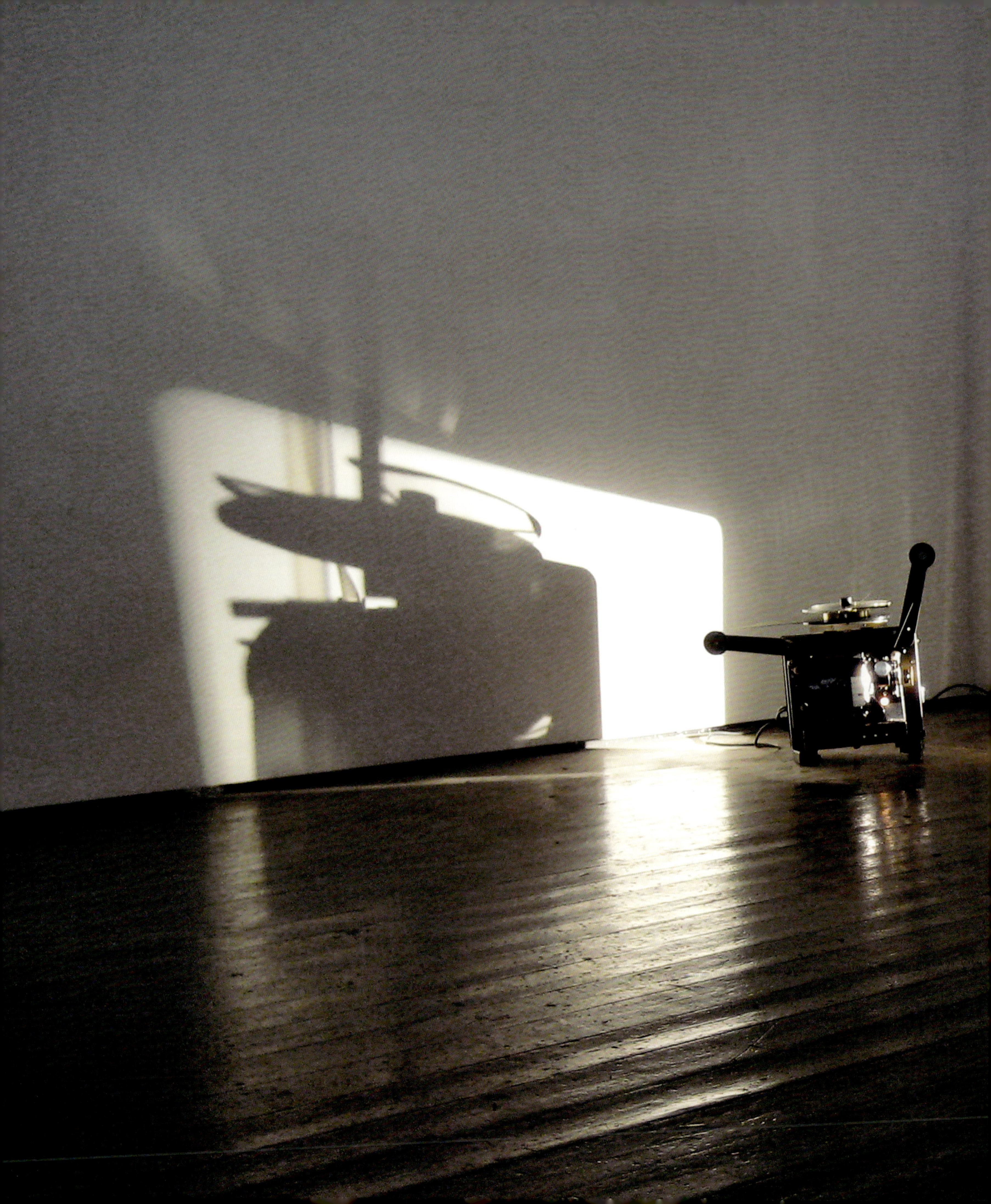

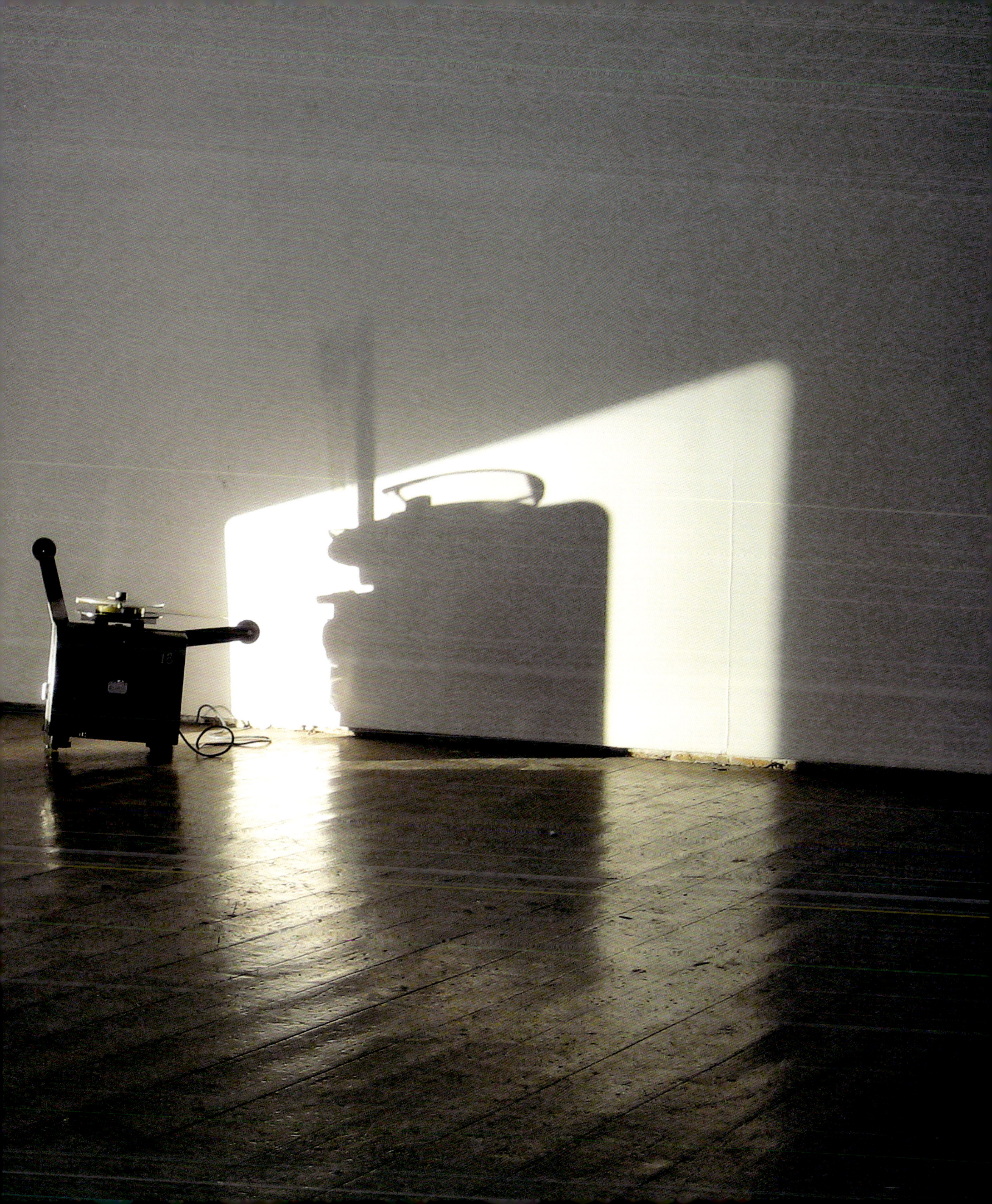

most probably lose its context in the future. The film shows an abandoned racetrack that has receded back into the landscape. I'm an observer of this record, holding a 35mm, approximately 15 kg handheld camera. I'm interested in how it relates to reality, not just as a pre-existent form, but as a potential condition or as an imagined object – a part of something that remains behind or constitutes a break within the narrative.

We circle the racetrack from an aerial view where the image resembles the geometric Nazca Drawings – large ancient geoglyphs in the Nazca Desert, in southern Peru. Some of these drawings are no longer readable, as the tools to translate them have been lost or haven't been transmitted to our generation. Suspended at the intersection of the present and past, and perhaps also of the future, the road to the racetrack emerges from the sand like an immense drawing, the stigmata of a now abandoned and forgotten modernist culture, ready to be transformed into something that's different and unexpected, not yet wholly expressed and probably inexpressible. I draw with the camera to trace the physicality of time.

Western Round Table is the name of a conference that took place in 1949 and apparently happened for the first time secretly in the Mojave desert and continued later at the Museum of Modern Art in San Francisco. Addressing contemporary artistic practices, the gathering included prominent male figures like Marcel Duchamp, Gregory Bateson, Frank Lloyd Wright and Arnold Schoenburg. Rather than describing a situation, I wanted to concretize, fragment and intervene in the condition of representation and of a place.

Two 16mm projectors placed together on the ground spool clear celluloid. Each creates a spotlight of white light on an adjacent wall into which the looming architectural shadow of its antagonist, the other projector, enters. The soundtrack is composed of extracts from two Fellini films cut so that the projectors appear to be conversing

below,
THE LONG ROAD, 2010
35MM FILM, COLOUR, OPTICAL SOUND
6 MIN. 14 SEC.

INSTALLATION VIEW AT CENTRE INTERNATIONAL D'ART ET DU PAYSAGE DE L'ÎLE DE VASSIVIÈRE, FRANCE, 2010

opposite,
THEY SHINE, 2007
35MM FILM, COLOUR, OPTICAL SOUND
4 MIN.

previous pages,
WESTERN ROUND TABLE, 2007
TWO 16MM FILM LOOPS, TWO PROJECTORS, OPTICAL SOUND, EACH 2 MIN.

INSTALLATION VIEW AT LUX, ZOO, LONDON, 2009

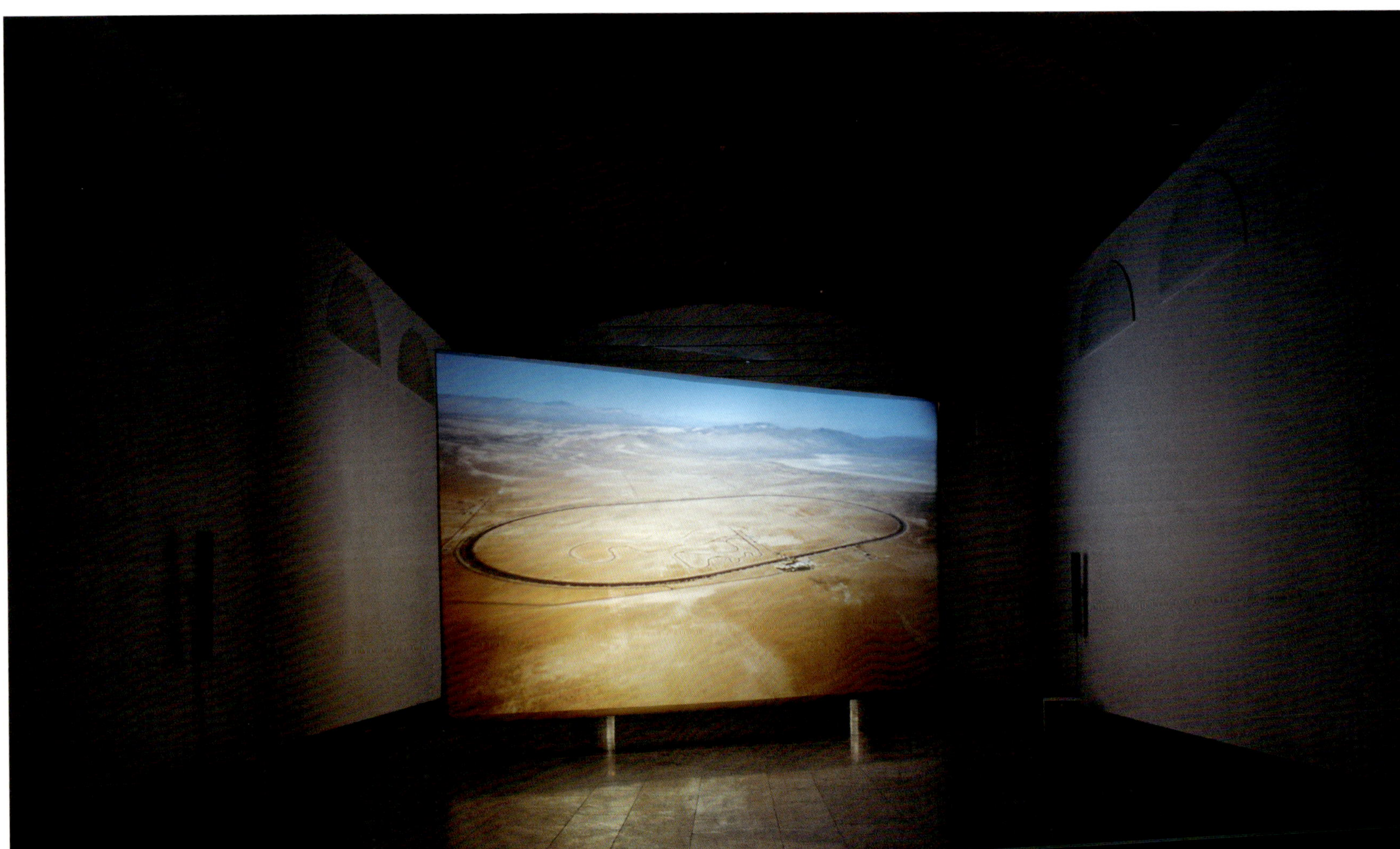

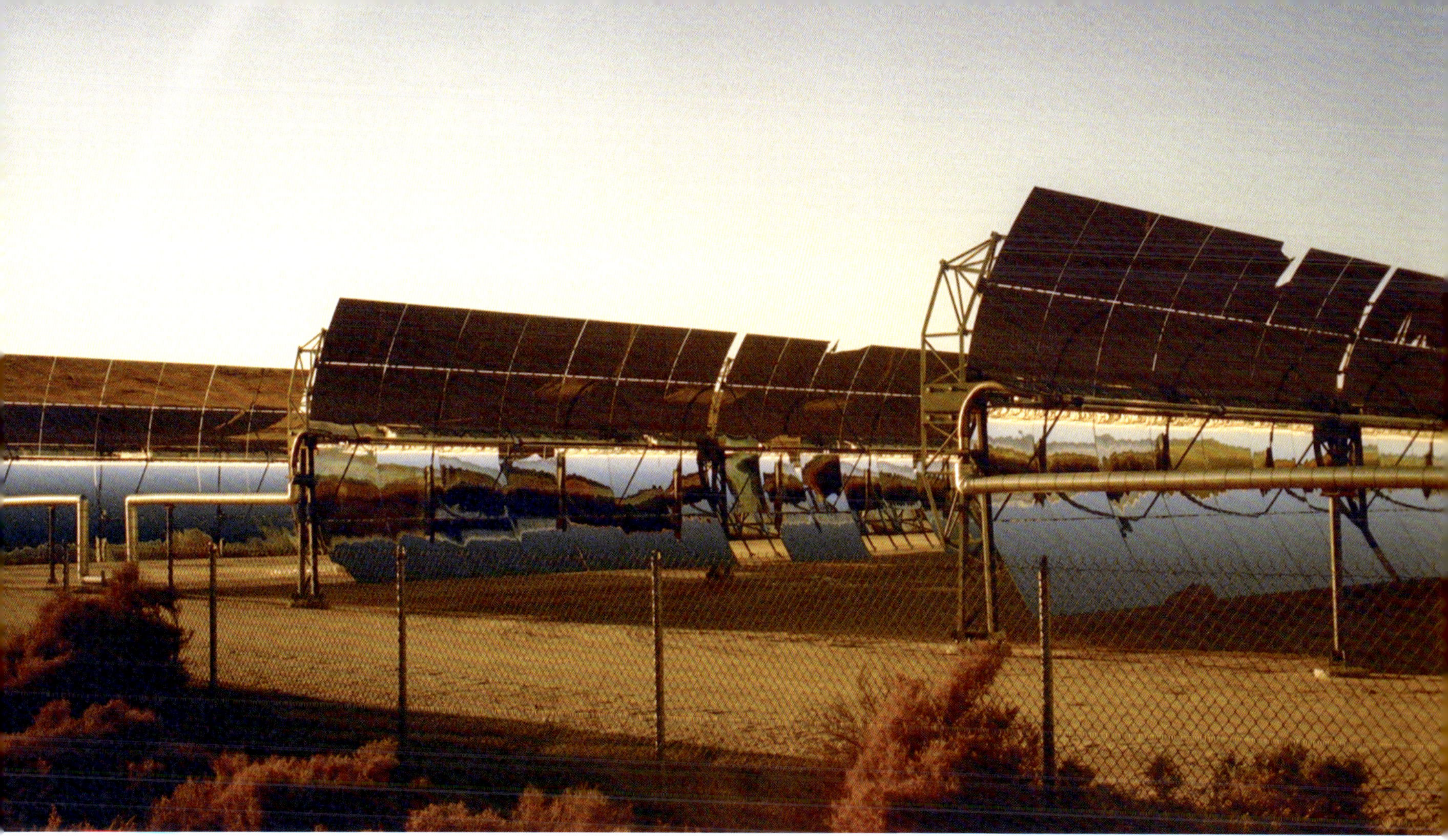

with each other. The space between the projectors opens a new space through fragmenting and translating the meaning constantly from one thing to another, keeping it in motion, or unstable and opening possibilities. It allows for a second becoming: something undergoes a certain metamorphosis by transforming its form and function. The work asks the viewers to resituate themselves in order to make sense of it.

This is also the case with the ongoing series *White Museum,* which I started in 2010. The projector beam visible in the night air delineates a fixed distance from the lens to a sharp-edged screen formed from the light hitting a surface. The space between the projector and the landscape undergoes a reordering of cinematic space – for me, an astronomical understanding of light, as distance travelled.

COMER: *Your installations often consider institutions, but they don't merely represent them on screen. The institution is drawn in and becomes part of the apparatus of the work and vice versa. In projects like* White Museum, *how do you consider the relationship between your work and the institutions and institutional architectures that frame it?*

BARBA: Responding to the museum architecture is one side I'm interested in, but I also understand the institution itself as a sort of community that represents different time layers with the present community that drives it. In all my films, I incorporate local voices, embodied experiences, historic and present documents into the fabrication. 'Museum Time' embodies many dialogues throughout different time zones, as do museum spaces. We often remember previous exhibitions in the museum spaces we inhabit, and traces of previous exhibitions remain in the room. I was thinking while installing, and even before, how *Aggregate States of Matters* at the Museum of Modern Art was in conversation with, for example, Sky Hopinka's video meditation on time or Sandra Mujinga's hologram *Flo*, both of which were on view at MoMA last year. I see museum spaces as possibilities to continue conversations; every exhibition remains inscribed in the building's memory.

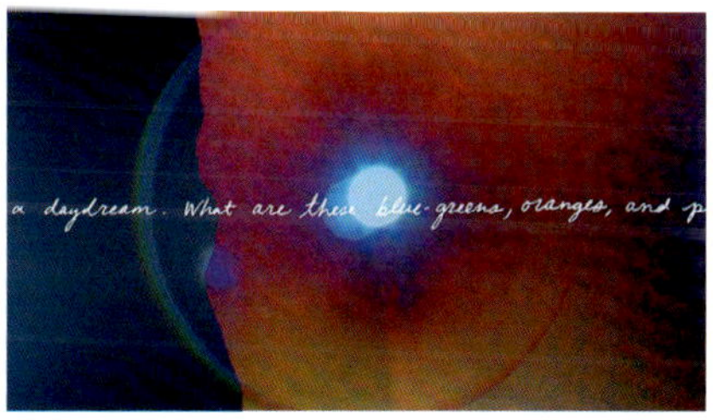

SKY HOPINKA
FAINTING SPELLS, 2018
THREE-CHANNEL COLOUR VIDEO, WITH SOUND
9 MIN. 45 SEC.

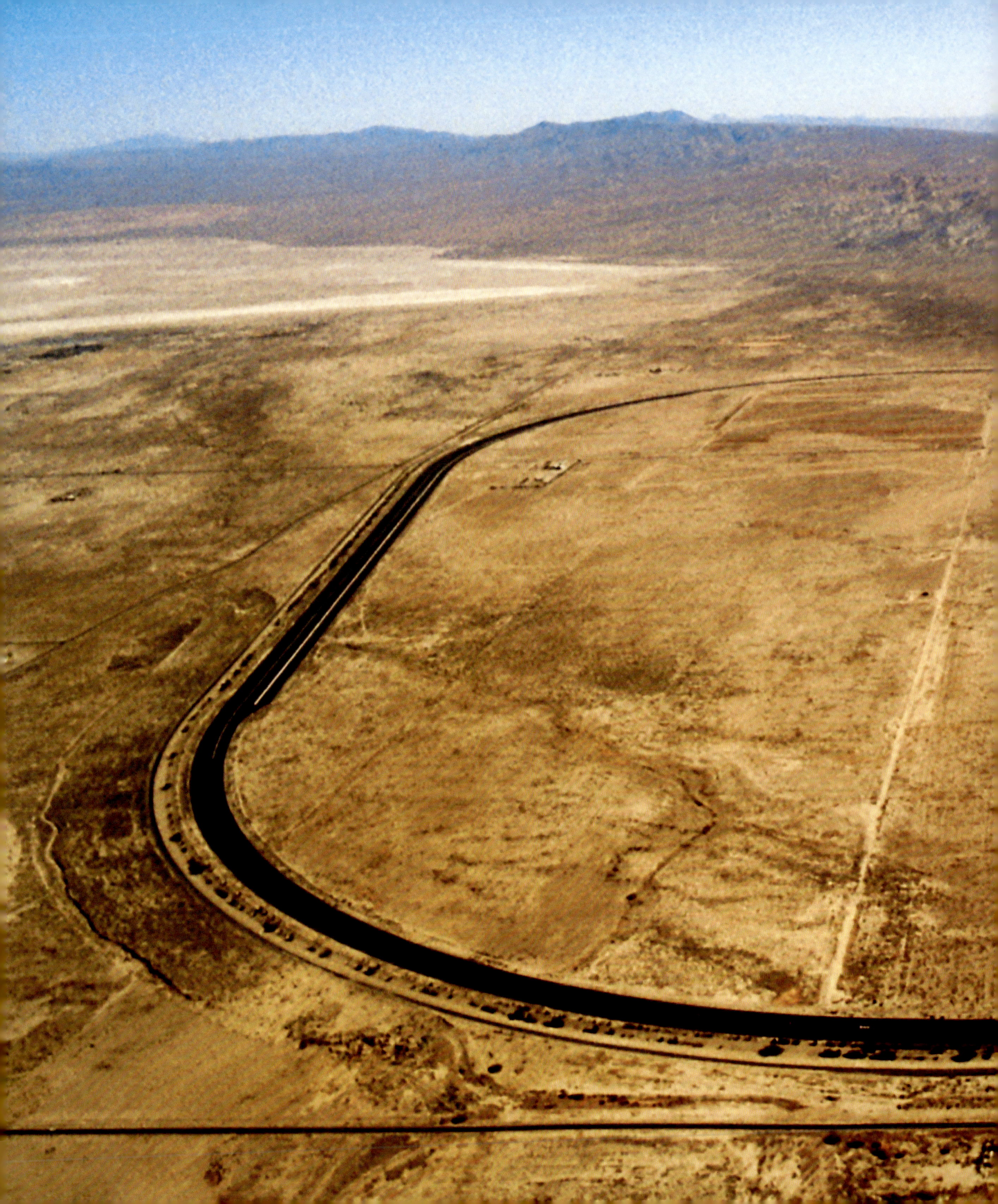

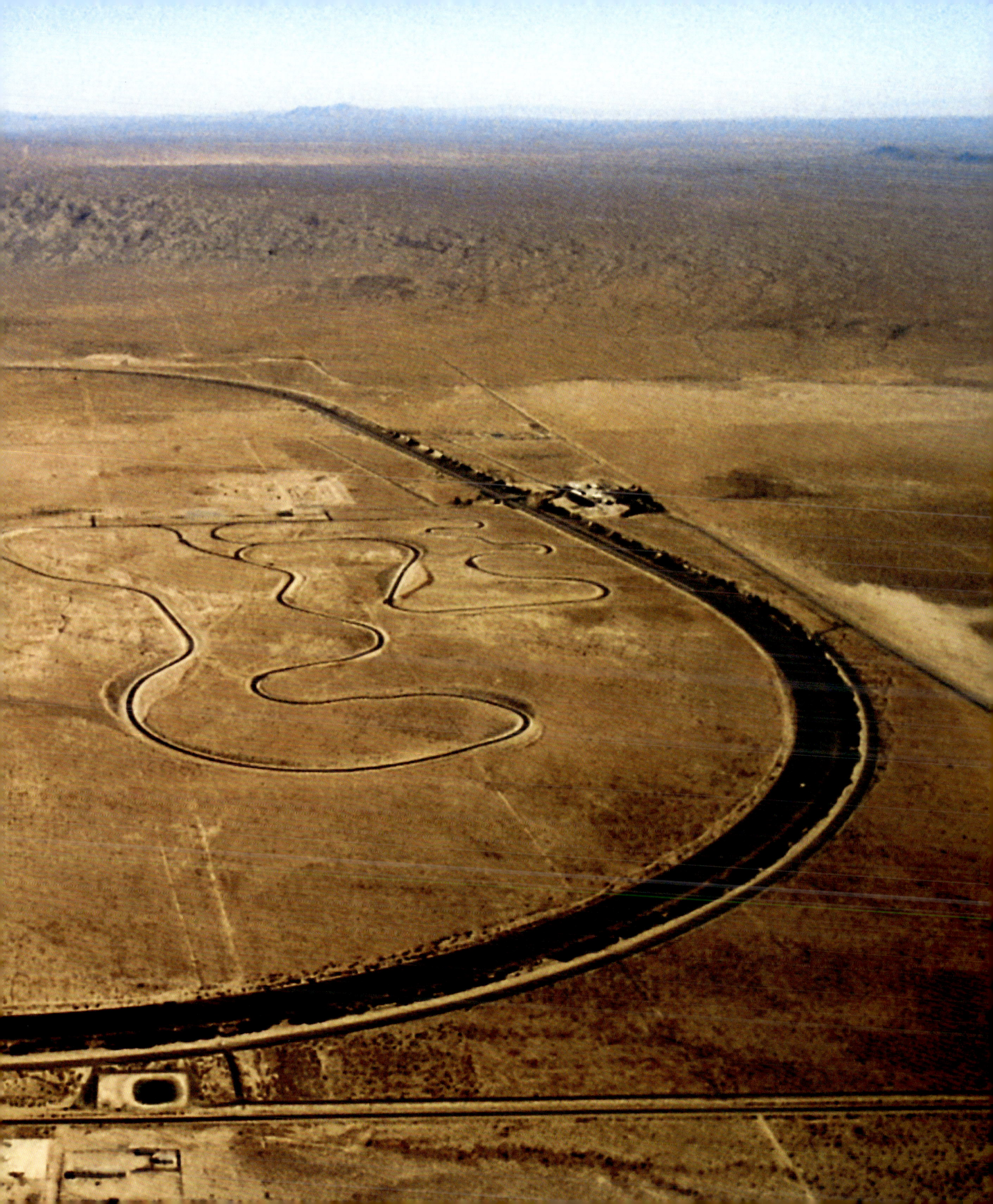

The Hidden Conference is a three-part film work exploring museum-storage systems; the work's title refers to imaginary conversations taking place between artworks inside these invisible spaces and between their creators, who often aren't contemporaries but whose artworks can continue to speak through different generations.

Works like *White Museum* push the boundaries of the museum architecture, extending the building through projected light to the outside, where it frames an urban situation or a landscape. This starts a dialogue with the history of the place where it stands and the stories it inhabits. It represents experienced time in a sort of astronomical understanding of the projected white light, which consists of all colours in the spectrum; a sort of condensed expression of different times, narratives and visual layers. Connecting the invisible narrative that lies outside of the museum, or drawing it to a complete body could be a sort of institutional critique.

There's a very direct response in my work to sound and cinema, which are often both created live. Images are made visible and edited through the sound. One of the projectors will be moved to project outside through the window, which will become a screen. Even if I work with film, I'm not interested in working in a completely darkened space. I invite daylight too, the movements of the sun and the space becoming slowly darker. Projections inscribe themselves within the architecture and outside of it, and these inscriptions have a graduation, starting very thin when it's pure daylight and becoming

below,
WAITING GROUNDS, 2007
16MM FILM, COLOUR
4 MIN.

opposite, from left,
ENIGMATIC WHISTLER, 2009
16MM FILM LOOP, MODIFIED PROJECTOR, OPTICAL SOUND

THE LONG ROAD, 2010
35MM FILM, COLOUR, OPTICAL SOUND
6 MIN. 14 SEC.

STATING THE REAL SUBLIME, 2009
16MM FILM, MODIFIED PROJECTOR

INSTALLATION VIEW AT TATE MODERN, LONDON, 2010

previous pages,
THE LONG ROAD, 2010
35MM FILM, COLOUR, OPTICAL SOUND
6 MIN. 14 SEC.

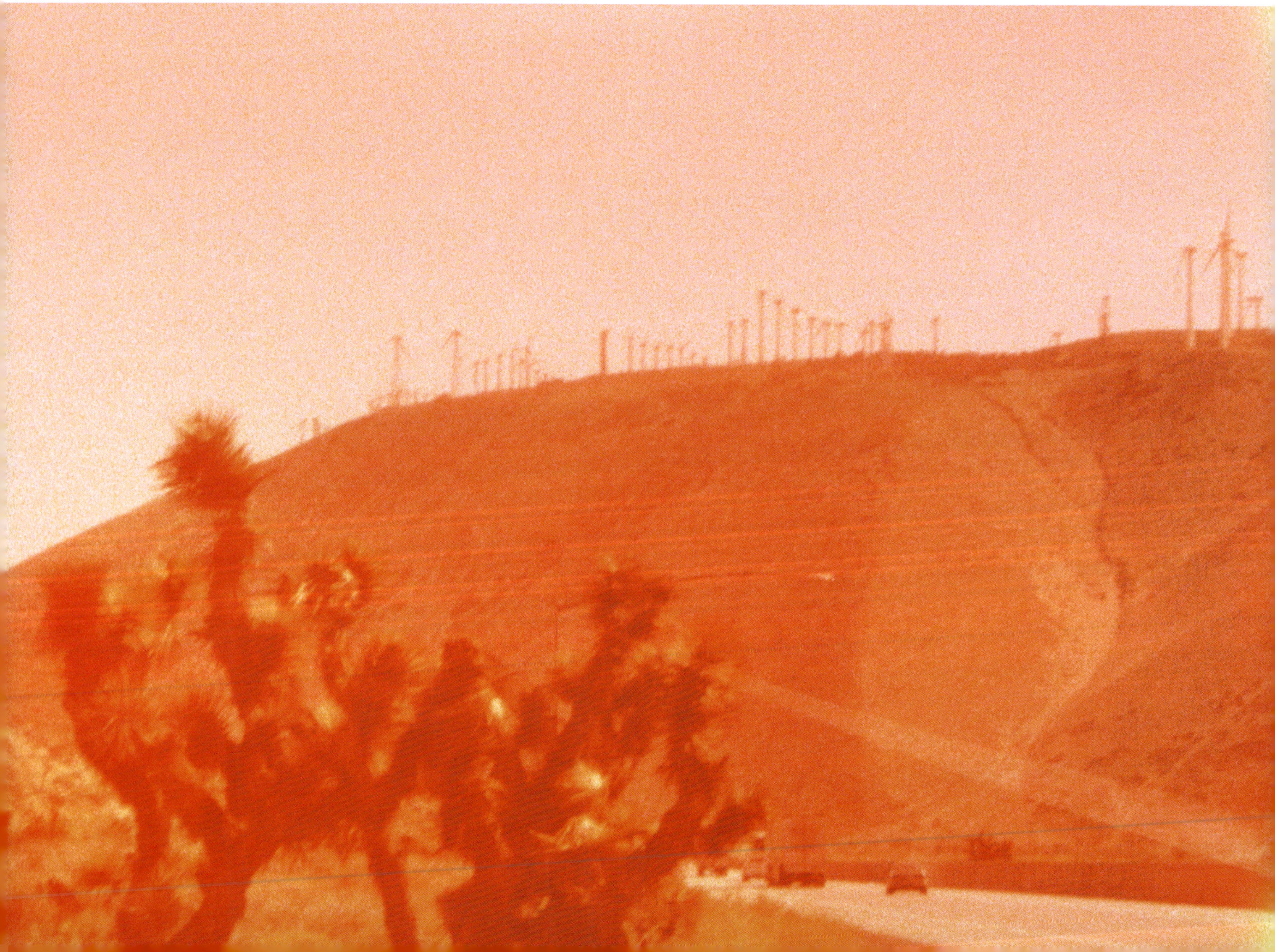

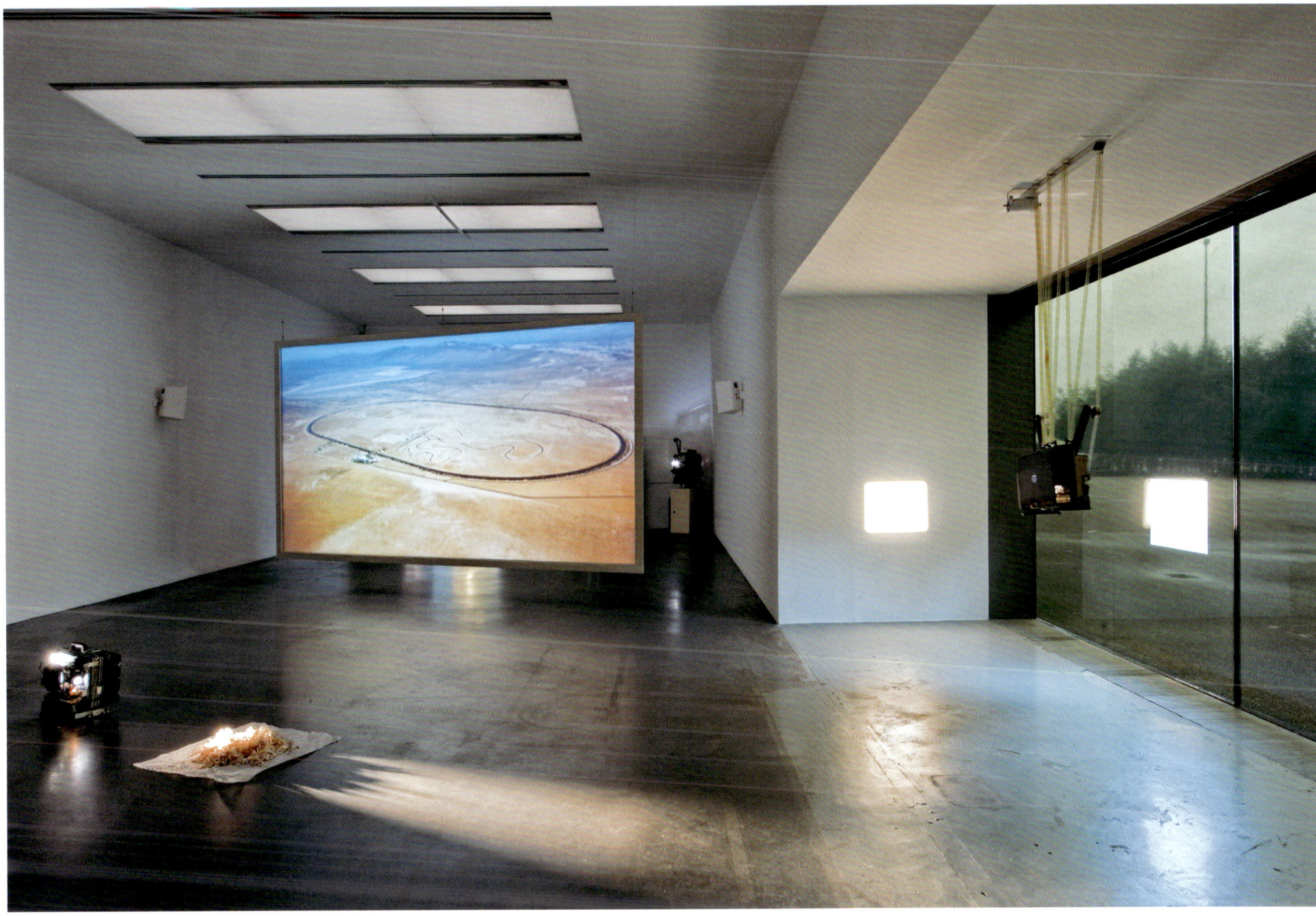

stronger and stronger, like a photographic exposure but with the architecture. And then it's a loop, as in an exhibition. Daylight comes back and it's a perpetual movement. The museum spaces actively participate in the notation of the exhibition.

I tend to create a performative frame when I make my films or objects, but also in exhibitions, landscape settings or within an institution. This frame outlines a conceptual practice but creates a space from which things can embark. One method is the use of the camera itself, which I introduced before as a drawing instrument, another to draw a performative frame within an exhibition setting, where a choreographed, looped notation takes place, again framed by the institution itself. The museum is the space where art gets to be public. When that happens, then art is really about all of us; it's about society and a public record about what you think and believe.

COMER: *How does the history of feminist theory and artists find a place in your work?*

BARBA: Feminist theory and art by feminists empowered me early on. They started to speak to me when I was growing up between Sicily and Germany, where I witnessed and reacted to constant unjust situations towards women and their freedom. The works and texts expressed this force for the right to choose their own voice, politically and conceptually. That was extremely inspiring and important.

Teresa de Lauretis, in 'Rethinking Women's Cinema, Aesthetics and Feminist Theory', elaborates on modes of aesthetic awareness and sensory perception. This was an important

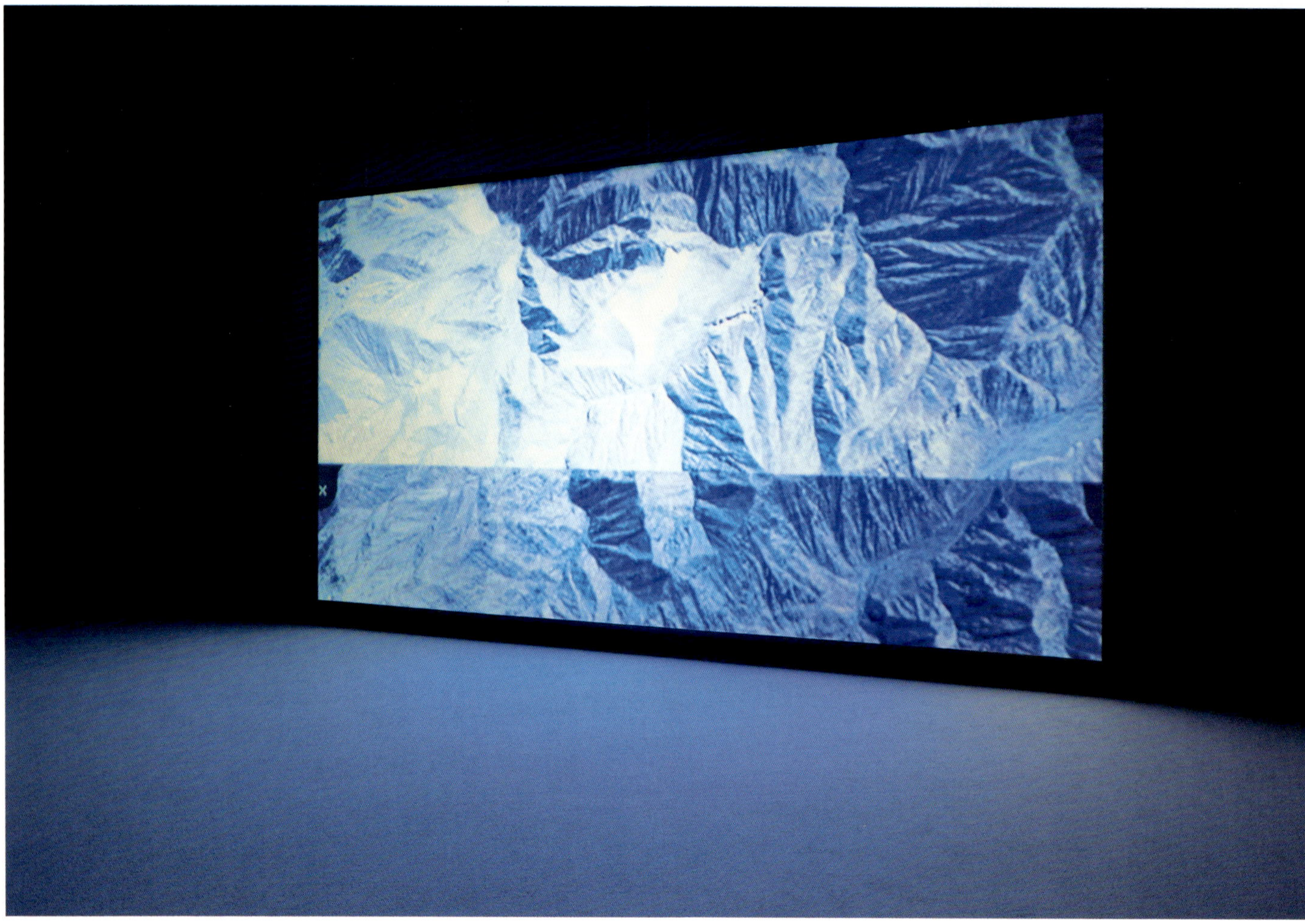

left,
AGGREGATE STATES OF MATTERS, 2019
35MM FILM, COLOUR, OPTICAL SOUND
21 MIN. 14 SEC.

INSTALLATION VIEW AT THE MUSEUM OF MODERN ART, NEW YORK, 2024

opposite and next pages,
AGGREGATE STATES OF MATTERS, 2019
35MM FILM, COLOUR, OPTICAL SOUND
21 MIN. 14 SEC.

early reading. I later understood my methodology of 'embarkation', which I started to establish in *Panzano*, in a similar sensory perception path. By 'embarkation', I mean a sort of 'release and reaching to' through experiencing and thinking. It's an abstract space in a suspended mode, where no time or scale references exist and an oscillating environment can be reached; it's a zone of speculation to bridge real gaps in knowledge. In this space, involuntary temporal connections are made, and these connections evoke new knowledge. People release stored memories in their bodies in front of the camera through the collective journey.

I also felt very close to Laura Mulvey's *Visual Pleasure and Narrative Cinema*, which helps free the look of the camera into its materiality in time and space and the look of the audience into dialectics, passionate detachment. It was an early desire to fragment the hierarchy in cinema and create another spatial sensorial experience.

Rosalind Krauss's legendary essay 'Sculpture in the Expanded Field' (1979) provided a framework for the understanding of sociopolitical dimensions of landscape and architecture in the practice of art, which is also essential for my work.

Studying with VALIE EXPORT and collaborating with Barbara Hammer for our performance at Jeu de Paume in 2012 have made important marks too, among others.

COMER: *How do you envision your role as a curator? I was particularly impressed by the collection exhibition you organized at the Museo Nacional Centro de Arte Reina Sofía in Madrid, in which VALIE EXPORT played a primary role.*

BARBA: Similar to the exercise of proposing a frame where concepts can evolve freely, I took on the invitation for a commission by Lynne Cooke at the Reina Sofía in 2009. The very generous invitation by the museum involved studying their huge collection on

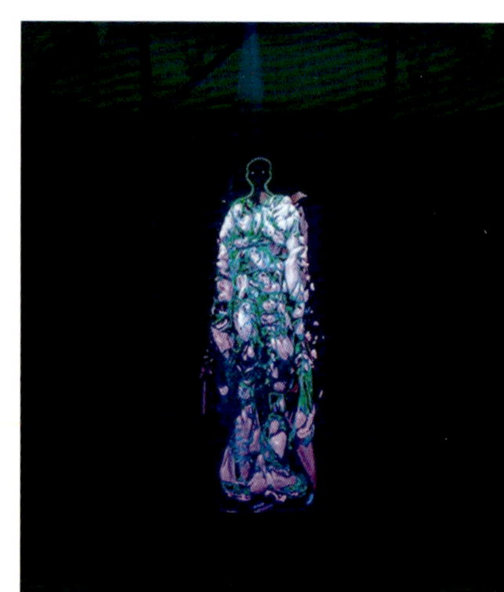

SANDRA MUJINGA
FLO, 2019
HIGH-DEFINITION VIDEO, COLOUR, SOUND
POLYCARBONATE PLATE, MDF, AND WOOD BEAMS
50 MIN. 13 SEC.

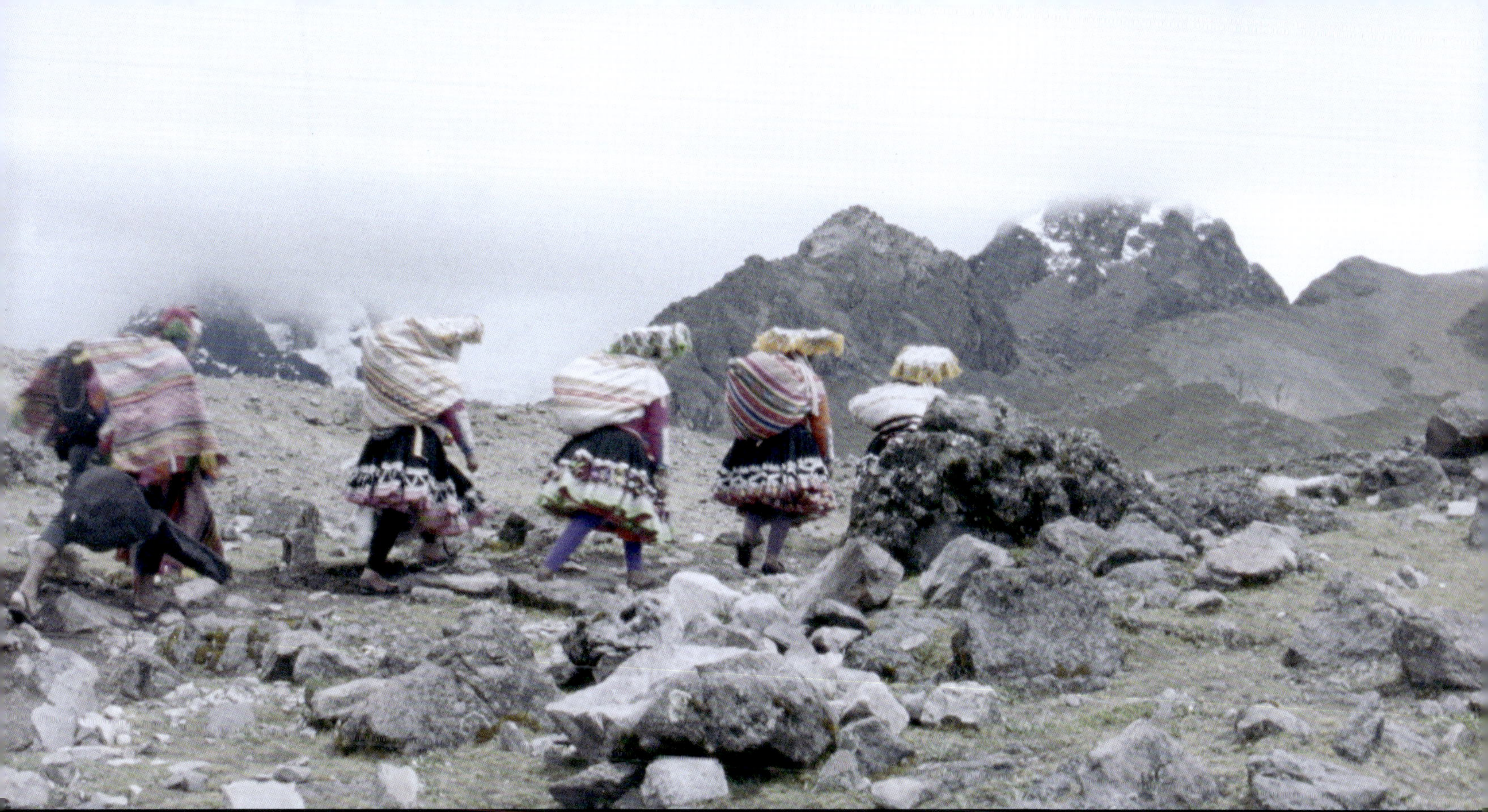

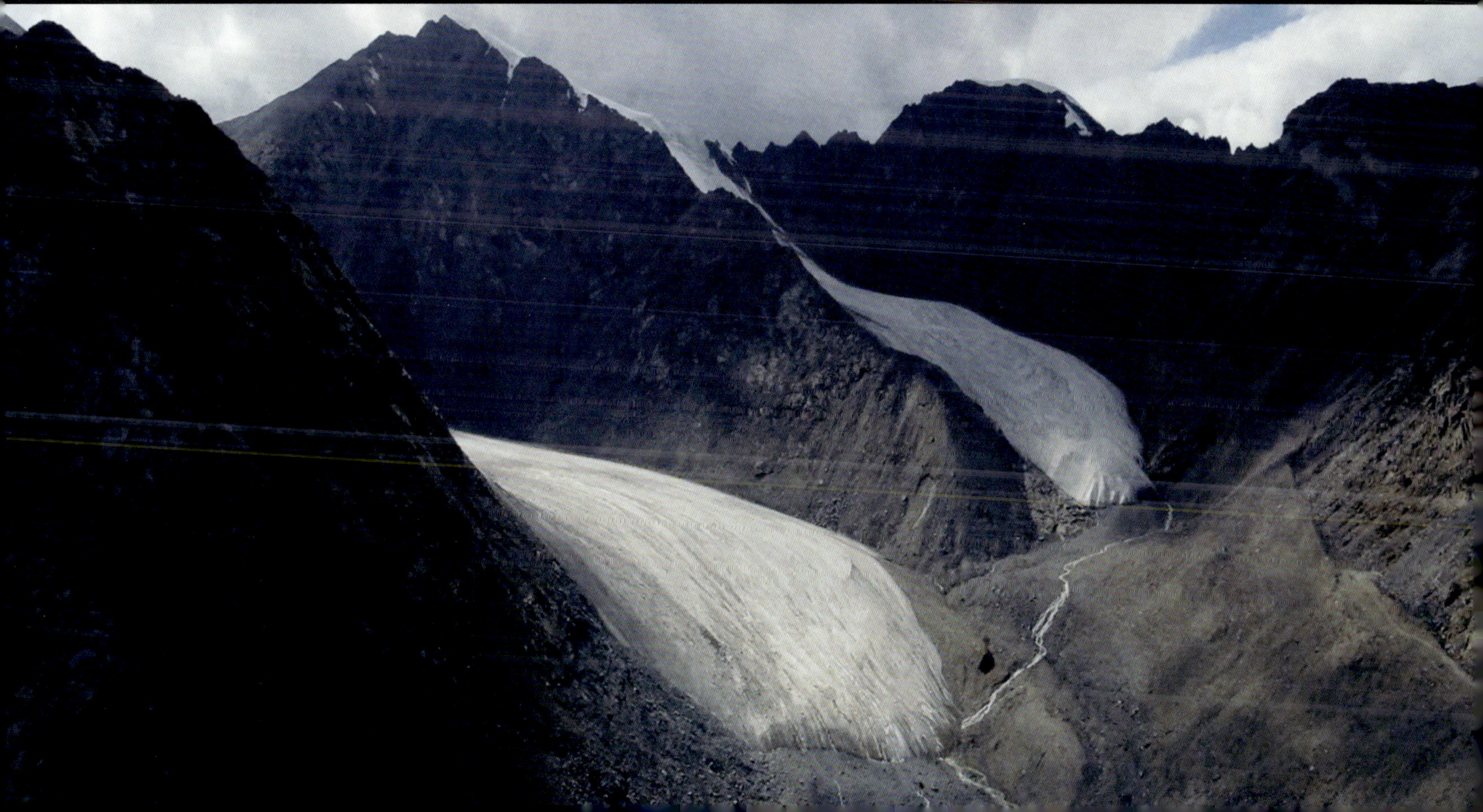

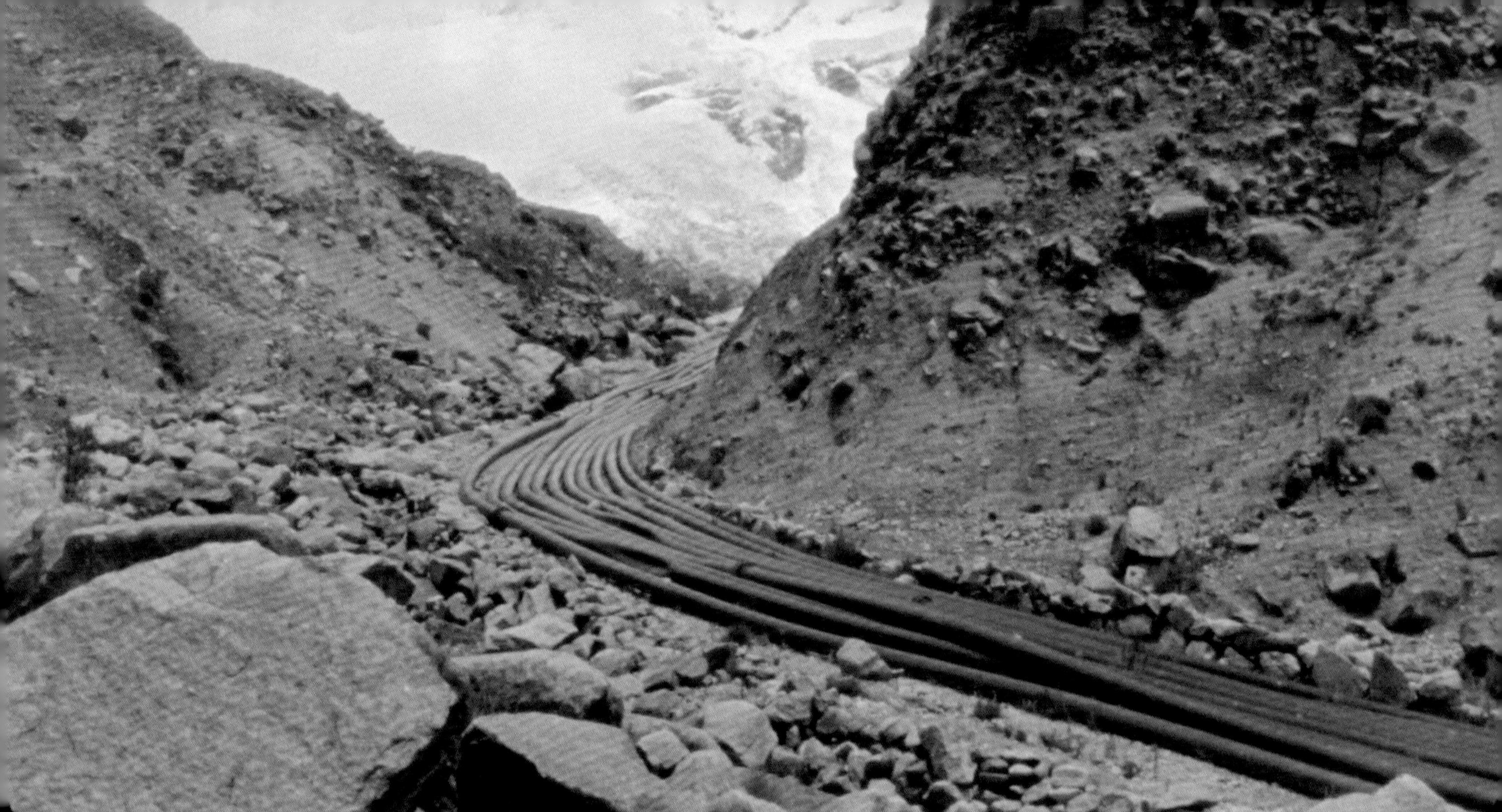

The impact in the White Mountain Range zone hasn't reached a point of collapse yet. As the glaciers are still providing water, hydric stress is
not yet present in the area, but this does not mean that the lack of water is not already noticeable.The water is not enough, and it is being consu
y the nearby villages because, according to the normative for hydric sources, it firstly must be used to cover the needs of the population, ar

White Mountain Range must give priority to personal consumption, the water left for sowing becomes scarce. But in the Black Mountain Ran
zone, given to the presence of hydric stress, the inhabitants do know how to use the little water they have in the most efficient way possible, r
zero waste. The difference between the two is that in the White [illegible] Range there are people who bring the water to their farm and when they
finish using it, they don't take it back to the source, so that waste of water still exists. People from the White Range say that the water won't end
s the gods will supply them with it forever, and that the glaciers will not disappear. Even though there are sectors that have already starte
the impact of the lack of water. They sow the whole year, they are used to that. The problem is that in the dry periods they need more water. The

for farming, but for grass. The biggest irrigation zones are Caraz, Yunguay y [illegible]. It will soon [illegible] they are being affected,
not only because of the lack of water, but also because of the frosts that are happening lately and that are damaging the farms. The glacier is i
fluencing the availability of the water, and that is already noticeable. In Huaraz, farming is not taking up the entire year time anymore, bu
Caraz and Yunguay areas it is still possible. And in the coastal zone, Chavimochic Project has already start having problems this year. Another

recently it was very clear that the tubes set in the lagoon could be used to manage the density of it. What do you think about this constructio
we have so many different versions about it. The thing is that this structure that Palcacocha has, it was made between the years 1972 and 1974,
is dam. It was made to regulate the run of the lagoon. It is designed for extraordinary events, as intense rains. But, when it was built it us

water. So the safety building done in the 70s does not guarantee the security of the lagoon anymore, because of how big in size it is.There a
[illegible] ice avalanches [illegible]
mass movements and avalanches happening constantly in different zones. If the avalanche impacts in the lagoon, having such a small dam, it ma
ollapse. As an emergency measure, this pipage has been installed in order to have a wall that can stop a wave if an avalanche happens. S

be studied in order to build another, better one, as this one is not useful anymore. The new design of the security building it is expected to fo
[illegible] constantly throughout different moments of the year in order to ma
he levels of the lagoon low. But it is still just a project. Anyway, asking the people, they always say that this crisis is too far away in the futur
and that nothing is going to really happen at the end, and this is [illegible] has already happened before. So I find it really odd that people a

Because a technician that is not inside the topic may say that nothing's happening as he cannot see any movement. But I say it mostly becau

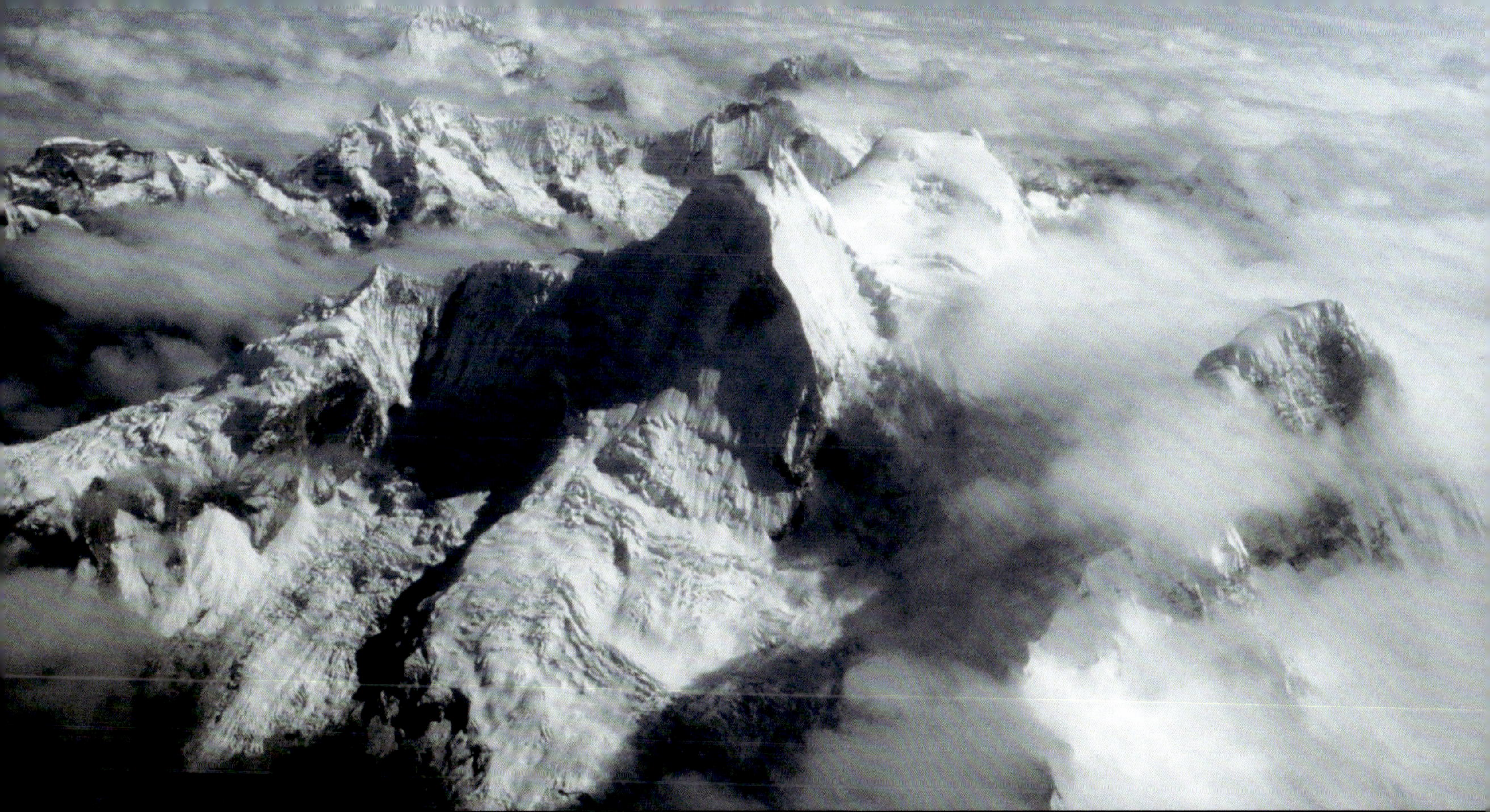

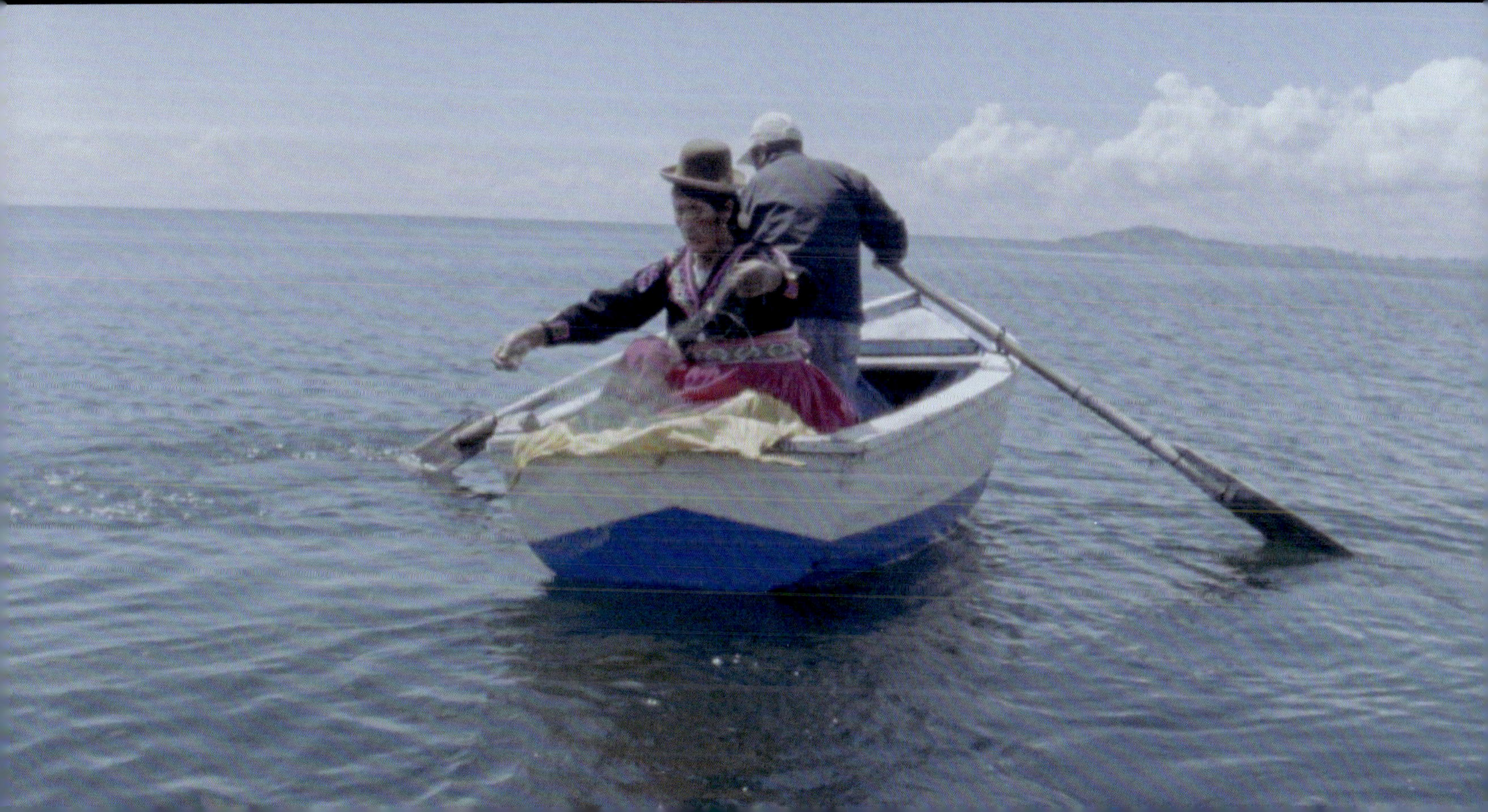

several visits throughout the year and to then propose an exhibition. I started this investigation around the role of works of art within the broader cultural setting. The exhibition I proposed was called: a curated conference. I presented forty-three works, including film and video, sculpture, painting, drawing and photography, in two connected galleries. I was interested to see what sorts of conversations could emerge from the different works in storage and by authors from different times, focusing on how ideas are given to the next generation, to another artist who isn't contemporary with them. I produced a diagram that was at the entrance of the exhibition about these different conversations that were taking place.

In the accompanying brochure, titled 'On the Future of Collective Strength within an Archive' (2010) I wrote: 'It is the aim of this conference to draw together a representation of artists from the twentieth and twenty-first centuries, and bring their informed opinions to bear on the significant questions of art.'

I juxtaposed and overlaid pieces made over the span of almost a century in close proximity. I was revisiting a specific technique for a kind of performativity and choreography that I'd already been using in my earlier exhibitions, where I was interested in how different works might switch on and off at different times to start different conversations, like a choir using a question-and-answer method. I used this method for the first time with my work *Coro Spezzato, the Future lasts One Day* (2009) presented at the 53rd Venice Biennale in the Palazzo delle Esposizioni.

Being so intensively involved with this, I started to think further about the question 'What is a museum collection?' Forgetting about authors for a moment and just thinking about the works and the ideas, what happens with ideas that aren't shown for a really long time but that may carry a thought that's extended further by another later work? I welcomed the anarchic outcome produced by a situation in which each artist speaks with their own voice in their own language, temperament and volume. Some of the artworks were recent additions but others had long been in the collection. I invited the artists through their works to explore the collective consciousness within the archive. What would emerge would be neither a consensual nor a coherent vision, but a 'Babel of voices'; the archive would be shown to be composed of dateless individual expressions that can be choreographed like a musical score.

I took the liberty of installing the artworks in a non-museological way and more as a drawing of voices within a conference setting. VALIE EXPORT's *Syntagma* (1983), Joan Jonas's *Vertical Roll* (1972), Dara Birnbaum's *Technology/Transformation: Wonder Woman* (1978–79), Yoko Ono's *Eye Blink* and George Maciunas's *Artype* (both 1966), as well as Paul Sietsema's *Figure 3* (2008) were all part of one workshop session.

Round-table discussions, workshops, a parallel session and keynote 'speeches' by Pablo Picasso, Mira Schendel, Louise Bourgeois, Martha Rosler and others were also part of the conference programme. These 'speakers' raised concerns that were expressed in my own practice too, like Picasso's: 'All I have ever made was made for the present and with the hope that it will always remain in the present.' I also shared George Maciunas's sense of collective identity when he termed this 'community of individuals grouping together a vast quantity of behaviors and attitudes … a "non-group" with no strict structures'. Bourgeois, for her part, addressed the ways in which visual works of art tell stories through the interplay of formal qualities: 'narrative becomes a tool not a meaning, a mediator not a solution'.

With this project, which formed and led to many other archive-related projects, I wanted to engage critically with the archive's discursive notion, offering an alternative to the norms of historical presentation, as I believe that artworks are ahistorical and timeless and therefore should also be heard when self-organized by themselves.

COMER: *I'm interested in how you invoke the conference as a model, particularly in a curated conference and in* The Hidden Conference. *In both instances, you draw on the archive, on museum storage, on forms of value that remain unseen but that*

THE HIDDEN CONFERENCE: ABOUT THE SHELF AND MANTEL, 2015
35MM FILM, COLOUR, OPTICAL SOUND
14 MIN.

INSTALLATION VIEW AT TATE MODERN, LONDON, 2023

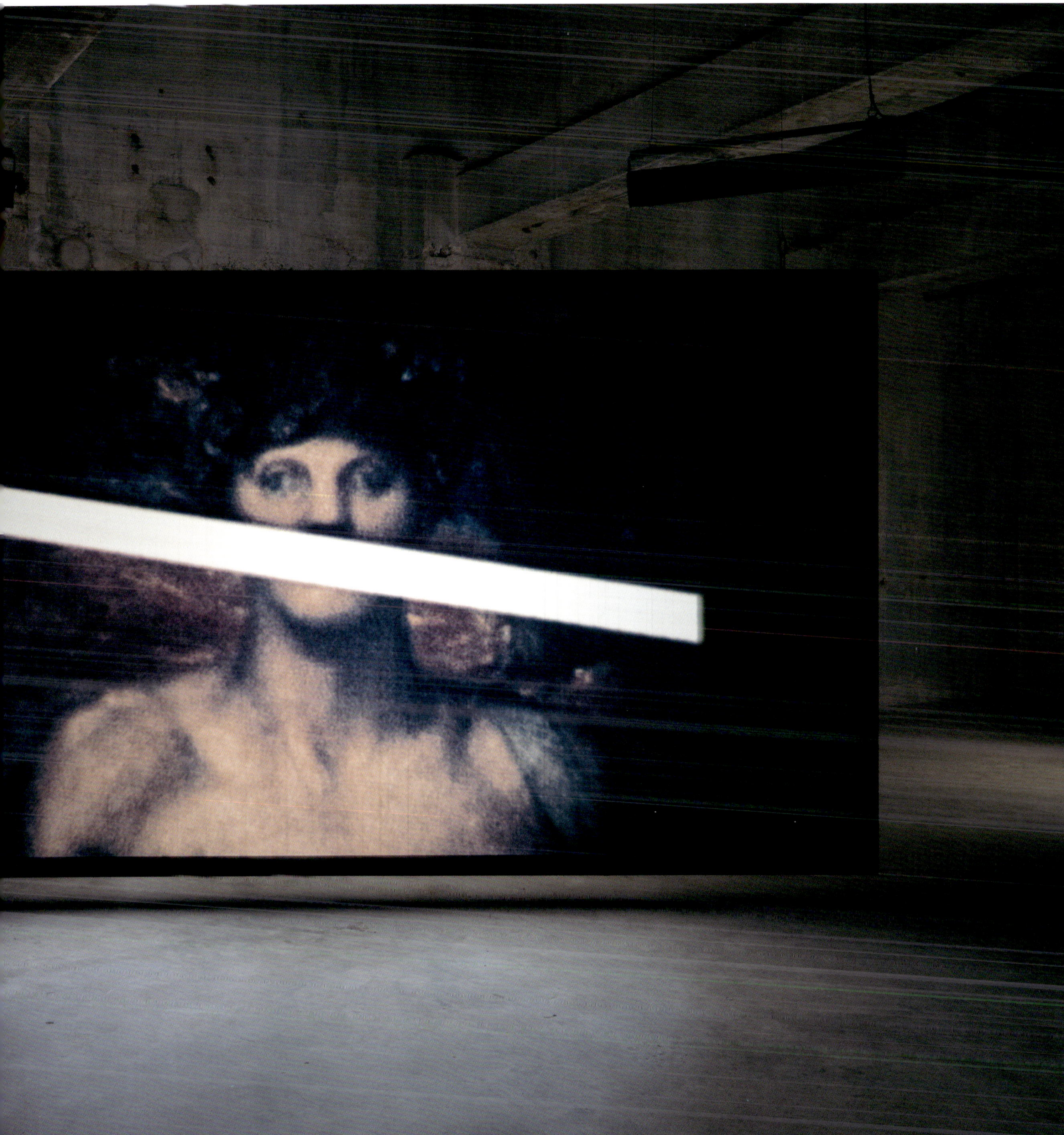

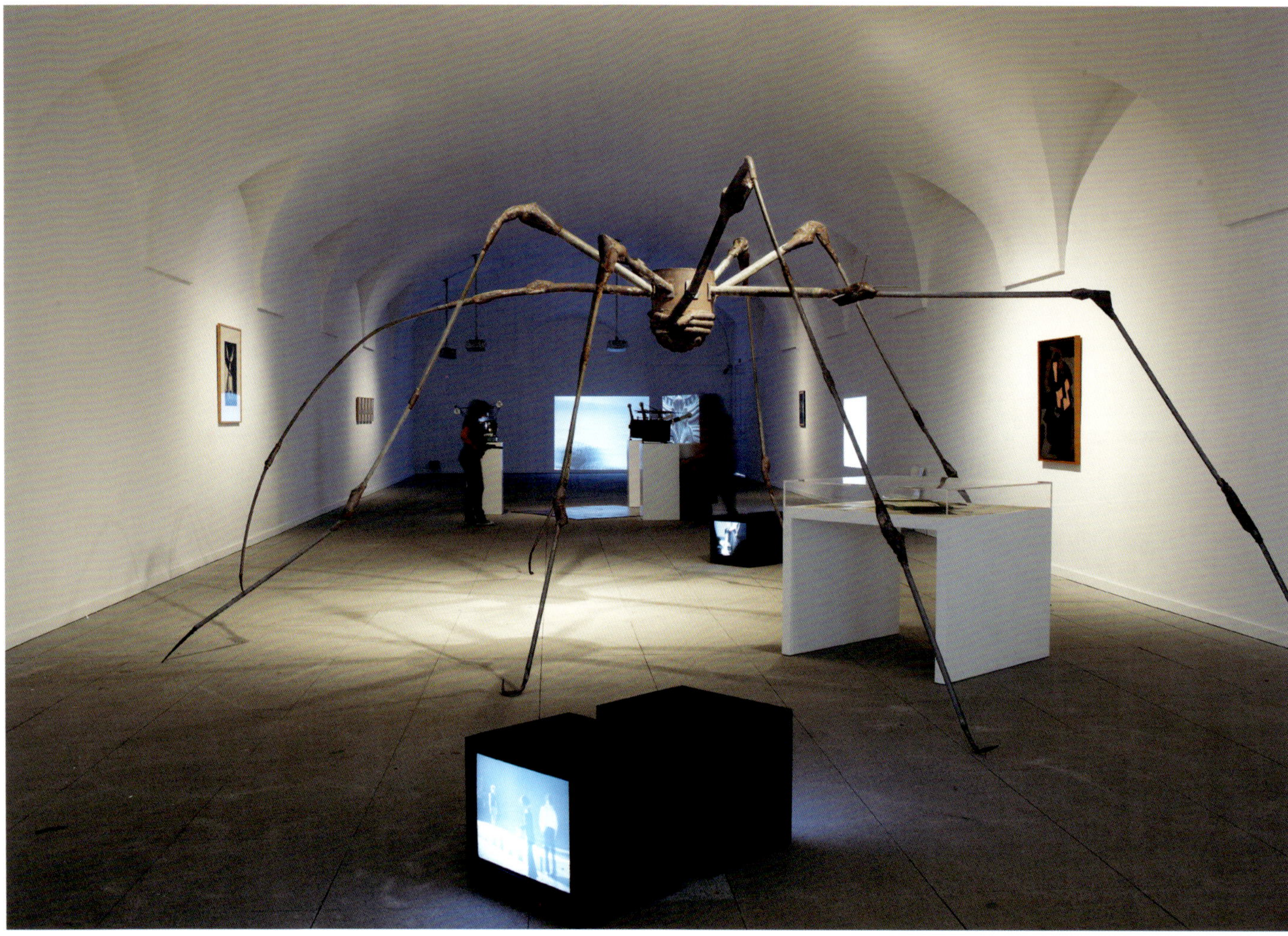

left and opposite:
EXHIBITION VIEW OF UNA CONFERENCIA COMISARIADA: SOBRE EL FUTURO DE LA FUERZA COLECTIVA DENTRO DEL ARCHIVO, ORGANIZED BY ROSA BARBA, MUSEO NACIONAL CENTRO DE ARTE REINA SOFÍA, MADRID, 2010

art on display includes
VALIE EXPORT
SYNTAGMA, 1983
16MM FILM, COLOUR, STEREO SOUND
18 MIN.

GUY DEBORD
SUR LE PASSAGE DE QUELQUES PERSONNES À TRAVERS UNE ASSEZ COURTE UNITÉ DE TEMPS, 1959
35MM FILM TRANSFERRED TO VIDEO, B/N, SOUND
19 MIN.

LOUISE BOURGEOIS
SPIDER, 1994
IRON, PAINT AND GALVANIZED IRON
248 X 803 X 597 CM

can accrue new meanings and associations when they're reanimated through display. There are many echoes and parallels in these projects with the procedures of cinema, in which the passage of light reanimates spectral forms from the past. There's a constant play between past and present, silent and sonic, withheld and disclosed, active and static. This isn't simply a polyvocal system, but one in which the many voices included occupy different states of being, of visibility. Does your approach to 'the conference' provide a structure that relates to your wider practice as a whole?

BARBA: The conference is a sort of community model that connects the artworks through their ongoing discussions and urgencies, responding to societal questions and forms as well as to the institution as a community idea, an active archive, where the work with the display itself acts as an active conference methodology. This has influenced and deepened my practice as whole.

At Reina Sofía, I started to examine the works themselves as material for a larger discussion on an ongoing, growing map where all works contribute to a discourse. Drawing a diagram while researching the archive helped me to formulate the idea. It became a sort of partition and each voice of the artist contributed to the rhythm and content of the deliberation. The reanimation through the choreography of the display added another cinematic dimension of what we imagine and what remains unseen or invisible; the juxtapositions asked new questions and created possible echoes through perpetual movement, their formal presentations, sound overlaps and spatial distribution.

Although I chose to omit my own works in the museum's collection from the exhibition – and by extension, my own voice from the actual discussion – I added my voice by selecting artists as the primary speakers whose aesthetics and work reflect the key

MARCEL DUCHAMP
LA MARIÉE MISE À NU PAR SES CÉLIBATAIRES MÊME (BOÎTE VERTE), 1934
PAPERBOARD, BLACK AND WHITE PHOTOGRAPHS, FABRIC AND HANDWRITTEN NOTES
33 X 28 X 3 CM

MARIA BLANCHARD
MUJER CON GUITARRA, 1917
OIL ON CANVAS
100 X 72 CM

MARTHA ROSLER
SEMIOTICS OF THE KITCHEN, 1975
BETACAM SP AND DVD BLACK AND WHITE VIDEO
6 MIN. 9 SEC.

DARA BIRNBAUM
TECHNOLOGY/TRANSFORMATION: WONDERWOMAN, 1978–79
VIDEO, COLOUR, SOUND
5 MIN. 50 SEC.

ROBERT BREER
RECREATION, 1956–57
16MM FILM, ALSO TRANSFERRED TO VIDEO, COLOUR, OPTICAL SOUND
2 MIN.

LILIANA PORTER
FOR YOU, 1999
16MM FILM TRANSFERRED TO VIDEO, COLOUR, SOUND
16 MIN.

JOAN JONAS
VERTICAL ROLL, 1972
VIDEO, B/N, SOUND
19 MIN. 38 SEC.

EWA PARTUM
EXCERPT FROM ACTIVE POETRY, POEM BY EWA, 1971–73
8MM FILM TRANSFERRED TO MINI DV, DIGITAL BETACAM AND DVD BLACK AND WHITE VIDEO, SILENT
5 MIN. 45 SEC.

CARL ANDRE
MAGNESIUM CROPPER PLAIN, 1969
MAGNESIUM AND COPPER
1 X 182 X 182 CM

DAVID LAMELAS
TO POUR MILK INTO A GLASS, 1972
16MM COLOUR FILM, SOUND AND SET OF 8 PHOTOGRAPHS
FILM LENGTH: 7 MIN. 35 SEC.
PHOTOGRAPHS: 235 X 26 CM

YOKO ONO
EYE BLINK, 1966
16MM BLACK AND WHITE FILM, SILENT
35 SEC.

GEORGE MACIUNAS
ARTYPE, 1966
16MM BLACK AND WHITE FILM, SILENT
2 MIN. 40 SEC.

PAUL SIETSEMA
FIGURE 3, 2008
16MM COLOUR/BLACK AND WHITE FILM PROJECTION, SILENT
16 MIN.

principles of my own practice. The archive became the literal foundation of my exhibition-as-conference, as the works on display were drawn exclusively from the museum's storage areas. I also use the term 'archive' in a more abstract sense, aligning with Hal Foster's notion of a system that 'structures the specific expressions of a given era'. I believe that artworks are 'ahistorical' or 'timeless', and, as such, they can organize themselves, coming together through the initiatives and themes proposed by their authors.

I wanted to critically engage with the ideology governing how the institution presents its collection elsewhere in its galleries, offering a subversive alternative to the museum's conventional norms of representational completeness and historical accountability. As Lynne Cooke observed, my project can also be understood through Theodor Adorno's 1953 essay on the Valéry Proust Museum. In this essay, Adorno argues that Valéry views the museum as a place where the art of the past is metaphorically put to death. He claims that 'museum and mausoleum are connected by more than phonetic resemblance', since museums act like family tombs for works of art, neutralizing culture in the process. However, in contrast to this embalming or reification of art, Proust envisioned the museum as a space where art could be reanimated, turning it into a site of active competition. My project echoes some of Proust's ideas, but with a notable difference: while Proust placed the responsibility for reanimating art in the hands of the spectator, I deliberately give that control to the artists themselves, allowing their works to embody their voices.

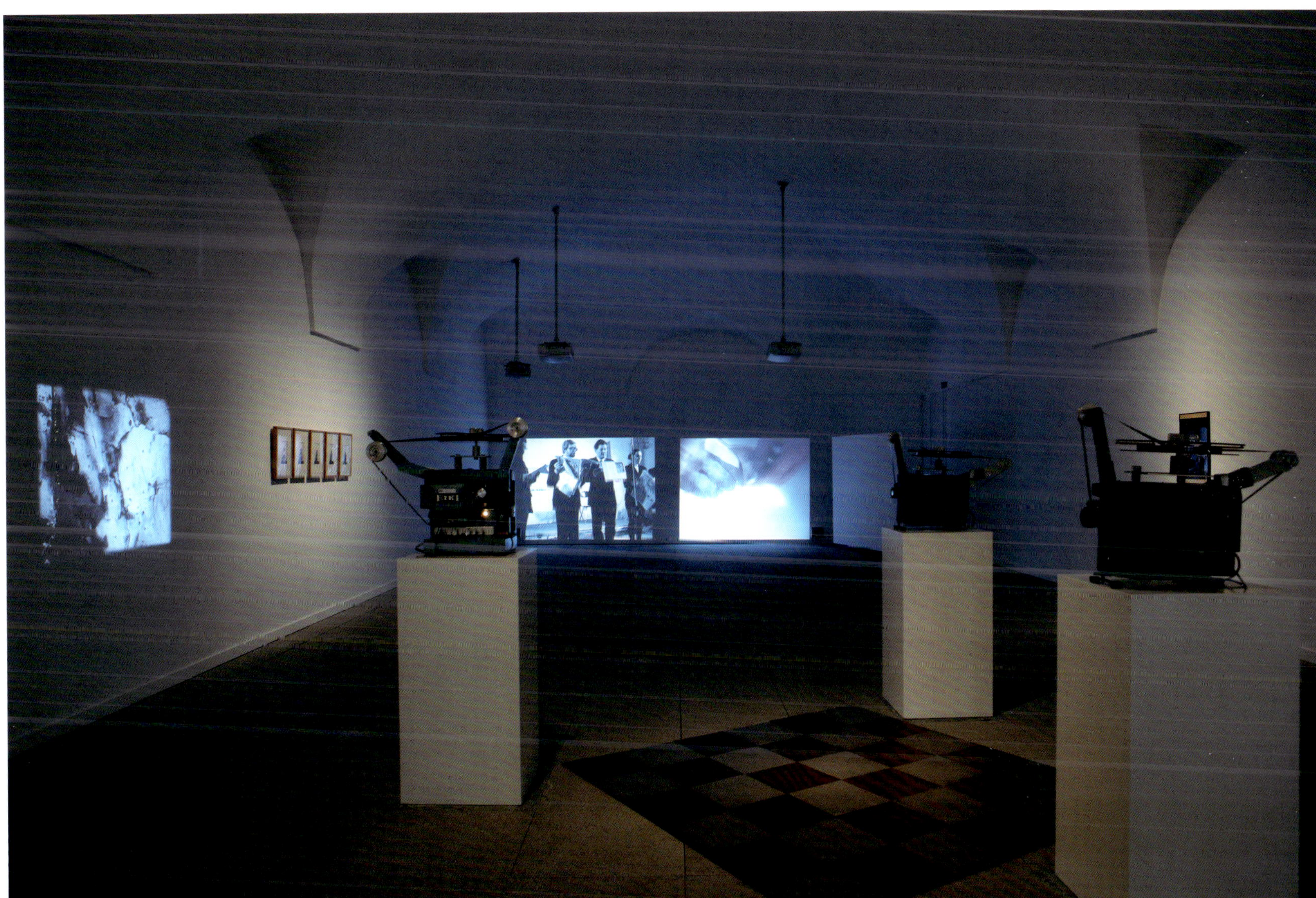

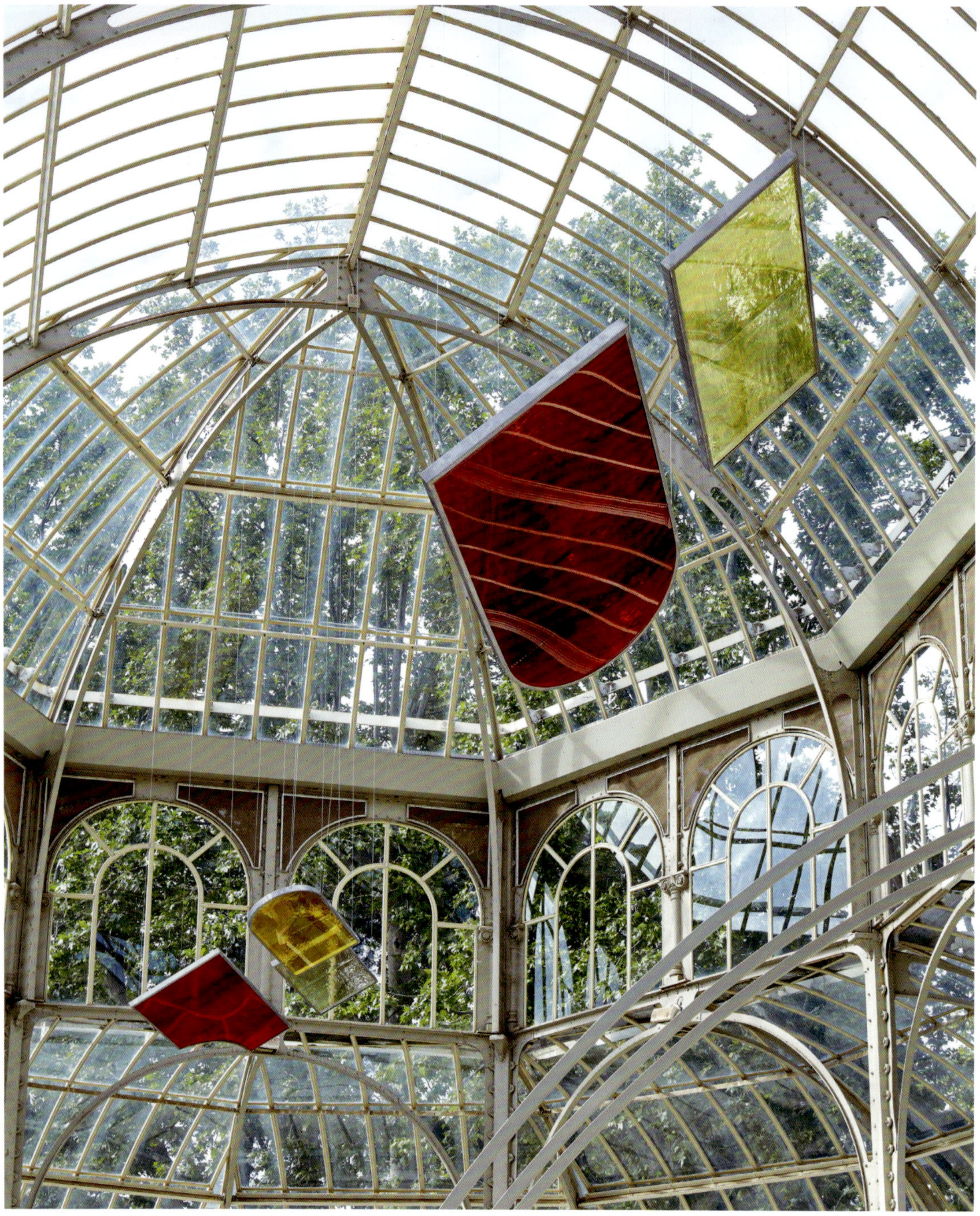

left and opposite,
SOLAR FLUX RECORDINGS,
2017
9 RECORDINGS, METAL,
COLOUR GLASS FILTERS,
ENGRAVED PLATES

INSTALLATION VIEW AT MUSEO
NACIONAL CENTRO DE ARTE
REINA SOFÍA, MADRID, 2017

In *The Hidden Conference* films, I entered museum storage facilities with my handheld camera, drawing and approaching the works as well capturing moments where sometimes works became visible through the mirroring inside or on top of another work, through shadows and proximity on the shelves, reflected in the communal space of the archive. Through the montage and the display of these three films, the conversation between the different museum archives grows and connects in new and unexpected ways. Indeed, the conference as a structure for my filmmaking and exhibition model became a very important tool for my practice. Some procedures existed already, like the inclusion of non-actors and the release of their inscribed memories, as well as including historical materials in my films with the attempt to create a new hybrid space where all of these elements inform each other. I understood these practices as an interwoven strategy that expanded further into the exhibition display.

COMER: *How have the forms of installation you've developed impacted your approach to making exhibitions and vice versa?*

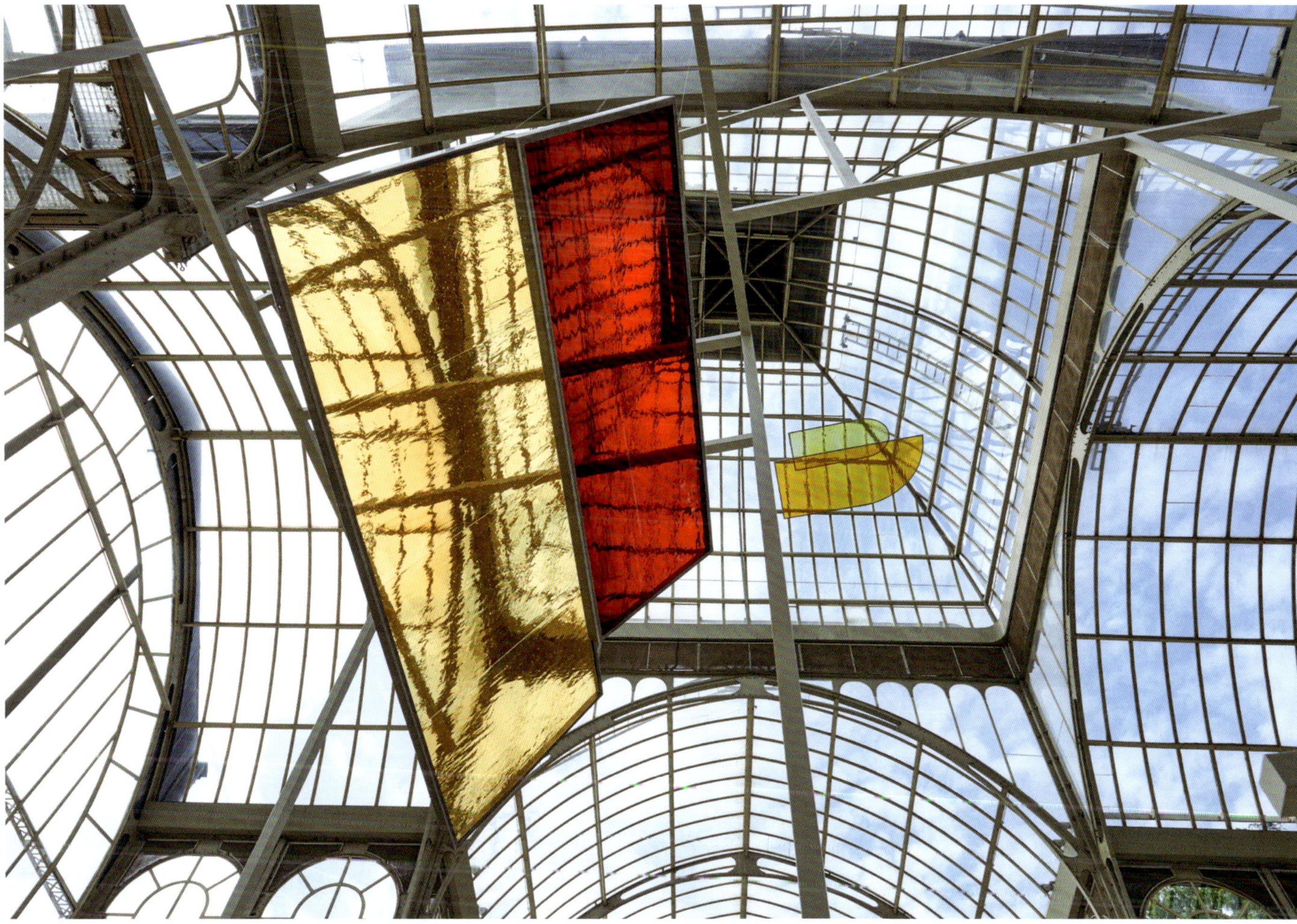

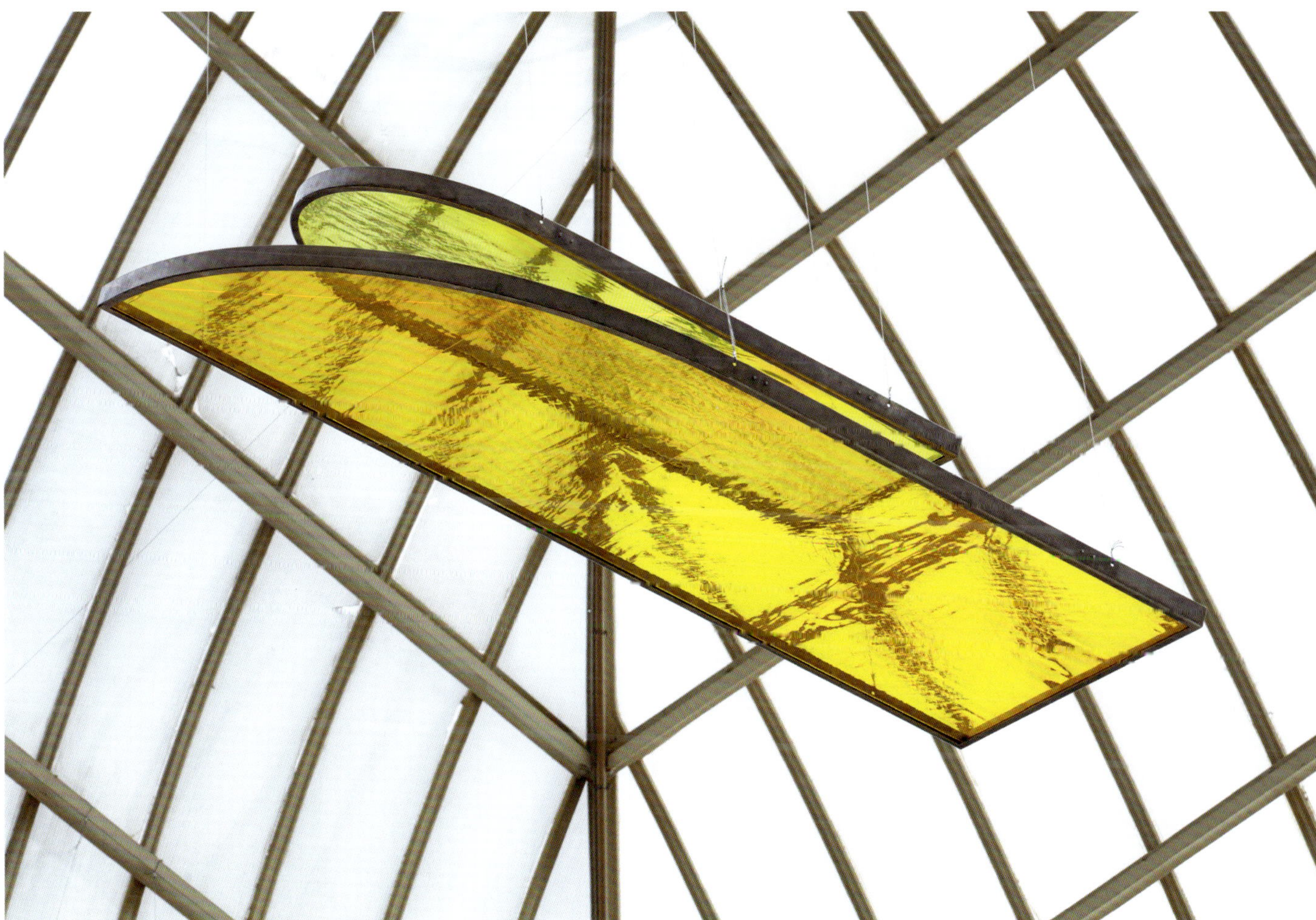

BARBA: The different installations over time have informed my approach to making exhibitions and developing them further. I see this as an unfinished exercise that grows constantly. The destabilizing effects of the stories, archival materials, forms and performativity are activated by my use of both fundamental concepts – time and language – in these non-traditional ways. Spatial examination unfolds through the deconstruction of the cinematic apparatus and filmic environment, as well as the institutions. The relationship between the works doesn't follow a linear chronology. Rather, in understanding the methods of history, speculative stories and text pieces that could add to voiceover narration or act as subtitles, official records and personal anecdotes come together in a choreographed activation. Maybe the distance or condition of the observer determines the result?

In a way, it becomes an active space that dissolves between a performance or an exhibition. I'm always interested in this moment when the piece can become performative by itself and creates a duration, with sequences during which some sculptures turn on and others turn off. A very complex endeavour in this sense was my exhibition at the Neue Nationalgalerie in 2021. Fifteen different works were choreographed and sequenced over a repeating forty-five-minute period. Even if the sequence repeated, one wouldn't enter the exact experience of the exhibition again, as the films were looped and the ends and beginnings shifted, fragmenting and translating the meaning and experience constantly from one thing to another, keeping it in motion or unstable. Adding the investigative form of play and its form of rupture is a method to reach the space of the sublime, which is a total space. In the words of the poet Susan Howe, it's 'a hum of the possible … neither legible, nor intelligible'.

I make deliberate decisions to unscrew cinema and reconfigure it through various expansions or contractions, up- and downscaling, suspending machinery and removing elements. That's how the new machine is produced and triggered. That trigger also results in the material having its own life, a life that articulates itself anew. Through choice and decision making, the material also reacts in its own way. Both actions are involved.

COMER: *To some extent, this interaction between elements speaks to a wider interest you have in collectivity and community. How did this become of interest to you and why is it such a focus in the work?*

BARBA: Even as far back as the mid-1990s, when I first began to work with film in my artistic studies, I had doubts about the cinematic apparatus that I'd inherited. I was overwhelmed by the overproduction and rigidity of all the elements that went into film, as well as by the overstimulation of the senses: the simultaneous overloading of both the audio and visual, according to a predetermined set of elements and standards that exist for presenting and consuming film in the cinema. Straight away, I developed a need to reduce those elements down to single tracks, giving each component much greater space – each gaining its own independent narrative layer – by playing around with and fragmenting them. This is evident in works like *Spacelength Thought*, *Stating the Real Sublime* (2009), *Boundaries of Consumption* (2012) and *One Way Out* (2009).

I also examined the possibility of activating the collective's subconscious as an artistic method in order to embark with it into an oscillating environment. I made works in search of the liminal, of spaces that exist in our world but only become visible through contrast with other spaces that they contest. Therefore, I use cinema in order to stage an intervention in a real space, confronting the division between public and private, fantasy and reality, to open up a hidden space – accessible through the interaction with the camera and the bodies.

My concern with the collective began early with my single-channel films, starting with *Panzano*, as 'collective performances' that have been recorded and conducted for my films and follow a precise set of negotiations and improvisation. In the terminology of contemporary dance and performance, 'choreography' and 'improvisation' are no longer antonyms, since improvisation can be included in choreographed pieces, as well as improvisation itself being sometimes choreographed. The organizing of the groups of

from left,
HEAR, THERE, WHERE THE ECHOES ARE, 2016–21
16MM PROJECTORS, 35MM PROJECTOR, GLASS FILTERS, SCREEN, SOUND, PERFORMATIVE ELEMENT

FROM SOURCE TO POEM, 2016
35MM FILM, COLOUR, OPTICAL SOUND
12 MIN

COLOR STUDIES, 2013
2 X 16MM FILM PROJECTORS, 2 X 16MM FILMS, SCREEN
EACH 2 MIN

THE LONG POEM MANIPULATES SPATIAL ORGANIZATIONS, 2014
MODIFIED PROJECTOR, PLINTH, STENCIL CUT, 16MM COLOUR FILM

INSTALLATION VIEW AT THE NEUE NATIONALGALERIE, BERLIN, 2021

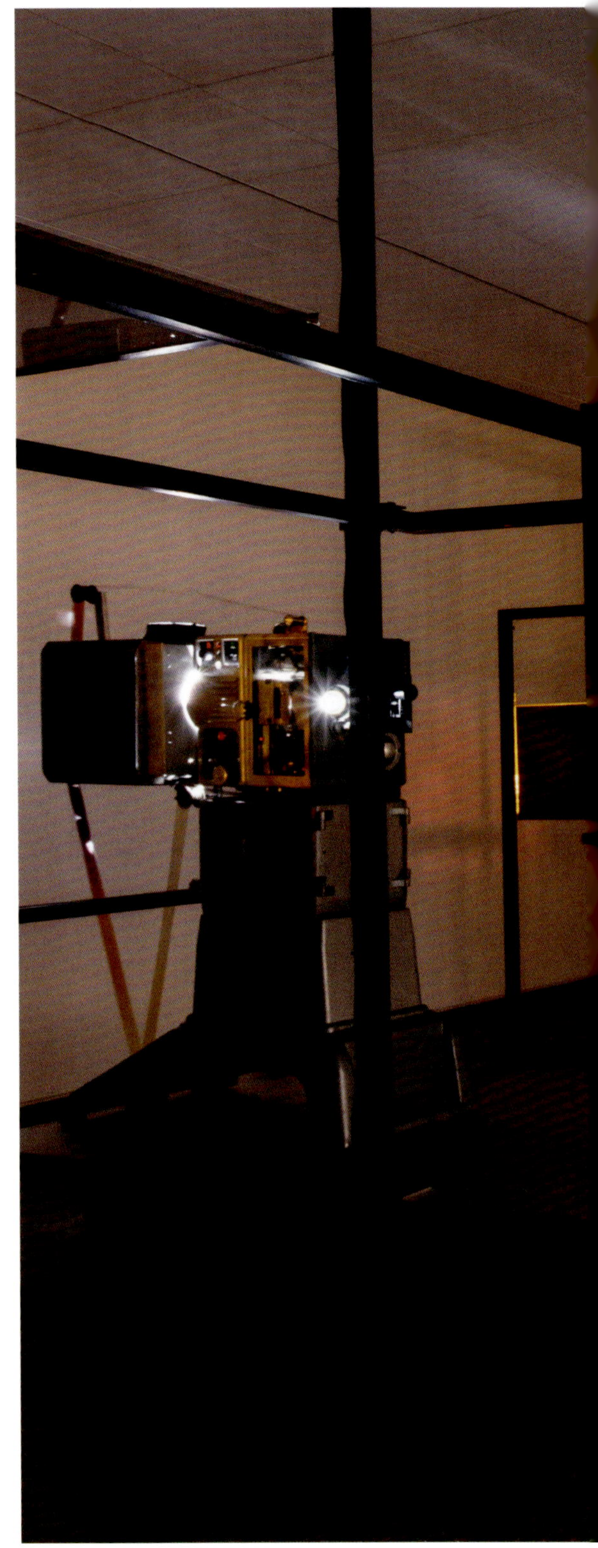

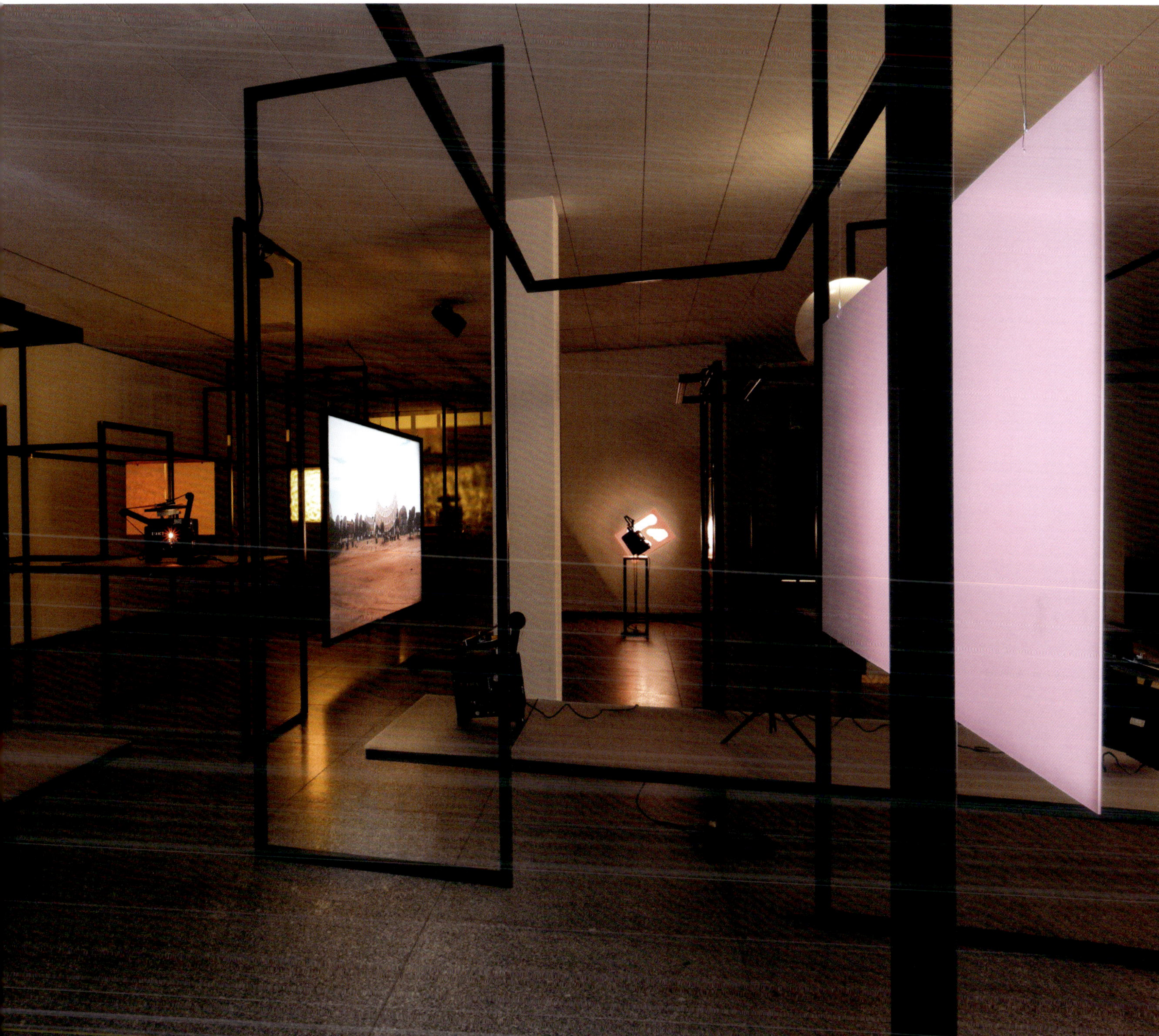

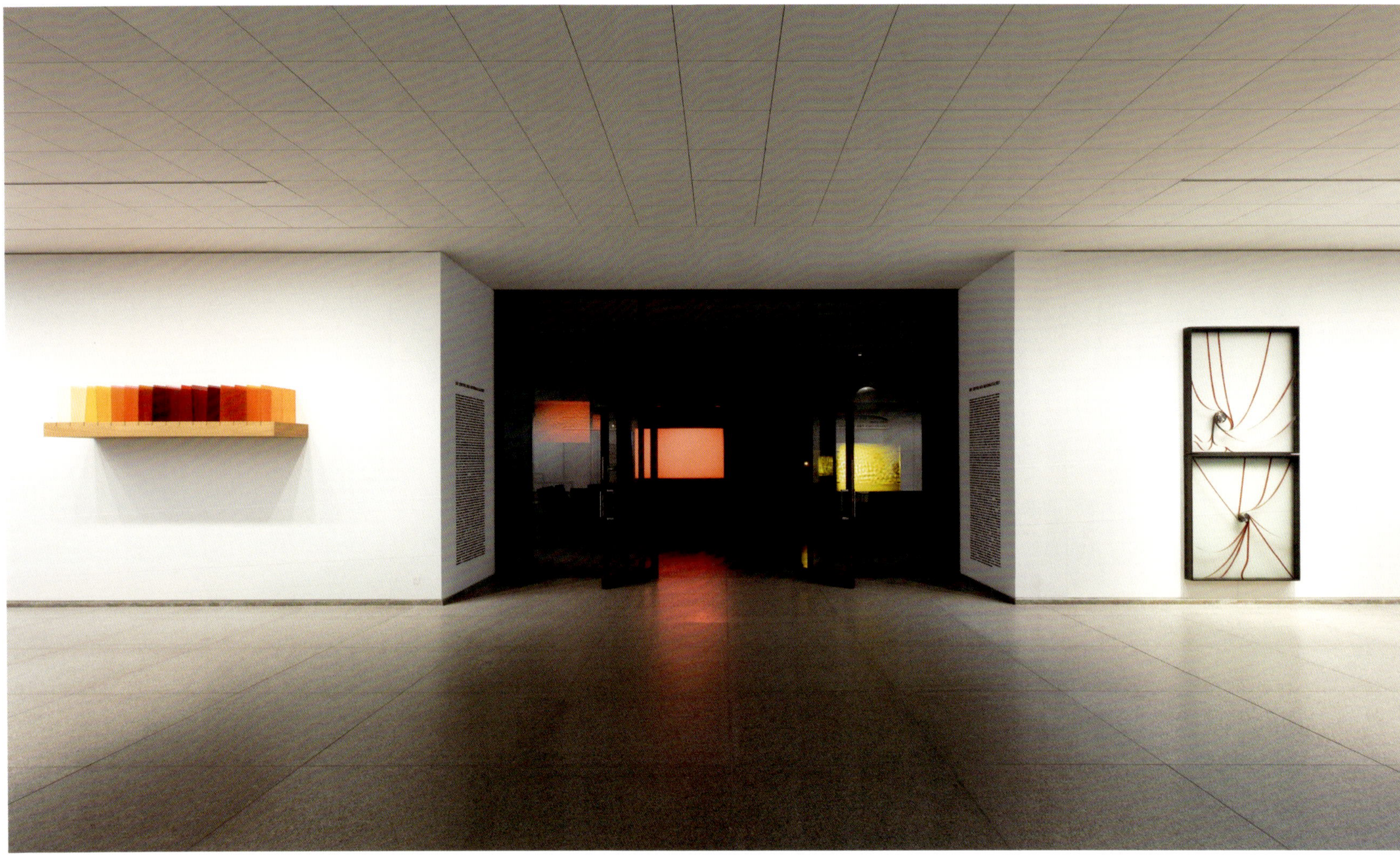

these 'actors', as I call them, into coherent performative entities is a result of a process where I instruct them in ways to envision the narrative and the film. They're invited to (re)act based on who they are and how they feel the narrative should be represented in the film, drawing on the individual histories and memories embedded in their bodies, which constitute a sort of physiological archive, and deciding how these histories should be released from their bodies. I believe that we constantly accumulate experiences and the knowledge that's produced from them in our bodies – a sort of 'mind-body memory', which often isn't released or converted into forms that can be put toward collective knowledge contributions.

COMER: *With the rapid transformations prompted by the surge of recent AI technologies, archives and collections have become valuable new forms of data to be mined and even exploited. Your work was already arguably to some extent at odds with the smooth surfaces and seamless spaces of the digital world. Do you want to resist or contradict some of these developments, or find new forms of friction and dialogue between the analogue past and the digital present? There's already much to learn from machines in your work. How does this shift in the era of machine learning?*

BARBA: I'm trying to produce ideas by introducing fissures, fragility and spatial explorations through resistance and contradiction to certain developments of the digital. Often, I'm in dialogue with it too, when exploring digital phenomena through an analogue lens.

In my installation projects, often the machinery – the hardware of cinema, the projector – is explored for its sculptural quality. It's the protagonist of the works, but also its own viewer. It resembles a fragile relic and evokes already archaic (and disappearing) techniques, equipment and modes of production. For example, in *Spacelength Thought*,

opposite, from left,
THIS SPACE POPULATED BY INFINITE COLORS, 2021
HANDBLOWN GLASS, WOOD
248 X 56 X 54 CM

HEAR, THERE, WHERE THE ECHOES ARE, 2016–21
16MM PROJECTORS, 35MM PROJECTOR, GLASS FILTERS, SCREEN, SOUND, PERFORMATIVE ELEMENT

UNCERTAIN THEME – AND THEREFORE ABSTRACT, 2021
STEEL, GLASS, MOTOR, 35MM FILM
EACH 123 X 140 X 12 CM

below, from left,
COLOR STUDIES, 2013
2 X 16MM FILM PROJECTORS, 2 X 16MM FILMS, SCREEN
EACH 2 MIN

CONDUCTOR, 2014
SILICONE MEMBRANE, MOTOR, SOUND
Ø 60 CM

FROM SOURCE TO POEM, 2016
35MM FILM, COLOUR, OPTICAL SOUND
12 MIN

INSTALLATION VIEW AT NEUE NATIONALGALERIE, BERLIN, 2021

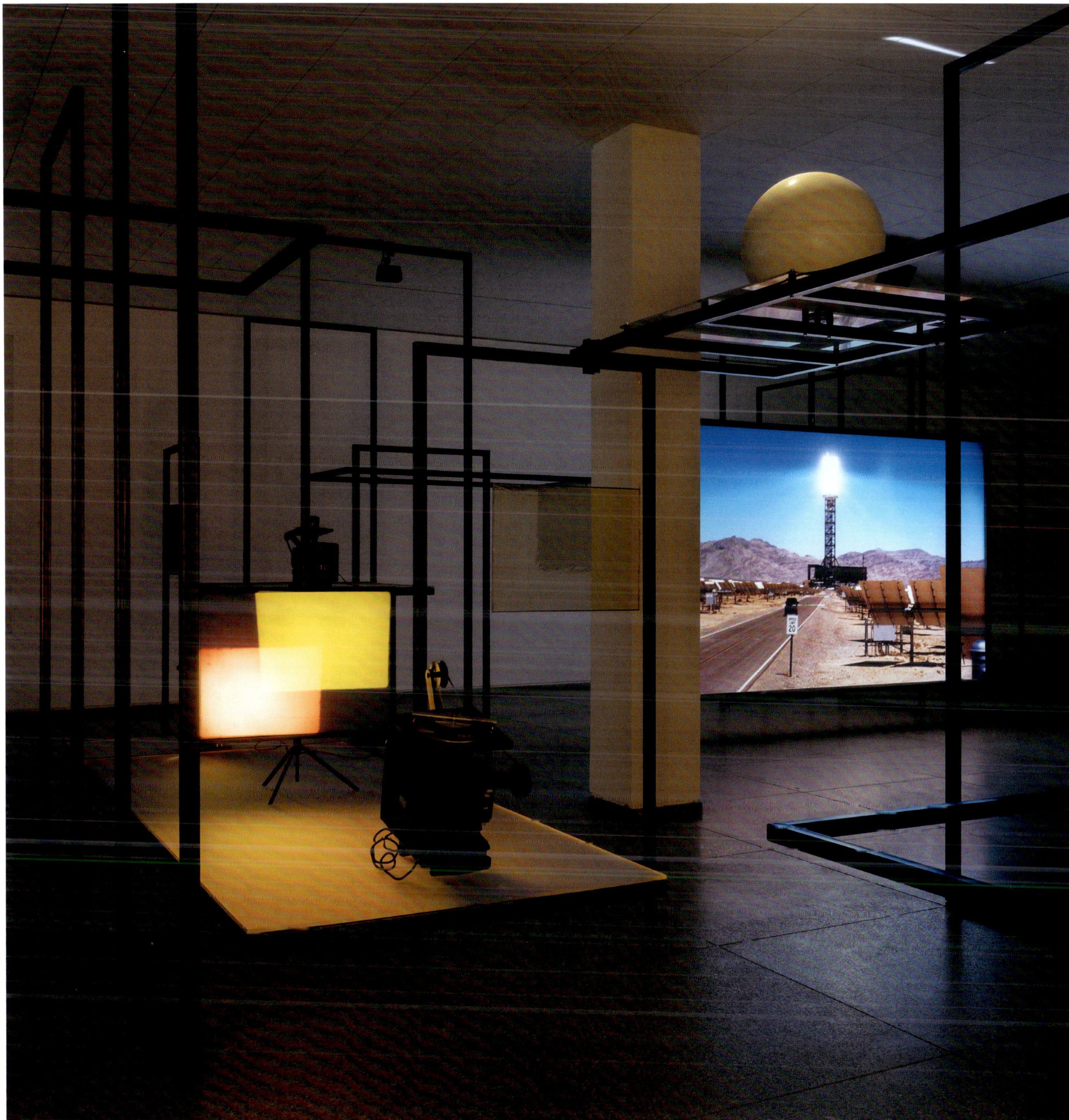

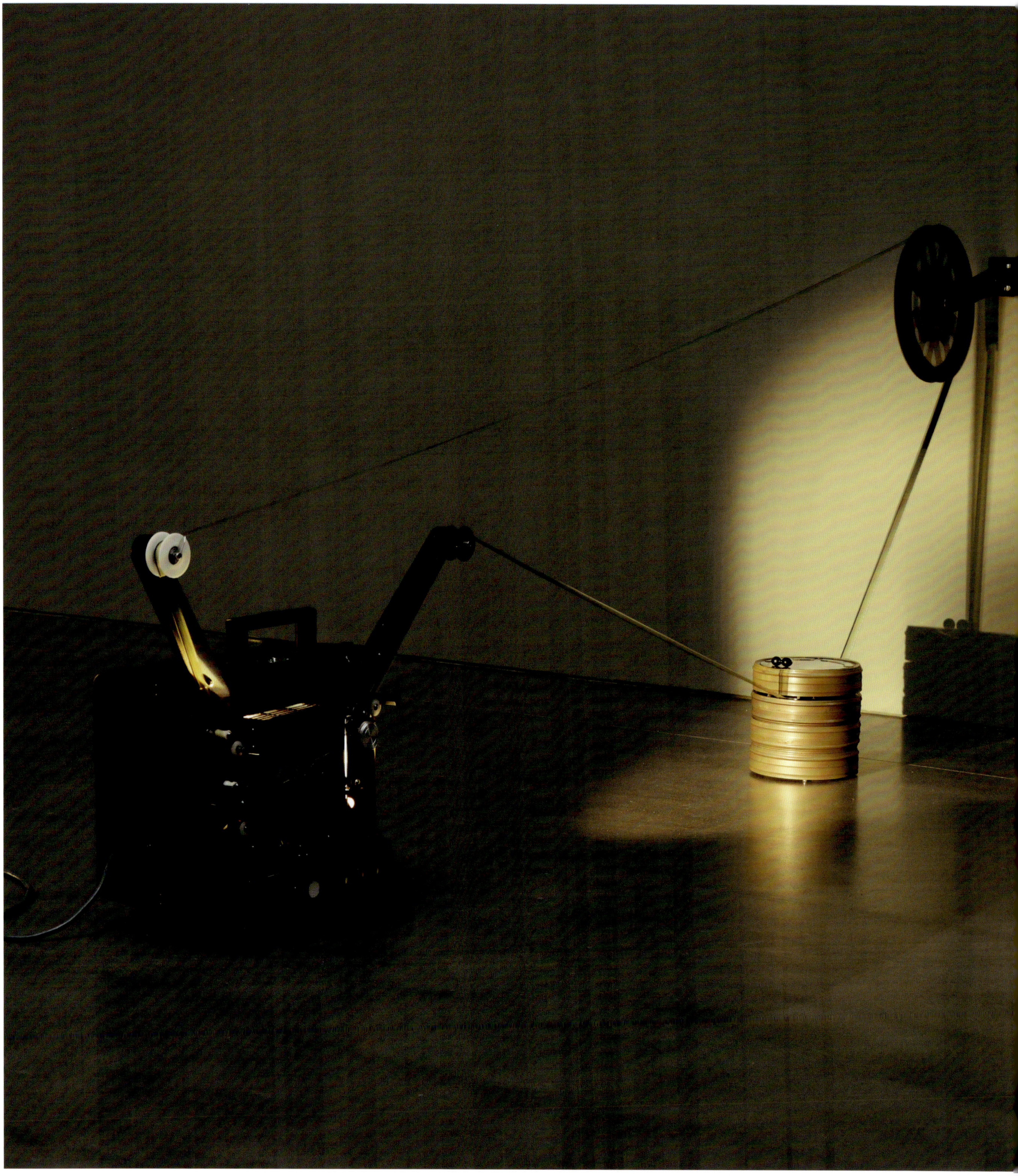

BOUNDARIES OF CONSUMPTION, 2012
16MM FILM, MODIFIED PROJECTOR, FILM CANS, 2 METAL SPHERES

INSTALLATION VIEW AT ALBERTINUM DRESDEN, 2015

which I mentioned earlier, much like a Turing machine, a mechanical code is being recited and revealed through the projection, creating a kind of poetry – an imagistic form of language. At the same time, the piece functions as an enigmatic machine and a transparent process. It presents language as an image produced through a sequence of code or data, embodying the principles of concrete poetry. In concrete poetry, the poet approaches language in a way in which it no longer serves to describe facts, thoughts, or emotions; instead, language itself becomes both the subject and the purpose of the poem, revealing its own inherent qualities through the use of a sort of physics particle method. Both in *Spacelength Thought* and in a Turing machine, an idea is constructed. My work refers to the idea and not the machine or the coding itself.

I'm rather interested in the idea as an abstract machine or an abstract methodology; the code that's created through the machine is the machine. It's a theoretical mechanism, a meta-machine that writes its own code. It represents an algorithm, a programme, or a sequence of symbols, whether these are letters, numbers or so on. These step-by-step manipulations of symbols or characters are written onto a tape, which can then theoretically be read and interpreted (in the sense of instructions) and become ideas. Any logical action can be reconstructed (much like digital code works). The typing machine acts as an author, but the production of the text doesn't adapt to human reading practices; it extends the production time of a single word, even a single letter, and moves at the pace of the celluloid. It's a manic writer, driven by a powerful production energy, endlessly inscribing text into film. The text producer projects only fragments onto the wall. The whole text is only readable during the exhibition after it has piled up on the floor. The film-text is produced on location, seconds before it's projected onto the wall, and remains and builds up on the floor as a winding cloud of printed film.

My aim is to release machines from their functionality with a sort of fragility or balancing act and make them explore other things. They can be used as one component of many to orchestrate a body of experience through working with the 'autonomy of the material' and with space in a very physical and almost tangible way. The significance of these interventions in the operation of the machines is that they may break the grip of utilitarian and functional definitions of the world and introduce new possibilities and shades of meaning and experience. Fragmenting and translating the meaning constantly from one thing to another, keeping it in motion or unstable, can open up these possibilities. It allows for a second becoming. By 'second becoming', I mean when something undergoes a certain metamorphosis by transforming its form and function. This process of rewiring or reworking the system thus results in a second becoming. These author-made machines aren't for transparent reading and consumption by the audience, but rather they can potentially open up new intellectual and emotional spaces for us.

I also introduce play as a stage or period of exploration where there's no immediate idea of reaching a goal. It's not constructed through production and it's not driven by a hope to earn something from the process. In play, there's no immediate notion of gain; it's rather an ongoing process of exploration and drift.

To use the contemporary language that defines the virtual and the physical in digital culture, with all the cinema hardware I use, I also produce kinds of software – which are almost immaterial applications through which I hope new mental or intellectual spaces are opened up for the viewer.

The new machine learning era often excludes spatial and collective relations. The digital seems to be a more democratic and accessible tool, but it also creates forms of exclusion and is less supportive of the collective. Licensing and intellectual property rights are less in the foreground, and the digital realm creates storytelling readymades.

COMER: *How do you think the documentary function of works like* Aggregate States of Matters *is transformed by the format of the installation? The viewer is inscribed within a system in which the hierarchies of cinema's various components are reconfigured; they become part of a ritual in the gallery that connects to the actions encountered on the screen in a distinctly physical – not purely visual or passive – manner. How have the strategies in your more abstract work impacted your approach to documenting subjects such as the Quechua and Uru-Iruito communities in Peru?*

BARBA: Looking for 'documents' in the landscape – which manifest themselves in sculptural ways, and which might grow into possibilities of fictional layers – is always an important method in my work. This process draws and expands on visual impressions and social interactions from my previous films, and also picks up on specific forms and appearances from shorter films that I shot in the desert.

Transformation in landscapes, whether it originates from its complex history of global development and human interventions or due to ecological concerns such as climate change, have long been the starting points for my films. My work *Outwardly from Earth's Center* focuses on Gotska Sandön, a small island in Sweden that drifts north due to tidal currents, moving one metre further away from the mainland every year. I constructed a narrative about how to tie the island to the sea; the act of anchoring the land to water transformed it from a mere object into a powerful idea. In the film, I begin with a specific subject and then explore the myriad possibilities that unfold from it. The narrative concludes with an aerial shot and hints at the idea of a potential solution. This work speculates on how the concept of documentation can evolve into a sculpture and reflect societal influences as an unintended consequence. There's a temporal element to a document or history, which we can observe or enter, and in my films, historical data is often transposed into a subjective voiceover or text layer. To quote Gilles Deleuze in his text *Desert Islands*, 'Some islands drifted away from the continent, but the island is also that toward which one drifts; other islands originated in the ocean, but the island is also the origin, radical and absolute.'

These speculative stories – articulated through voiceover, subtitles and text pieces from non-actors – are temporally indeterminate and are drawn from both official records and the personal anecdotes of people who live close to the subjects I investigate, often drawing on a core of facts, characters and places that populate established histories, recorded information and documented sources about the locations I film. I interview people around those sites by asking the questions that I'd like to pose in my film, even though I don't repeat these questions in the work. The different views I collect help me add layers to my construction while also helping to define the desire of a society composed of rational and irrational occurrences, enabling a deeper understanding and respect of the world we share.

An important methodology for me when working with this society – which can also be a memory of a community introduced through work in archives – is the inclusion of language that enters from a participating group and introduces a movement of thought, thus providing a 'real' movement into the image. The fiction in my work comes from this kind of modulation of text. Flicker here means the becoming legible of the illegibility of the text.

A core that immediately deteriorates. I introduce other possibilities into the text, or the people I include in my films introduce wishes or visions for a subject that isn't real. These act as instruments to push the idea further. These wishes are anchored in real statements of people or from literature; for example, in *From Source to Poem*, the idea of the Library of Babel correlates with the Library of Congress.

In *Aggregate States of Matters*, I thought of a title through which I could describe a physical state of a landscape, but also a collective experience that reflects different time layers from past to future – something that's at the same time a power unit but also liquid material; a psychological landscape in transformation and a sort of magnetic field between its inhabitants. This psychological landscape gets projected into the exhibition space and the experiences are passed on to the exhibition audience.

While preparing, but also shooting *Aggregate States of Matters*, I interviewed many people from several Indigenous communities – including Quechua communities and the Uru-Iruito community – as well as local archivists and geologists. With

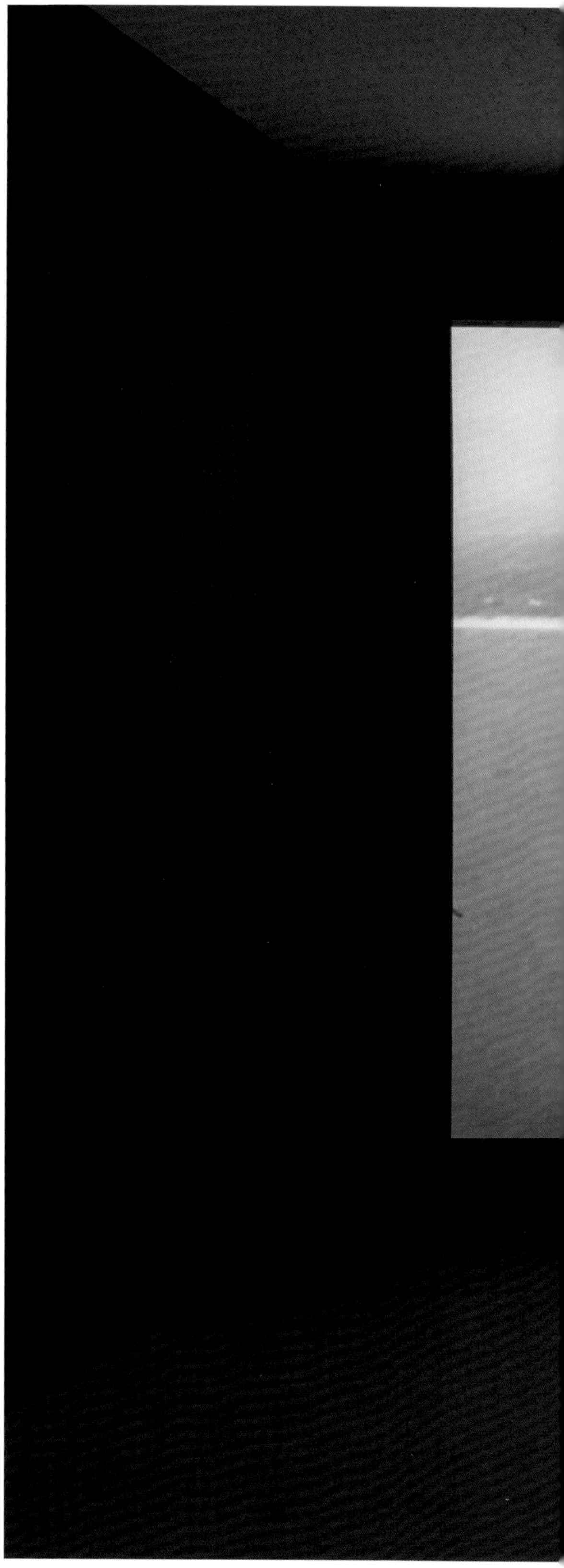

OUTWARDLY FROM EARTH'S CENTER, 2007
16MM FILM TRANSFERRED TO VIDEO, COLOUR, SOUND
22 MIN.

INSTALLATION VIEW AT CENTER FOR CONTEMPORARY ART, KITAKYUSHU, 2019

next pages,
OUTWARDLY FROM EARTH'S CENTER, 2007
16MM FILM TRANSFERRED TO VIDEO, COLOUR, SOUND
22 MIN

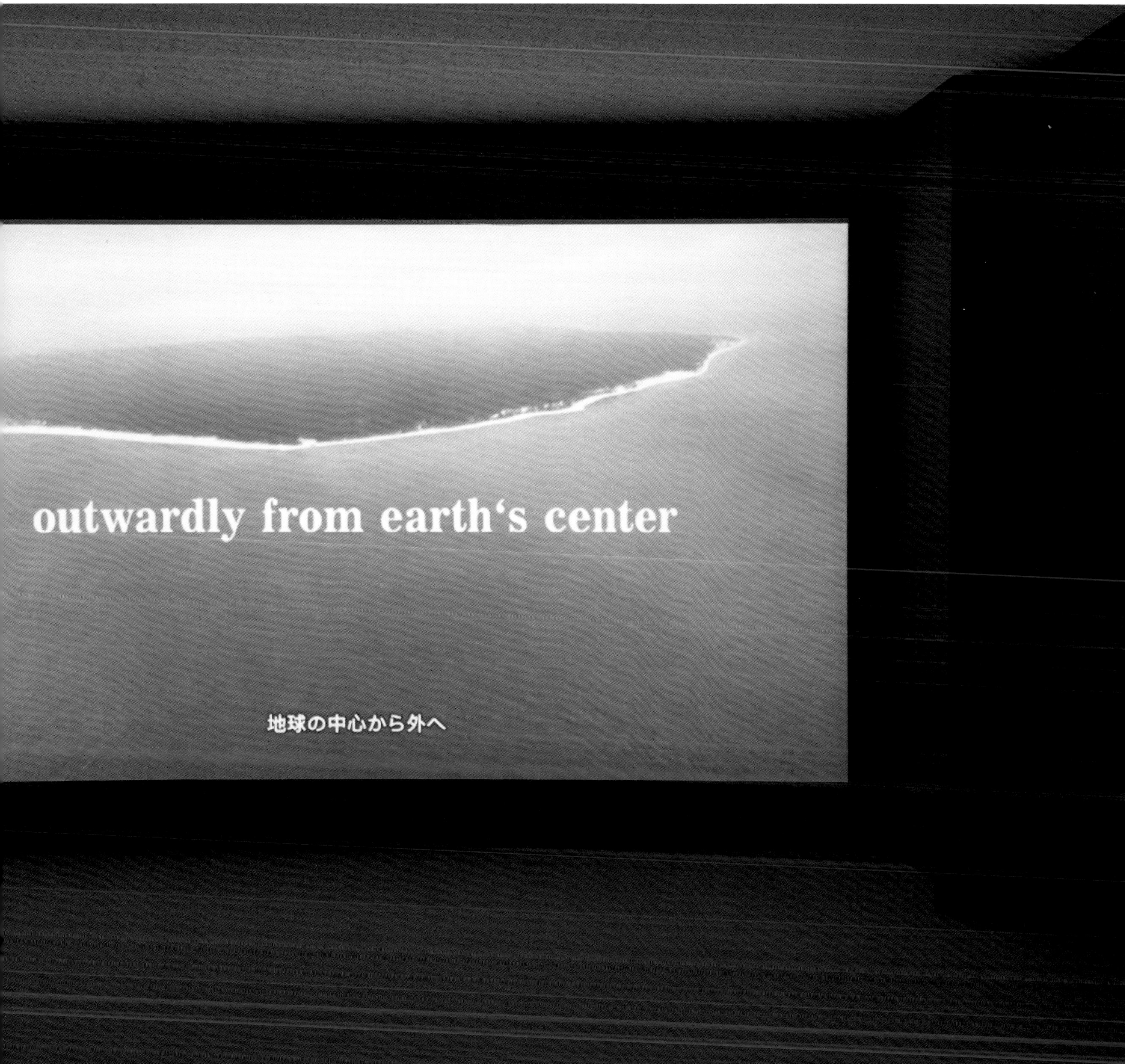
outwardly from earth's center
地球の中心から外へ

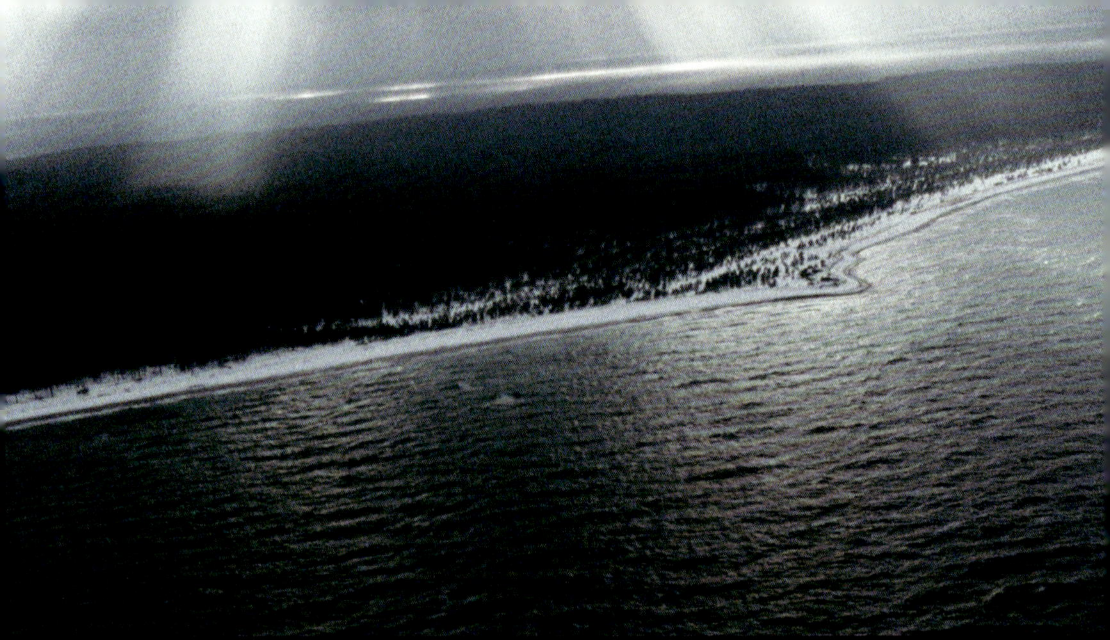

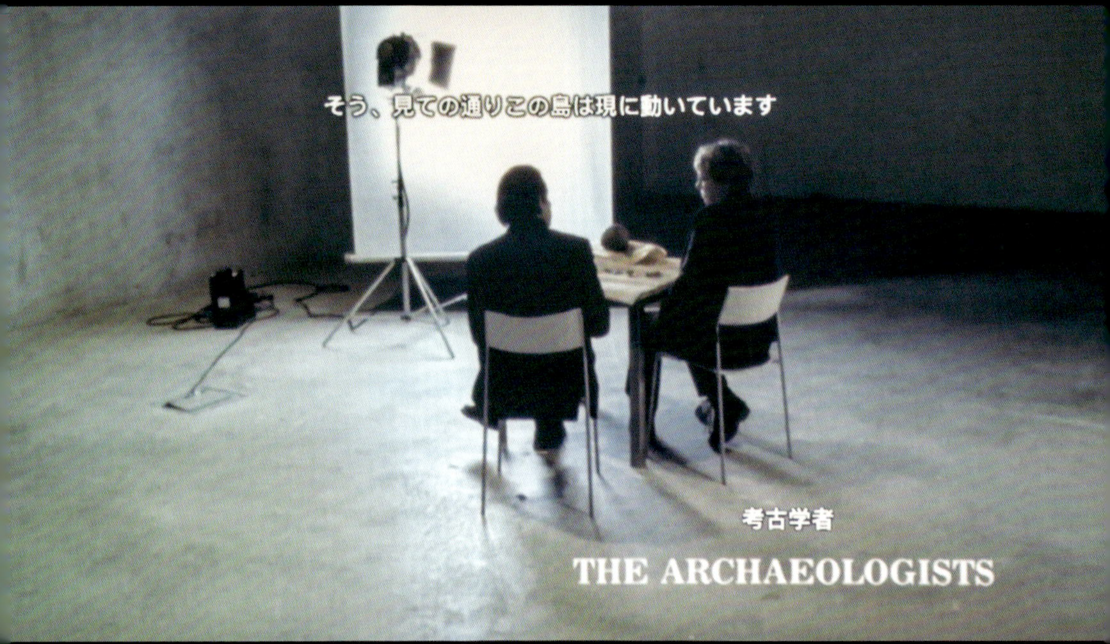
そう、見ての通りこの島は現に動いています
考古学者
THE ARCHAEOLOGISTS

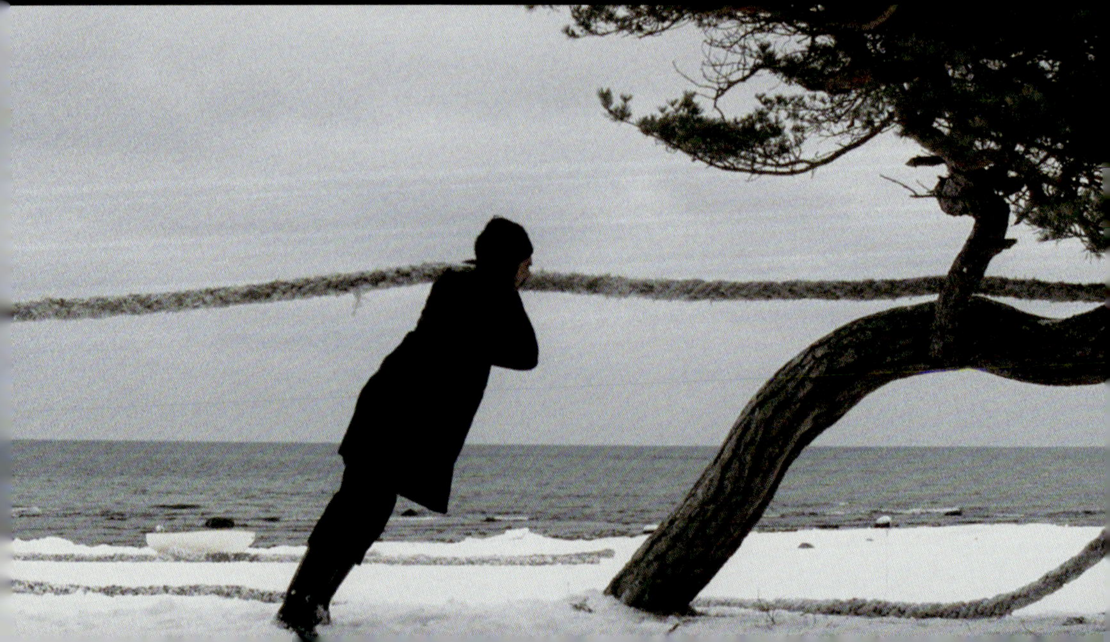

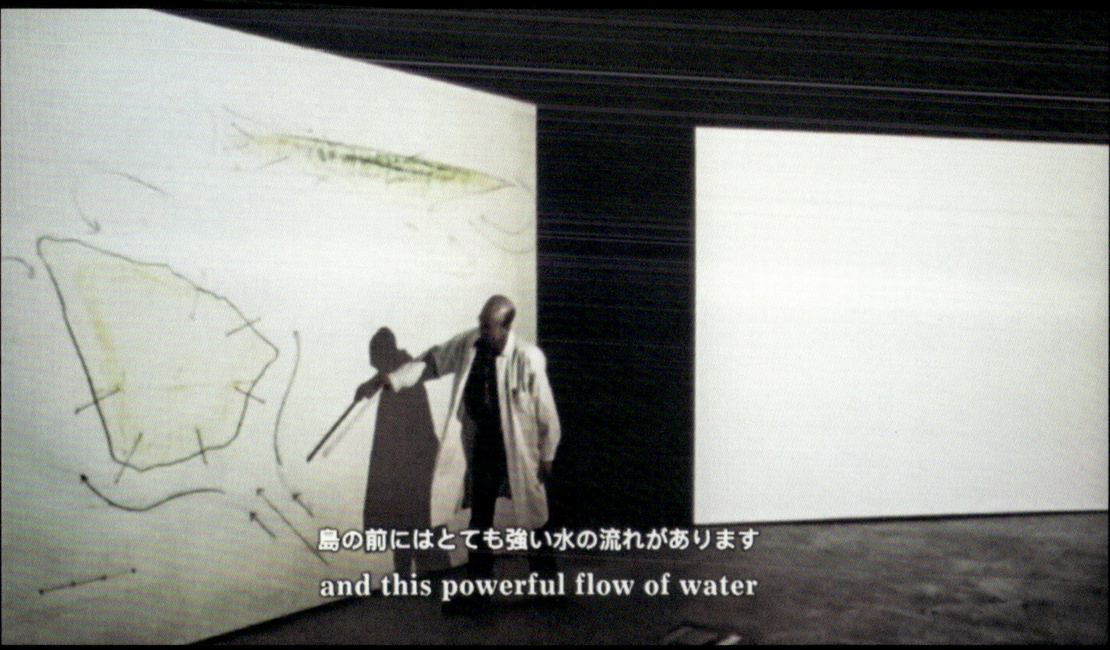
島の前にはとても強い水の流れがあります
and this powerful flow of water

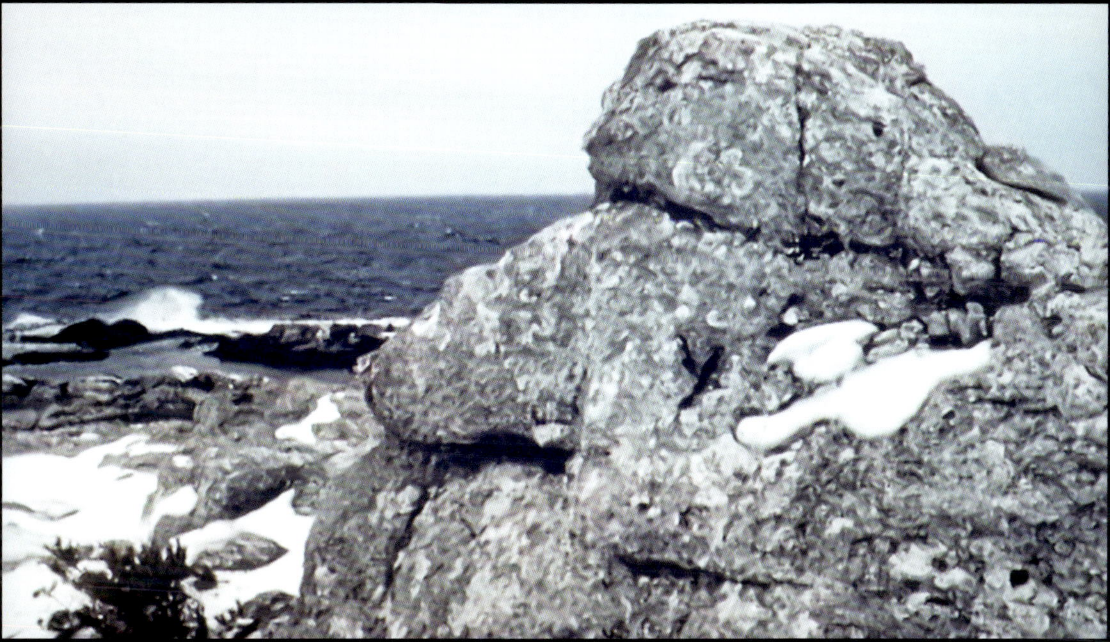

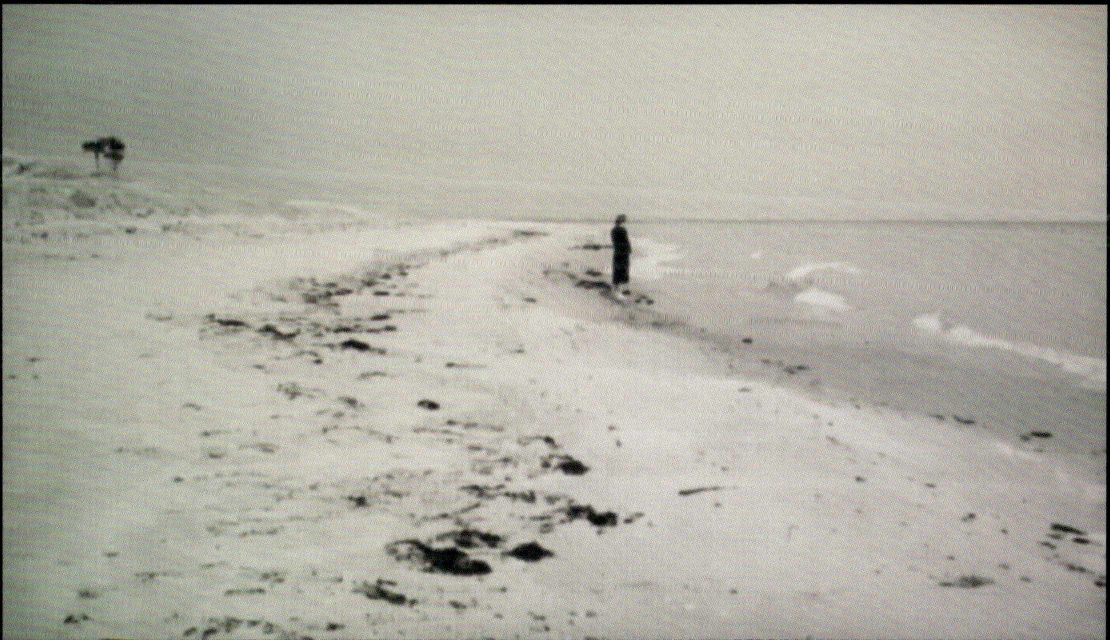

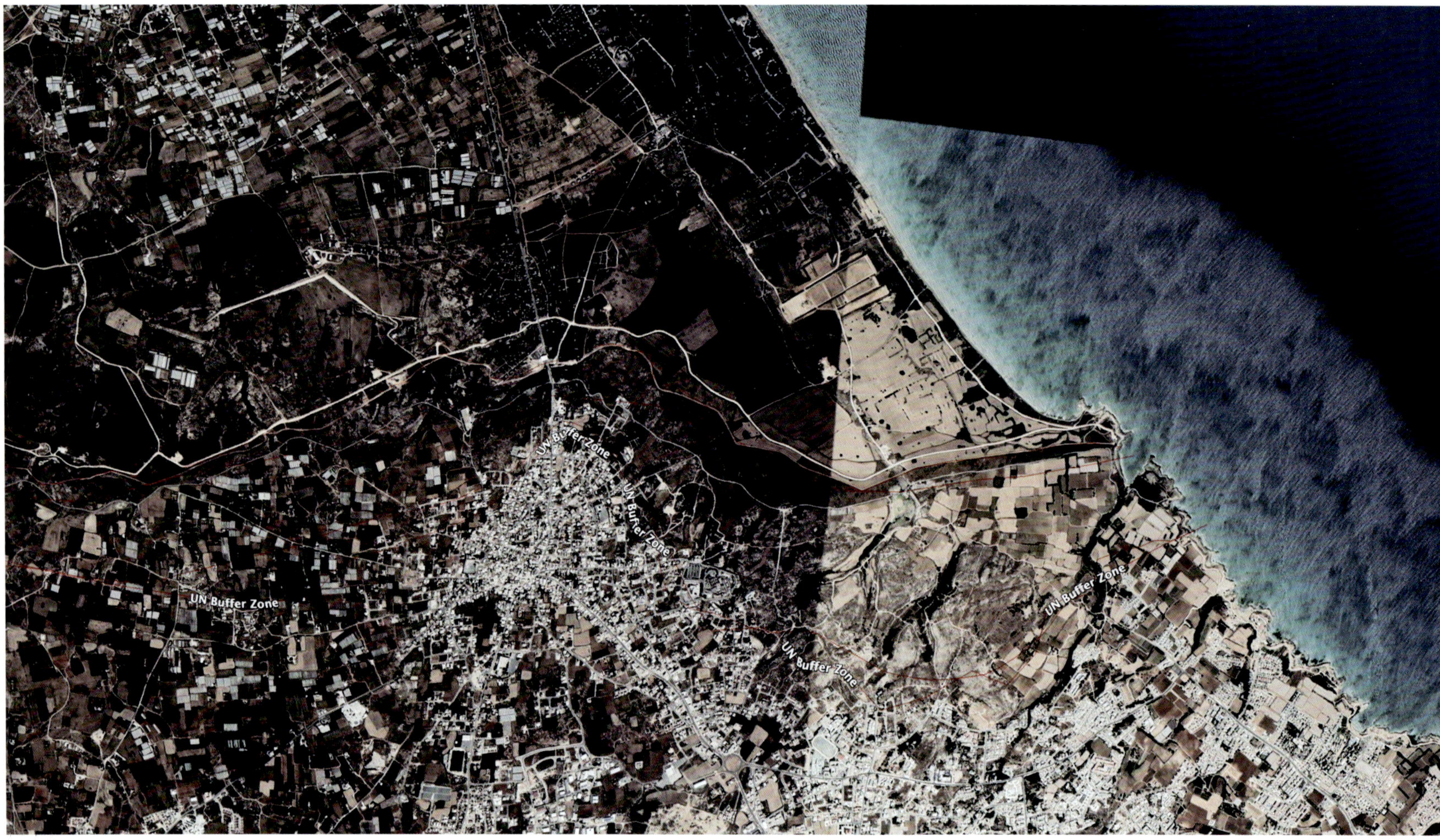

particular respect to the experiences of the Indigenous communities that were relayed to me, and which are shared orally throughout generations, I didn't want to include them as voiceovers but rather find a way for these stories to become part of the landscape as well, letting the voices appear as a visual transcription and at the same time inhabit the image. The text layers build up and keep moving, so that a linear reading isn't really possible. I'm always interested in finding ways to fragment language into forms where a non-chronological sense of time can be introduced to the viewer/reader.

COMER: *Your project* Inside the Outset: Evoking a Space of Passage, *an open-air site in Cyprus, is a fascinating example of how you provide space for both the afterlives and the active spaces of cinema to coincide. This is an important work in which the relationship between the film and the land it records are more than symbiotic or indexical. The frame itself produces the encounter, but also becomes part of its afterlife, part of the system of entropy that erodes both land and celluloid, but also a prompt for new forms of community formation. How did you develop this project, and how does it engage with the specificity of Cyprus?*

BARBA: In 2013, I was invited by Point Centre for Contemporary Art in Nicosia to explore the island and propose a project. After that I proposed to build a cinema sculpture in the Buffer zone that has marked the separation between the North and South since 1974. I envisioned the location of this open-air installation to function as a meeting point for members of all communities on the island, a place where people could freely walk to. The idea was to build an amphitheatre with a permeable screen on which films could be watched from both the southern and the northern side. Working with this political landscape, I aimed to counterbalance existing images of conflict with an emphatic expression of solidarity and openness, thus transforming the image of division into a shared experience.

left,
INSIDE THE OUTSET: EVOKING A SPACE OF PASSAGE, 2021
16MM FILM TRANSFERRED TO DIGITAL AND 8K FILM, SOUND, 31 MIN. 15 SEC

below,
INSIDE THE OUTSET: EVOKING A SPACE OF PASSAGE, 2021
OPEN AIR CINEMA SPACE
RAMMED EARTH SCREEN, APPROXIMATE OVERALL OPEN-AIR SCREENING AREA: 555 CM
30.5 X 30.5 M
SCREEN SIZE: 450 X 800 CM

INSTALLATION VIEW AT THE BUFFER ZONE, DERYNEIA, CYPRUS, 2021

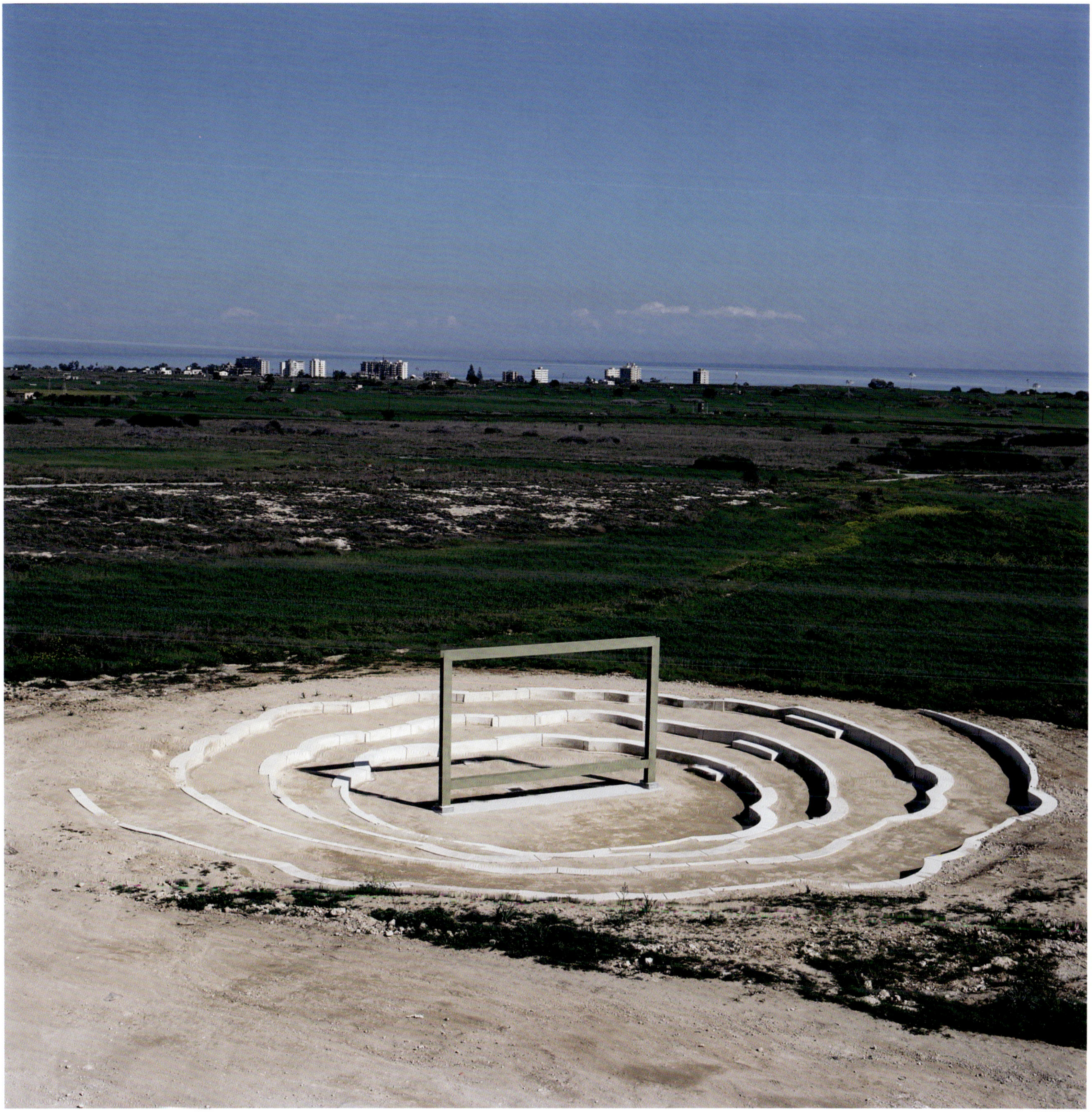

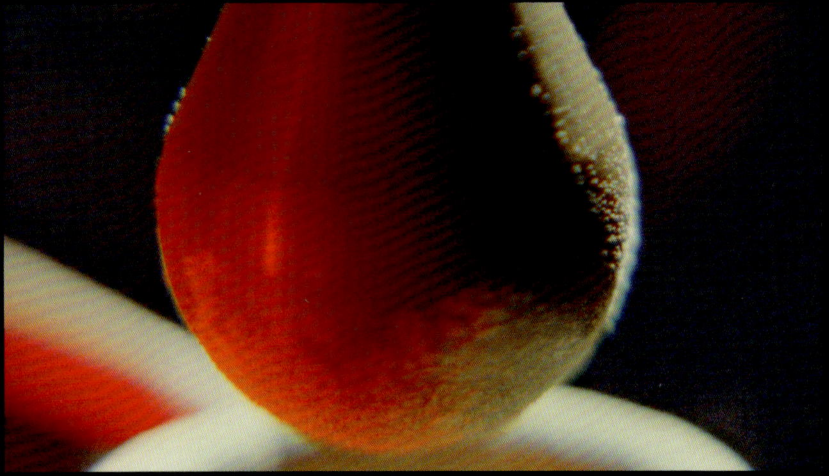
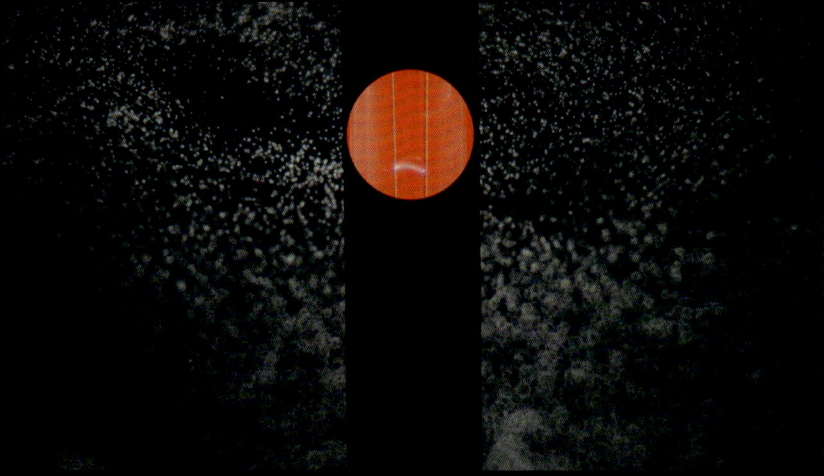
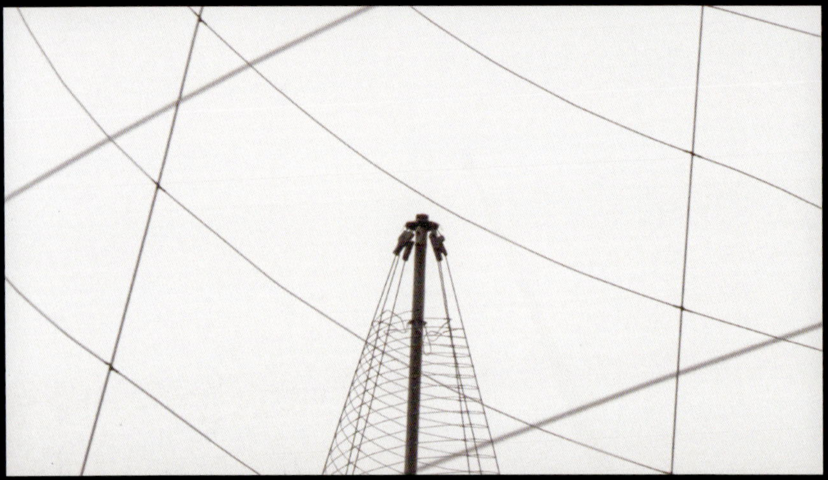
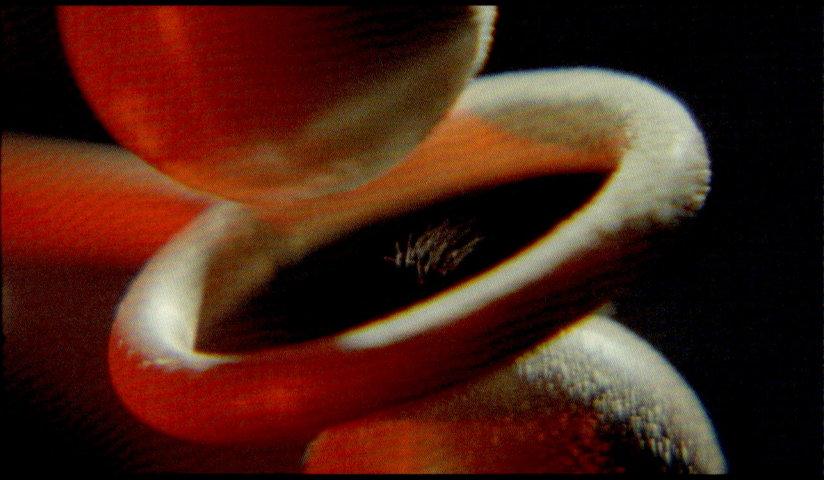
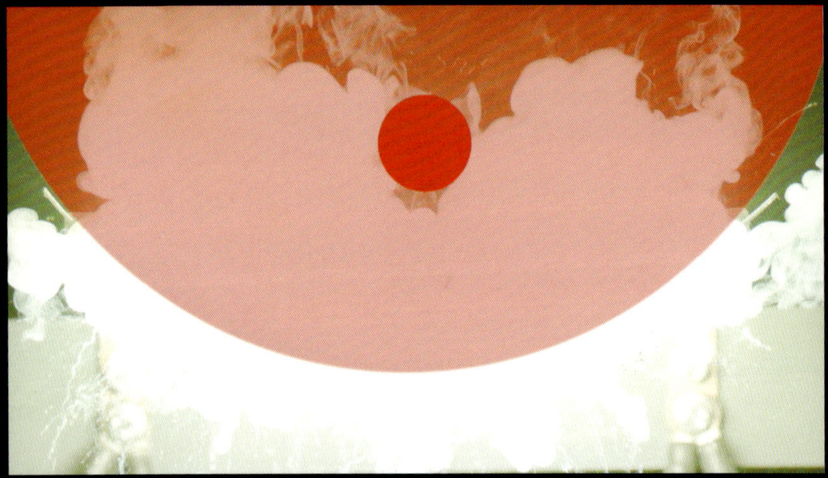
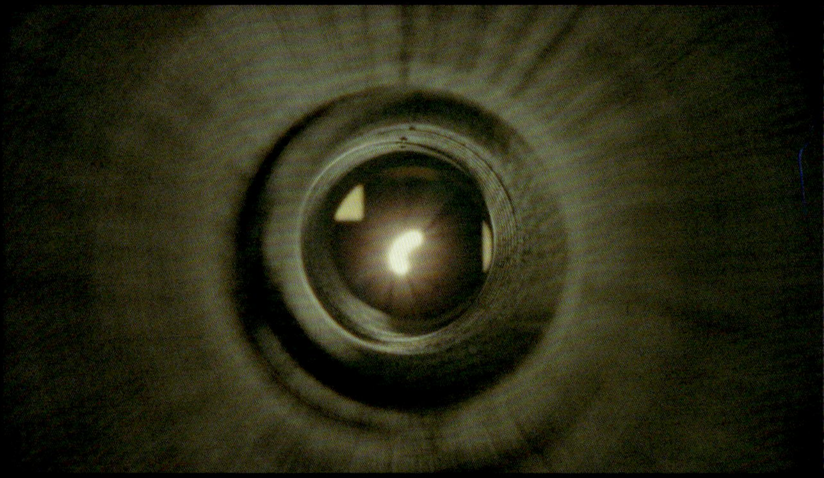
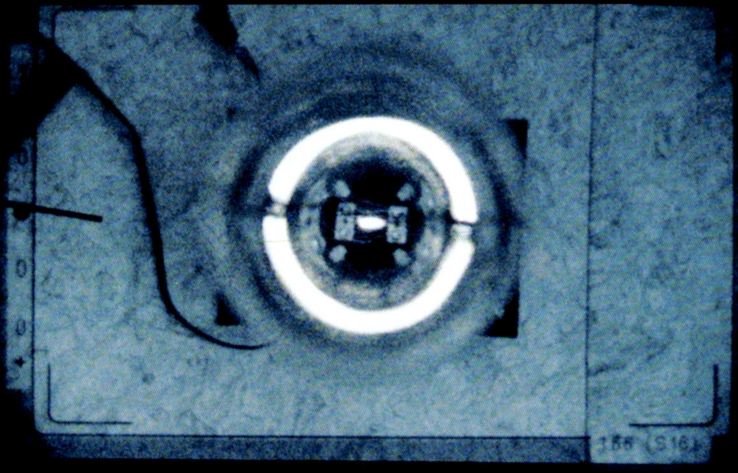
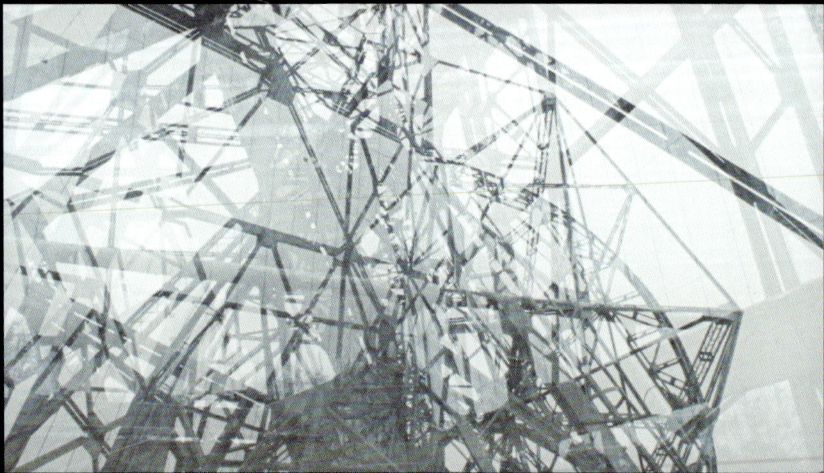

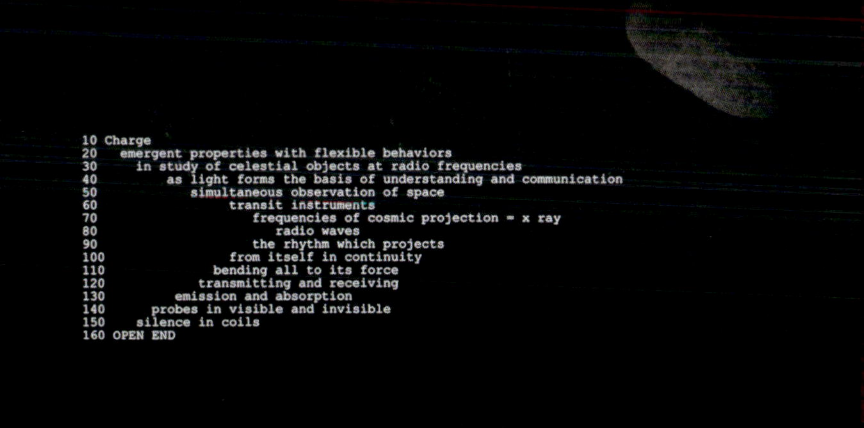
10 Charge
20 emergent properties with flexible behaviors
30 in study of celestial objects at radio frequencies
40 as light forms the basis of understanding and communication
50 simultaneous observation of space
60 transit instruments
70 frequencies of cosmic projection = x ray
80 radio waves
90 the rhythm which projects
100 from itself in continuity
110 bending all to its force
120 transmitting and receiving
130 emission and absorption
140 probes in visible and invisible
150 silence in coils
160 OPEN END

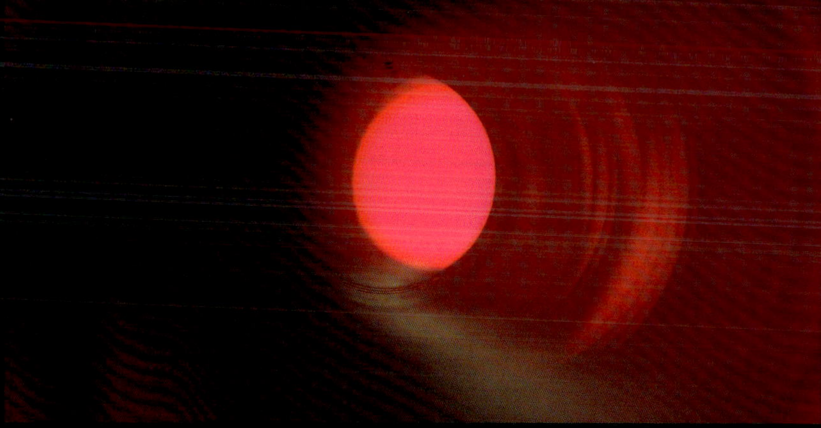

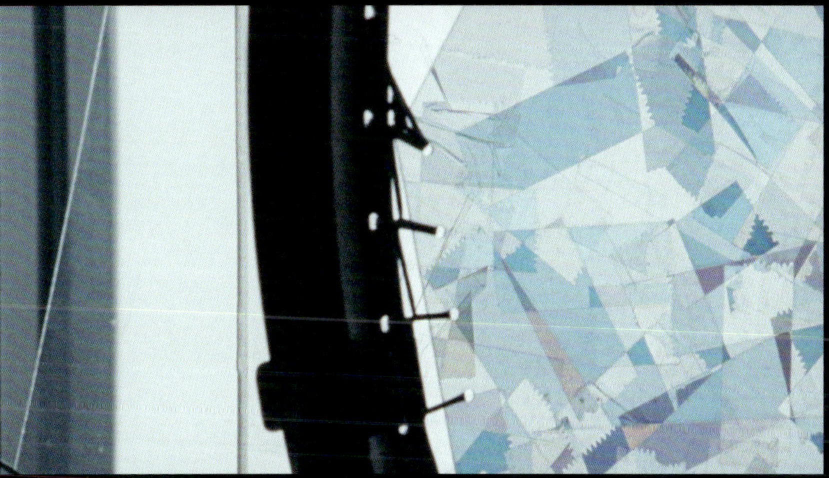

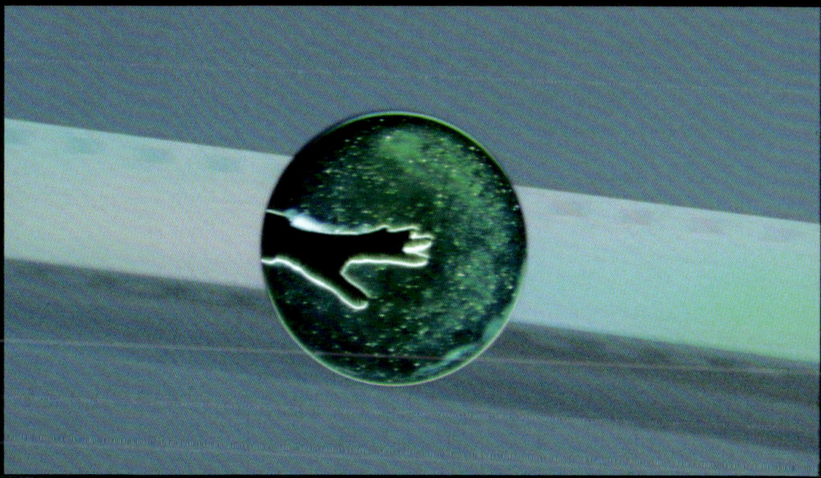

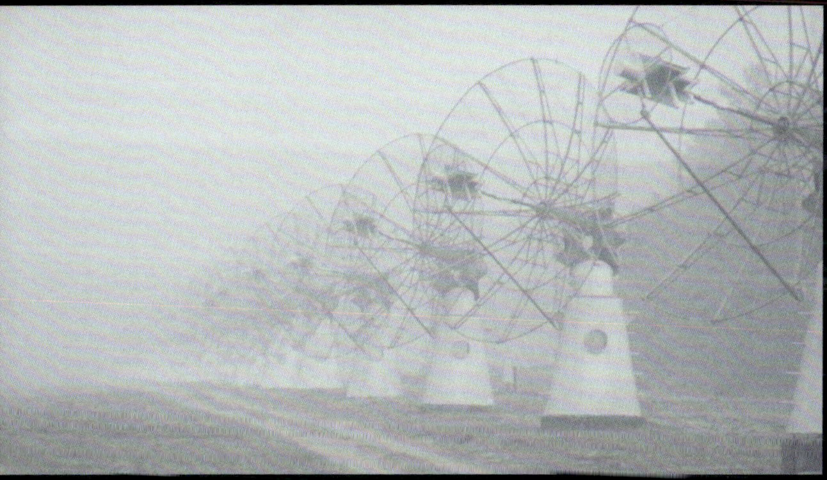

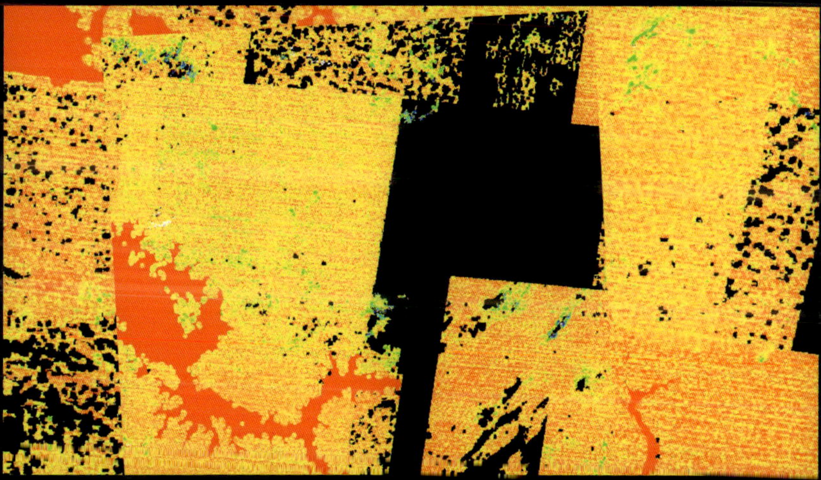

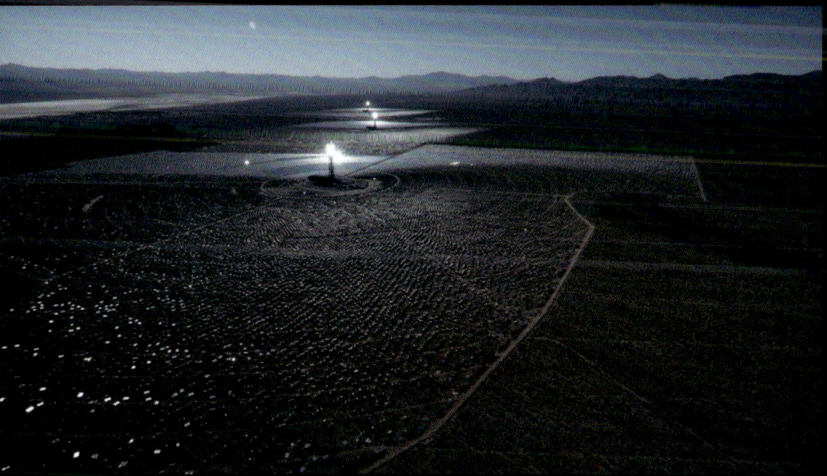

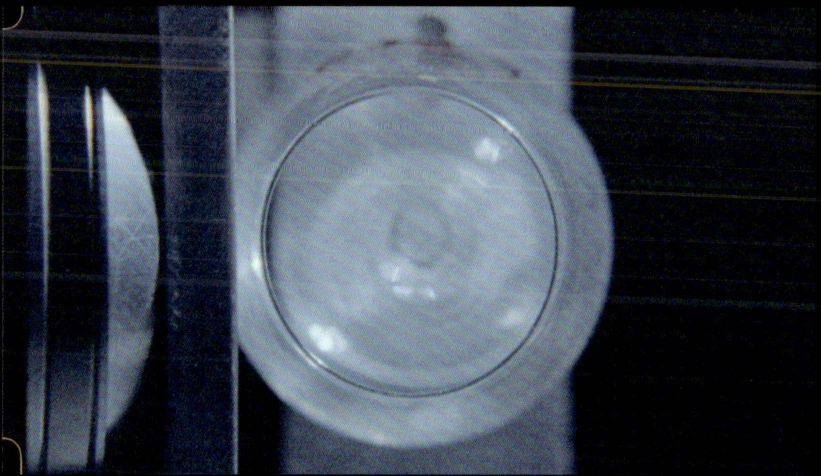

previous pages and opposite,
CHARGE, 2025
35MM FILM, COLOUR, OPTICAL SOUND
25 MIN. 33 SEC.

For the construction of the Open-Air Cinema, I focused on incorporating the theatre into Deryneia's natural environment, avoiding materials alien to the landscape. In collaboration with architect Maya Shopova, I worked with rammed-earth material on site. The earth materials that shape the amphitheatre will deteriorate in the future, maybe sooner rather than later, with the effects of erosion and climate change, underlining also that the conflict might be a temporary one.

The screen is positioned in the centre of the surrounding seating, and a screen positioned in the centre faces both sides. When there's no activity, the screen material is detached and the landscape on one South side and sea view on the North complete the picture. It was a proposition to interact with the screen as an architectural space that also incorporates a specific geopolitics.

I proposed an installation in this non-populated UN neutral zone as a place where both sides could go without claiming it for a certain side. We finally inaugurated it on one evening in the summer of 2021 with a screening of the film I shot over the course of seven years alongside short films by other artist filmmakers from the North and the South of the island. When you look through the screen, you see on one side the city of Famagusta abandoned in 1974 and on the other the town of Deryneia. The frame is basically offering the unification of both sides or just a conversation about this possibility. It's more of an ephemeral proposal.

COMER: *Your work continues to push the relationships between sound and image, between the live bodies of the spectator, the artist/performer, and that of the cinematic apparatus. For your project at MoMA, you're giving voice to the machine of filmic technology and also to the machine of the museum itself. These voices aren't autonomous, but produced by integrating these systems together, literally giving sonic form to the ghosts in the wires. Light and sound are fugitive materials that become activated through the mechanics of projection and also the projection of the human voice. How do you think these relationships have evolved in your work, and how has involving live performers pushed it in new directions?*

BARBA: In my project at MoMA, I experiment further with methods and rhythms of editing the exhibition and the relationship between sound, image, the sculptural works, the museum architecture and the intervals of performance. Sound is produced by conducting image and light in front of and beyond the lens. The performers are pushing these possibilities further while testing them out live.

These relationships have expanded the transmission of sound from body to machine in symphony with both light and space. The exhibition has been conceived with an understanding of the museum as a machine, a stage and at the same time a laboratory. This is also explored and reflected in the new film *Charge* (2025), which occupies the large screen. After *Charge* is projected, the screen is illuminated by a blank film projection, which gives light to the ten sculptures in the space until *Charge* begins again. The exhibition can be seen as one fragmented work, a spatial film, or a mechanical ballet within the museum architecture. It's situated inside and outside the building at the same time. The window façade turns into a membrane, which seems to push the light inside out. The performers create further physical interruptions, sonic gestures that link bodies, machines, light and sound in a unique continuum. A special form of cinema is created in that moment while it emerges out of the notation of the exhibition. The transmitter and receiver are fluent in both directions.

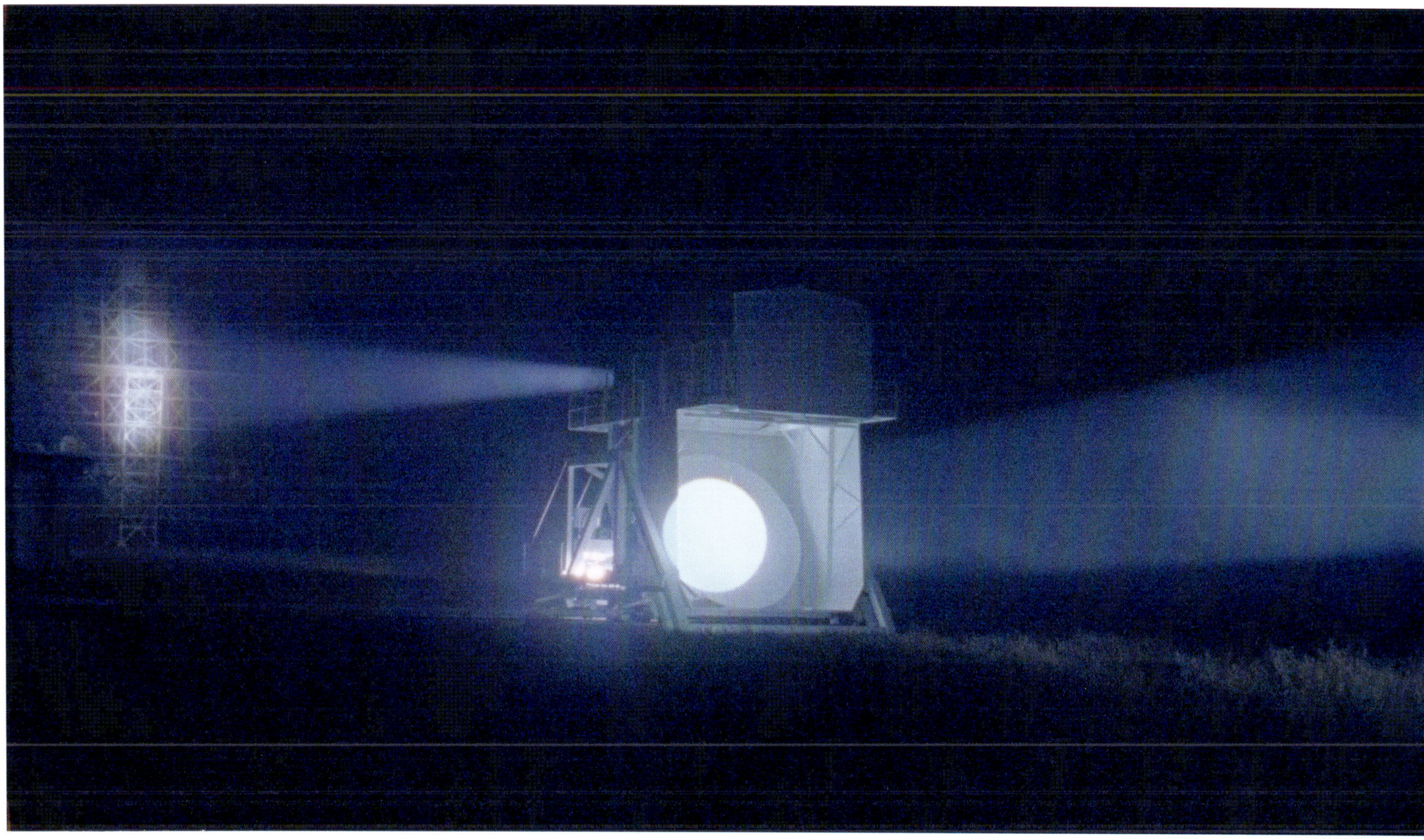

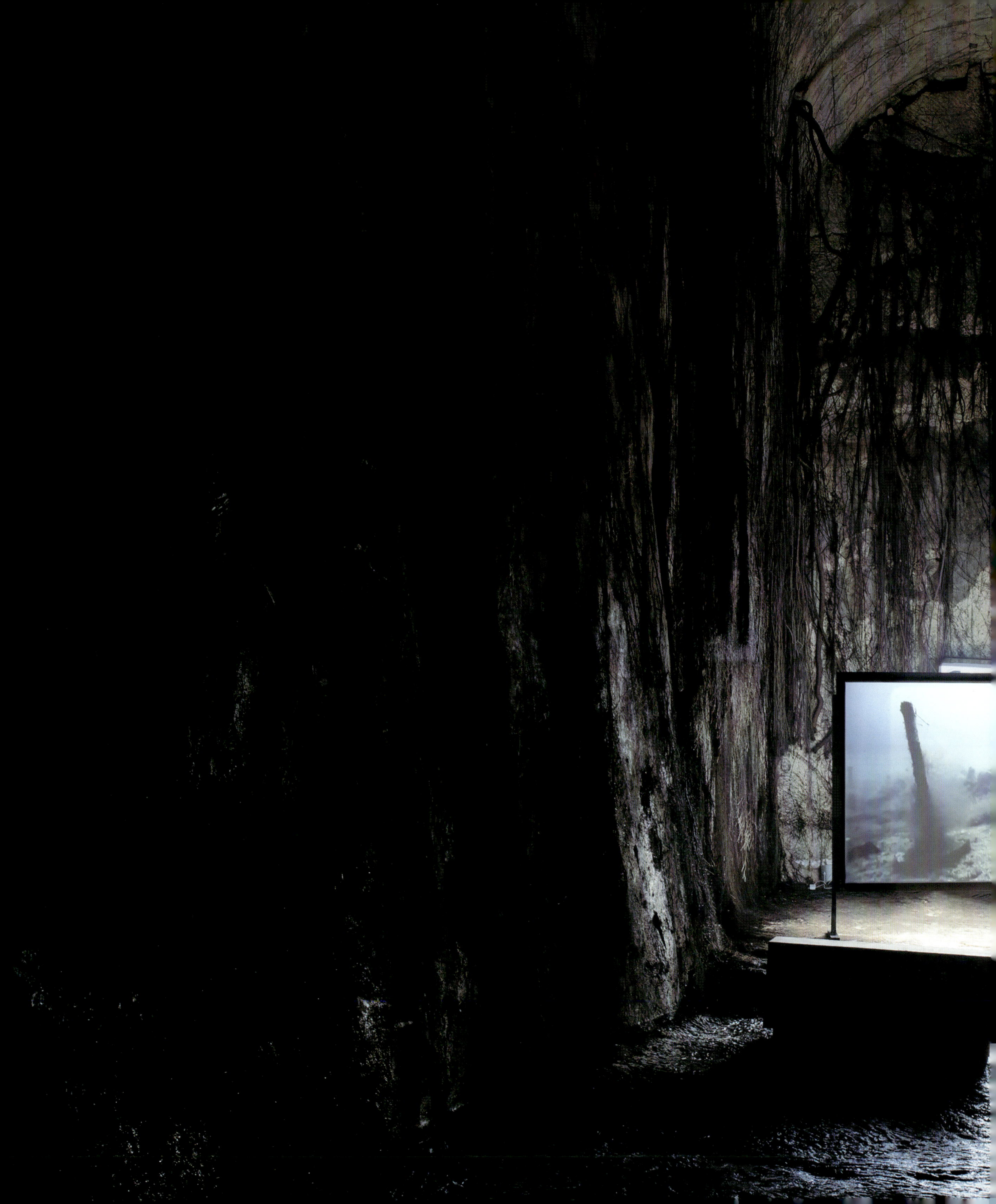

051 SURVEY

Interrogating the Qualities of Space

Shanay Jhaveri

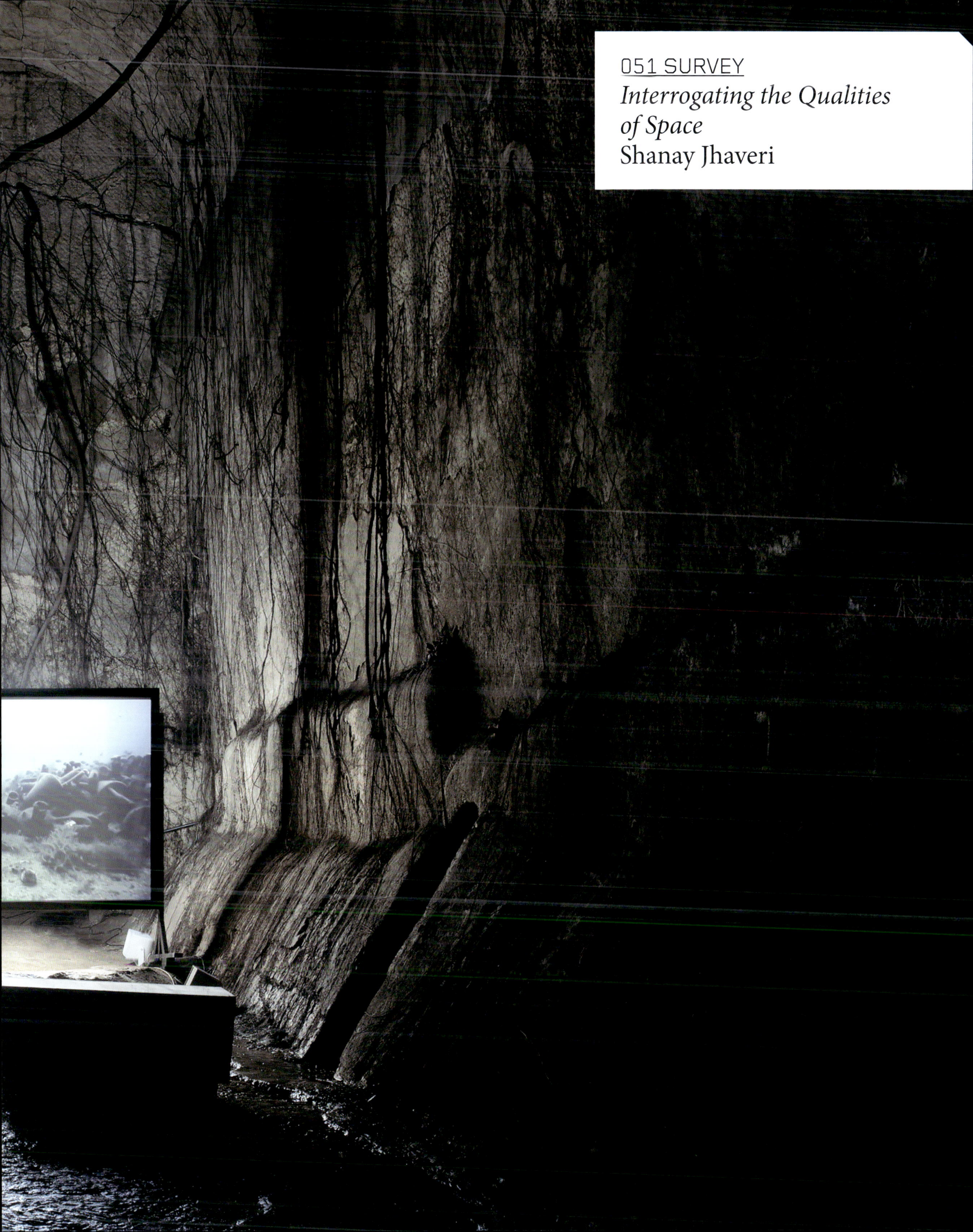

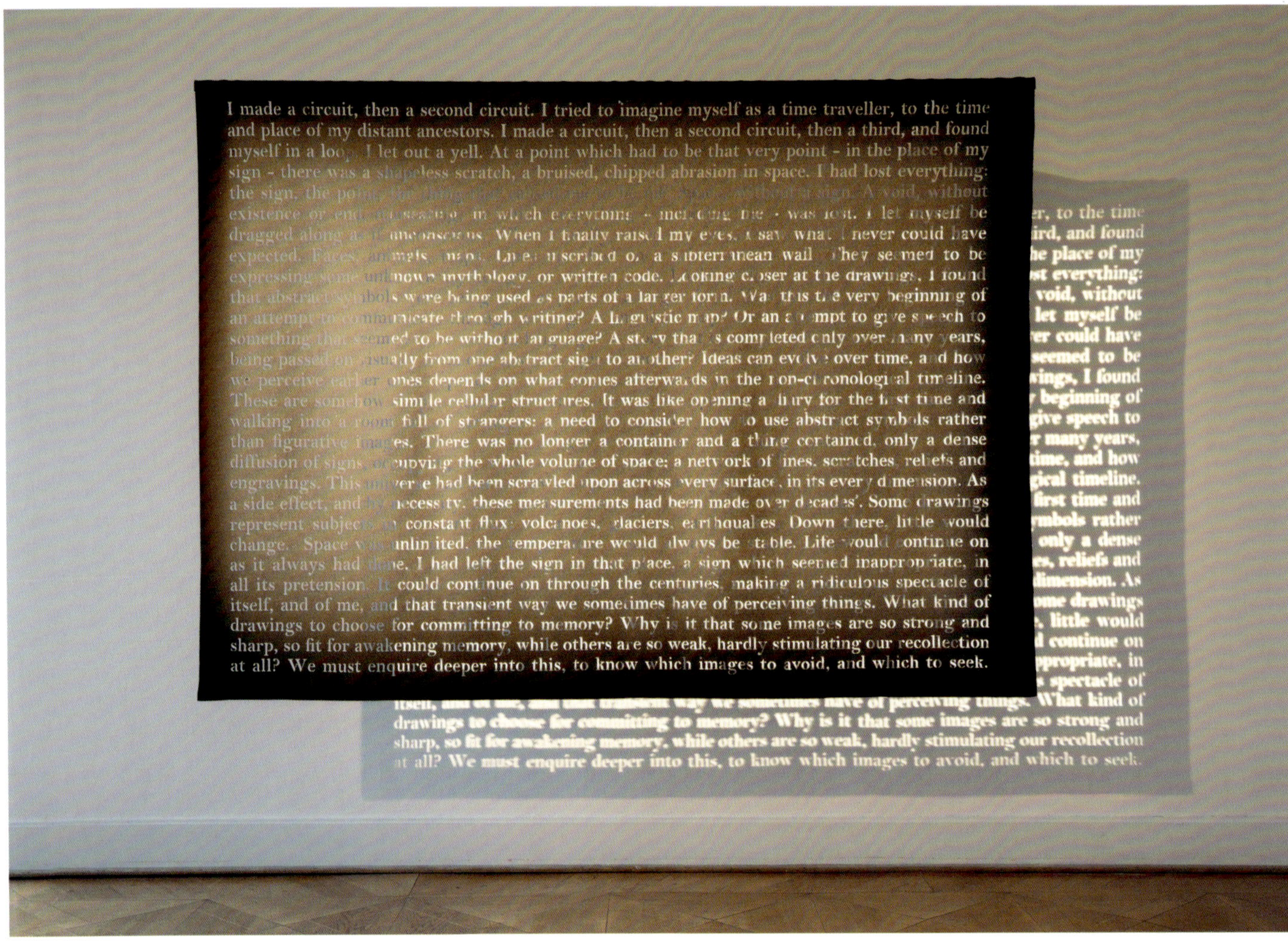

left,
I MADE A CIRCUIT AND THEN A SECOND CIRCUIT, 2010
CUTOUT TEXT ON FELT, SPOTLIGHT
180 X 240 CM

INSTALLATION VIEW AT KUNSTVEREIN BRAUNSCHWEIG, GERMANY, 2011

previous pages,
INSIDE THE OUTSET: EVOKING A SPACE OF PASSAGE, 2021
16MM FILM TRANSFERRED TO DIGITAL AND 8K FILM, SOUND
31 MIN. 15 SEC.

INSTALLATION VIEW AT THE MALTA BIENNALE, VALLETTA, 2024

In Rosa Barba's installations *Stating the Real Sublime* and *One Way Out*, both completed in 2009, simple constituents like accumulating particles of dust or air passing through a ventilation tube become vital presences. Her careful placement of a film projector in each work creates the conditions for a single strip of celluloid film to interact with these imperceptible elements of the environment. In *Stating the Real Sublime*, a film strip spools onto the ground from an elegantly suspended projector, seemingly defying gravity, while in *One Way Out* the celluloid strip performs a counter action, ascending upwards via a hanging suction mechanism into a tin pipe. In each instance, the projector casts what appears to be a blank image. However, what gradually emerges is an array of marks and scratches, the result of the celluloid strip's contact with the particles of dust or rubbing up against the pipe during the course of an exhibition. These works function not only as simply formal exercises in which the apparatuses of cinema are deployed to explore film's materiality, but as Barba has stated, become 'instruments to interrogate the qualities of space'.[1]

Over the course of a two-decade-long practice, Barba has consciously and consistently exceeded the bounds and conditions of conventional exhibition spaces through her deft choreography of the screen, the projector, the film strip – all constituent components of cinema – to explore existing architectures. She also seeks to create alternative experiences, 'that open narrative possibilities by dissolving the barriers between the space of the projection and the space of the spectator as well as the space beyond'.[2] It is this opening of possibilities that is subtly manifest in *Stating the Real Sublime* and *One Way Out*, where the traces of what is left behind by the exchange of the film strips and the environment of the gallery aspires to provoke a recognition of the space itself, as well as how the visitor might engage with it and the status of the objects on display. In each case, the projector and film strip are enacting real-time existence through their interaction with the unseen elements of the environment in which they are installed. They should now cease to be apprehended as fixed in or outside of time; instead, they seek to activate spatio-temporal awareness through a sensory encounter that is both visual and auditory. The latter is made manifest in *One Way Out*, whose optical soundtrack is reinforced by the acoustics of the pipe. In Barba's own words, in response to the advent of newer immersive technologies that wash over a visitor, she has sought to intensify her own 'strategies of fragmentation'[3] by 'dismantling the status quo of cinema', to destabilize what has regulated and anchored modes of visitor's perceptions. This of course takes on different connotations and implications depending on the site and location of the work.

background, from left,
STATING THE REAL SUBLIME, 2009
16MM, MODIFIED PROJECTOR

SPACELENGTH THOUGHT, 2012
16MM FILM, PROJECTOR, TYPEWRITER, PLINTH

ONE WAY OUT, 2009
16MM FILM, OPTICAL SOUND, PROJECTOR, VENTILATOR, TUBE

foreground, from left,
SENSIBLE SUNS, 2025
ACRYLIC GLASS, POLARIZATION FILMS, STEEL, ALUMINIUM, MOTORS AND LED LIGHT
90 X 68 X 45 CM

WIREPIECE, 2022
16MM FILM PROJECTOR, 16MM FILM, LENS, DRUM STRING, BRIDGE SADDLE PIECE, PICKUP MICHROPHONE, PREAMP, PLINTH

OFF SPLINTERED TIME, 2021
GLASS, MOTORS, LED LIGHT, 35MM FILM
80 X 80 X 70 CM

INSTALLATION VIEW AT THE MUSEUM OF MODERN ART, NEW YORK, 2025

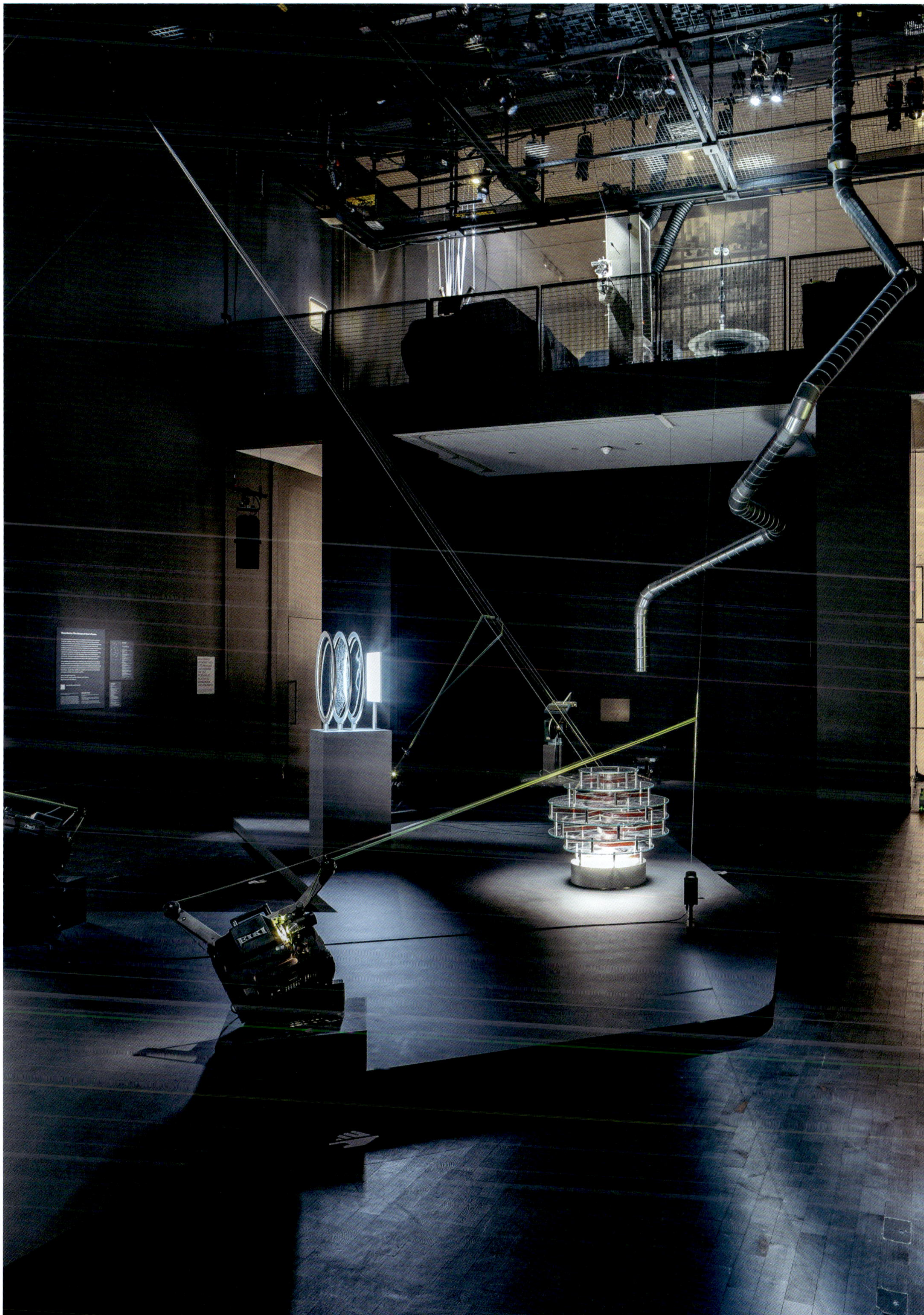

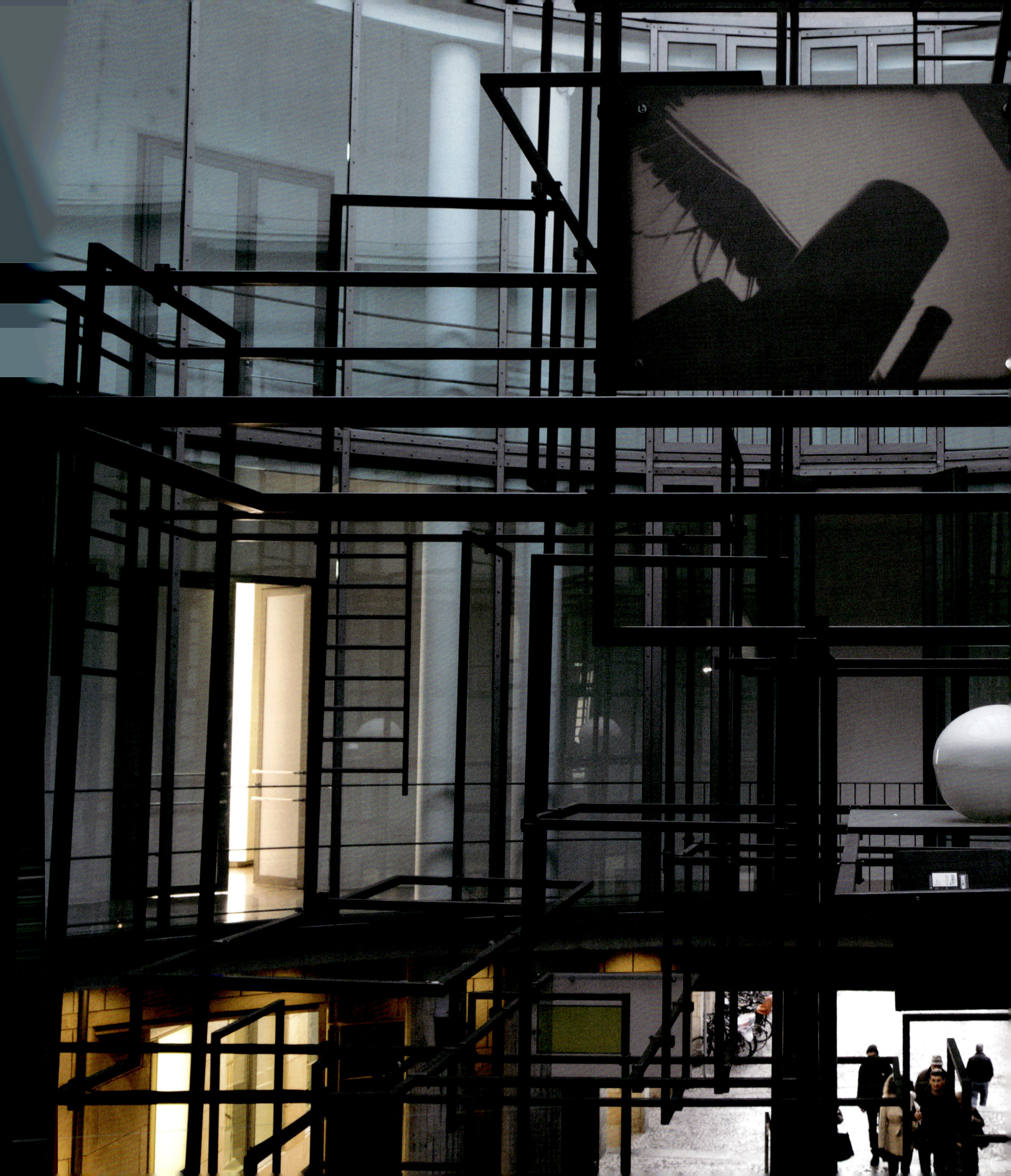

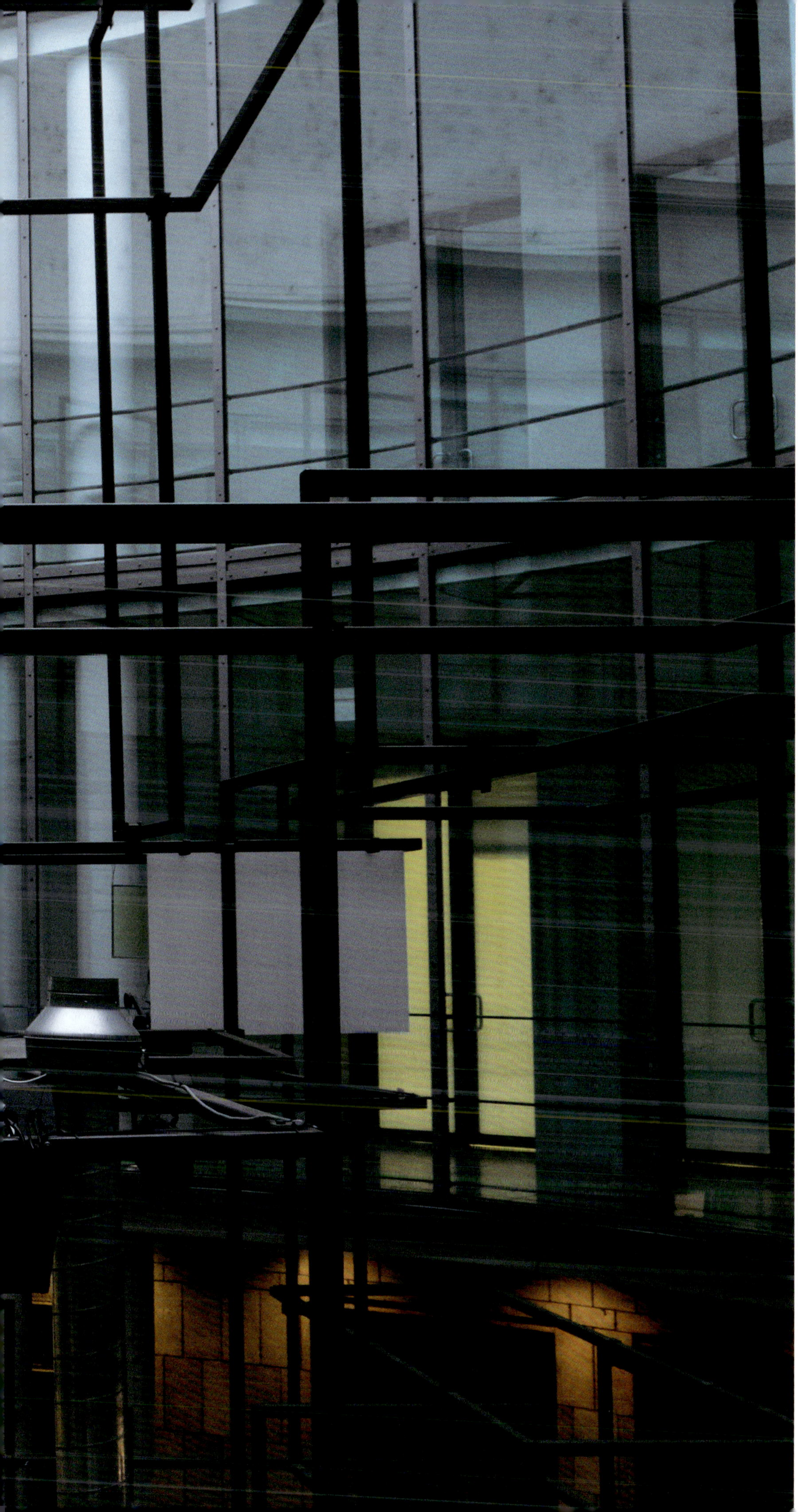

BLIND VOLUMES, 2016
80 STEEL FRAMES,
PLATFORMS, SCREENS

ABOVE THE PLATE AND RECEIVER, 2016
16MM FILM, OPTICAL SOUND,
5 MIN

CONDUCTOR, 2014
SILICONE MEMBRANE, MOTOR,
SOUND
Ø 60 CM

INSTALLATION VIEW AT SCHIRN KUNSTHALLE, FRANKFURT, 2016

The body of the museum, its own physicality, was the first ground of Barba's intervention. In 2010, she produced a work, *White Museum*, that has subsequently had numerous iterations, but the essential elements of this piece are a projector, white film and the existing architecture of a museum. The white light emitted from a 70mm projector, is directed outwards from the museum through a window, casting a frame onto an exterior landscape, cityscape, streetscape, which becomes visible only after sunset. Each landscape is inscribed with its own history, and through the act of selecting where the frame falls, Barba awakens these layers of time. It is a call to collective memory, how histories are remembered, forgotten or suppressed. By co-opting the architecture of the museum and transforming it into a projection booth, Barba repurposes, animates, the architecture of the museum. It is no longer a vault, a container, a monolith but an active entity brought into correspondence with the surrounding landscape. Boundaries are collapsed and it is this dismantling, or maybe the recasting of limits, that becomes Barba's enduring subject.

This is extended when she begins to probe the spatial configurations of museums and art galleries that inherently recommend certain norms of viewing and display, turning them into recurrent locations for her investigations. An invitation from the Schirn Kunsthalle in Frankfurt offered Barba a key occasion to further her own inquiries in the form of the ambitious installation *Blind Volumes* (2016), which was conceived to fill the lobby of the institution. What attracted Barba to the rotunda was that it was an intermediary space where visitors gather and through which they pass before they enter the exhibition galleries. It was precisely the accessibility of the rotunda, with no thresholds to cross, no tickets to be bought or reception to pass by that interested her. Developing the work over two years, she started with a physical model

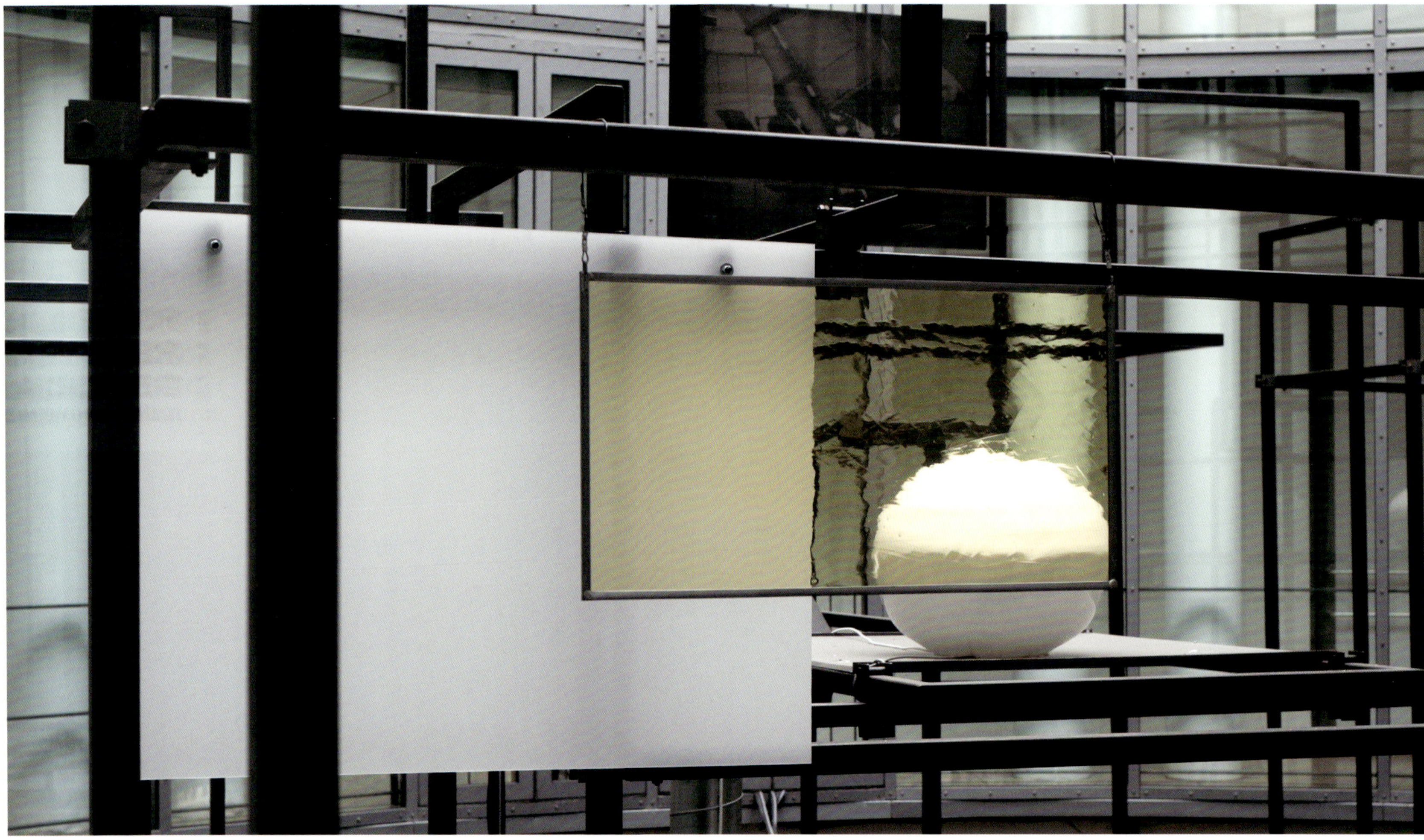

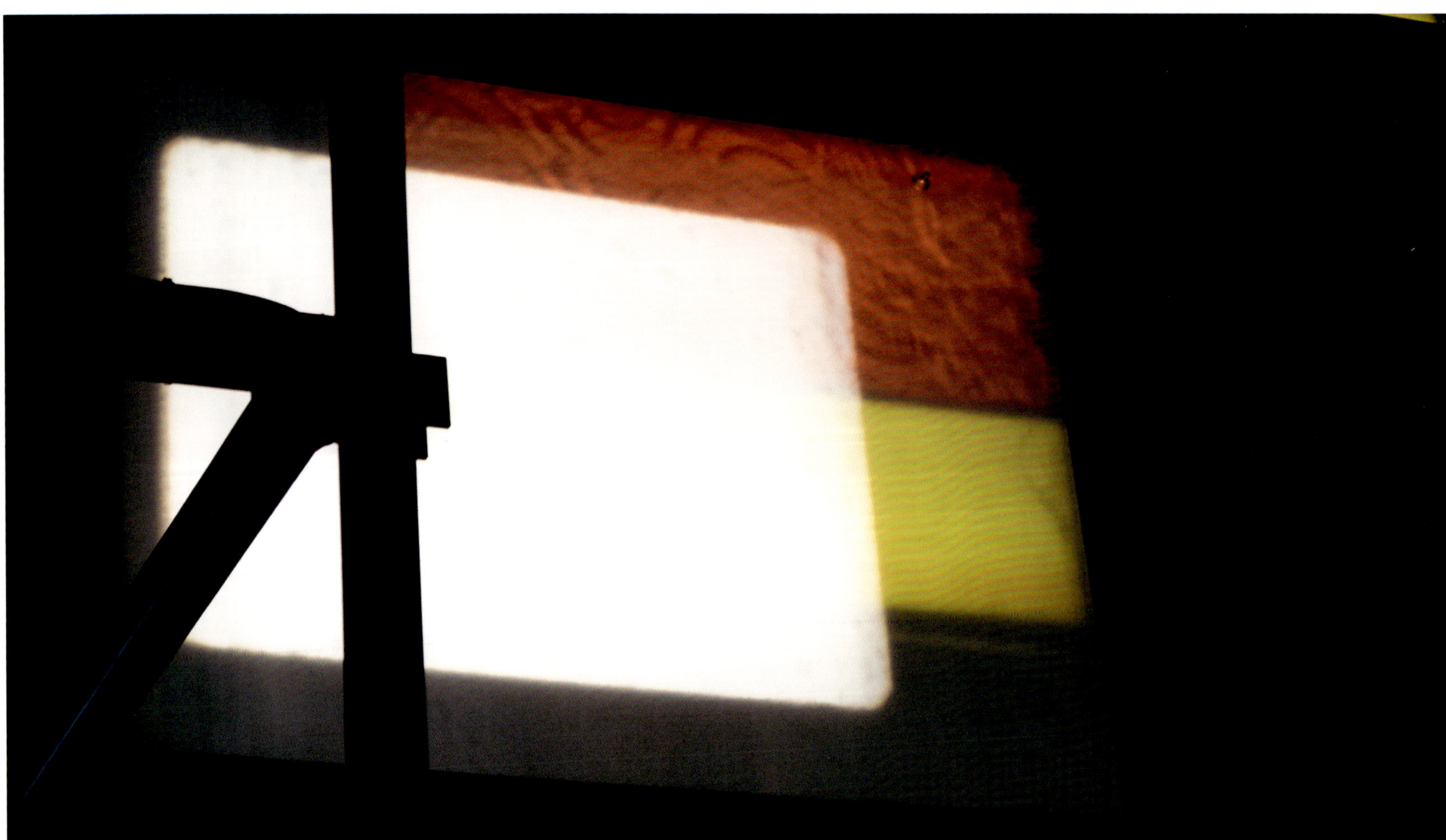

right,
BLIND VOLUMES, 2016
80 STEEL FRAMES,
PLATFORMS, SCREENS

HEAR, THERE, WHERE THE ECHOES ARE, 2016–21
5 X 16MM PROJECTOR, 4 GLASS FILTERS, 35MM PROJECTOR, SCREENS, SOUND

opposite, from top,
BLIND VOLUMES, 2016
80 STEEL FRAMES,
PLATFORMS, SCREENS

CONDUCTOR, 2014
SILICONE MEMBRANE, MOTOR, SOUND
Ø. 60 CM

BLIND VOLUMES, 2016
80 STEEL FRAMES,
PLATFORMS, SCREENS

HEAR, THERE, WHERE THE ECHOES ARE, 2016–21
5 X 16MM PROJECTOR, 4 GLASS FILTERS, 35MM PROJECTOR, SCREENS, SOUND

INSTALLATION VIEW AT SCHIRN KUNSTHALLE, FRANKFURT, 2016

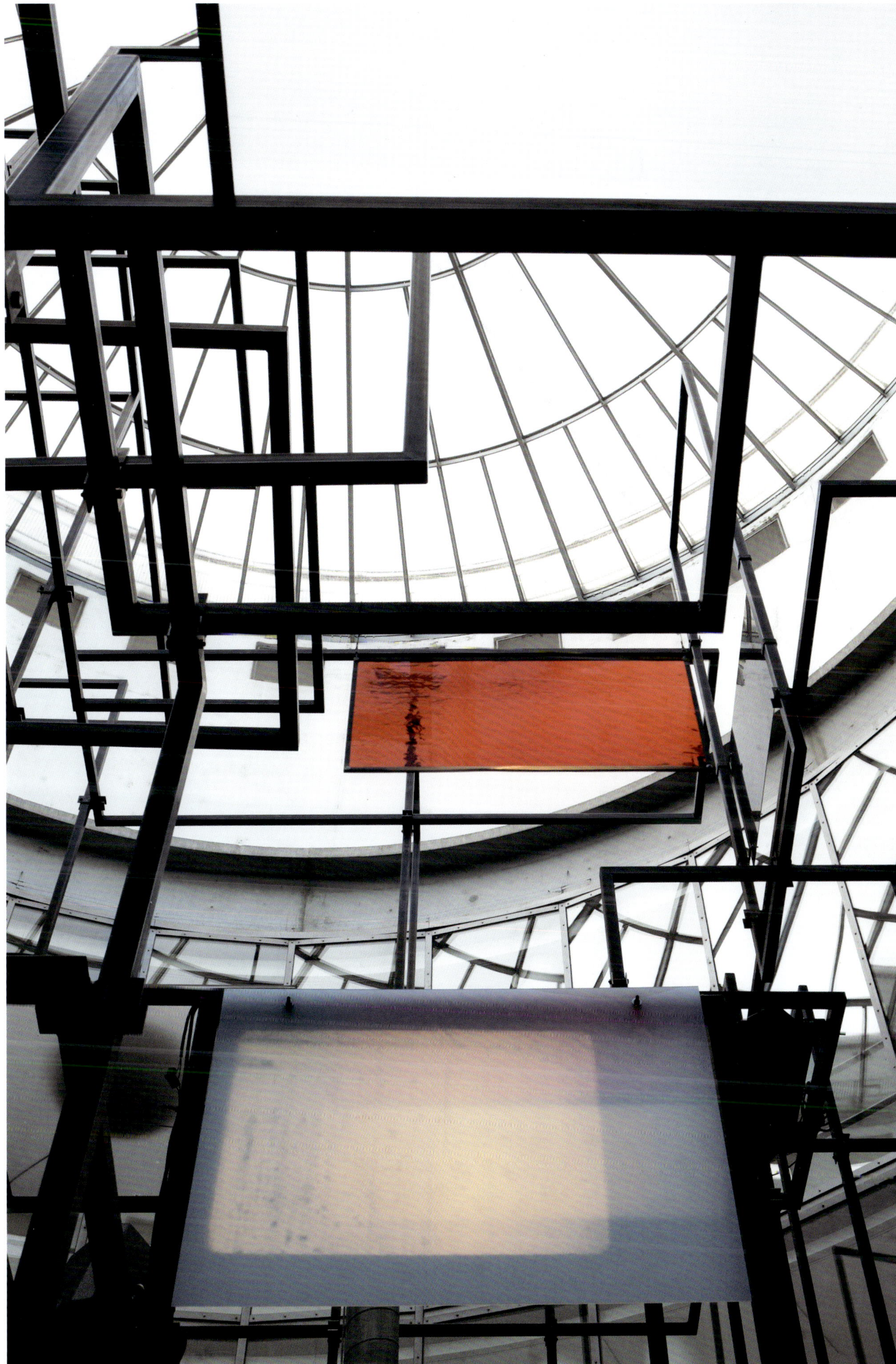

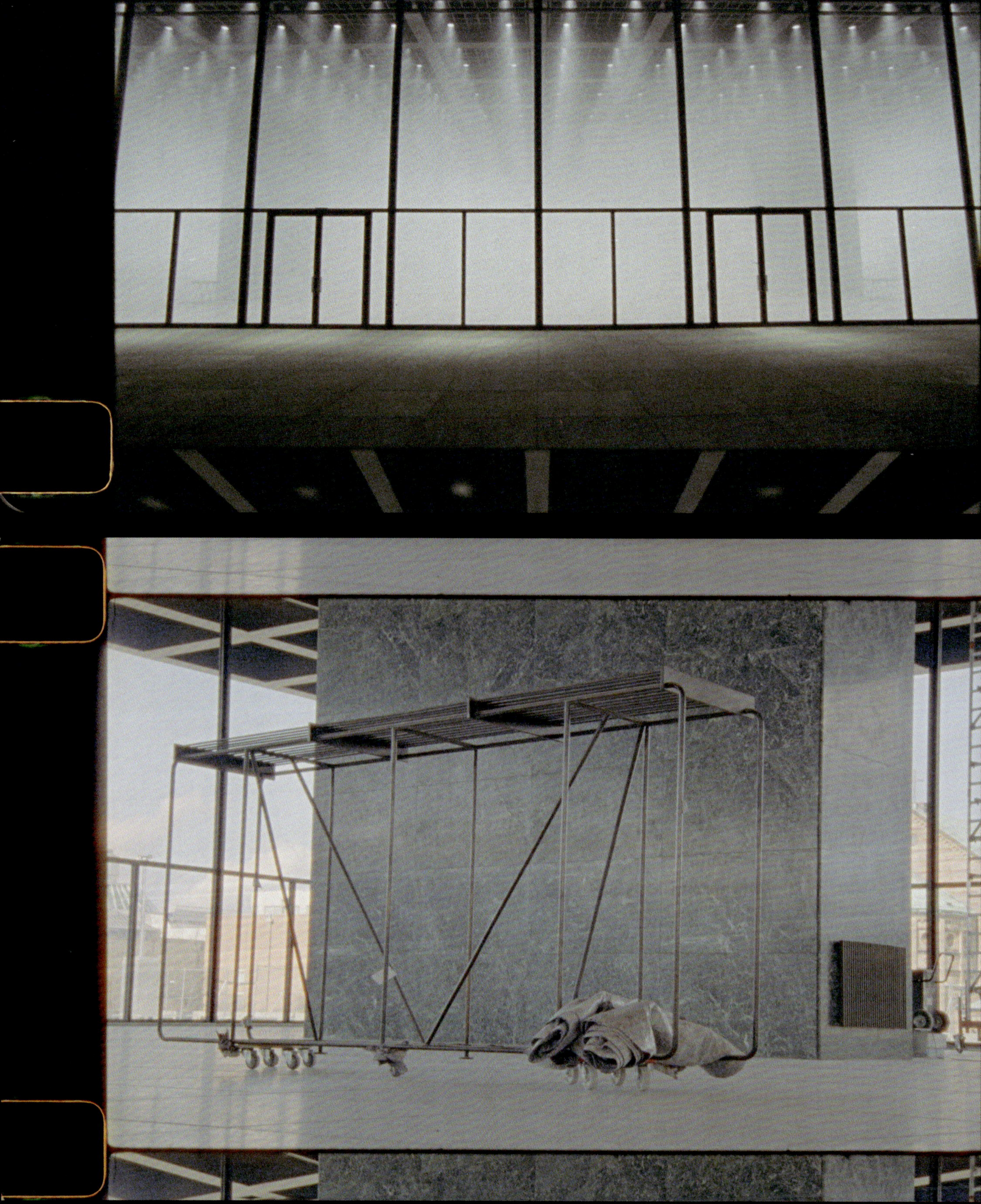

opposite,
PLASTIC LIMITS – FOR THE PROJECTION OF OTHER ARCHITECTURES, 2021
35MM FILM, COLOUR, OPTICAL SOUND
14 MIN. 40 SEC.

next pages,
THE HIDDEN CONFERENCE: A FRACTURED PLAY, 2011
35MM FILM, COLOUR, OPTICAL SOUND
5 MIN.

INSTALLATION VIEW AT TATE MODERN, LONDON, 2023

and then refined the form of the structure by sketching digitally. The final installation, which Barba has described as a 'stage', would stand 12 metres tall, a series of eighty geometric interlocking steel frames that occupied the entire rotunda. Within the steel structure, she embedded a number of her other films to be projected on a loop, as well as sculptural works including *One Way Out*. The placement of these pieces throughout the vertically stacked structure was guided by her desire to explore in an embodied fashion the principles behind montage. This freed her up to produce a dynamic setting, where each artwork becomes a protagonist, a satellite, a note, which visitors can choose to apprehend either on its own or as a part of a larger composition that lasted the length of a quarter of an hour and would then repeat. Barba was intent on privileging the visitor's own sense of mobility and discernment while walking through the structure and viewing it from different elevated vantage points at their own pace. With *Blind Volumes*, she created a work that could not be experienced in a linear manner, or ever viewed in its entirety. Instead, an understanding of it would emerge out of shifting perspectives seen from different levels.

Barba's occupation of the Schirn's rotunda inaugurates a new approach in her practice when engaging museum architectures, which can be described as 'site-responsive' rather than 'site-specific'. The notion of 'site responsive' was formulated by Joanne More in 2017 to describe artistic interventions that are made for a particular site but are not permanent and continue to travel and adapt themselves to other locations following the original display. Notably, these works are generally 'critical interjections' that 'temporarily stimulate the site' enabling a 'reconsideration of the site, its displays and meanings'.[4] It can be proposed that this is exactly what Barba was striving for with *Blind Volumes* at the Schirn, catalysing a reconsideration of a site and its function, an approach she would continue in future iterations at Malmö Kunsthall and, most provocatively, at the Neue Nationalagalerie in 2021.

Barba was the first living female artist to have a solo exhibition in the Neue Nationalgalerie, Mies van der Rohe's last major building, following a six-year renovation. Her exhibition, which was hosted in the downstairs galleries (upstairs was an Alexander Calder exhibition), pivoted around an adapted configuration of *Blind Volumes*. The footprint of the steel framework would be derived from one of Van der Rohe's unrealised projects, the Brick Country House, which was conceived in 1924. Van der Rohe himself would say that with the Brick Country House design 'I have abandoned the usual concept of enclosed rooms and striven for a series of spatial effects rather than a row of individual rooms. The wall loses its enclosing character and serves only to articulate the house organism.'[5] Clearly, in its intention not to have pronounced definitions or boundaries between rooms, his original design pivots on an asymmetric logic. There is little alignment, with the architect resisting the placement of conventional entry and exit points that would orient a front or back to the house, and prioritizing an openness that bestows the architecture with a certain rhythm. All of this resounds with Barba's own experimentation with dissolving barriers and prioritizing interactive engagement.

The floorplan seemed like an apt source of inspiration for how to physically organize and define the space of her exhibition and to begin to dialogue with the concepts that underpinned Van der Rohe's legacy. This is taken further when she opts to dialogue with the Neue Nationalgalerie itself in the film *Plastic Limits: For the Projection of Other Architectures* (2021), one of the fifteen films and sculptural works housed in her *Blind Volumes/Backstein*. In *Plastic Limits*, shot during the renovation of the Neue Nationalgalerie, the building becomes a site of cross-examination of the very principles that Van der Rohe formulated around transparency and openness. In a dramatic and awe-inspiring sequence, filmed from the exterior, the entire structure is seen filling up with fog. The simple act of releasing a thick cloud into the Neue Nationalgalerie, obscuring its clear lines, blocking the vista through the pillar-less building, throws into relief the associations of freedom courted by the architect, his pursuit of 'universal space'. Introducing a literal lack of clarity into an edifice of a certain modernist ideal of purity, Barba is rendering this historical space contemporary, and counteracting the building from imposing itself on the work. Rather, she creates a productive exchange, a reciprocity that allows the site itself to be appreciated differently, as something living in time rather than simply being a monument.

Barba is clearly conscious that a building with such history can not only serve as a framework for her piece, but can also participate in expanding its context. This mode of inquiry goes back to her primary intention to generate an awareness of the conditions in which art is displayed and the meanings it imparts. So while *Blind Volumes/Backstein* and *Plastic Limits* preoccupy themselves with modernist architecture and its vocabulary of expression, Barba's trio of 35mm films *The Hidden Conference* (2010–15), expands her project by venturing into the storage systems of three museums – the Neue Nationalgalerie in Berlin, Musei Capitolini in Rome and Tate in London. In these films, Barba's handheld camera slowly pans across artworks kept in dim lighting, stacked on racks, wrapped in plastic in climate-controlled conditions, occasionally being moved by automated machines. Through the configuration of screens showing the three films, Barba orchestrates a 'meeting of the artworks' in different storage units and storerooms.

The opening text of the first film, *About the Discontinuous History of Things We See and Don't See* (2010), reads: 'at an unspecified point in time, a witness observes the silent encounter of artworks from different epochs'. The storeroom becomes a space in which the objects are released, if only temporarily, from the curatorial narratives of curated displays and can commune with one another, while at rest from the gaze of the public, many times

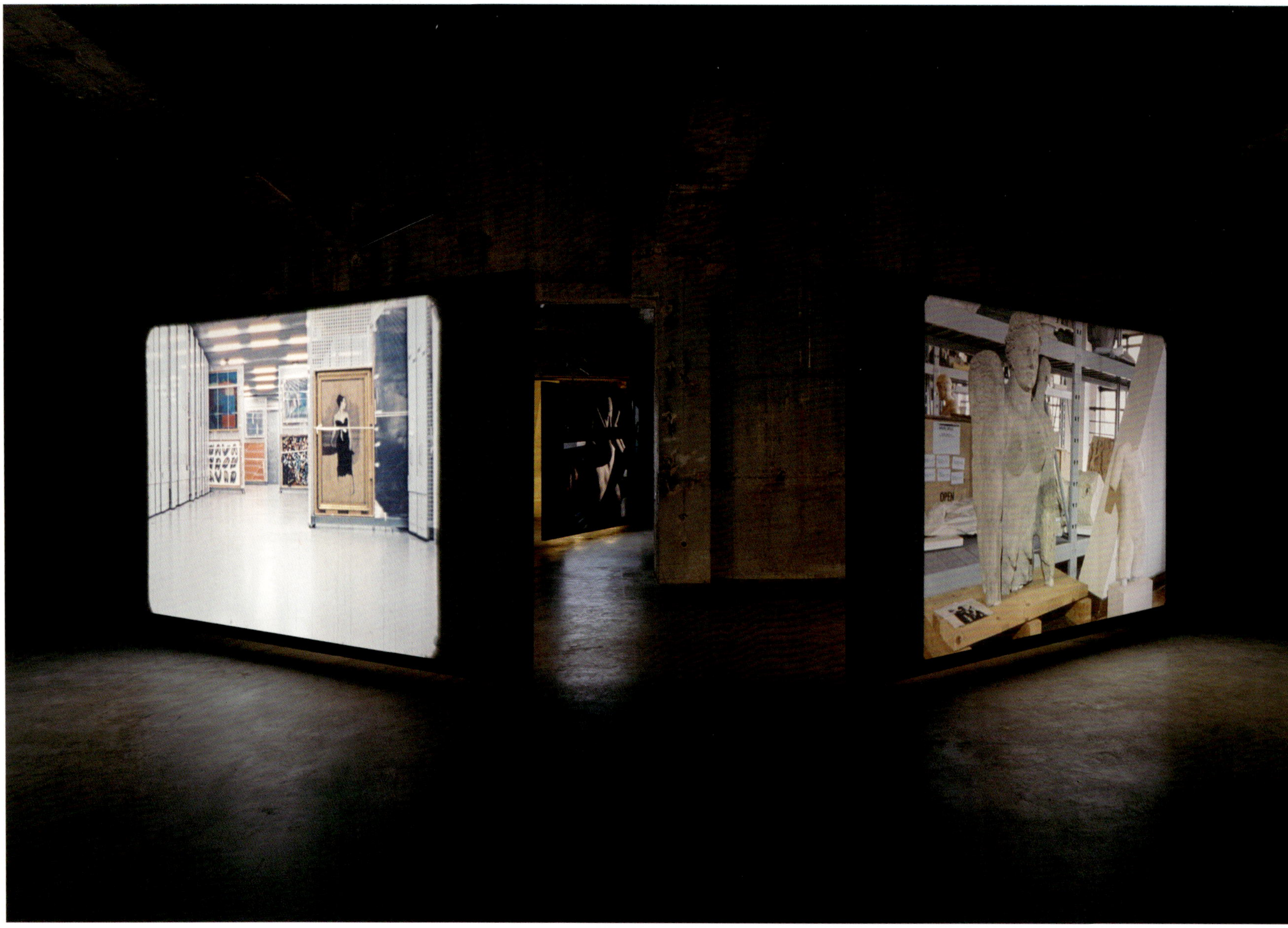

on the instruction of conservators to ensure their own preservation. The concern (or anxiety) for their material well-being allowing a reprieve. Being able to observe the works outside of the context of the museum's public spaces only confirms and underscores how museums impact and at times control the manner in which these objects are appreciated and understood. Seeing them released from narrative contracts, unexpectedly coming into contact with one another, the surprise from seeing them cross one another in a passage way, sharing space momentarily, reiterates the burdens they have to shoulder as cultural signifiers, instrumentalized more often than not as markers to animate overarching frameworks presented by these institutions. In this way *The Hidden Conference* demonstrates the potential for a speculative, counter art history, while also exposing that the lingering spectre of the institution, the weight of its collecting practice, cannot be forgotten.

The impulses behind the need to preserve also motivates Barba's 2016 35mm film *From Source to Poem,* which was shot in the National Audio Visual Conservation Center (NAVCC) at the Library of Congress in Culpeper, Virginia, the largest media archive in the world, a record of sounds and images and associated technologies. As in *The Hidden Conference*, Barba focuses on the nature of how this cultural output is being archived. However, unlike the objects in museums, this media archive begins to amount to what she describes as 'white noise', since here the emphasis is not on display but on obsessive storage and the sense of control inherent in that action. This is amplified by the fact that NAVCC is housed in a bunker built in 1968 in the midst of the Cold War, the paranoia of that moment a driving force behind its mission. Sequences of solar plants in the desert, where electricity is collected, are juxtaposed with texts about the NAVCC, and the soundtrack is a tapestry of free source material from Library of Congress where the archive 'enables the memoralization of voices, shapes, times, ideas':[6] interviews with field workers, vocal groups and migrants, excerpts from Hispanic literature, readings by poets, and the oral histories of women.

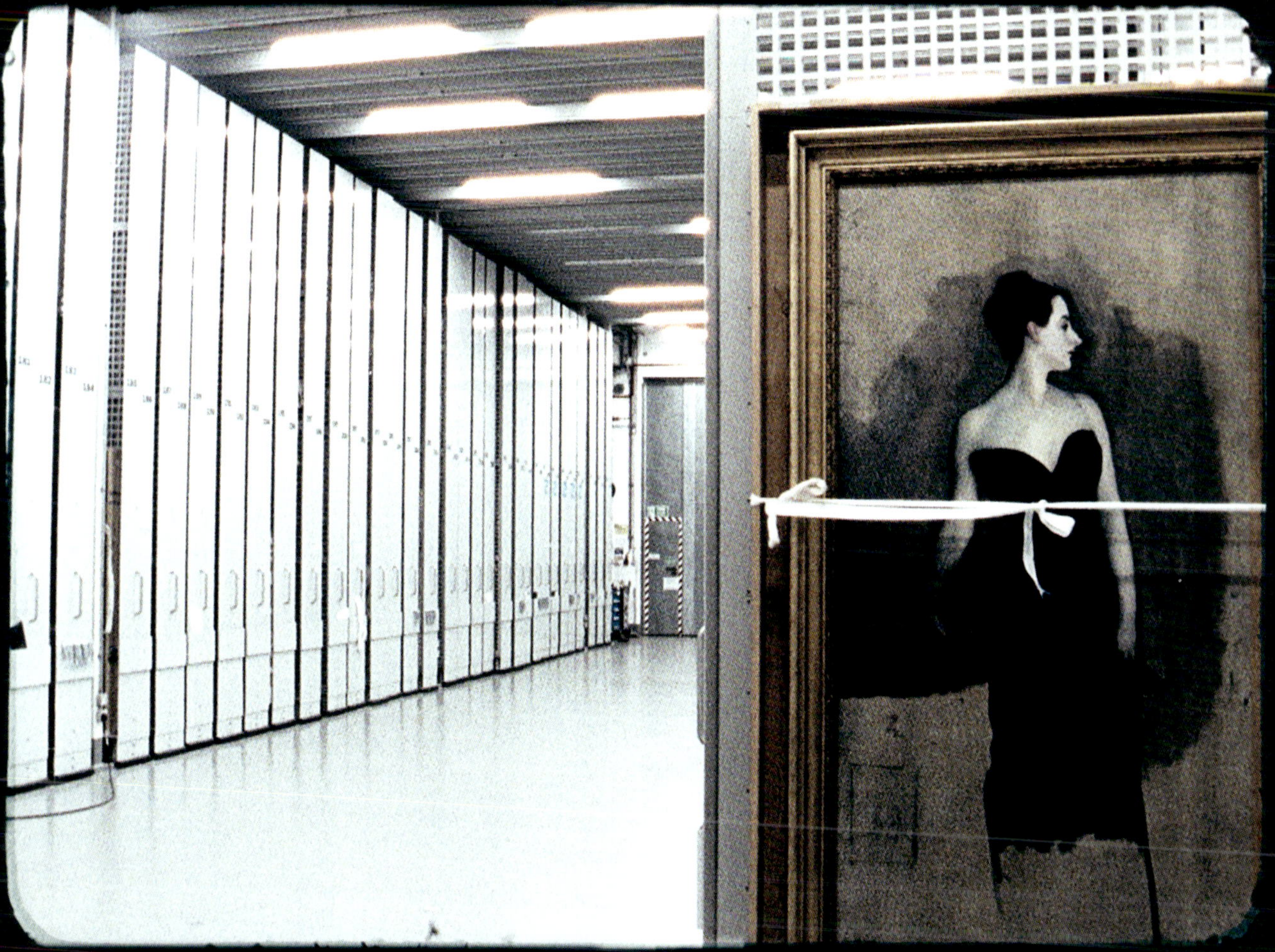

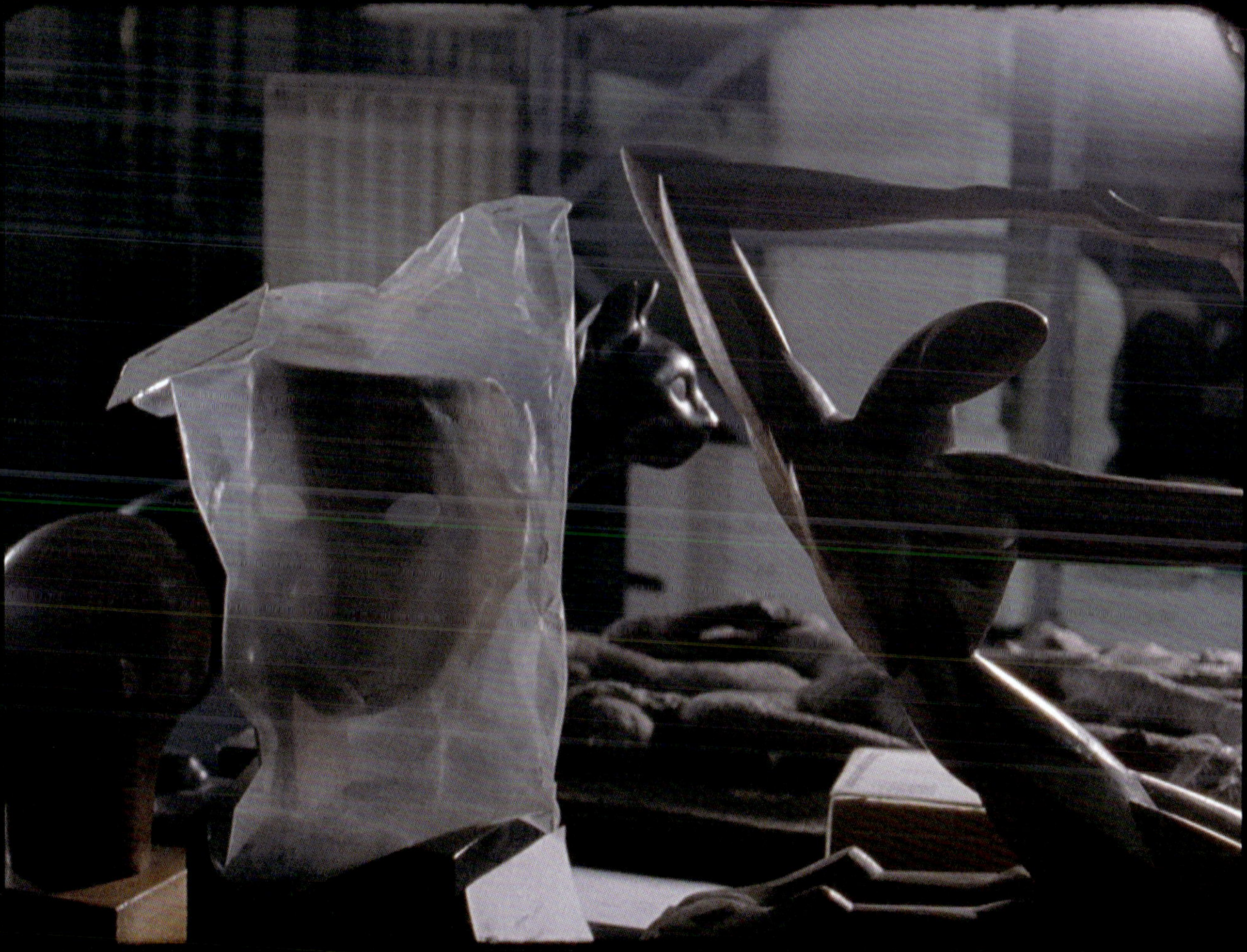

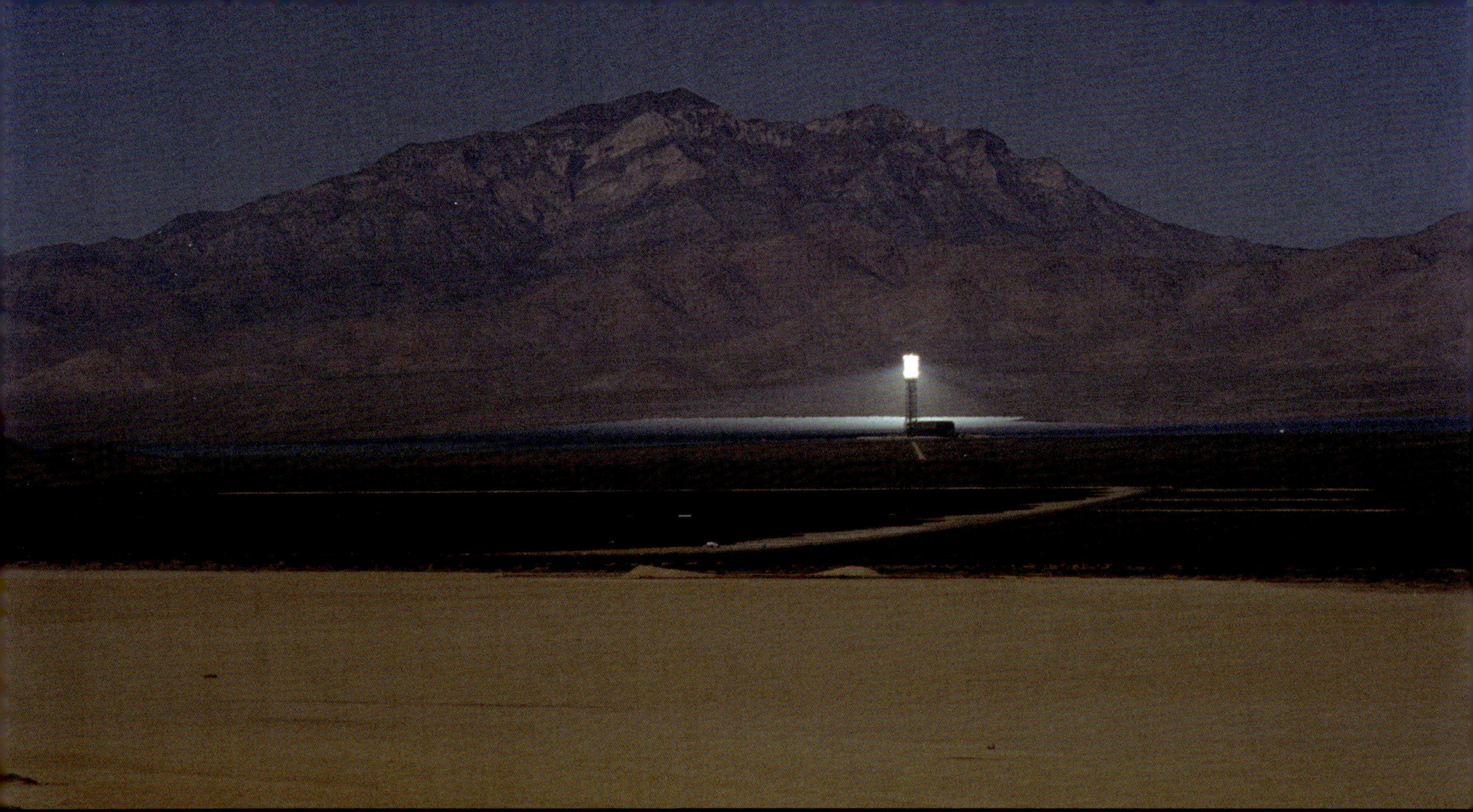
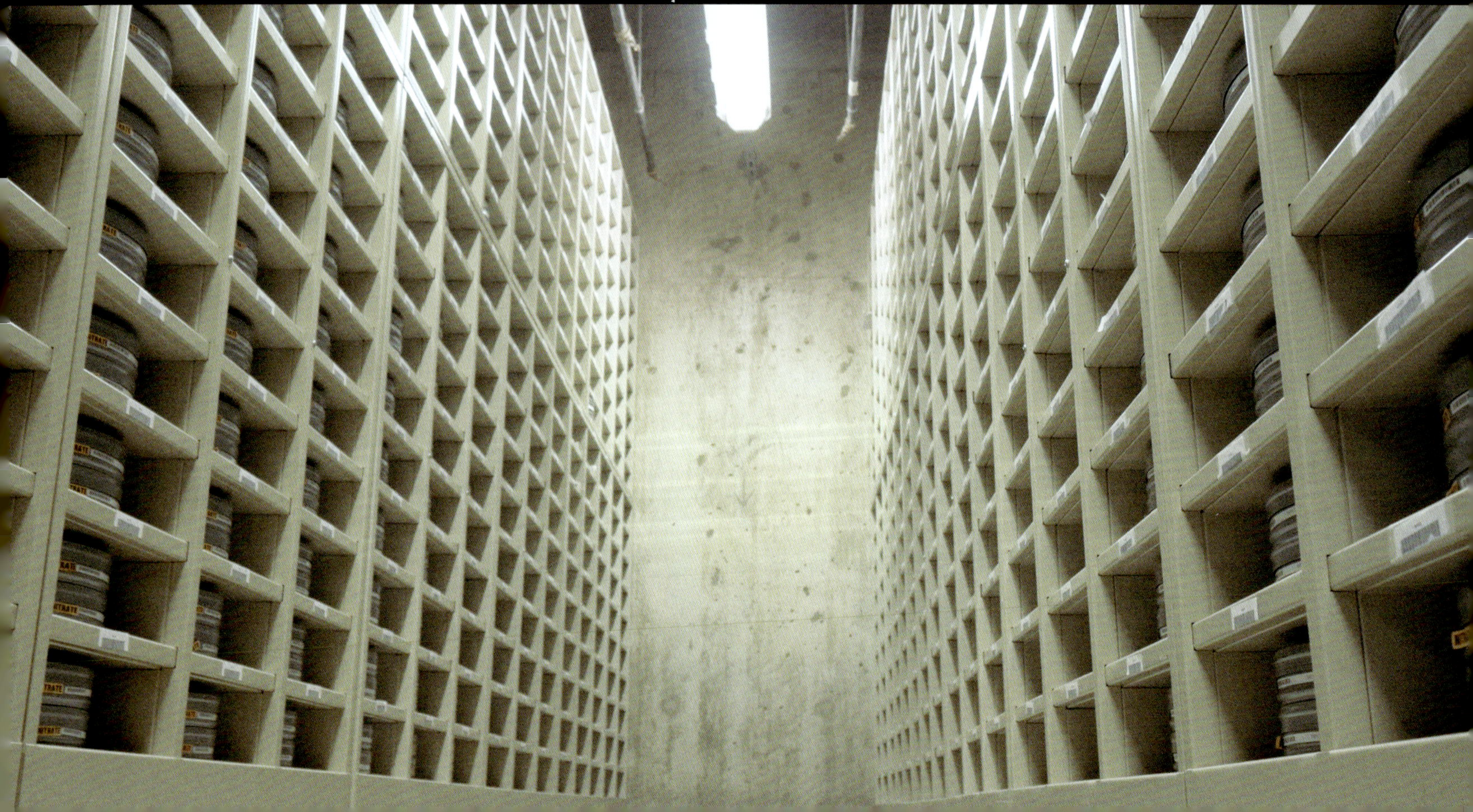

opposite,
FROM SOURCE TO POEM, 2016
35MM FILM, COLOUR, OPTICAL SOUND
12 MIN.

below, ,
FROM SOURCE TO POEM, 2016
35MM FILM, COLOUR, OPTICAL SOUND
12 MIN.

INSTALLATION VIEW AT CAPC MUSÉE D'ART CONTEMPORAIN DE BORDEAUX, 2016

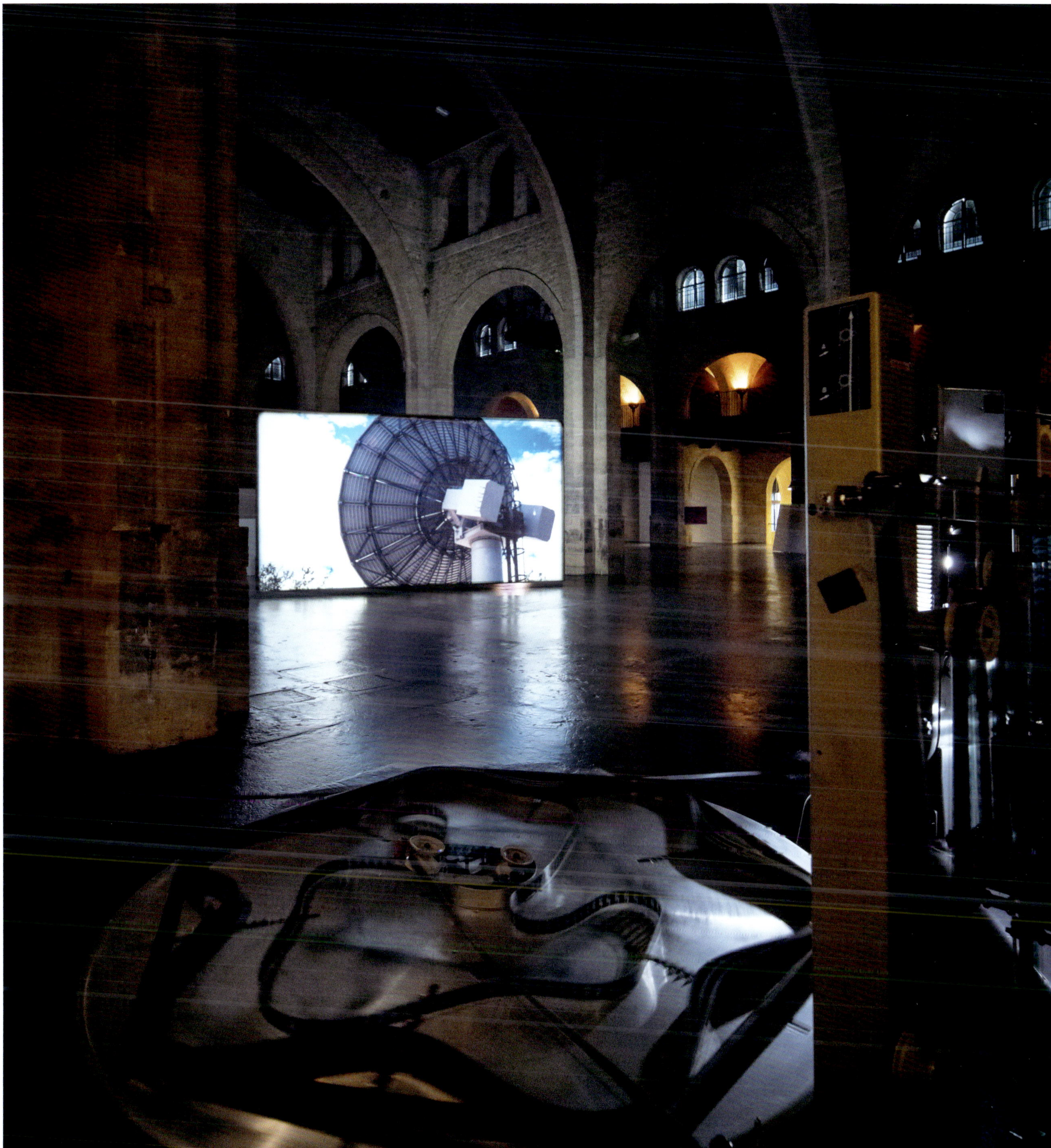

DISSEMINATE AND HOLD, 2016
16MM FILM TRANSFERRED TO DIGITAL, SOUND
21 MIN. 13 SEC.

Another work from 2016, *Disseminate and Hold* also begins with a polyphony of voices, as Barba's camera, filming from a driving car, makes its way around São Paulo on the Minhocão (giant earthworm), an elevated highway completed in 1969 to link the east and west sides of the bourgeoning city. This highway, extending for more than three kilometres, has a contested reputation and history, finished during the height of the Brazilian military dictatorship. Grafitti-covered apartment blocks pass by while the voice of one individual becomes clearer, that of Luciano, who shares with the viewer that he used to live at the corner of the Minhocão and General Jardim. He is followed by Lourdes Cassapulo, who recounts that he lived so near to the highway that the 'window of my bedroom seemed like it was close enough to touch'. The reminiscences of local residents continue, and what emerges is a portrait of a community and how the Minhocão, a remnant of another era of political power, is being reclaimed and reused today. One interviewee recalls 'I was amazed by the buildings around me. I imagined the people … how they might pass over above, and … how people were living together in the Minhocão'. Another states, 'I salute the Minhocão … because it's … a part of my life.' The film ends with Barba's camera at street level on a Sunday morning tracking along the highway, passing residents walking, exercising, idling, sitting, chatting. This confirms Barba's contention that the Minhocão has become 'this public body' and that 'you can expand the public's voice – maybe in a much more powerful way – if you take over architecture in the city'.[7]

Disseminate and Hold is not the first time that Barba has taken to exploring and mapping urban landscapes and infrastructure projects. With *A Private Tableaux* (2010), filmed in Liverpool, she found herself not on street level looking up at the built environment, but underground, following the sound from the ventilation towers that pump the air under the tunnels of the River Mersey. In the process, she chanced upon scores of white chalk drawings made over 100 years – a notational system formulated by the generations of engineers when they checked the stability of the tunnel. Barba's shaky hand-held camera, lit by a torch, analyses this vast collective drawing, following its lines and marks that surveyed the cracks in the vault caused by the overhead traffic. For Barba, it remains curious, enigmatic, recalling archaic cave art, as the subtitles of the films suggest, or 'automatic writing'. What the film enacts is the layering of her own articulation of these drawings over the engineers' intent, reading into them a host of other interpretations and images like flying machines or portraits of people's faces. Unable to gauge the functional meaning of these drawings, she is still ready to enter into a dialogue with them, making this vast enterprise of tunnels, this urban infrastructure, if not intelligible, then relatable. A century's worth of mark-making, made in response to the changing nature of an urban environment, becomes inscribed within another system of looking and contemporary engagement. Crucially, it also situates the engineers as central, acknowledging their exchange with the infrastructure, their practice and knowledge of this architecture as worthy of study, consideration and a springboard for the imagination.

Through her repeated inquiries into urban infrastructure, cityscapes and built space, and on occasion what they house, Barba comes back to the individual, the person, the group, the collective. A contemporary appraisal of the Minhocão comes via the interviewees who experience it; the network of tunnels in Liverpool are animated by the drawings of the engineers. Similarly, the architecture of the NAVCC in Culpeper and its archive is permeated by a chorus of voices, who throw into relief the distance between the act of collecting and compressing data and the reality of lived experience. *A Private Tableaux, Disseminate and Hold* and *From Source to Poem* all

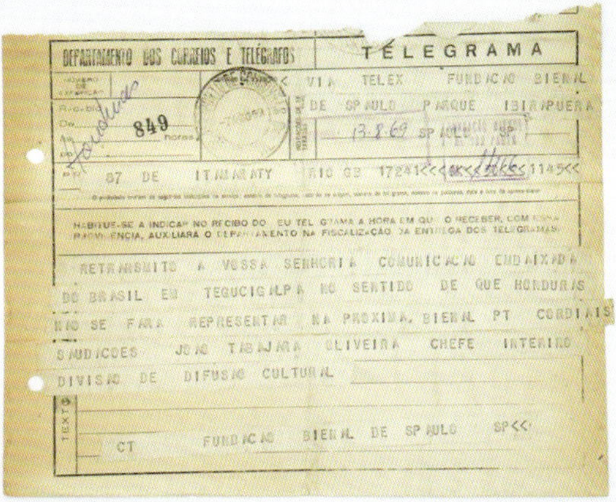

DEPARTAMENTO DOS CORREIOS E TELÉGRAFOS

TELEGRAMA

849

VIA TELEX FUNDICAO BIENAL DE SPAULO PARQUE IBIRAPUERA

13.8.69 SP

PR 87 DE ITAMARATY RIO GB 17241<<

HABITUE-SE A INDICAR NO RECIBO DO SEU TELEGRAMA A HORA EM QUE O RECEBER. COM ESSA PROVIDENCIA, AUXILIARA O DEPARTAMENTO NA FISCALIZAÇÃO DA ENTREGA DOS TELEGRAMAS.

RETRANSMITO A VOSSA SENHORIA COMUNICACAO EMBAIXADA DO BRASIL EM TEGUCIGALPA NO SENTIDO DE QUE HONDURAS NAO SE FARA REPRESENTAR NA PROXIMA BIENAL PT CORDIAIS SAUDACOES JOAO TABAJARA OLIVEIRA CHEFE INTERINO DIVISAO DE DIFUSAO CULTURAL

CT FUNDACAO BIENAL DE SPAULO SP<<

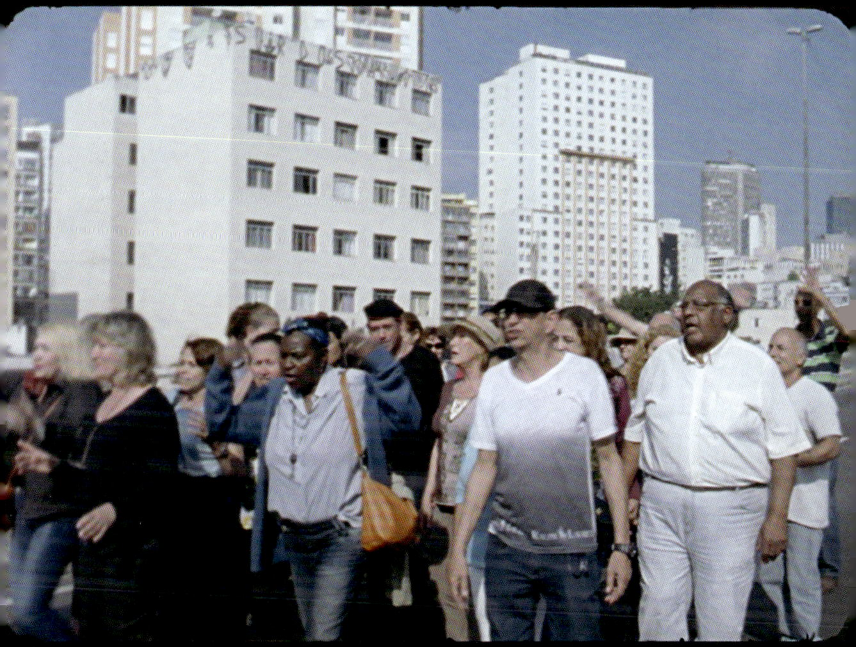

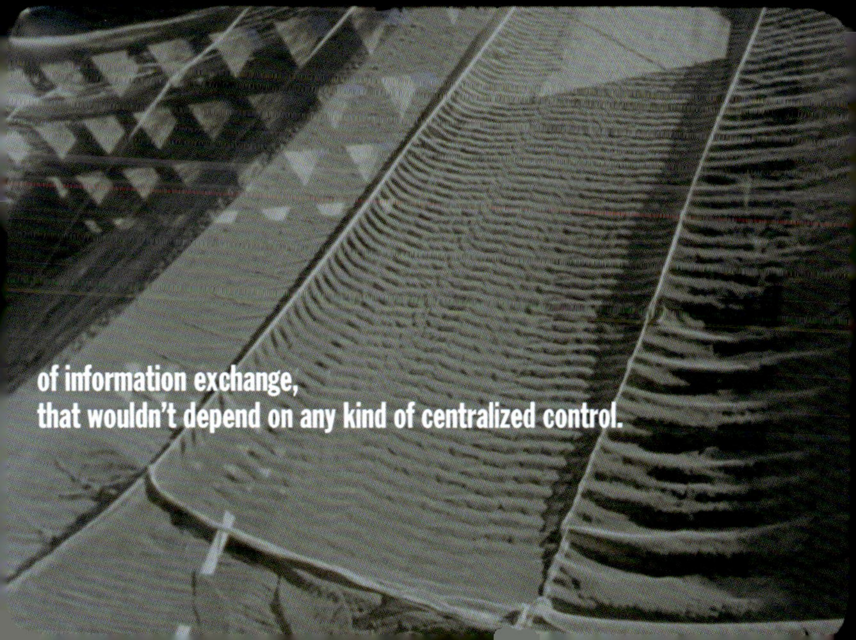

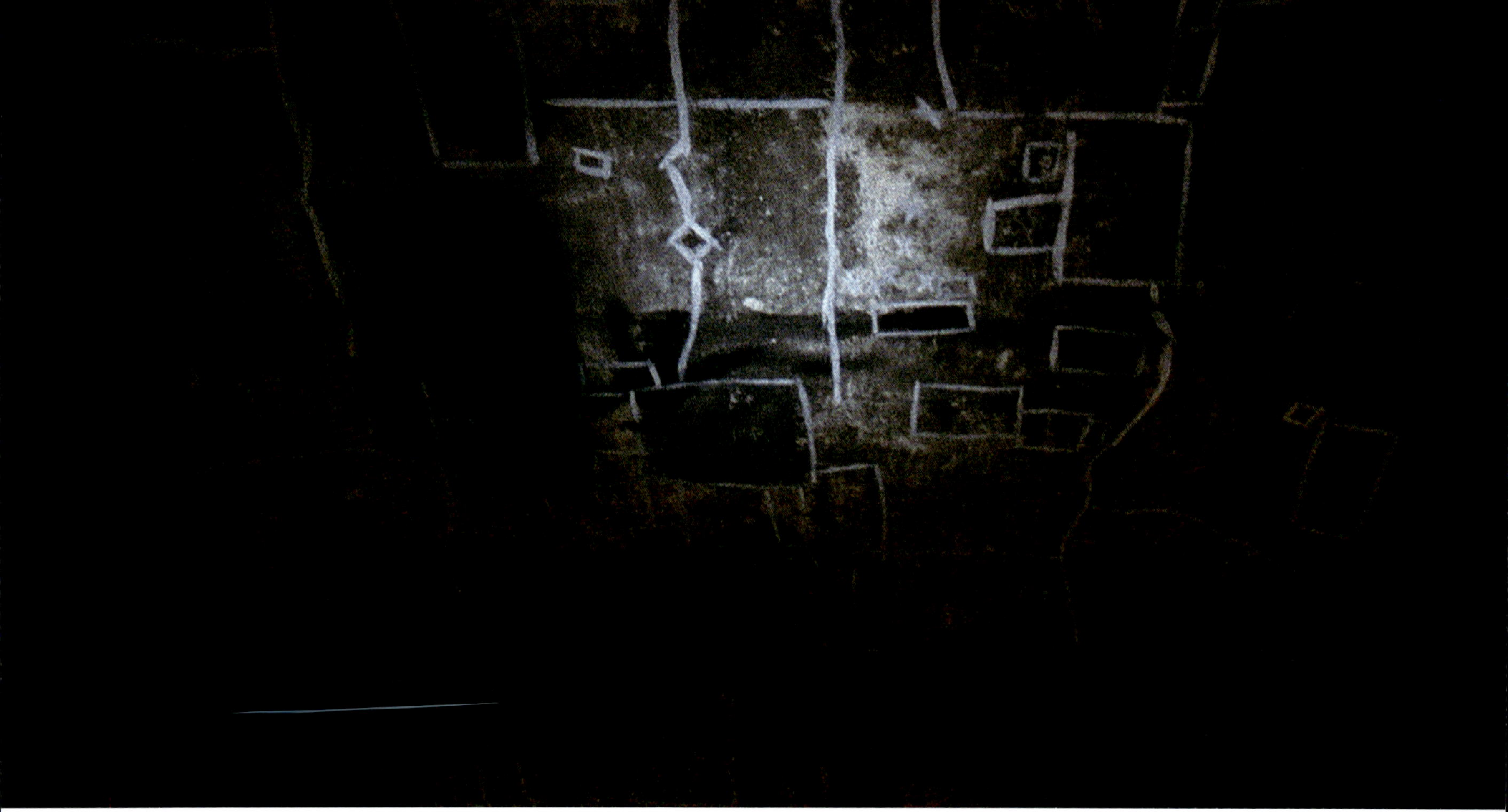

illustrate Barba navigating the spatial and physical configurations of the museum and the archive, stressing the inextricable and intimate relationship that exists between architectures and peoples. She has stated that what is of critical significance to her is the 'notion of [how] space as architecture relates to the community that shares those spaces, geographically and mentally'.[8]

This commitment to examining and revealing how certain communities stake out space for themselves within a larger moving social order, and how shifting political circumstances affect them, traces back to Barba's first longer film, *Panzano* (2000), a collaboration with Ulrike Molsen. This 16mm film follows a group of older people who shared a home in the town of Panzano in the Chianti region of Tuscany that had been released from the mental-care-homes system as part a change in government policy in the 1970s. Barba came to this town as a student in 1998 and spent six months there, during which time she developed relationships with the residents of the home, who would become the protagonists of the film. Barba invited Valeria, Dino and Claudio to choose their own roles in the film – roles that they did not inhabit or play in their daily lives. During the shoot, which lasted between 1998 and 2000, a loose plot was developed, with each of the invited protagonists given ample room to improvise. The film never explicitly mentions the back stories of Valeria, Dino and Claudio; there is no establishing context – they are just shown to be living in a house, having organized themselves into some sort of family unit. Only gradually does it begin emerge that each of them is navigating mental instability, and that they are individuals who have been neglected by the Italian heath-care system. Their mental, emotional makeup is mirrored in the elliptical quality of the editing of the film, generating an anxious atmosphere. The interactions between them are captured with a full range of emotions on display – quarrelsome, playful, sharp and tender – their role-playing taking cues from established social codes and conventions that then start to fray. The home, while a setting for the film and literal place of inhabitation for the three protagonists, undeniably functions allegorically. The film asks whether it offers refuge from social structures, in a society that seems to have forsaken them, or whether it cuts them off from that society. The lexicons of the alienated and disenfranchised are made to comingle with the tropes of domestic architecture, creating a tension between finding a sense of belonging and deep isolation. As Barba recounts, 'the cast's determined – albeit untrained – performances reveal the sincerity of their own desire to bring this fantasy to life, to belong to and be in the house they inhabit in the film … here the "having" of a place or home in society became something to be thematized.'[9]

opposite,
A PRIVATE TABLEAUX, 2010
16MM FILM, COLOUR, OPTICAL SOUND
7 MIN

below,
A PRIVATE TABLEAUX, 2010
16MM FILM, COLOUR, OPTICAL SOUND
7 MIN

INSTALLATION VIEW AT AT CONTEMPORARY ART CENTRE (ŠIUOLAIKINIO MENO CENTRAS) VILNIUS, 2014

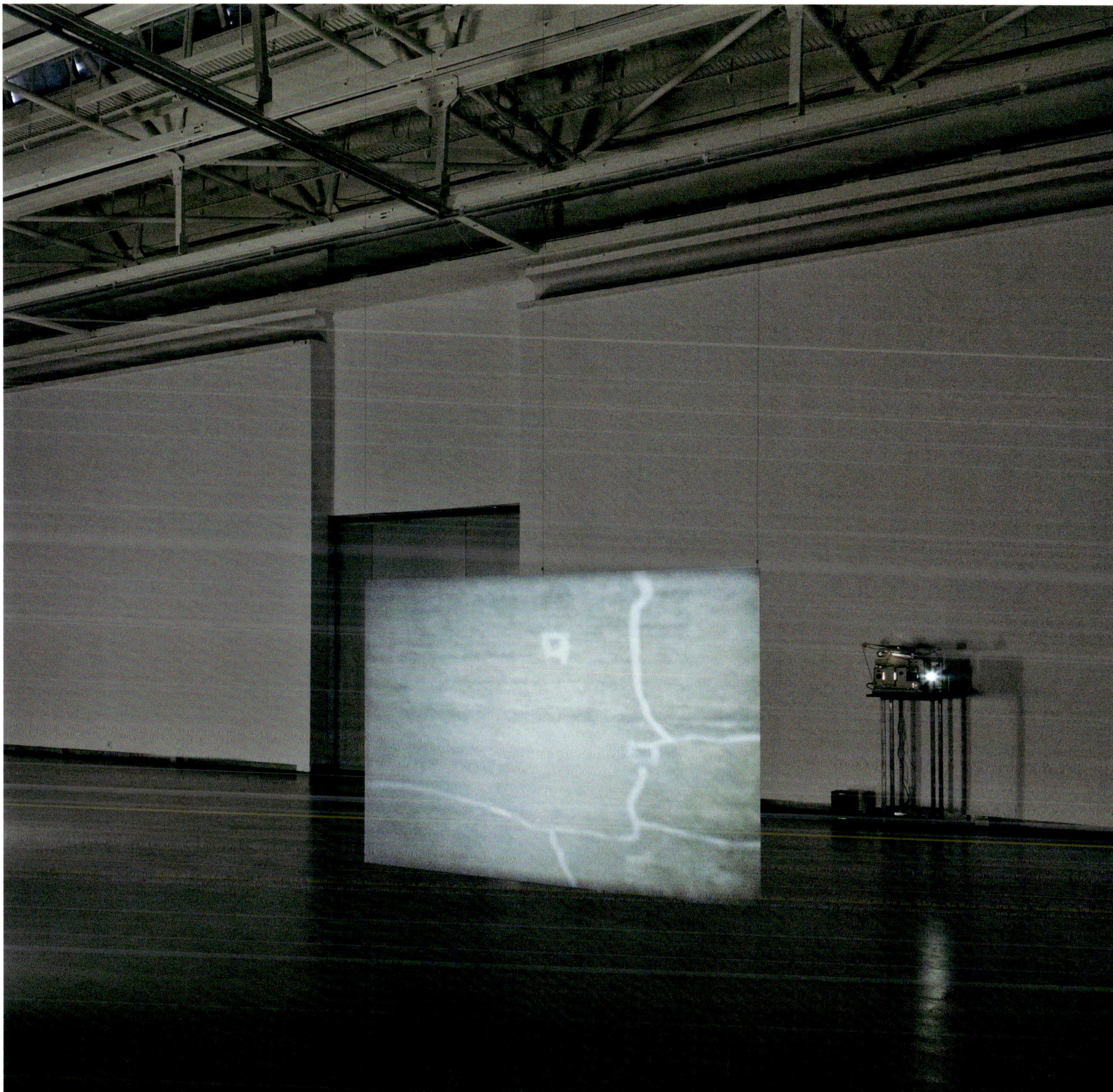

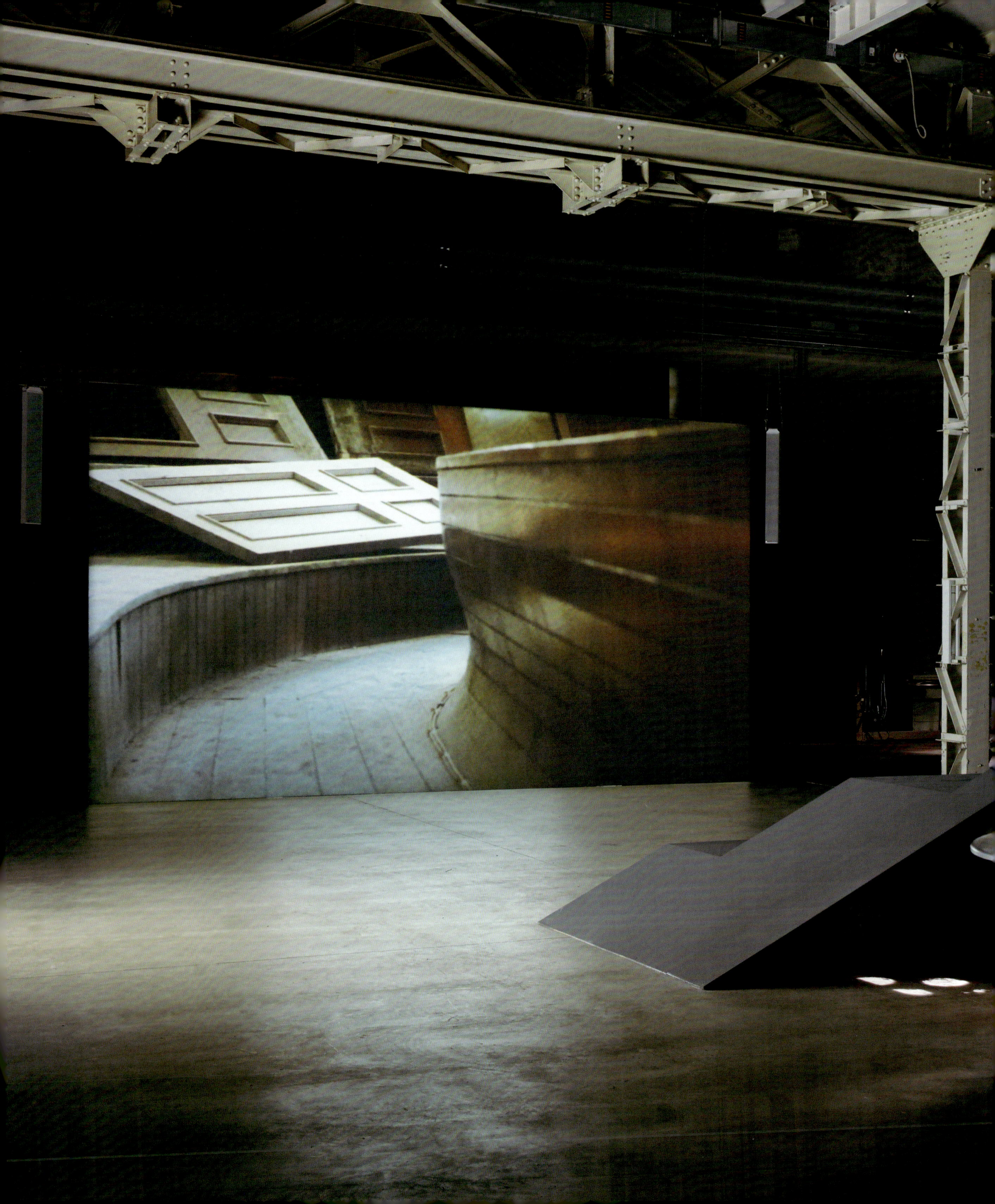

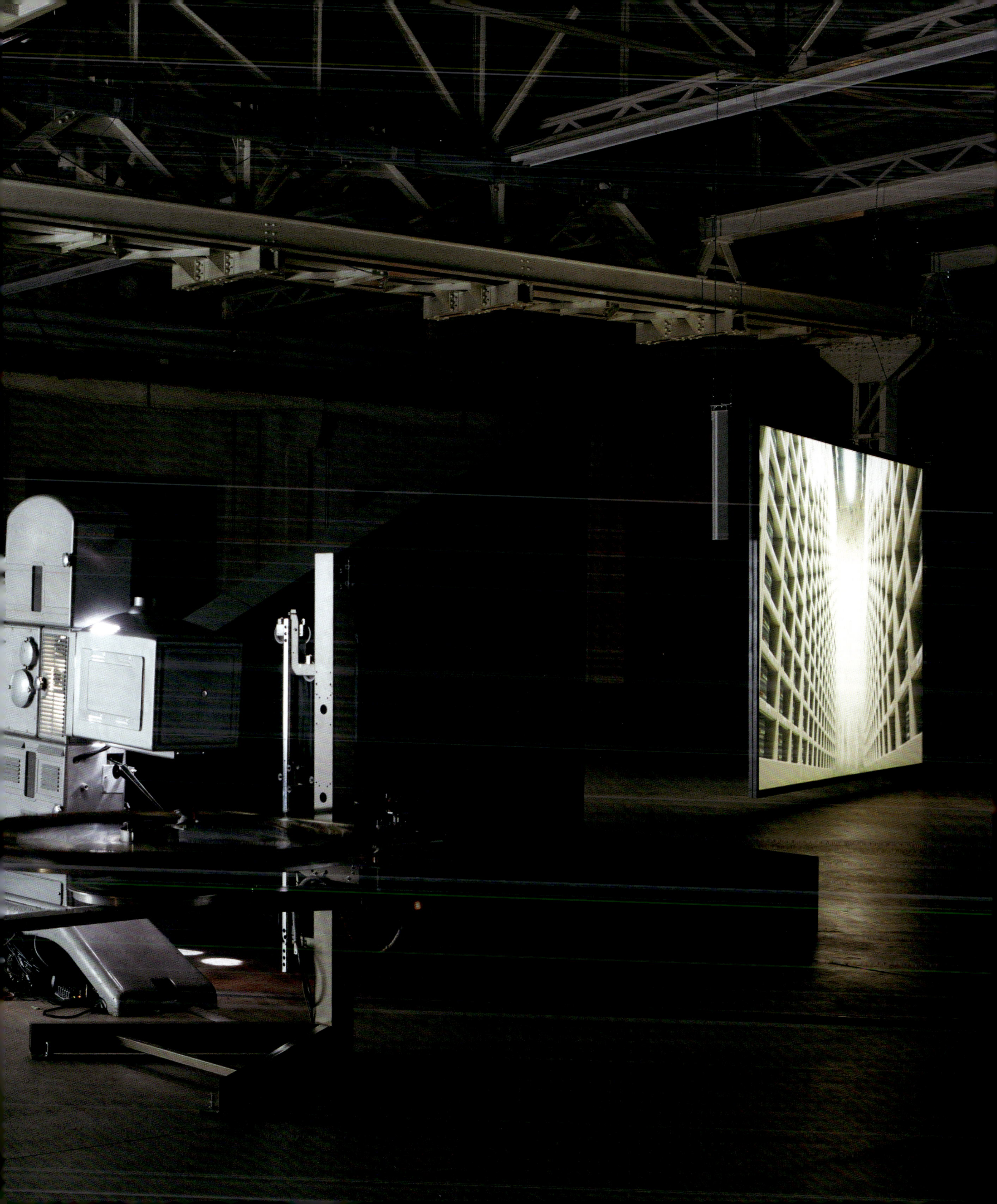

opposite,
SUBCONSCIOUS SOCIETY, A FEATURE, 2014
35MM FILM, COLOUR, OPTICAL SOUND,
40 MIN.

previous pages,
SUBCONSCIOUS SOCIETY, A FEATURE, 2014
35MM FILM, COLOUR, OPTICAL SOUND,
40 MIN.

INSTALLATION VIEW AT PIRELLI HANGARBICOCCA, MILAN, 2017

Another improvised, temporary community of individuals is brought together in *Subconscious Society, A Feature* (2014), a film of abandoned, dilapidated architectures from across England. The forgotten Wesleyan chapel, Albert Hall, in the centre of Manchester becomes a central site, a space for a group of individuals to gather whose fractured stories and reminiscences are communicated in voiceover and text. They reflect on the building itself, its various functions, but also on the outmoded, on what no longer has function or ceases to be relevant as society transforms itself, shedding the post-industrial and sliding into the digital. Here Barba is yet again digging into the memories of a local community. Their collective mental state reverberates with the broken-down, derelict condition of Albert Hall. Many of her actors had never been on a plane, or travelled at all, reinforcing their deep ties to this location. The film ponders what might be possible in a collective act of adaptation and rehabilitation as they attempt to form a new way to live and be together.

This sense of collective possibility also haunts what is perhaps Barba's boldest sculptural intervention, *Inside the Outset: Evoking a Space of Passage* (2021),[10] an open-air cinema built on the eastern side of Cyprus. It is located in the periphery of the village of Deryneia, within the 180-km-long, UN-controlled Buffer Zone that runs across the island, dividing it between the Turkish-speaking North and the Greek-speaking South, a line that was introduced in 1974. First proposed by Barba in 2013, the open-air cinema was constructed after seven years of preparation in collaboration with the Point Art Centre for Contemporary Art and the United Nations. When she visited Cyprus, she was intrigued by the 'buffer zone' and the lack of communication and exchange of culture between the two sides. She then set out to find a suitable location for a project. She finally alighted on a spot from where you could see both a mosque and a church on either side, where an open-air cinema could be situated and people from both communities could access and view the same film without any border controls. To construct the cinema, Barba imagined an amphitheatre-like space, collaborating with local architects, who under the supervision of Maya Shopova, used only local materials. Sculpting into the terrain, they created a circular arena with integrated step seating, at the centre of which is a simple pale green metal frame, the choice of colour allowing it to blend unobtrusively into the surroundings.

Inside the Outset: Evoking a Space of Passage is the grandest evocation of Barba's 'site responsive' strategy. It shares with previous works like *Blind Volumes* the commitment to provide accessibility, and with other works the urge to transform or interrogate, raising questions around built architectures in order to shift their relationship with the communities that visit them or live in proximity to them. Sensitive to the fact that this would be the first structure to be installed in that area since 1974, Barba did not want to court permanence, to establish a monument. Instead, by using earth materials, she created something that was discrete, gentle and that will gradually disintegrate, dissolving back into the earth, but while there will temporarily stimulate the site, altering normative patterns, perceptions and ways of being.

For the time the open-air cinema is to exist, its life-cycle determined by the natural elements from which it is made, it should be a meeting point, a place where communities can come together and watch a film simultaneously in a space that Barba has literally carved out. In her own words, it is an example of a space that 'we can engage in – not creating new safe and amusing spaces, or new completed imaginary story worlds. Rather opening spaces that are unpredictable, playful and perhaps scary. We don't know what we will find there; these are the places where new things can occur.'[11] The first screening took place on September 2021, and since then the open-air cinema has lain dormant due to political tensions. Will these political currents shift and allow the cinema to be activated again, or will it become moribund, like the abandoned architectures of Barba's other films? What is to become of the openness and generosity that guided and shaped the project; the promise, perseverance and enthusiasm that drove its extended development? As these questions linger over Barba's open-air cinema, one can hope that what inspired the project will reverberate. And yet, even if it were never to be activated again, there will always be that one time when the dream machine of cinema did kick into action and it became a space where communities did coexist, did come together and contemplate the future and all its possibilities. It happened once, and it can happen again.

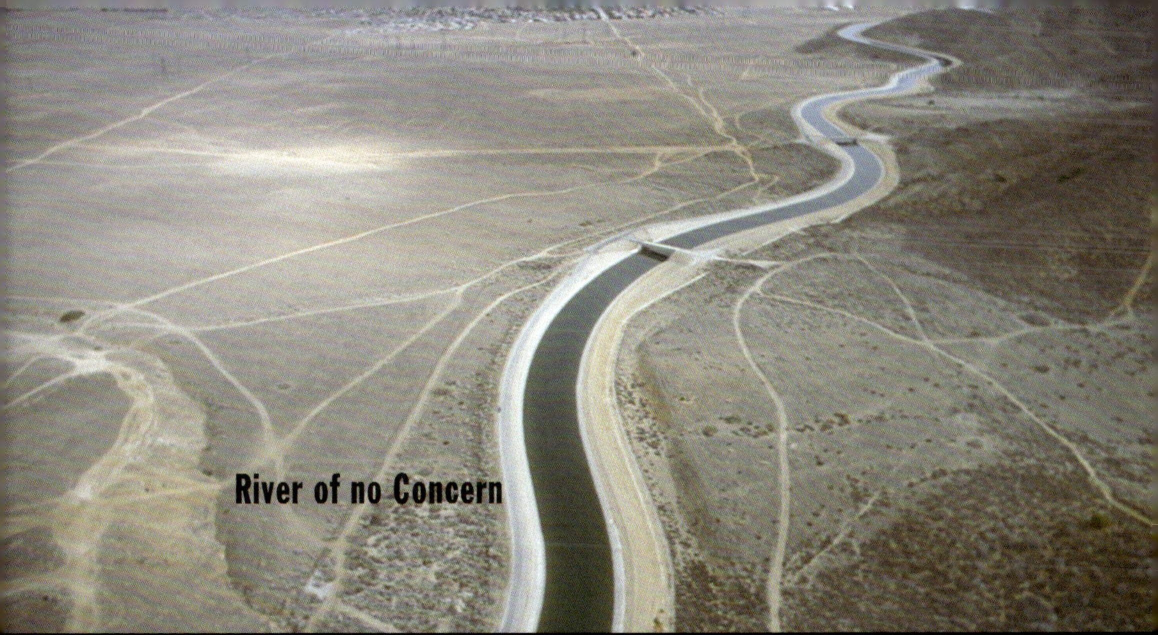
River of no Concern
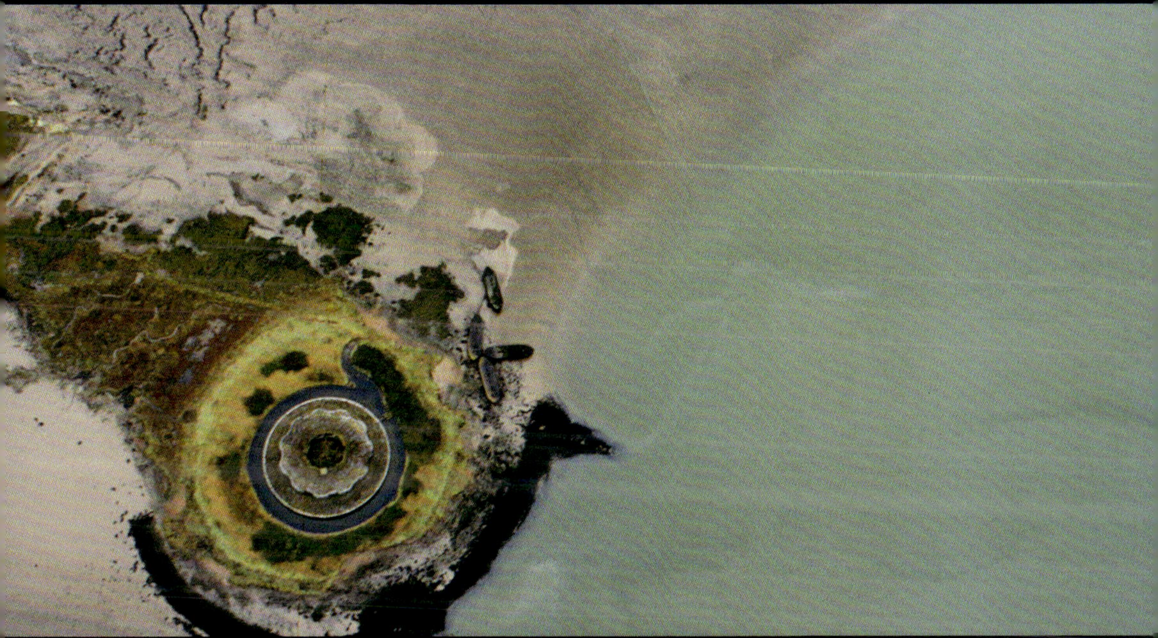
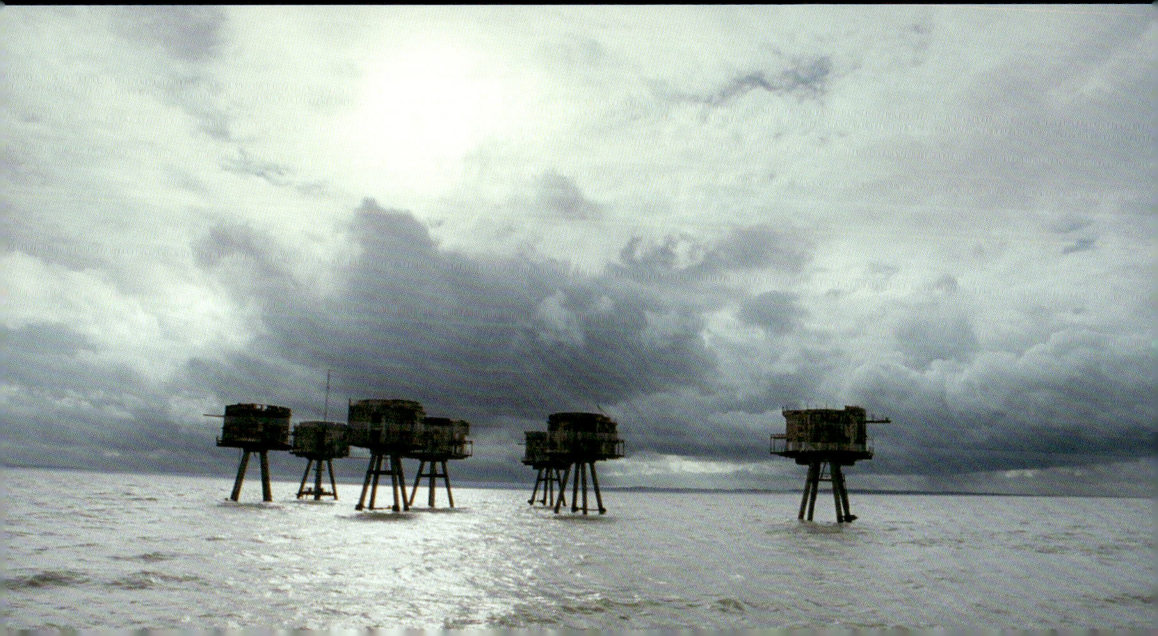

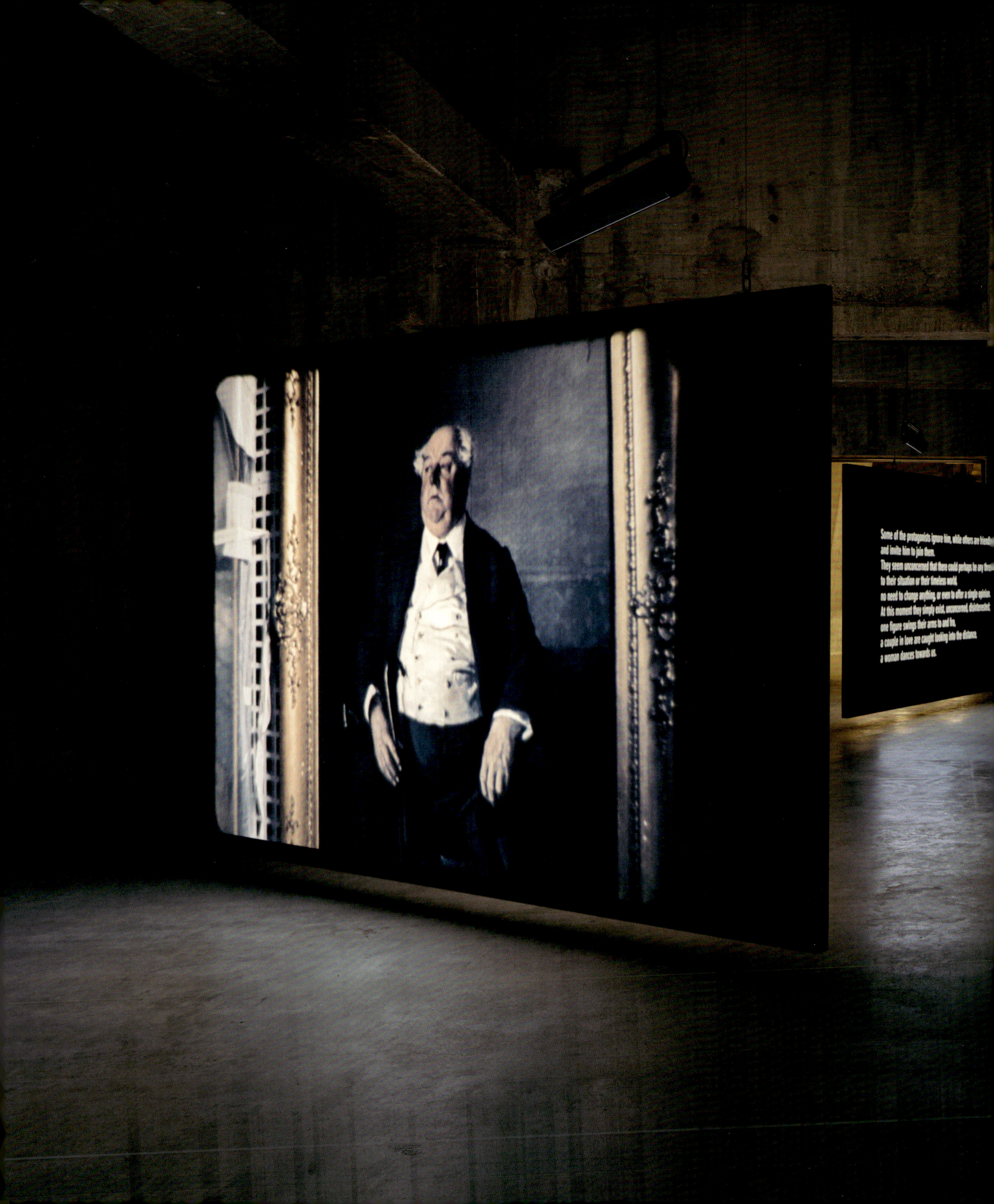
Some of the protagonists ignore him, while others are
and invite him to join them.
They seem unconcerned that there could perhaps be any
to their situation or their timeless world,
no need to change anything, or even to offer a single opinion.
At this moment they simply exist, unconcerned, disinterested:
one figure swings their arms to and fro,
a couple in love are caught looking into the distance,
a woman dances towards us.

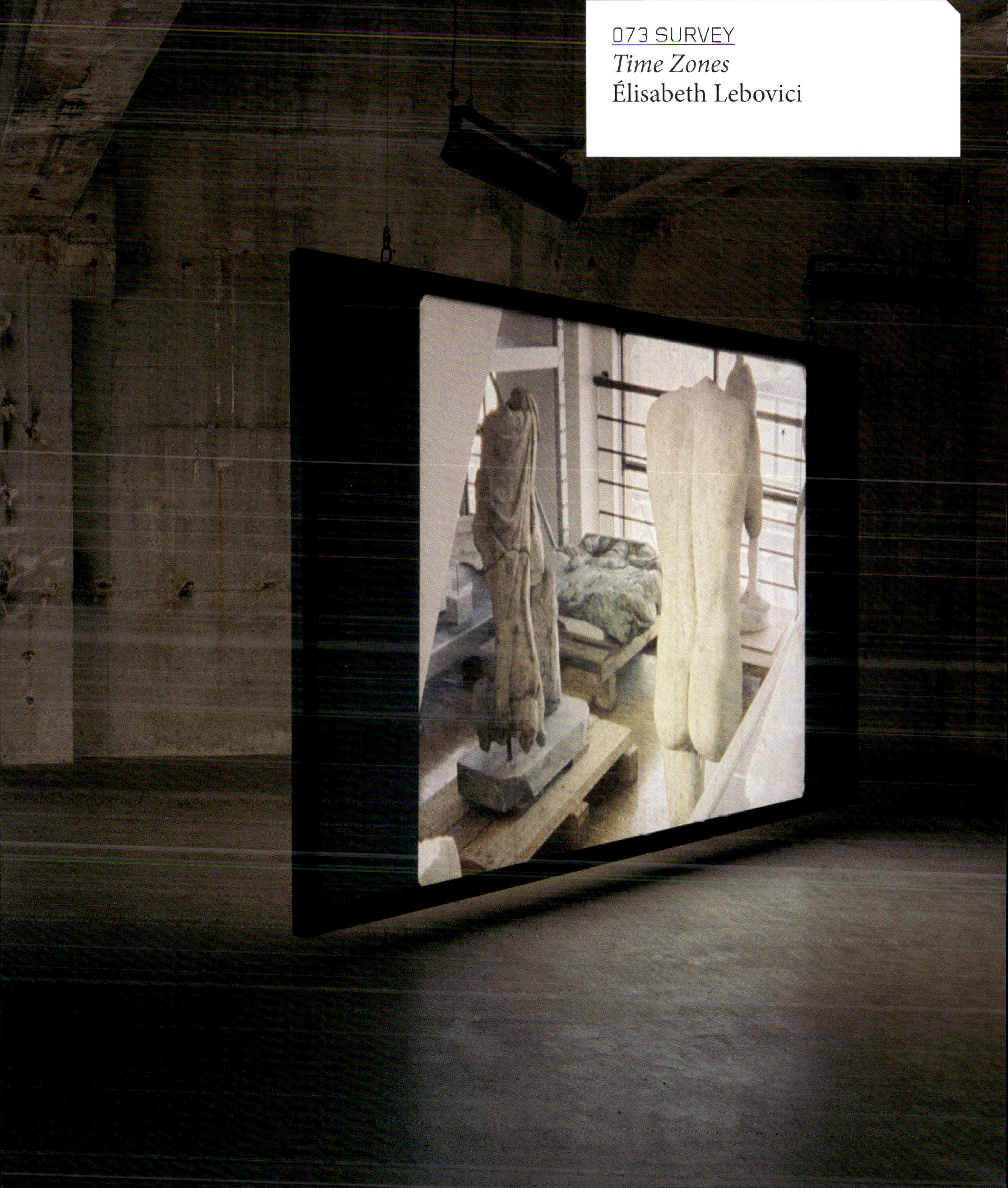

073 SURVEY

Time Zones

Élisabeth Lebovici

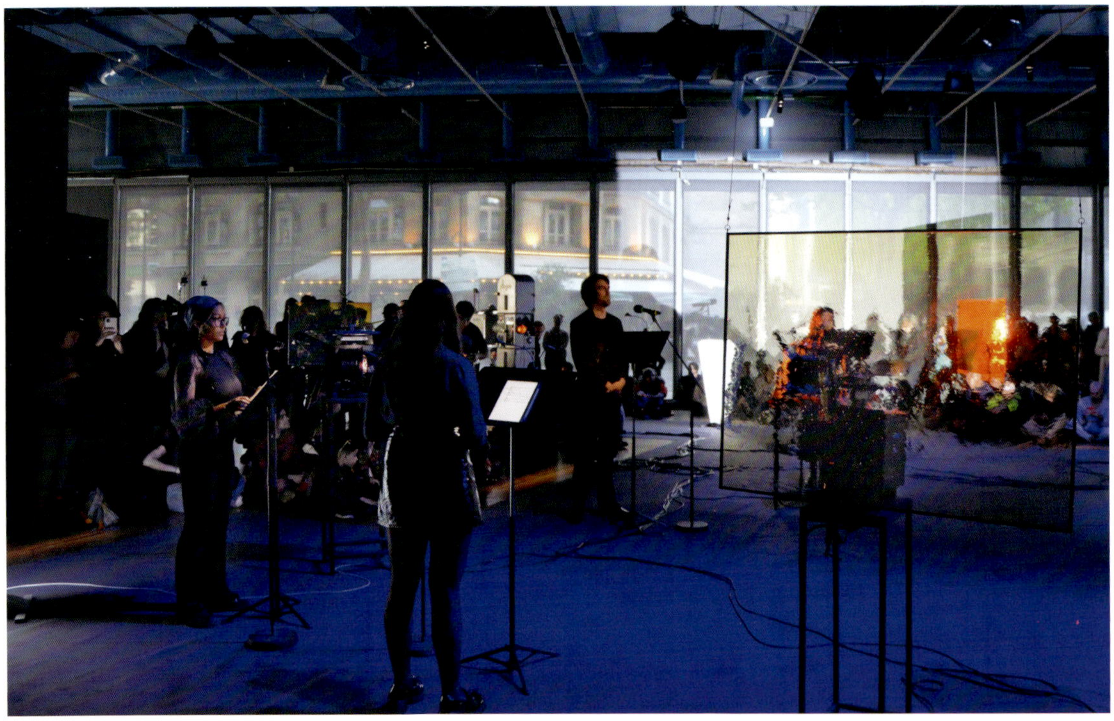

left and opposite,
VOICE ENGINE, 2021–23
VOICE AND PROJECTORS
SCORE WITH COMPOSER AND PERFORMER ERIC D. CLARK, ACCOMPANIED BY ALEX AIKIU, FLORENT BAFFI, SHIRLEY-SOA BERNARD, SARA BRUNEL, RITA FILIPE AND CHRISTIANE PRINCE.

INSTALLATION VIEW AT CENTRE POMPIDOU, PARIS, 2023

previous pages, from left,
THE HIDDEN CONFERENCE: ABOUT THE DISCONTINUOUS HISTORY OF THINGS WE SEE AND DON'T SEE, 2010
35MM FILM, PROJECTION, DRESDEN D1 PROJECTOR, COLOUR, OPTICAL SOUND
11 MIN. 8 SEC.

THE HIDDEN CONFERENCE: A FRACTURED PLAY, 2011
35MM FILM, PROJECTION, DRESDEN D1 PROJECTOR, COLOUR, OPTICAL SOUND
5 MIN. 29 SEC.

THE HIDDEN CONFERENCE: ABOUT THE SHELF AND MANTEL, 2015
35MM FILM, PROJECTION, DRESDEN D1 PROJECTOR, COLOUR, OPTICAL SOUND
13 MIN. 59 SEC.

INSTALLATION VIEW AT TATE MODERN, LONDON, 2023

This is where I began writing, from a position of rethinking. A modification of experience, a movement inside precipitated by all the things outside.[1]

These words from Ian White, who was Rosa Barba's friend and mine too, bring us together and hold me back. They are the connection to the writing of this text. In this monograph, my stance is that of an art critic, a receiver. My starting point is how the works impact me – in their production, in the artist's physical and mental creative area, but also in their circulation, their afterglow, their presence at each event in space and time, at every exhibition. Whether at an evening performance at the Pompidou Centre (Paris, France), at an introduction to the artist at the Esther Schipper gallery – which represents her – in Berlin, at a one-night event in Marfa (Texas, USA) at the end of a residency, at the Centre International d'Art et du Paysage at Vassivière (Limousin, France) and its surroundings, in a former food warehouse for products from colonial plantations[2] converted into a contemporary art museum (CAPC Musée d'Art Contemporain de Bordeaux), in a publication, book or set of photographs, viewed by the artist as an exhibition of *Printed Cinema*,[3] or again at a fleeting installation in Alexander Calder's former studio in Saché (Touraine, France), I experienced each of these as an arrangement, or rather, as a *composition*. Pleasingly, this term is primarily used in relation to music, which is essential in the case of Barba, who initially trained in music and modern dance. I often think back to the concert tours organised between 1995 and 1997, which she accompanied with a light show. She would carry, install, adjust her Super-8 and 16mm projectors for hours before each evening performance, then crawl onto the stage, with sticky tape in her mouth, to mend the film, which had broken in the heat of the action.[4] When she was a projectionist in Cologne, during her studies, I remember her taking care to make a smooth changeover between one reel of film and the loading of the next. This description of activities, which includes the artist's body, and that of her materials makes me think of an account of her earlier life, and of how, from adolescence, Barba observed the world through an analogue camera, then a Super-8 cine camera, then 16mm, developing her films herself and using her family and social environment as subject matter, while at the same time exploring non-narrative images: 'I think it was a mode of understanding how the camera gave me freedom.'[5]

But the term 'composing' also implies the bringing together of disparate, varied mechanisms, and using them in a way that is often unusual or, at the very least, imaginative, but which can throw us off balance and undermine our usual practices. In each of the happenings referred to above, and in many others too, the artist arranges various spatial organisations of filmic time that, individually and together, react to the places and times of her intervention. The verb 'to compose' is also close to the verb 'to compromise'. It shows me where I am, here and now: I have to compromise with my memory. This is where writing starts, or rather restarts,[6] as it recalls things that have been forgotten and omitted, and restores an experience, or the experiments that Barba is constantly conducting, to the present day. They must indeed be approached 'from a position of rewriting'. Composing, after all, is reconfiguring the space of meetings and distributions.

This can be seen at MoMA in New York, on the floor housing the contemporary art collections. Barba's work is exhibited in two rooms, as two contiguous acts

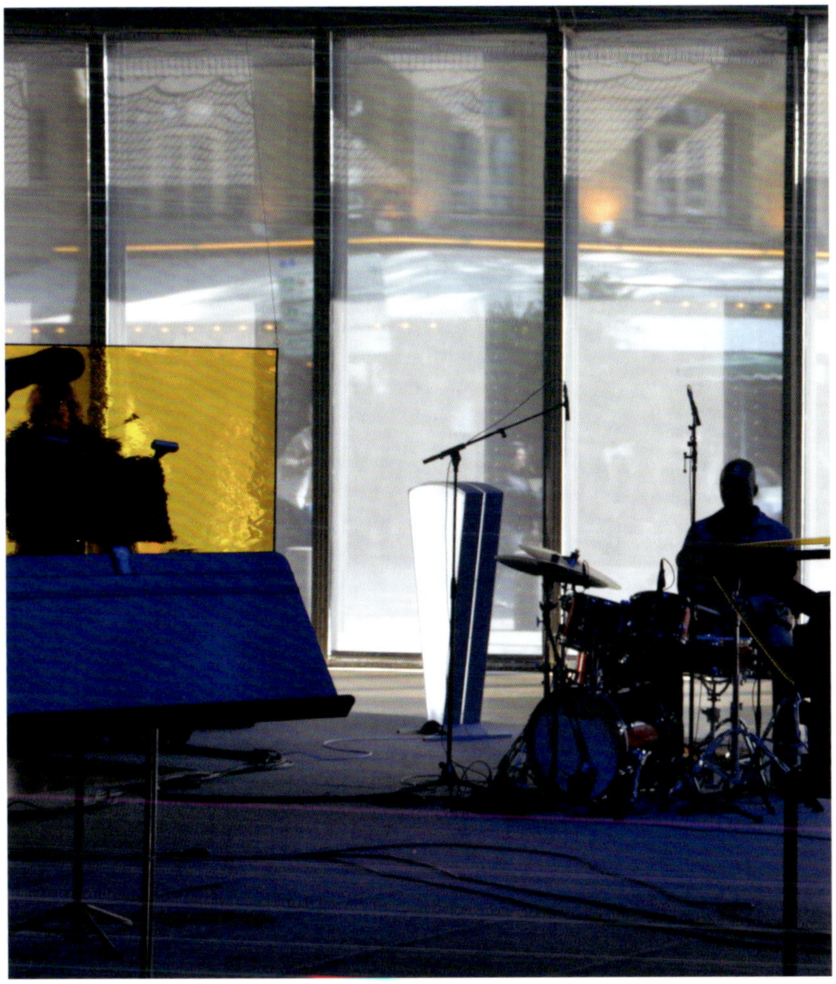

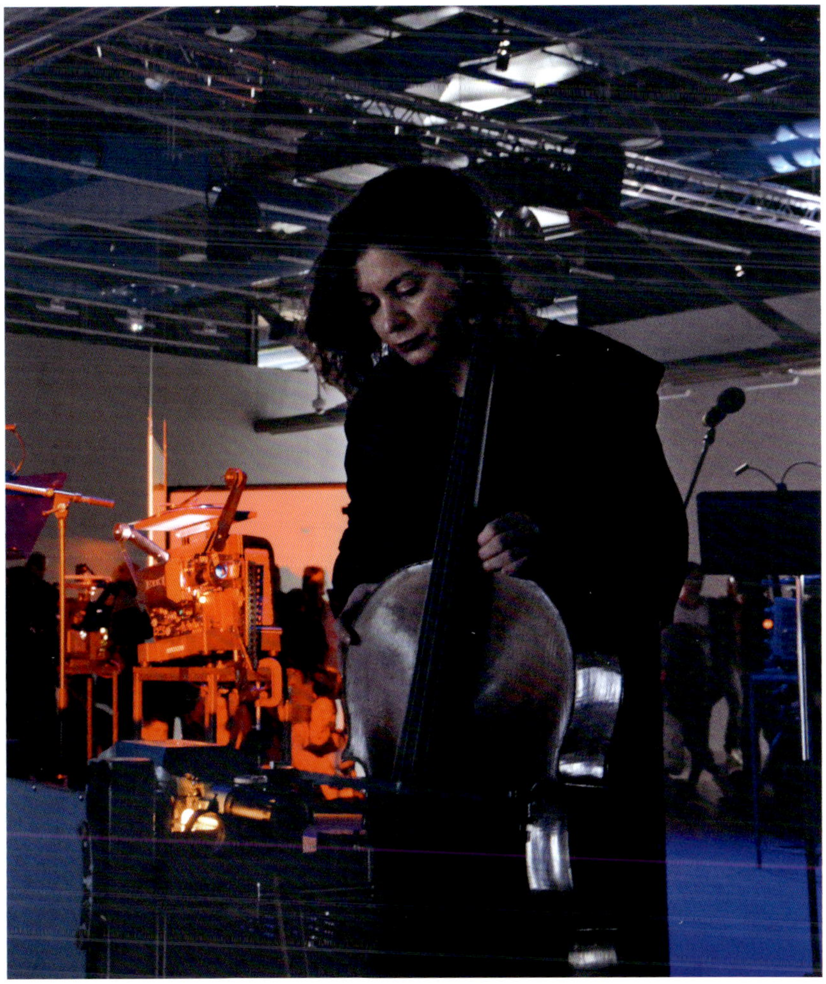

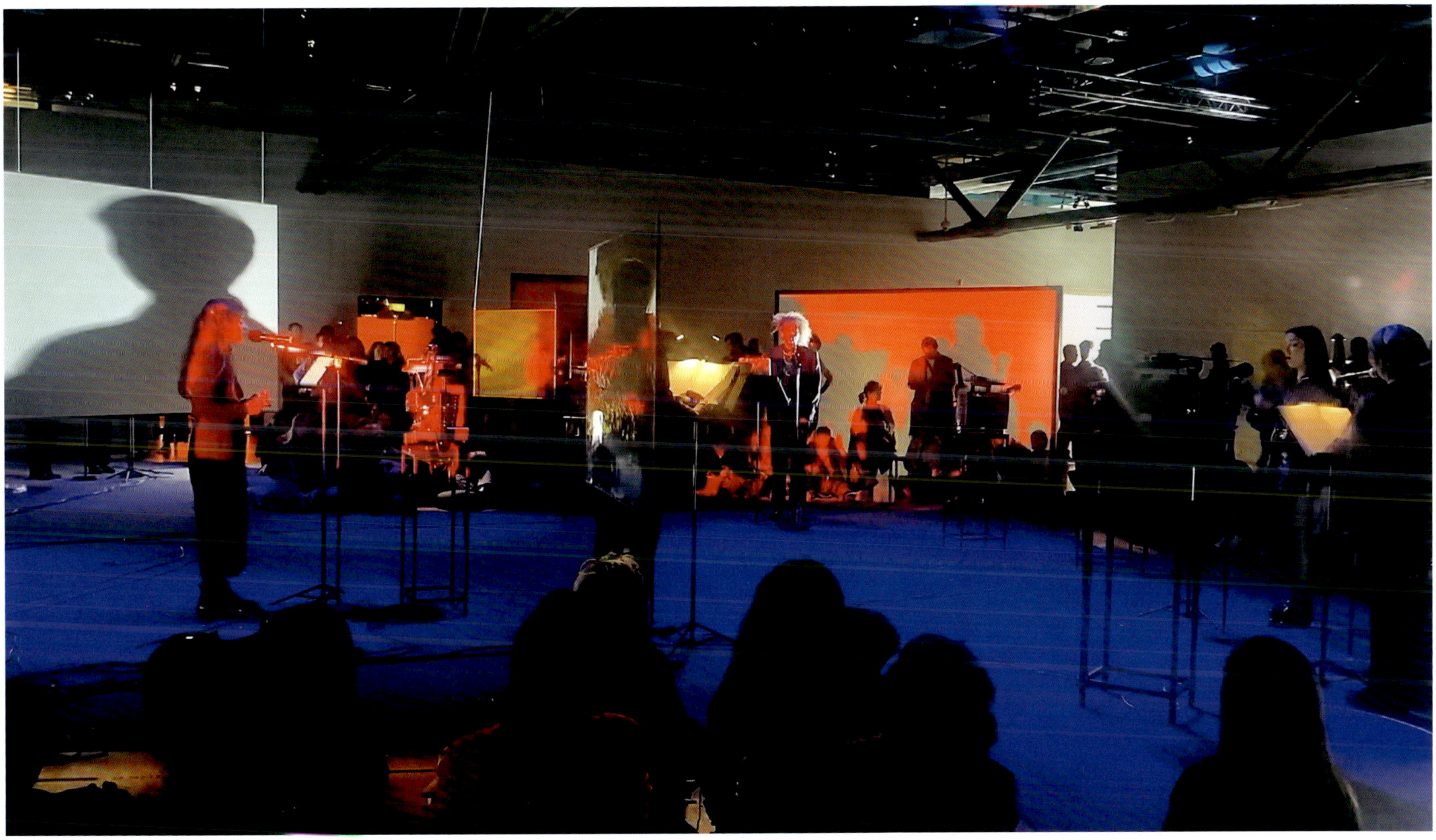

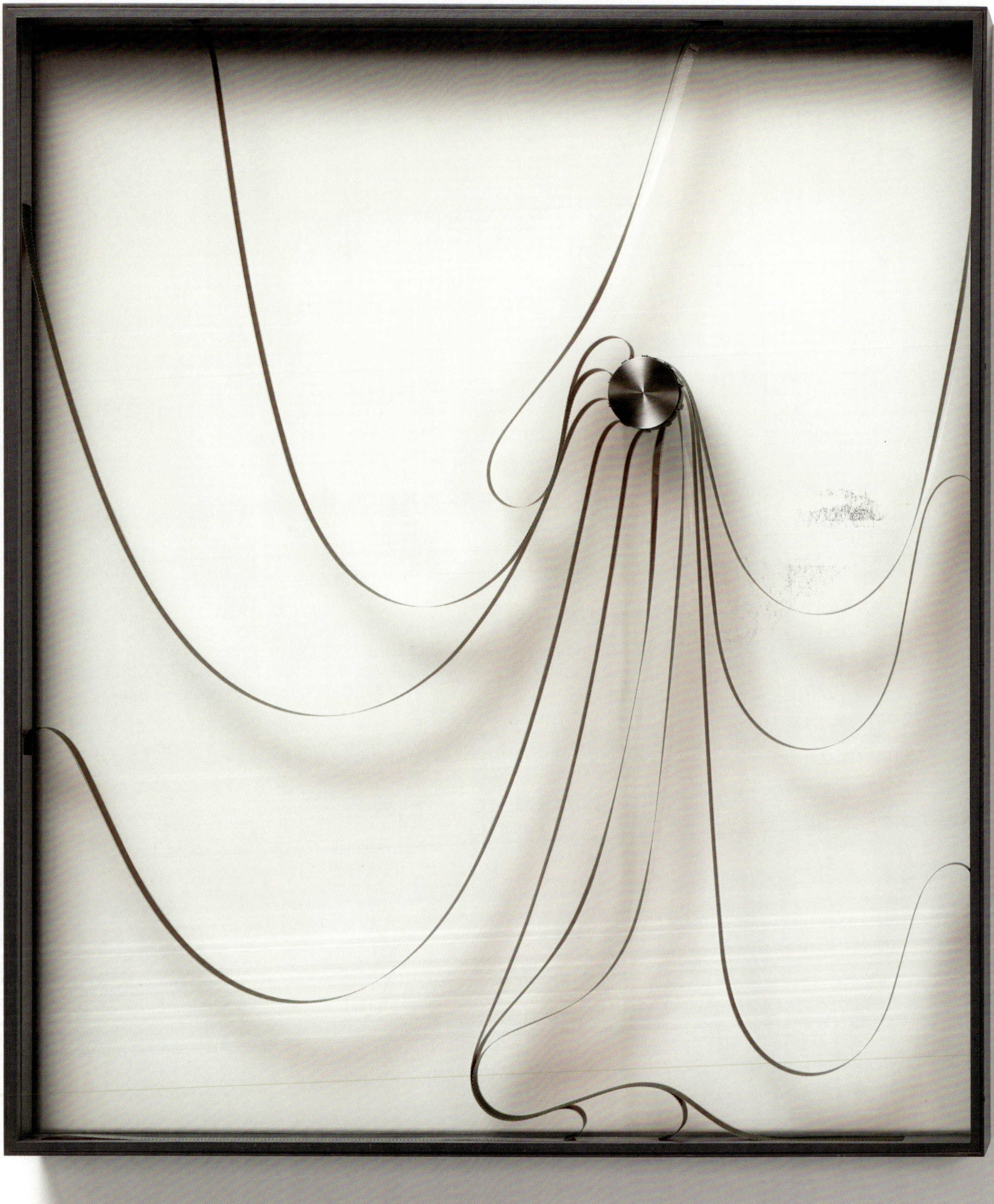

right,
UNCERTAIN THEME – AND THEREFORE ABSTRACT (DETAIL), 2021 STEEL, GLASS, MOTOR, 35MM FILM
123 X 140 X 12 CM

opposite,
UNCERTAIN THEME – AND THEREFORE ABSTRACT, 2021 STEEL, GLASS, MOTOR, 35MM FILM
123 X 140 X 12 CM

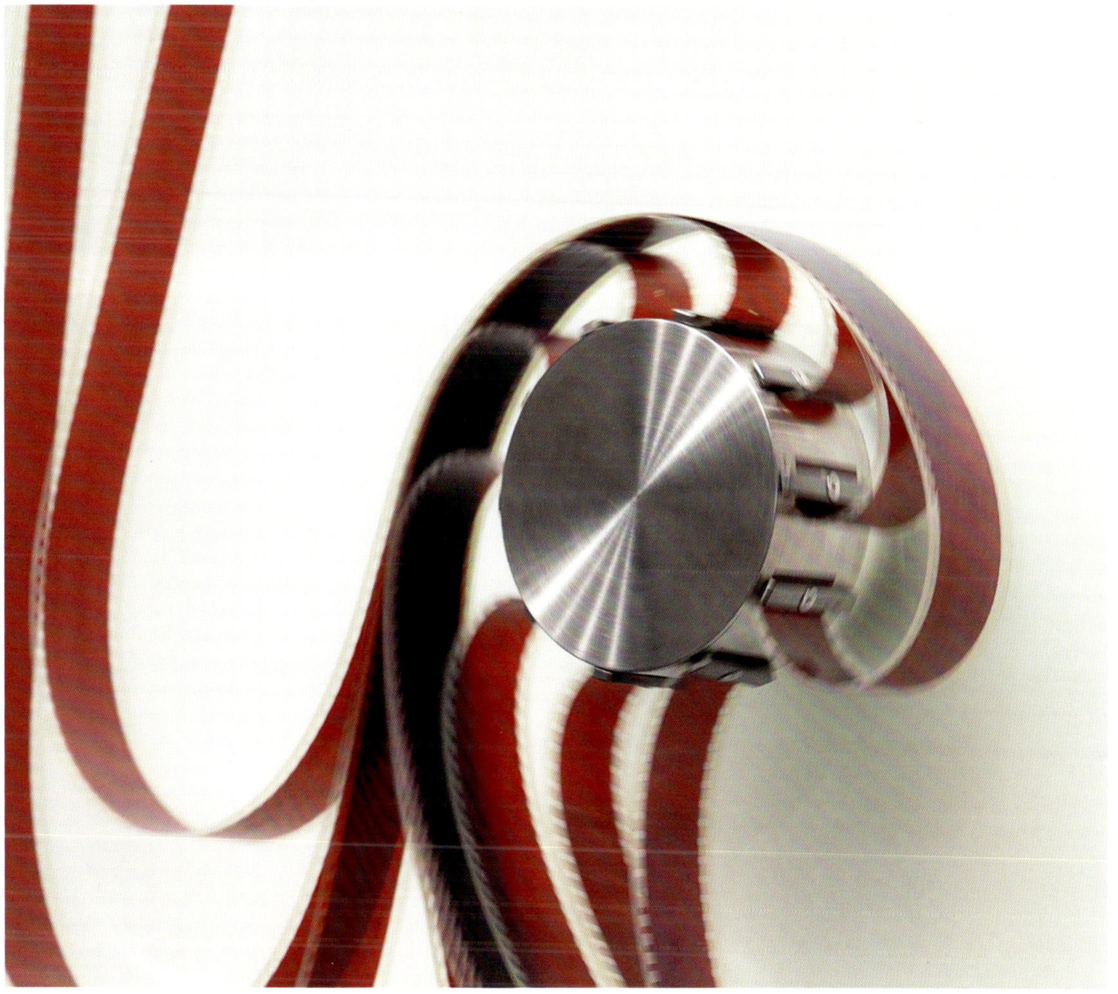

separated by a wall. *Uncertain Theme – and Therefore Abstract* (2021) is a transparent box containing a ribbon of film that winds and unwinds around a constantly rotating mechanism. Its ongoing, staccato dance constructs its own time, separate from ours. In this piece, 'the fatigued formal trope of the loop'[7] performs both a choreography and a strip-tease, as the raw film is stripped naked, not dressed with images. In the same way, Duchamp, for *The Large Glass* – otherwise known as *The Bride Stripped Bare by her Bachelors, Even* (1915–23) – organized a vision of the object and through the object. In Barba's work, to use the words of Giuliana Bruno, 'sightseeing' becomes 'site-seeing',[8] a journey, moving, *travelling*. This is so even when, as in *Weavers* (2023) – the weaving of films – it seems fixed. In these blue or red pieces, 16mm film is looped through and around a 35mm celluloid strip (both bearing images filmed by the artist), stretched on a metal frame. They are suspended like a mobile, in a clear reference to Calder, in whose studio they were woven collectively using a local basketry technique from the village of Villaines-les-Rochers. They rotate slowly in the air, alternating between transparent colours and opaque metallic reflections, between folding screens and cinema screens. At the same time, the frames are constantly intertwined, as are the strips of film, containing phrases such as 'final images' or 'Never cut this fragment', which form a poem created randomly. *Weavers* calmly conjugates the thought of movement.

While presented as a stand-alone 'sculpture', *Uncertain Theme – and Therefore Abstract* also acts as a shift of gear or link to the second installation, *Aggregate States of Matters* (2019), in a move from white museum walls to a darker room. In this room, the eye is drawn not only to the screen. The machinery of the 35mm projector is in itself a sculptural event, producing light, air, movement and a soundtrack. Its lamp emits a beam of light, while visitors can hear the noises from the ventilator needed to cool down the lamp, as well as those made by the moving film, as the workings of the machine become part of the music of the film itself. This monstrous, kinetic machine[9] is what we see first, just as striking as the moving images parading across the large screen opposite. This screen, moreover, is not placed directly facing the spectators, like a mirror. Instead of forming the fourth wall, as in the classic theatre arrangement – the missing wall that frames the action – it has pulled away at an acute angle, is set on a diagonal, shifting the viewers' perspective and preventing them from becoming completely absorbed in the film being screened.
In the language of dialectical materialism, the process of producing the exhibition does not end with the product. The installation must compromise, come to terms with its technological environment, which is part and parcel of the exhibition. I am reminded of the 1970s deconstructions – particularly in Francophone film theory – that analyse the 'dispositive'[10] as an ideology or even

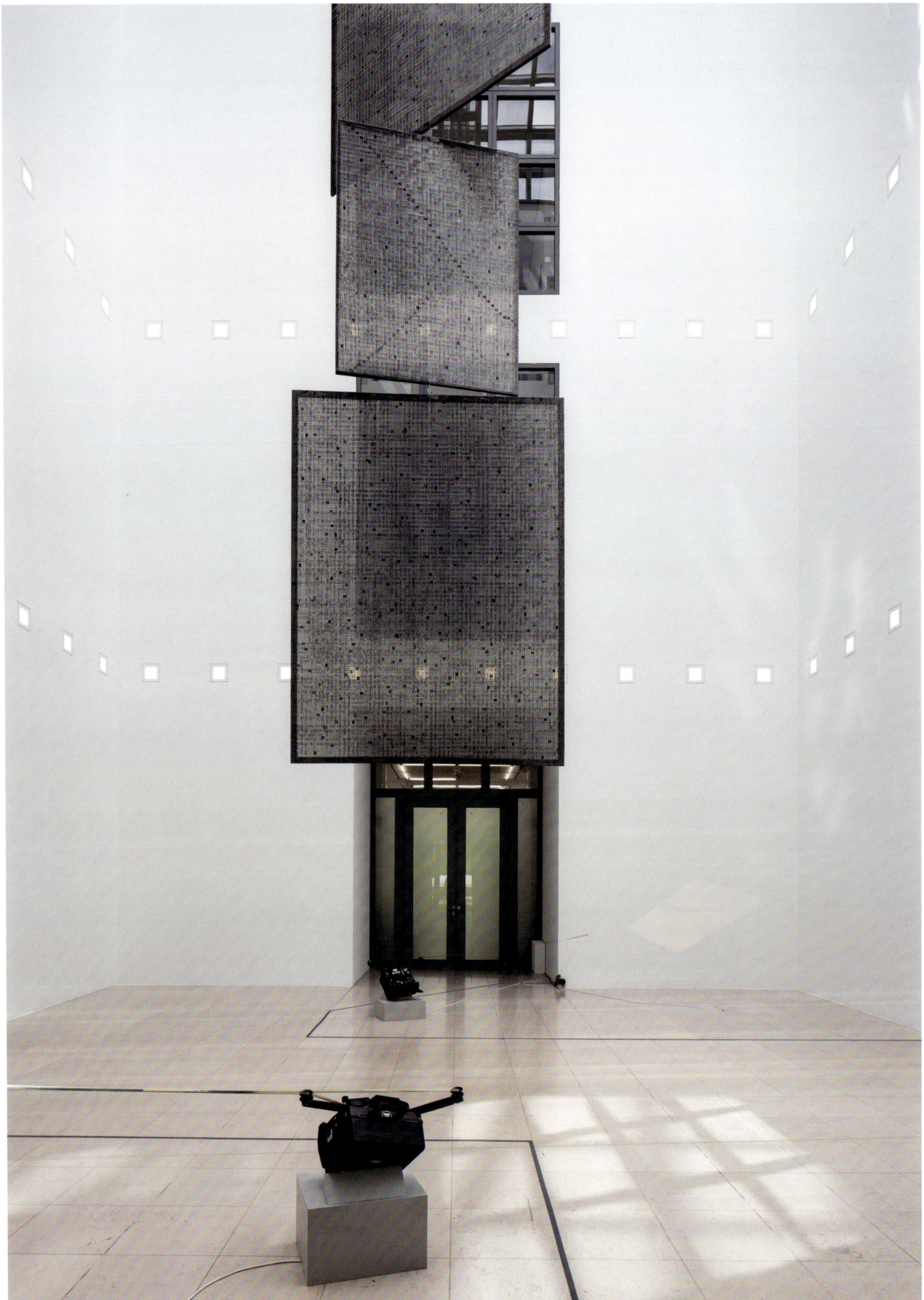

left,
WEAVERS, 2021
35MM AND 16MM FILM, METAL FRAME, AND DISCO BALL MOTOR

WIREPIECE, 2022
16MM PROJECTOR, 16MM FILM, LENS, DRUM STRING, BRIDGE SADDLE PIECE, PICKUP MICHROPHONE, PRE-AMP, SPEAKER, PLINTHS

INSTALLATION VIEW AT HAMBURGER KUNSTHALLE, HAMBURG, 2024

opposite,
STATING THE REAL SUBLIME, 2009
16MM FILM, MODIFIED PROJECTOR

INSTALLATION VIEW AT TATE MODERN, LONDON, 2010

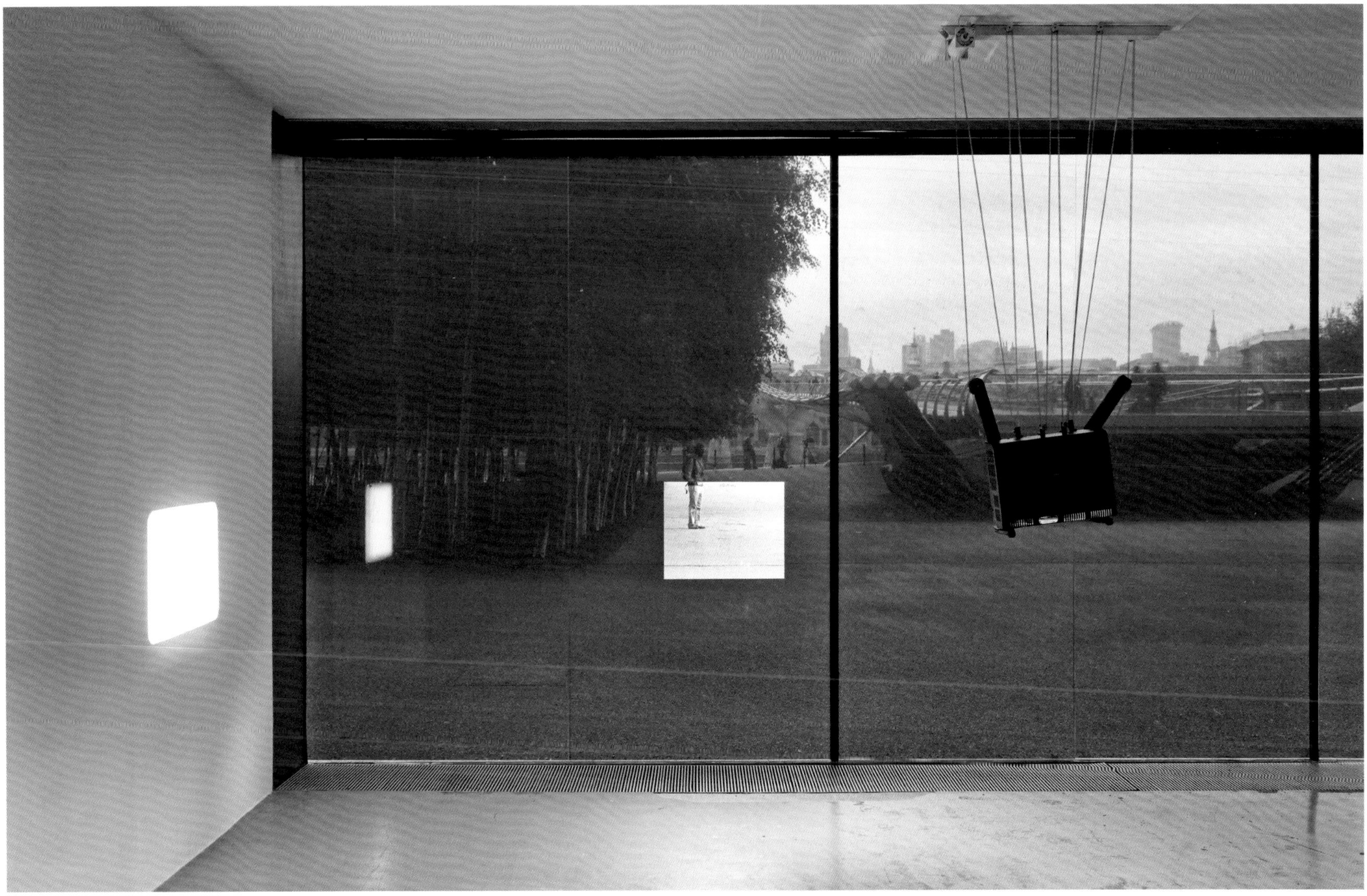

as an idealistic ritual. In these, the cinema space was compared to Plato's cave, the stillness of the spectators to a state of conscious or less conscious sleep; their gaze was compared to psychic regression, and the film to a fake reality. This allowed, at least, some displacement to take place. These analyses pushed the focus of the film off-camera, *sideways*, away from a direct, head-on view and towards the projection of the film and its effect on a third person, their body, their gaze, their emotions, but also their space and time, which were thus included in the conversation.

In mainstream cinema, reality is equated with what is visible; the technology is therefore concealed and rendered invisible by the projected object. In Barba's work, however, the equipment and the screen are not only visible, but include the *projection*, a term that refers to the space of the film, its performance at an exhibition, as much as to its mental construction.[11] Film comes out of the closet: 'If the situation and condition of industrial cinema ultimately read as Barba's (meta)subject', writes White, 'what is effected is a kind of turning inside out of that situation and condition such that it becomes surface content and might be occupied and dismantled at the same time and by its own means.'[12] Disassembled from its patriarchal functional order, technology is reintegrated, together with its herstory, its stories, its vocabulary, its institutions, its economy, the network of relationships it constructs. To this can be added the traces produced by time, signs of ageing or marks of endurance, this ongoing construction site, where we see at work that 'curious ability of inanimate things to animate, to act, to produce effects dramatic and subtle', which Jane Bennett refers to as their 'material vibrancy'.[13]

I recall an intensely fragile sculpture, made up of a 16mm projector suspended from the ceiling by a diaphanous loop of film. The film spins through the body of the device, which projects an area of light, where it can, where it is hanging (*Stating the Real Sublime*, 2009). The screen gradually accumulates specks of dirt over the course of the exhibition. This is not the triumph of technology (fetishism) versus the authoritarian narrative of film (cinephilia). Neither do we have to choose between the movement of the 'physical film' and the 'projected film'.[14] In Barba's work, these binaries have disappeared. *They are combined* in the very matter of a space whose 'competence is deduced from [its] performance' rather than being

opposite, from top,
BLIND VOLUMES, 2016
80 STEEL FRAMES,
PLATFORMS, SCREENS

FROM SOURCE TO POEM, 2016
35MM FILM, COLOUR, OPTICAL
SOUND, 12 MIN.

INSTALLATION VIEW AT MALMO
KONSTHALL, 2017

assumed before any action takes place. Barba describes it as a place 'where the environment, the screen and the projection can be combined and pushed forward to create another spatiotemporal dimension … and a new foundation for thinking and acting through destabilizing the old hierarchy of the old components of cinema, by freeing them from their original use and letting them interact in new and unforeseen ways'.[15] Film, a *dated* practice, or film, a *projected* practice, are replaced by the creation of a 'Chthulucene'[16] cinematographic space. This brings me to Donna Haraway, who speaks of the 'thick present' of this type of film, which slows down all descriptions and does away with any definitions.[17] In both its methodology and its actions, this thickness contrasts with the illusion of mastery coming from a viewpoint situated outside time, looking down on events and thus at a distance. Barba, we can see, holds the camera in her hand or on her shoulder, postures that she compares to those of an artist drawing.[18] The proximity and instability of one body affects the other.[19] Deconstructing the transcendence of dominant ways of framing, Barba's methods create multiple local viewpoints, directing the gaze to disproportionate arrangements of time and place, 'since things, living or inanimate, have … their own way of being in time'.[20] Chronology, in these cases, gives way to 'polychrony'.[21]

This is what interests me here.

In the space-time established in the exhibition room, several timescapes interact, side by side.[22] Should we focus on the timescape composed in the museum – the conversation between the works, or between these works and the museum collections, both those on display and those which remain invisible,[23] and with past or future exhibitions?[24] Or should we discuss the technological landscape, shown both in its own movement – its reflexive dimension – and in the movement that it translates to the screen – its transitive dimension?[25] Is the work alluding to the landscape filmed around Lake Titicaca and the day-to-day life of the Perca Indigenous People, the Quechua community, to whom the lake gives the resources 'to live, to wear, even housing'[26] and which is being contaminated by the mining industry? Or to the altered landscape of the glaciers, which can be seen on the surface of the screen, where abrupt changes of colour, format and film quality create irregularities, flaws and cracks in the smooth surface of the film? Is the artist evoking the complex temporality that, thanks to its sudden bursts of colour and untimely white frames, the montage imputes to geopolitical situations? Is the work highlighting the slow deterioration of the landscape, separated from the rituals and lifestyles of an endangered people, as we read in a text appearing on the surface of the screen, and mixing bursts of language with the mountains? Should we focus on this desertification, which implies both a disappearance (of a way of creating worlds) and a naturalisation (of a group of humans gobbled up by colonial expansion)? Are we to picture a landscape moving in a time and space invisible to the Western eye, trained since the seventeenth century to see nature separately from human society and relationships – concepts that the European nations created to objectivise their own destiny, their own historical trajectory? Or is this installation referring to a geological era, prior to any human way of relating to the world? How can we give shape to that which contains us?

In her work, Barba adds to her stories the very substance of the instruments and tools that she presents to us: filmmaking material, with its series of darknesses (the darkness inside the camera, the chemical black of the photographic film); the light modulation of the projection; the white membrane of the screen; the meditative cycle of the loop; the lack of start- and end-point; the constant repetition up to a breaking point; the breathing spaces, the 'editorial'[27] rhythm of the white frames; the almost strobe-like vibrations of the projector; the texture of the various noises, of the electronic jingles or the projection and ventilation technology, the music marking the movement, incomprehensible conversations … In both analogue and digital film, the texture of the projection reacts with the subject matter, recorded and reported back from the place of observation. Thinking again of *Aggregate States of Matters* at MoMA, this area of the Andes, to which Barba has twice returned,[28] has experienced a slow decay of the resources and traditions of the Indigenous peoples, imperceptible to the 'naked' eye (*Aggregate States of Matters*). In *Bending to Earth* (2015), the view, filmed from a helicopter with a handheld camera, of fields used to store uranium waste, arranged as a regular series of blueish rectangles, also gives historical context to the present and to the collective ways of preserving the memory of these radioactive materials, rather than ignoring an environmental disaster that will last far longer than a human lifetime.

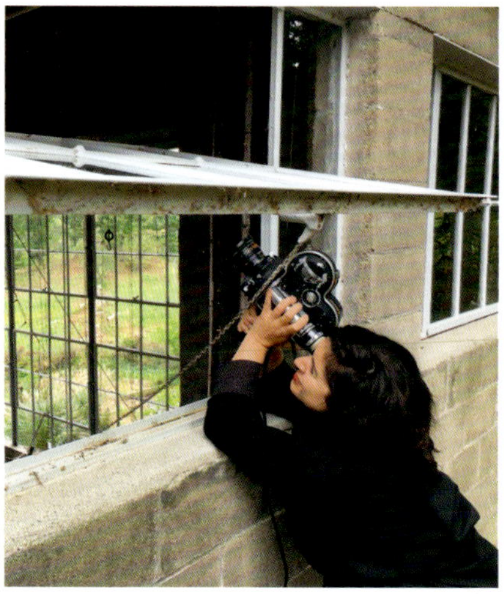

THE ARTIST FILMING ENIGMATIC WHISPER (2017) AT ALEXANDER CALDER'S ROXBURY STUDIO, CONNECTICUT, 2016

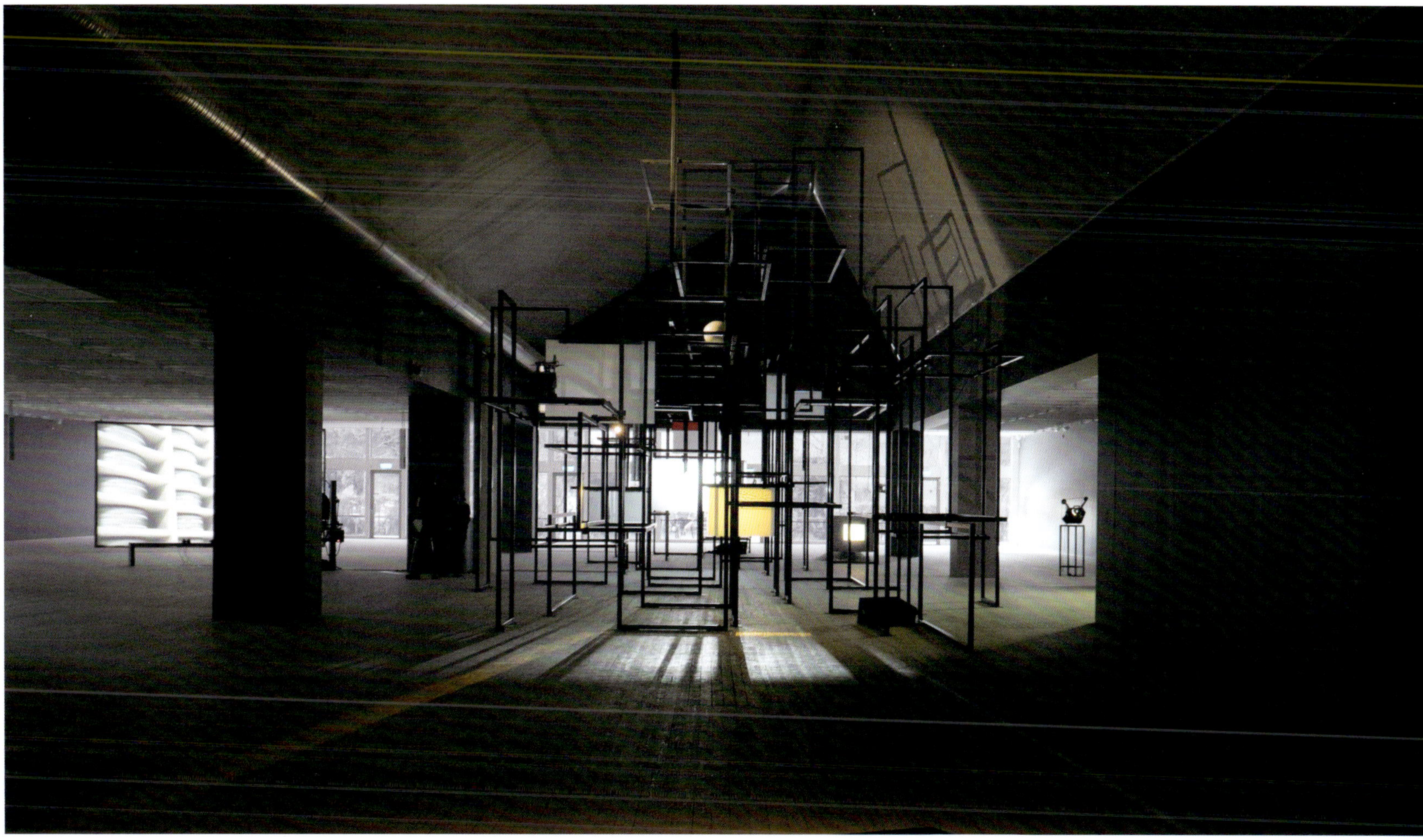

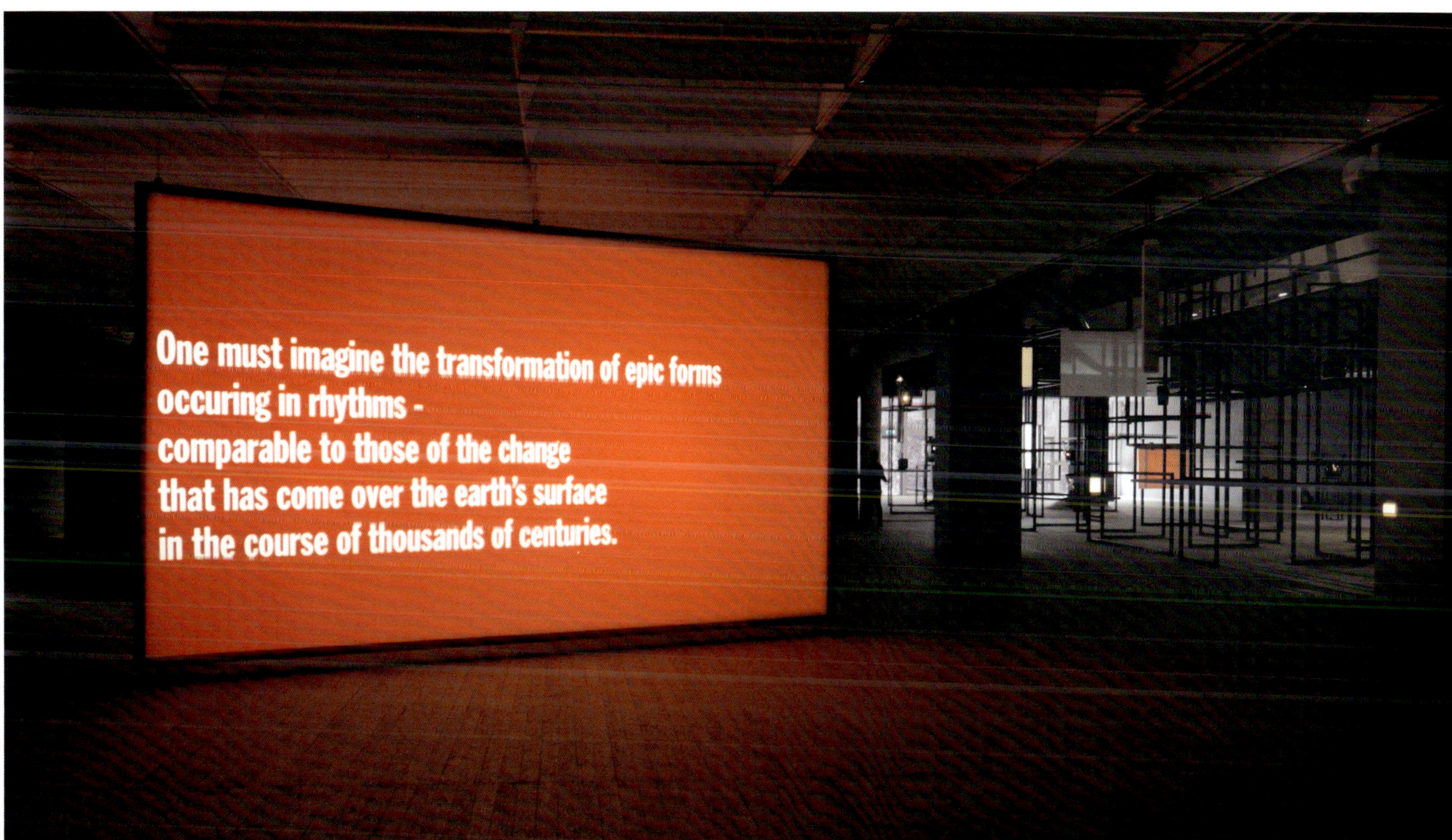
One must imagine the transformation of epic forms
occuring in rhythms -
comparable to those of the change
that has come over the earth's surface
in the course of thousands of centuries.

In another installation, on an island, the postmodern building designed by Aldo Rossi and Xavier Fabre houses a huge 70mm projector, set into a high, square window. Day and night, this beacon sends out, over the lake and the surrounding area, a powerful, pulsating beam of white light. It transforms the water into a screen, which, in salvos of bubbles, emits dull sounds of underwater explosions (*White Museum [Vassivière]*, 2010).[29] It thus commemorates the engulfing of the village that previously stood there, before the administrative decision was taken to submerge it and convert the area into a place for tourism. During the whole course of the exhibition, the same spectacle is repeated, for the benefit of the only inhabitant of the artificial island who refused to move – and, by extension, of all those who were relocated.

Another piece focuses on the dust built up on the photographic plates observed by the astronomer Henrietta Swan Leavitt at the Harvard College Observatory. She discovered a relationship between the luminosity of the Cepheids – variable stars – and the rhythm of their pulsations, enabling astronomers to measure the distance between Earth and other galaxies. But this debris of the passing of time can also be understood as reflecting on how discoveries and research done by women were rendered invisible, how these women were nicknamed 'the computers' and were banned from using the telescope, and of how the credit for their work was taken by 'great men' (*Send Me Sky, Henrietta*, 2018). In other words, the narrative as it is generally understood is radically changed. It is constructed as a sort of tracery, in line with the recent approach contributed by the social sciences to science and the description of science. In Barba's work, film is interwoven with astronomy, just as the architecture of experience is interwoven with its tools (those of the Hirsch Observatory,[30] for example: the telescopes, methodologies, surveys, validation, storage), their technological condition

below and opposite,
WHITE MUSEUM (VASSIVIÈRE)
2010
70MM WHITE FILM, PROJECTOR

INSTALLATION VIEW AT CENTRE INTERNATIONAL D'ART ET DU PAYSAGE DE L'ÎLE DE VASSIVIÈRE, FRANCE, 2010

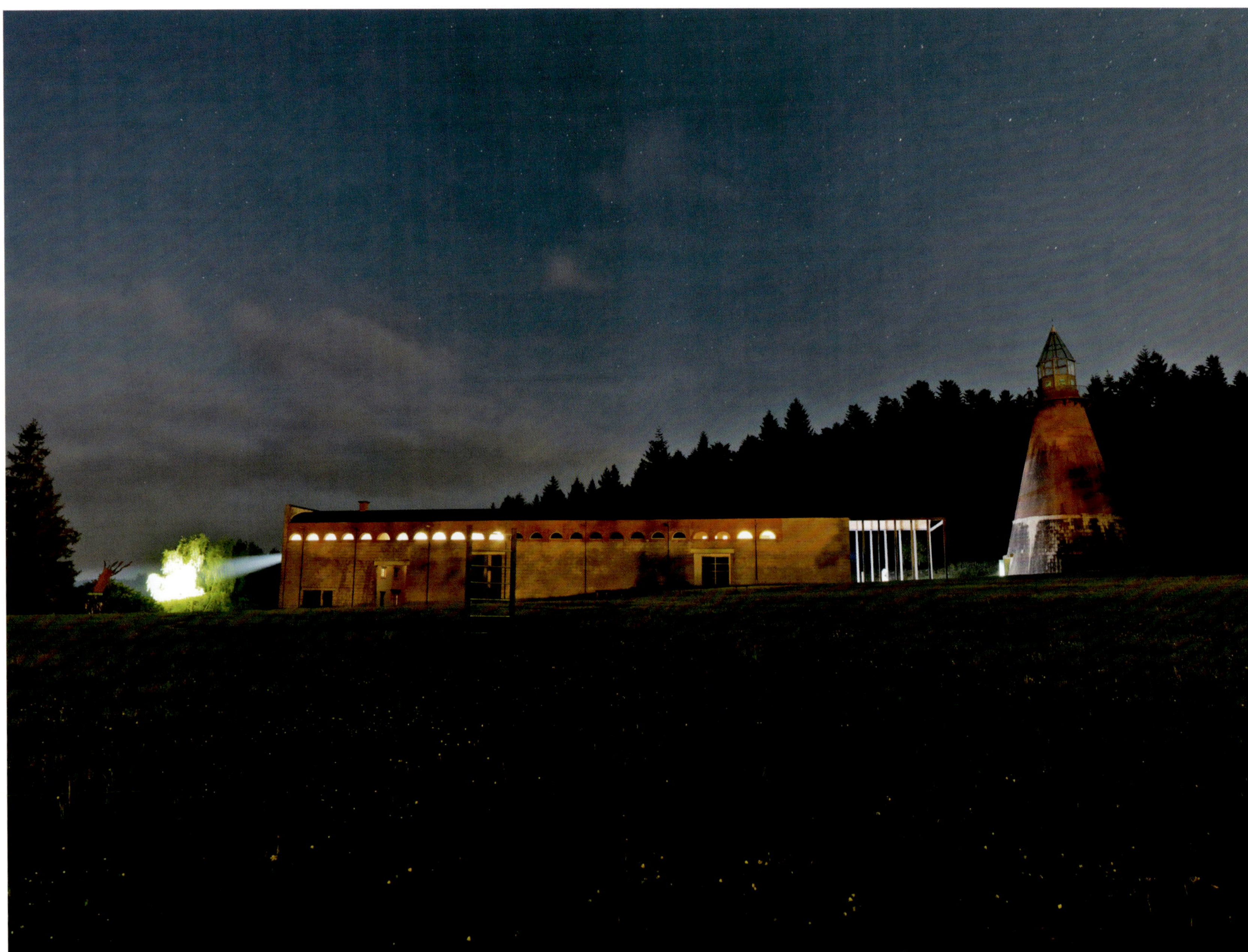

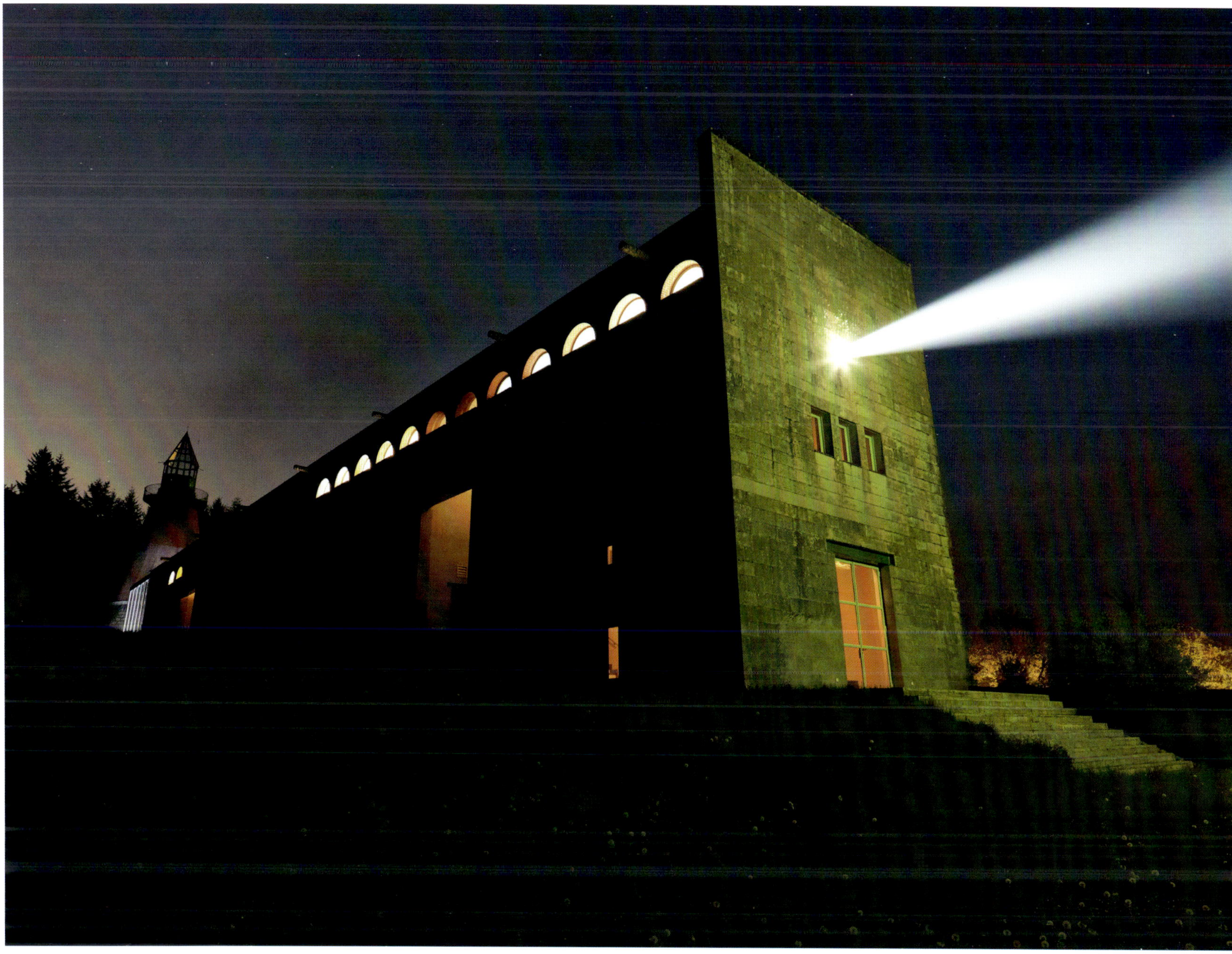

but also their possible fictions, the organisation of the work, the transmission space, those who are part of it, those who are silenced, etc. In short, the social construction of scientific activity interacts with its subject to produce situated knowledge (*The Color Out Of Space*, 2015), with each exhibition constructing a new situation. Barba also re-enacts the many, varied uses – scientific and medical, surveillance, military, etc. – made of film in its early days (not just modern-day film, ordered around economic structures of distribution, demonstration and production geared to capitalist profit), so as to understand them not just from the inside, but as devices that activate certain types of relationships or connections.

We know, wrote Isabelle Stengers in 2009, although she placed this 'knowledge' in inverted commas: 'We now "know"', she wrote, 'that the ice is melting far more quickly than predicted, in both the Arctic and the Antarctic, and that the glaciologists are having to correct their models on this point. [...] The models need to be corrected, the most pessimistic forecasts generated by simulations are seeming more probable. In sum, in this new era, we are no longer dealing only with nature which "must be protected" against damage caused by humans, but also with nature which is able, for good, to disrupt our knowledge and our lives.' [31]

Outwardly from Earth's Center (2007) opens with an aerial view of an island, and suddenly reverses the perspective, observing the water from on land, from the lighthouse-keeper's station, with its observation instruments and its light, equipped with parabolic reflectors mounted on a turning framework. The use of mirrors, then of rotating lenses, was a technical invention that meant that,

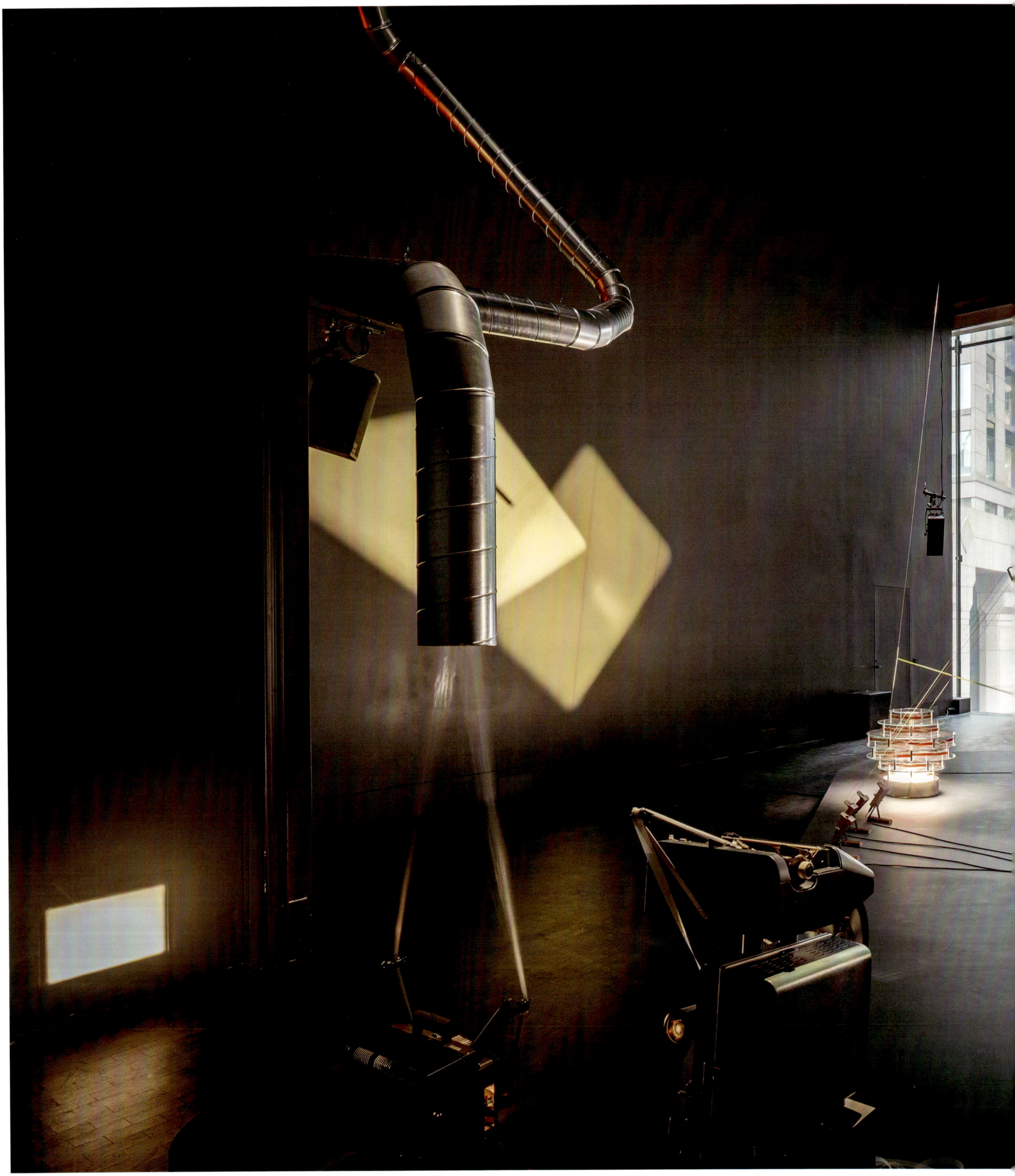

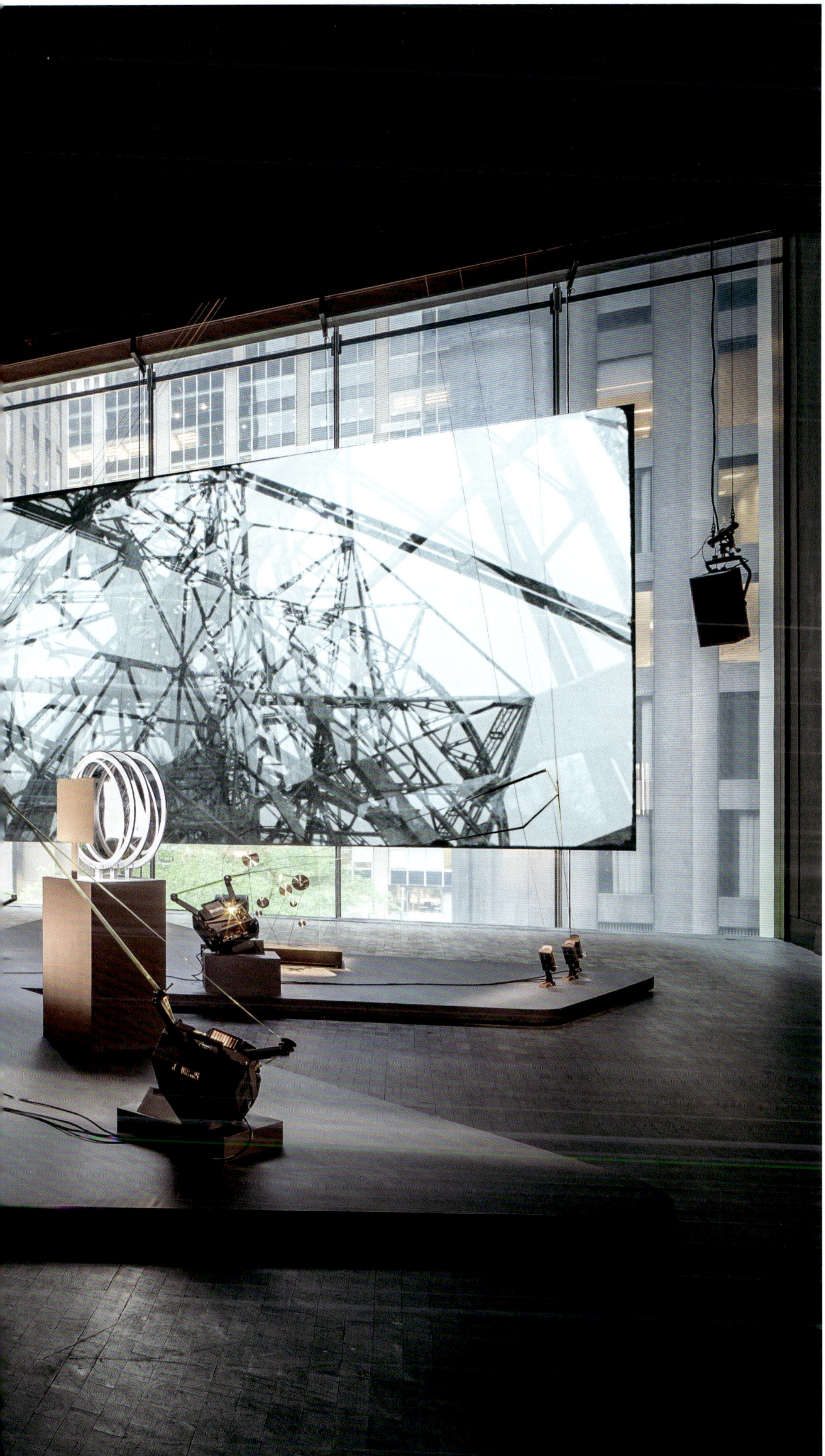

background, from left,
OFF SPLINTERED TIME, 2021
GLASS, MOTORS, LED LIGHT, 35MM FILM
80 X 80 X 70 CM

CHARGE, 2025
35MM FILM, COLOUR, SOUND
25 MIN. 33 SEC.

SENSIBLE SUNS, 2025
ACRYLIC GLASS, POLARIZATION FILMS, STEEL, ALUMINIUM, MOTORS AND LED LIGHT
90 X 60 X 45 CM

WIREPIECE, 2022
16MM FILM PROJECTOR, 16MM FILM, LENS, DRUM STRING, BRIDGE SADDLE PIECE, PICKUP MICROPHONE, PRE-AMP, PLINT

WIREPIECE, DOUBLE STOPS, 2025
16MM PROJECTOR, 16MM FILM, LENS, DRUM STRINGS, BRIDGE SADDLE PIECES, PICKUP MICROPHONES, PRE-AMPS, PLINTH

WIREPIECE, TRIPLE STOPS, 2025
16MM PROJECTOR, 16MM FILM, LENS, DRUM STRING, BRIDGE SADDLE PIECE, PICKUP MICROPHONE, PRE-AMP, AND PLINTH

foreground, from left,
ONE WAY OUT, 2009
16MM FILM, OPTICAL SOUND, PROJECTOR, VENTILATOR, TUBE

SPACELENGTH THOUGHT, 2012
16MM FILM, PROJECTOR, TYPE-WRITER, PLINTH

INSTALLATION VIEW AT THE MUSEUM OF MODERN ART, NEW YORK, 2025

OUTWARDLY FROM EARTH'S CENTER, 2007
16MM FILM TRANSFERRED TO VIDEO, COLOUR, SOUND
22 MIN.

INSTALLATION VIEW AT CENTER FOR CONTEMPORARY ART, KITAKYUSHU, 2019

from the eighteenth century, the turning beam could produce periods of darkness and light, creating a rhythm that could be identified by sailors. We next hear from the experts, all men: the Archaeologist, then the Architect, then the Politician, who make their 'professional observations'.[32] The island of Gosta Sandön is drifting one metre per year towards the North Pole. It is up to the community of nameless inhabitants, living the island from the inside and intimately bound up with this local situation, to take action – action that will impact the projected film. The screen too becomes an island, and the islanders work together to construct a sculpture of ropes and wooden pillars, to pull it back from the sea and keep it with them.

We 'know', writes Gilles Deleuze, that there are two sorts of islands:[32] continental and original islands. The former are created when they split from the mainland, and the sea comes between two pieces of land. The latter were already there, tied to the sea. Geography adds nothing to what our imagination was already telling us: 'Dreams of islands, whether nightmarish or joyous, are dreams about separation, that you have already broken loose, are far from the mainland, lost and alone – or they are dreams of starting over from nothing, of re-creating, beginning again.'[34] Separation and re-creation are not mutually exclusive, as long as some attempt is made to reach a composition.

A first application of these ideas can be found in *Panzano* (2000), a collaboration between Barba, Ulrike Molsen, and Valeria, Claudio and Dino. These three survivors of one of the mental-health communities that became widespread in Europe from the 1970s, particularly in Italy,[35] live together on their island. In *Panzano*, unlike in a documentary, there is no 'proper distance' between them and us. As in institutional psychotherapy, the collective housing and sharing of tasks have resulted in the creation of a sort of projection, in which the media (the camera, the television, the talent show) are 'agents' just as much as the threshold of the house, the people, the roles with which they identify, the characters they become when they hear the unexpected noises made by the recording equipment, which itself also 'figures' in the action. The film's ecosystem is not the Tuscan village of Panzano, but the screen itself, which shifts from optical to haptic sensations, with overexposures, compositions that combine the physicality of all the actors, including the technology. The spectral capacities of these features provide some 'play', since a character can disappear or reappear in a blinding beam of light. The eye of the camera is combined with all the virtual, potential stories and chemical effects of layering, the cracks and crevices between the outside and the inside, reality and the real, sinking down into each other.

As Barba explains, when she was in the US to attend the screening of *Panzano*, she was strongly impacted by Leslie Thornton's cycle of anti-establishment films, *Peggy and Fred in Hell* (1984–89). In four episodes, the series follows two children growing up in an apocalyptic, waste-strewn landscape, who spend each day looking for a place where they can live, i.e. *where they can play*. It begins in a junkyard of twentieth-century technology, with tangles of electric cables, light bulbs, tools, cathode-ray monitors. The children improvise short film clips, as if they were on television, while the films gradually bring together, into a 'semiotic chaos', scientific documents, various tones and uses of film, the digital effects of video, in a hybrid production, somewhere between ethnography and science fiction,[36] according to Thornton. From this work, Barba has particularly retained the relationship of trust, not just between the camera and the children, but also with the environment through which they are wandering, in 'the detritus of prior cultures, cast loose in a world of post-apocalyptic splendor'.[37]

As Janet Bennet explains, this work is not contrasting the dull and passive matter of things with our vibrant life as humans. 'The quarantines of matter and life encourage us to ignore the vitality of matter and the lively powers of material formations, such as … the way our trash is not "away" in landfills but generating lively streams of chemicals and volatile winds of methane as we speak.'[38] Filmed from the lake, the environment itself, the fresh water of Lake Titicaca fills with algae and industrial waste (*Aggregate States of Matters*). Underwater, the cargo of amphorae and ceramics, 2,400 years old, from the boat that sank near the village of Mazotos in Cyprus, acts, at one and the same time, as an archaeological reserve, a historical map of maritime trade, an amusement park, a reef for many species, including for the humans who colonise the island, and as a reflection concerning the 'buffer zone' in Cyprus that separates the north from the south of the island (*Inside the Outset – Evoking a Space of Passage*, 2021). Seen first from a car, then from an aircraft, the large loop of an abandoned racetrack appears like a trace fossil in the desert (*The Long Road*, 2010) or prehistoric remains. 'Whether kin to the ancient Nazca lines only rediscovered as a result of air travel, or to the industrial-scale incursions that Robert Smithson and his peers made into remote desert terrain in the post-war years, this elliptical incision in the Earth's surface is similarly subject to decay and the predations of time. The soundtrack mingles techno electronic sounds, from which haunting micro-tonal phrases emerge intermittently, with the throaty voice of Robert Creeley reading from his poem "The Long Road"',[39] comments Lynne Cooke. The space of the desert joins with the timeframe of the deserted track, the 'second nature' of future remains with their legends and myths.

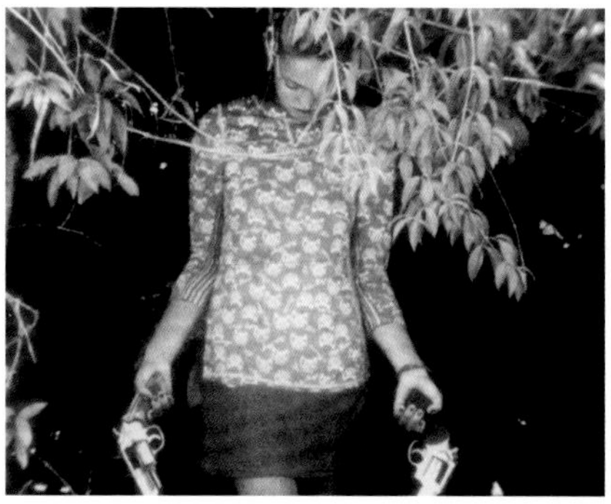

LESLIE THORNTON
PEGGY & FRED IN HELL, 1985
FILM
20 MIN.

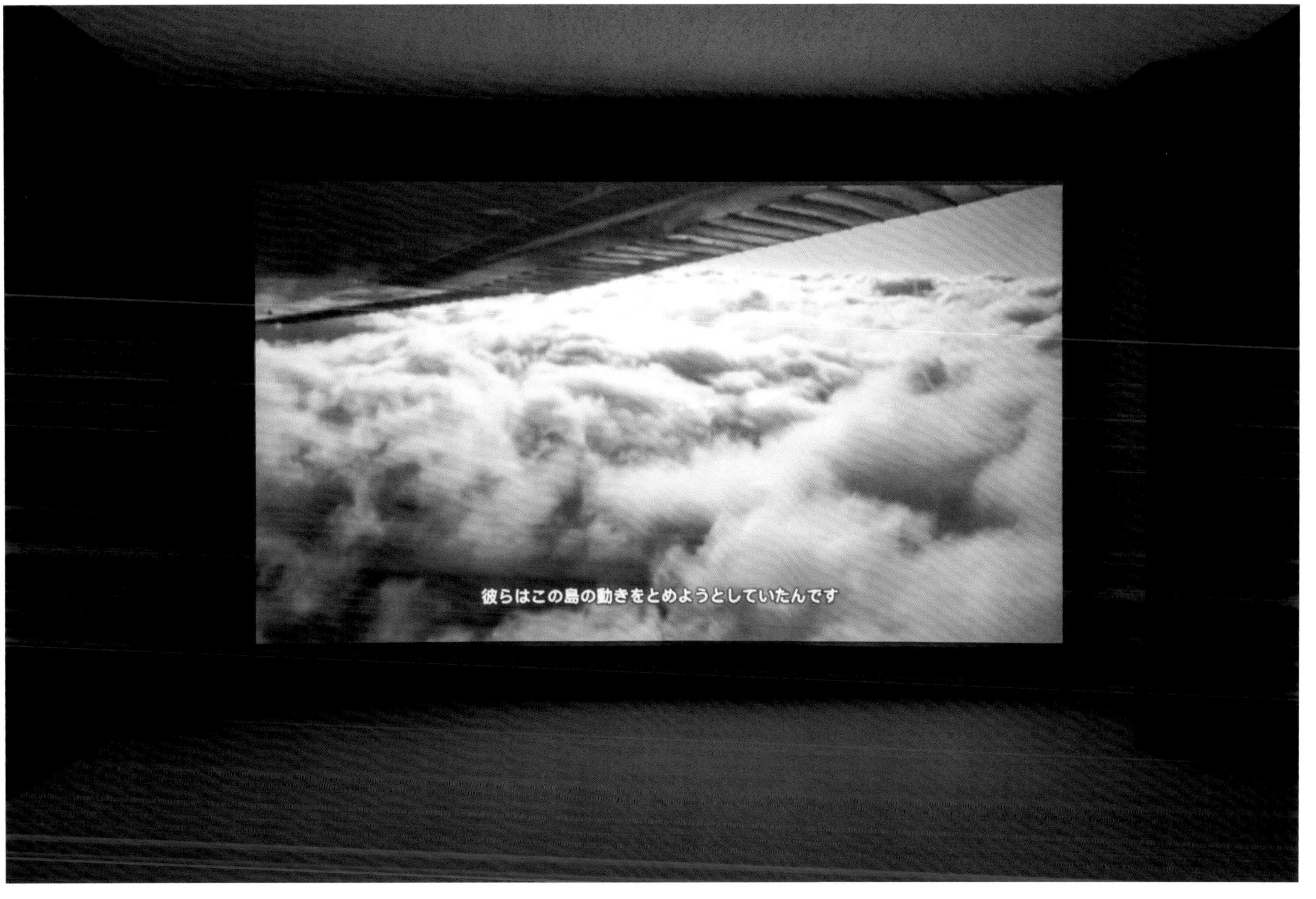
彼らはこの島の動きをとめようとしていたんです

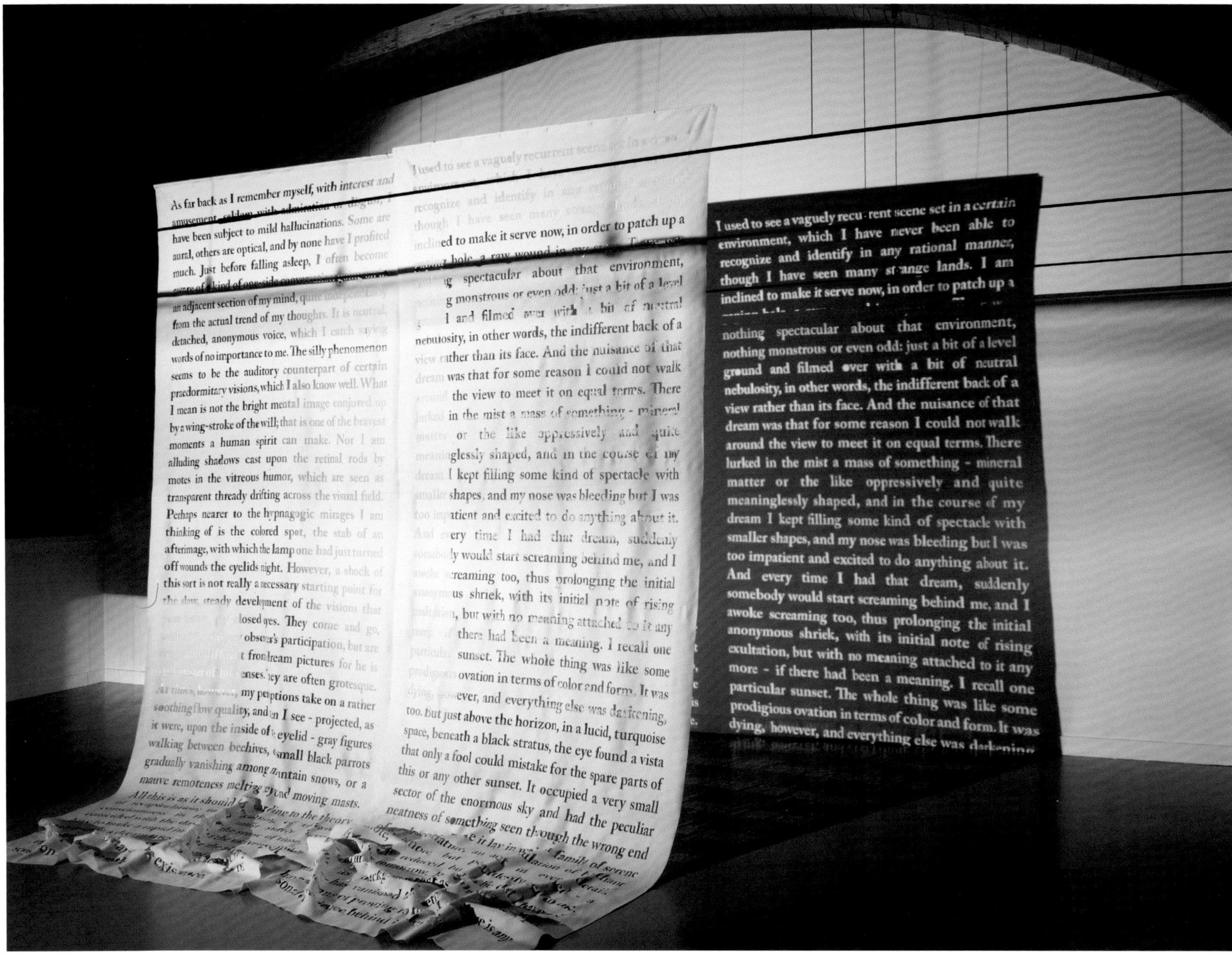

These are not foundational myths. The artist is not discovering the 'primitive scene' of an original tale, but rather telling a story, starting *from a position of rethinking*. So, in *They Shine* (2007), we hear people from the local communities of the Mojave Desert in California commenting on the choreography of hundreds of enormous solar panels held out like shields. The conversation we hear gives the panels greater meaning, like that of a native ritual honouring technology. The local spirits conjured up here produce unexpected stories of a living environment, where human and non-human life exist intimately side by side.

'The locus of agency is always a human-nonhuman work group.'[40] This, I think, is where Barba moves and works. Her terrain can be found in those stores of energy, technological junkyards and dumps from which people have been evacuated, relocated, alienated. Her work consists precisely in renewing agency by reversing the separation that deserted the deserts, isolated the islands, rerouted the routes, reserved the reserves for silence. She does this by getting artefacts (from the Capitoline Museum in Rome, the Neue Nationalgalerie in Berlin, Tate in London: the three components of *The Hidden Conference,* 2010–15) to engage in conversation. She reassigns, from its daily hustle and bustle, a stretch of the 'Minhocão', the 'giant earthworm' urban highway in São Paulo, built during the dictatorship and then neglected (*Disseminate and Hold,* 2016). Each of these archival pieces of architecture entrenches a mechanism of expectation, which places the present clearly in its historical context, thus opening up a store of potential secret conversations. *Subconscious Society*[41] mixes noises and words with simultaneous images, sound archives and music composed by Jan St Werner, together with a type of leitmotiv chosen by Tim Ganes. These disparate echoes

opposite,
THE INDIFFERENT BACK OF A VIEW RATHER THAN ITS FACE, 2009
CUT-OUT TEXT ON FELT
450 X 180 CM

INSTALLATION VIEW AT CENTRE INTERNATIONAL D'ART ET DU PAYSAGE ILE DE VASSIVÈRE, FRANCE, 2010

below, from left,
THE HIDDEN CONFERENCE: A FRACTURED PLAY, 2011
35MM FILM, COLOUR, OPTICAL SOUND
5 MIN.

THE HIDDEN CONFERENCE: ABOUT THE DISCONTINUOUS HISTORY OF THINGS WE SEE AND DON'T SEE, 2010
35MM FILM, COLOUR, OPTICAL SOUND
13 MIN. 40 SEC.

TIME AS PERSPECTIVE, 2012
35MM FILM, COLOUR, OPTICAL SOUND
12 MIN.

INSTALLATION VIEW AT ALBERTINUM, DRESDEN, 2015

merge with views from an approaching aircraft, boat and hovercraft, imprinting their respective trepidation on the images. Industrial sites around Manchester, with their crumbling seaside jetties, maritime fortifications emerging on stilts like insects, alternate with figures meeting in Manchester's Albert Hall, a cathedral of capitalism in the early twentieth century, and then, until the end of the 1960s, of BBC radio culture. The actors carefully examine items that they do not really understand, relics from the age of mechanical reproduction and analogue technology, such as BBC machinery and Margate's *Dreamland*, the town's amusement park, now also fallen silent. The idea of 'amusement' is of course closely linked to the notion of film, and to the 'cinema of attractions', which 'bases itself on … its ability to show something'.[42] Contrary to arguments that portray cinema as a voyeuristic art, here spectators experience its ability to show, in a dramatization generated by fragments of narrative combining science, technoscience and science fiction. The 'disasters depicted and the disasters that threaten them might equally be read as actual and fictional'.[43] For what differentiates fictions from ideologies is that their role is not to hide reality, but rather to construct it, with whatever darknesses or lights – those of the projected images and those of the machines included in the installation's live performance.

To complicate things further, the simultaneous presentation of these pieces by Barba, exhibited together, each in its own timeframe, enhances their meaning rather than detracting from it, as she removes any notion of irreversibility. Friedrich Kittler describes this as the role of media technology, from writing to digital technology: 'in media technology, time itself becomes one of several variables that can be manipulated'.[44] Referring to writing, he gives the example of the invention of blanks, spaces

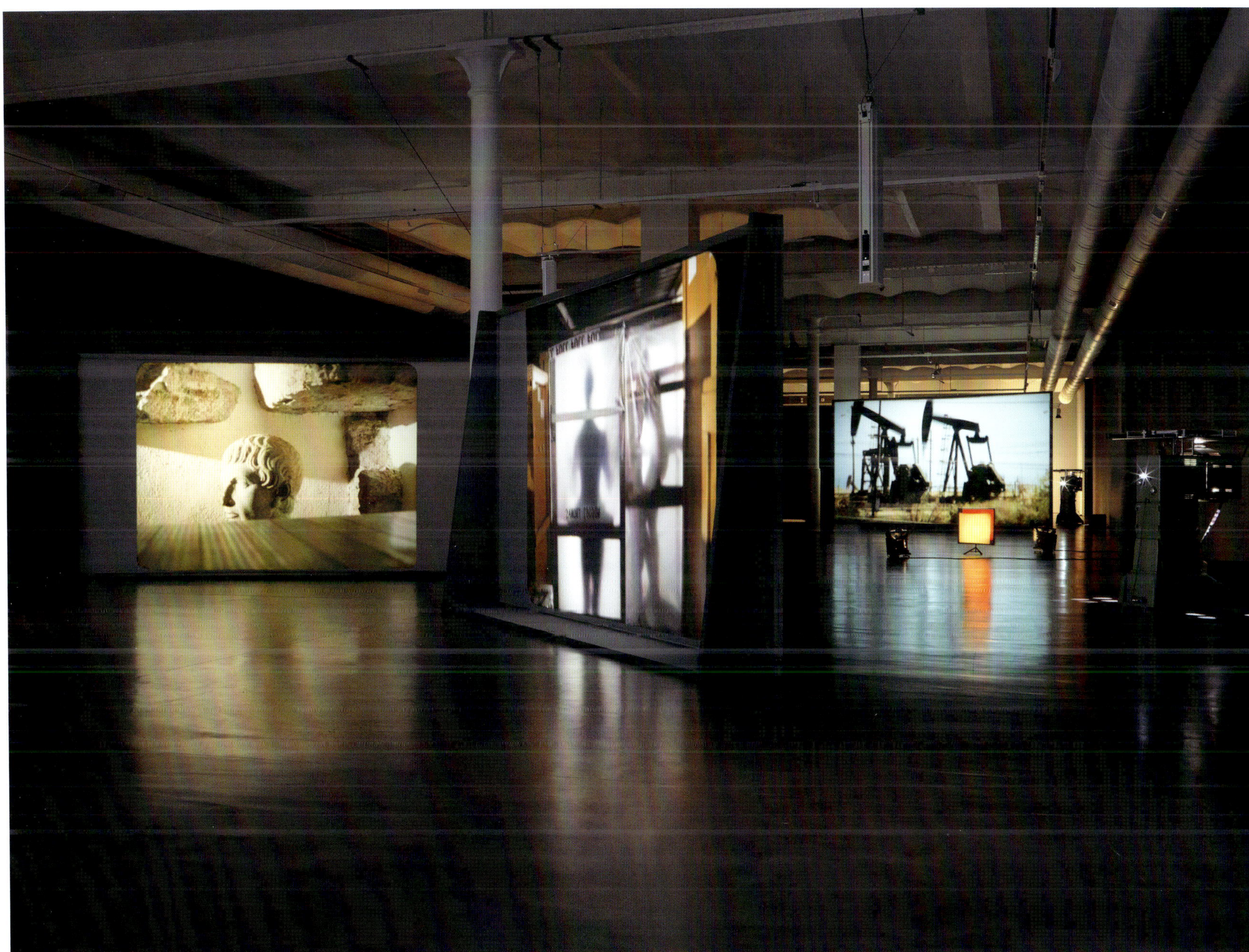

in alphabetical writing, which Barba uses even in her filmmaking style. In the spatial transition between the technologies of writing and of analogue media, writes Kittler, inscription gives way to the collision of surfaces.[45] This is what happened in the great nave of the CAPC Musée d'Art Contemporain de Bordeaux (2016), and in the Pirelli HangarBicocca in Milan (2017), in *Hear, There, Where the Echoes Are* (2016). The space, which can never be seen as a whole, splits into various viewpoints, governed by the beat of a drum. Basking in the particular acoustics of the space, the percussionist Chad Taylor, one of Barba's musician friends, plays with brio. He has left, he might come back. But the drumming has already started up again with its bursts of sound and syncopation. Amplified, it continues on its way, then doubles back, encouraging visitors to listen, to feel in their bodies as well as observing the intense visual effects. This synchronisation with sound is at the heart of, or is maybe the purpose of, the flashes of light, from 16mm and 35mm projectors, illuminating Plexiglas panels coloured by red and yellow blown-glass filters, and painting pictures on the screens; the strips of film are transposed into images and sounds. In some works, such as *Enigmatic Whisper* (2017) in Milan, this projection is also intertwined with the very design of the exhibition. In Calder's studio in Roxbury, left just as it was found on the artist's death, the content and coloured geometrical shapes, the reflecting metal foils, the mobiles – in differing stages of completion – join in the dance. The screening of the film melts into the installation around it, and vice versa, mixing two different timeframes. The spectators move diagonally, projecting their shadows into the light, and thus including their travelling in the narrative, which continues to take shape, never completed, always unpredictable. As Barba writes: 'I'm trying to find that space that is not waiting for me',[46] or for the spectators. The base structures act as screens, and, supporting the projectors, give them too a breathing space between movements. At times, the sound of the drums stops, and the play of colour and light also slows. During the time of silence, a slanted screen lights up when a projector is turned on.

In Milan, in Bordeaux, *From Source to Poem* (2016) runs through the development of Western audiovisual technology, obsessively stored, arranged and packed into the 140 kilometres of galleries of a former bunker in Culpeper, Virginia. The camera pans through the basement areas, along corridors, offices, shelving, piles of metal cannisters, wiring, cardboard boxes full

below,
ENIGMATIC WHISPER, 2017
16MM FILM, COLOUR, OPTICAL SOUND
8 MIN

opposite, from left,
TIME AS PERSPECTIVE, 2012
35MM FILM, COLOUR, OPTICAL SOUND
12 MIN

COLOR STUDIES, 2013
2 X 16MM FILM PROJECTORS, 2 X 16MM FILM, SCREEN, EACH 2 MIN

COLOR CLOCKS: VERTICALS LEAN OCCASIONALLY CONSISTENTLY AWAY FROM VIEWPOINTS, 2012
35MM FILM, MOTORS, ALUMINIUM, PLEXIGLASS
84 X 123 X 16 CM

STATING THE REAL SUBLIME, 2009
16MM FILM, MODIFIED PROJECTOR

INSTALLATION VIEW AT MIT LIST VISUAL ARTS CENTER, CAMBRIDGE, MASSACHUSETTS, 2015

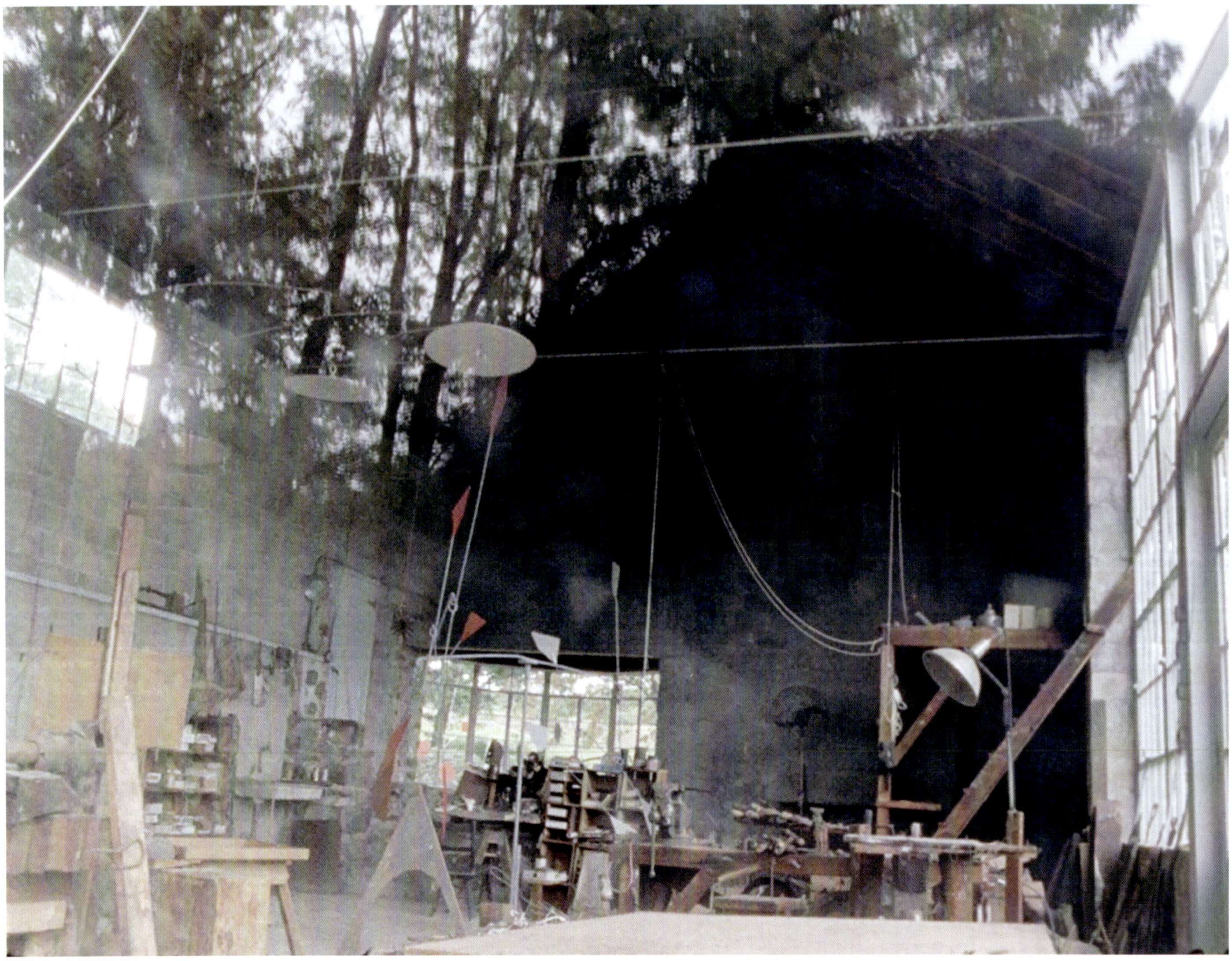

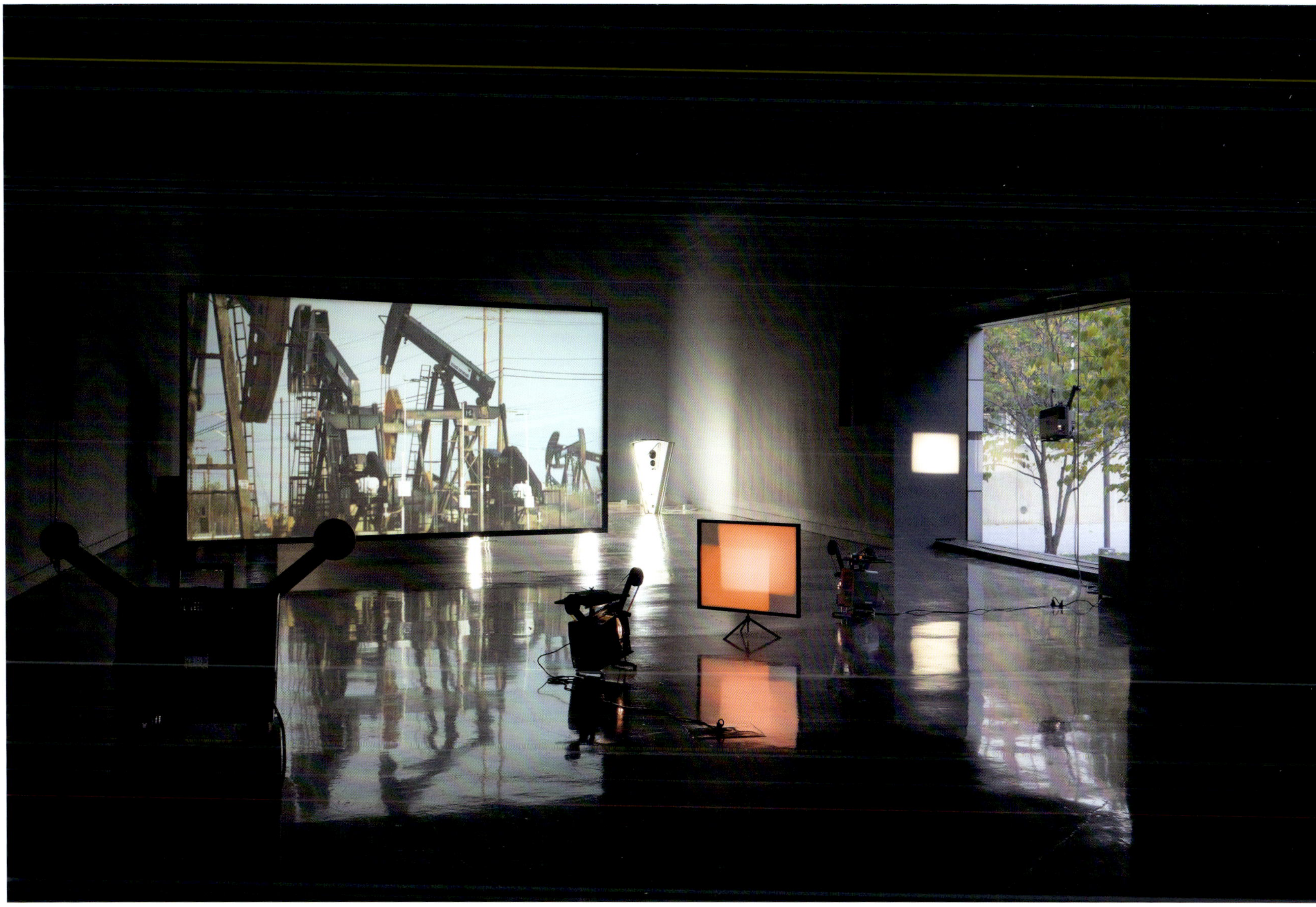

of cassettes, headphones and various types of projection equipment. Time, here, becomes tactile, inscribed in each of the coding systems and in how they are stored. We hear the voice of a former slave, recorded in the 1930s by the WPA (Work Projects Administration), and other superimposed words – from rural workers, native American poets – from the depths of analogue history. As well as the compressed time of this journey into the archives, the rush of poetry generated by each of these silenced words, a series of pulses of light are emitted by lamps from the power plants. Their interaction undermines any sort of linearity, in a deregulated present. As Kittler comments: 'data processing becomes the process by which temporal order becomes moveable and reversible in the very experience of space'.[47] It is also a way of describing the exhibition.

Time as Perspective (2012) shows a pattern of oil wells, with pumpjacks pumping continuously, regularly, mechanically in the Texan desert, in an 'all-over' approach that covers the whole screen. This chthonic vision of the work of machines provides a disturbing parallel to Kafka's 'machine',[48] which, in the penal colony, inscribes the sentence of the condemned men into their backs. The judicial machine progressively destroys the men's bodies, which are emptied of blood. Barba's work includes many deserts applying the colony's 'touch of law': not only the Texas oil drilling, and not just solar energy destined for thermal power plants (*They Shine*). She also considers the population expelled from their homes, from these areas; the destruction of human, animal and plant life; the polluting of thousands of kilometres so that countries can join the Nuclear Club of nations and carry out research on survival in a radioactive environment.[49] In the desert, the texture of the extraction seems to carve itself directly into the vagueness that spreads to the performance of the film. On the screen, the blurred outlines produce an impression of radioactivity that clouds the vision (*Radiant Exposures – Facts Run on Light Beams These Days,* 2022). From time to time, the sentence appears as a series of phrases on the surface of the screen, never long enough to enable us to read them easily. This is a way, I think, of deterritorializing writing, of showing the power and power relations behind it. As in Kafka's book, 'it's not calligraphy for school children'.[50] We need to get used to reading slowly, to a type of reading that

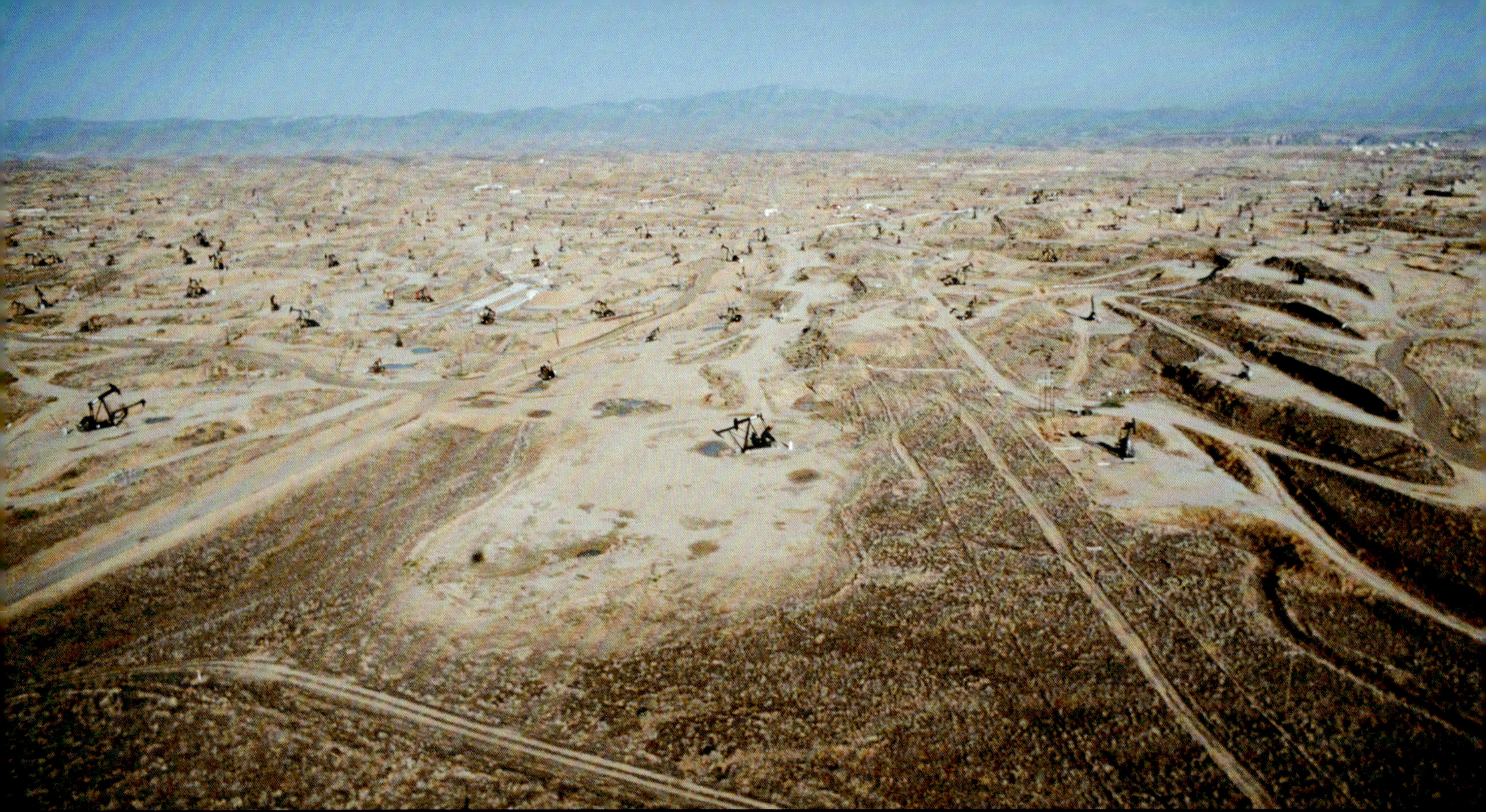

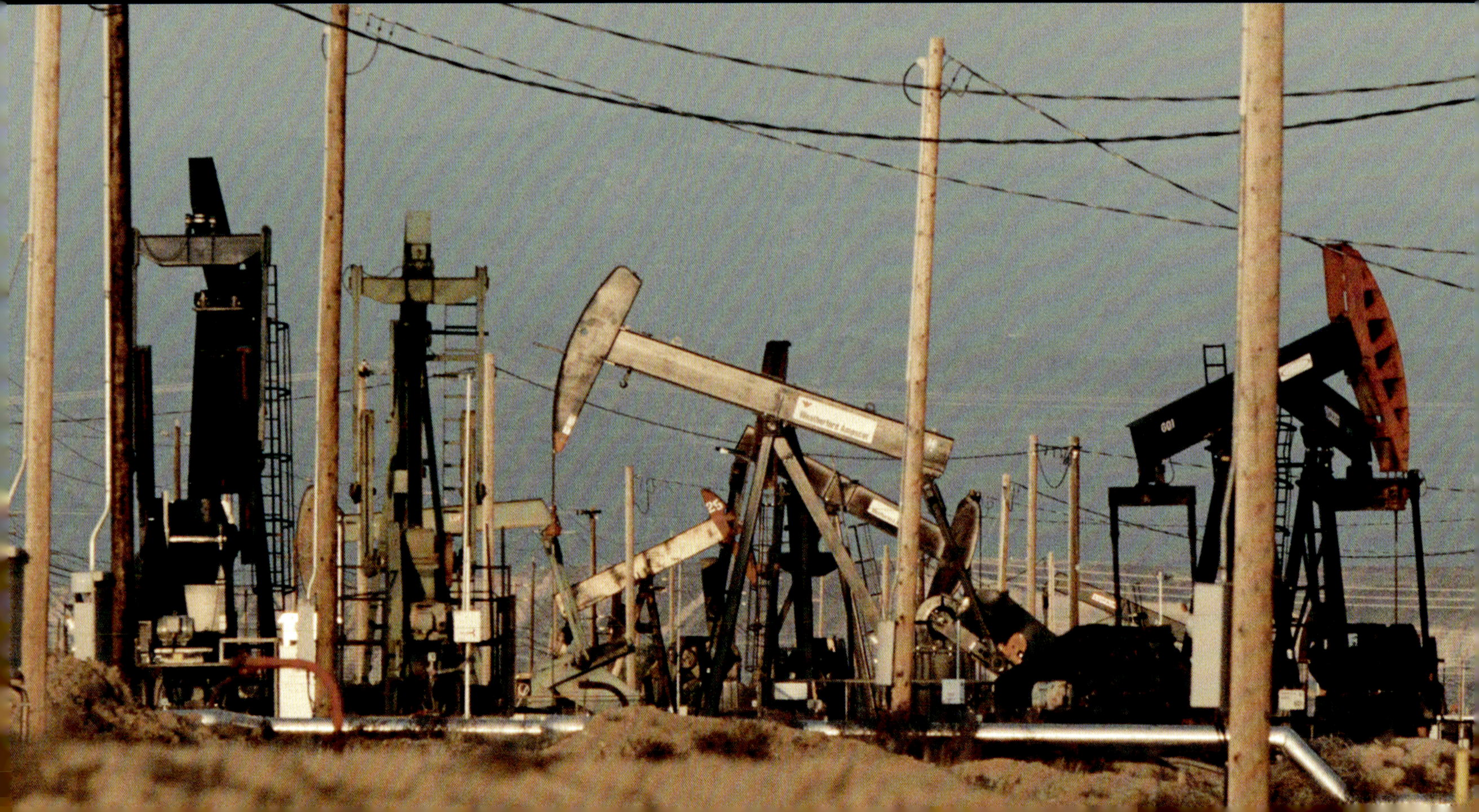

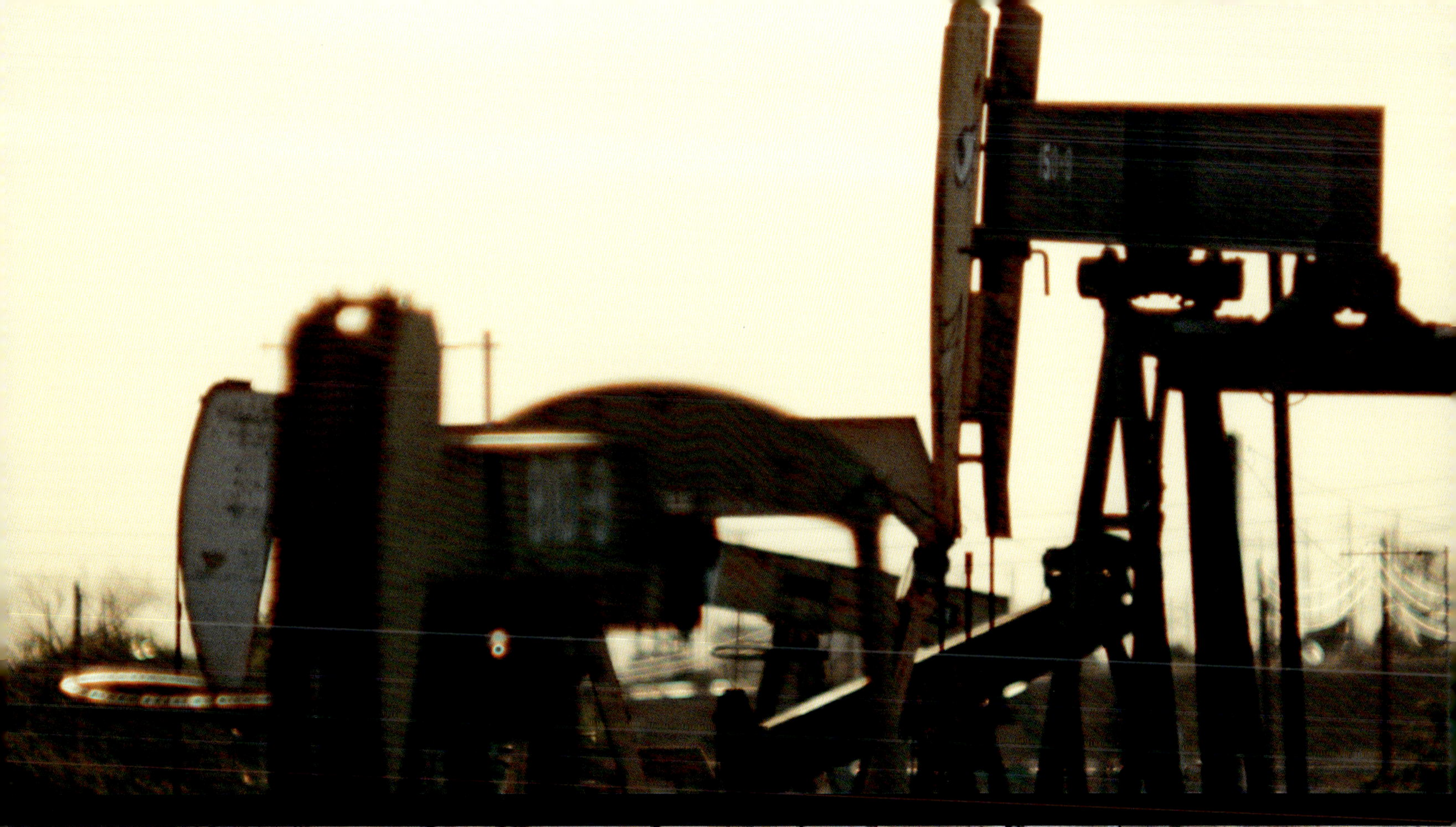

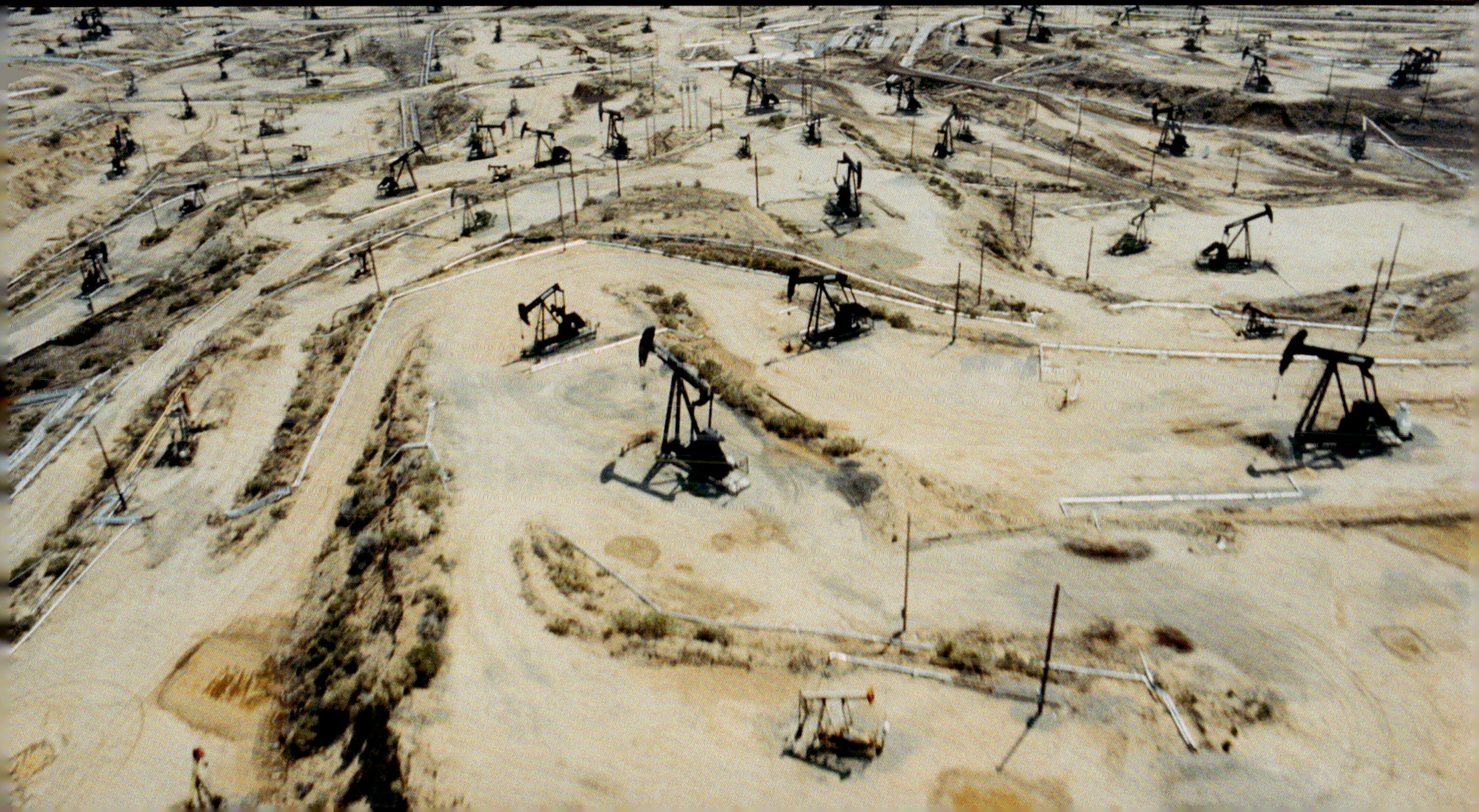

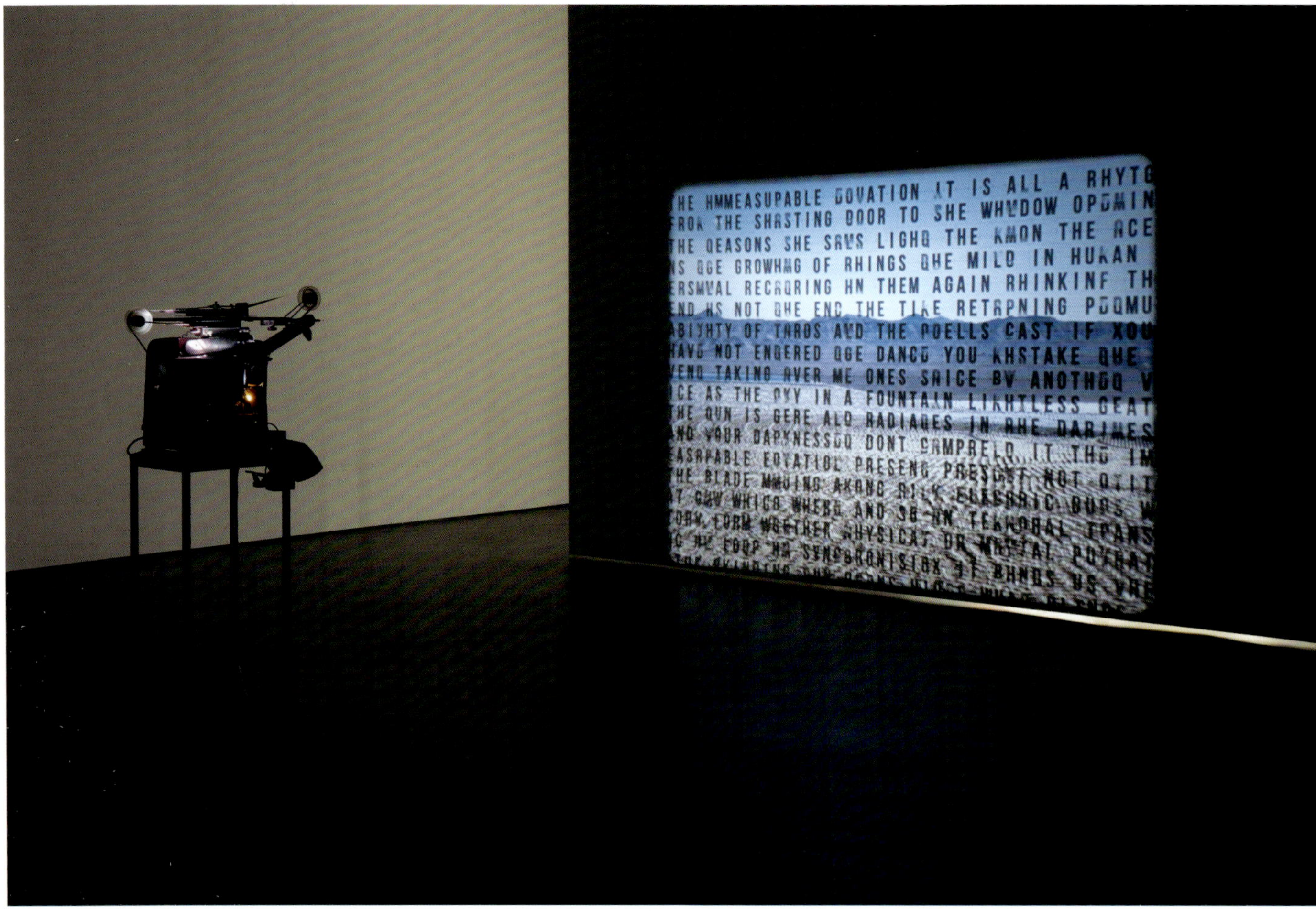

left,
RADIANT EXPOSURES – FACTS RUN ON LIGHT BEAMS THESE DAYS, 2022
16MM FILM, COLOUR, OPTICAL SOUND
6 MIN.

INSTALLATION VIEW AT ESTHER SCHIPPER, BERLIN, 2022

previous pages,
TIME AS PERSPECTIVE, 2012
35MM FILM, COLOUR, OPTICAL SOUND
12 MIN.

is difficult, partial, cruel. *The Indifferent Back of a View Rather Than Its Face* (2009) presents a large rectangle of white material, with letters cut out; a projector shines light onto this screen, producing a luminous silhouette on the wall behind. To the spectator, it looks like the skin of someone whose back is turned. It also recalls the film material used by Barba: perforated silver emulsion film, the format of which (8, 16 or 35mm) is, incidentally, determined by the number of holes. These perforations, necessary for recording and screening, also evoke the effect of the slender harrow of Kafka's cold punishment machine. Perforate and perform: the words are close, the differences are ultra-thin, like skin and its mental image.

'Does he know his sentence?' 'No', said the officer, eager to go on with his explanations, but the traveller interrupted him: 'He doesn't know the sentence that has been passed on him?' 'No', said the officer again … and then continued: 'There would be no point in telling him. He will experience it on his own body.'[51]

There are no preliminaries. A typewriter types its monologue onto the film, and the text that appears projected onto a wall is constantly escaping us, while the celluloid skin marked with the letters spills onto the ground (this is also what happens to Kafka's 'machine', which vomits up its entrails). The ribbon of film irreversibly printed with letters falls into a heap, into swirls (*Spacelength Thought*, 2012). A projector, tilted at 45 degrees and shining a rectangle of light, produces individual stencilled letters, through coloured filters, cut into the celluloid film: T - H - E - L - O - N - G - P - O - E – M. The writing is printed onto the body of the screen. There would be no point in telling it.

Here I cut to a 1968 work by Joan Jonas. *Wind* is a Super-8 film. It transposes a performance that took place indoors (*Oad Lau*, 1968) to the outdoors, to a snowy landscape in Nova Scotia. A very strong wind is blowing. It batters the performers. It forces them to react to their environment, impeding their gestures. The choreography is like a burlesque mechanism, further shaken by the jumps in the film. The characters, seen from a distance, are in a constant struggle with their coats, buffeted by the wind. The reflections of the small mirrors decorating some of their clothing create an impression of fragmentation, on top of these silent and invisible factors, which define the piece as much as the human actors. The links between causes and effects are dissolved away in this sculpture, which finds its own balance in destabilisation, and vice versa.

I see a clear link between *Wind* and the resistance generated by the works of Barba. Resistance, that is, in the electrical as much as in the political sense of the term. This resistance needs to be, literally, *worked out*: performed. Links must be made, so that the island holds firm. Cyprus is an island where the breaking of links

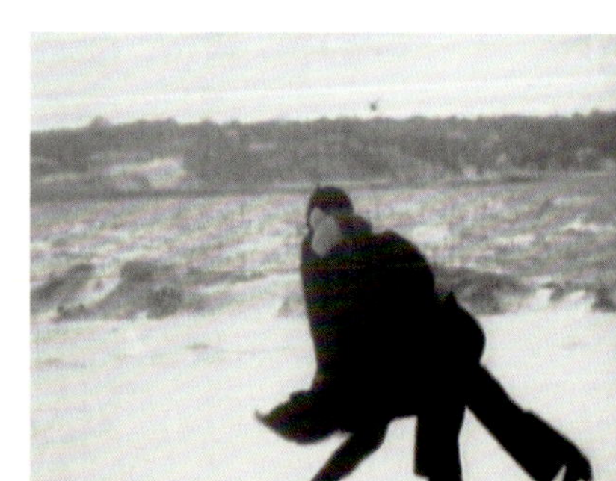

JOAN JONAS
WIND, 1968
16MM FILM
5 MIN.

SOLAR FLUX RECORDINGS, 2022
STEEL TABLE, COLOUR GLASS PLATES, 35MM FILM, PROJECTOR, LOOPER
STEEL TABLE AND COLOUR GLASS PLATES DIMENSIONS: 130 X 100 X 55 CM
FILM DURATION: 11 MIN.

INSTALLATION VIEW AT ESTHER SCHIPPER, BERLIN, 2022

is a living environment. The division of the island is portrayed by a third separation: a buffer zone known as the 'Green Line'. The camera moves along this line: tufts of grass, disused tracks and an abandoned building, glass doors; the painted sign 'UN99', showing the domination and control by the United Nations. On the large, rectangular building, an inscription in ageing capital letters makes partial reference to its past as an 'International Airport'. Resistance kicks in, rises up in the physical space of Cyprus's internal border. Machines dig, heap up, level out tiers for an auditorium in the ancient Greek style: two semicircles of open-air seating, either side of the demarcation line. In the centre is a supporting framework for a screen, a light-sensitive membrane, which can be watched from both sides. The 'buffer zone', once isolated, has become an island. The plural thickness of its time entangles the construction work with the action in the film, which has recorded not only the process, but also the material and non-material traces of it: the screen, the auditorium, and the projective force of the groups or individuals who will invite each other along to be involved on *both sides*.[52] The performativity of the film, as an installation, is the effect of its storytelling – of its ability to tell a story that becomes real, is incarnated in something tangible. It may remain in this condition for ten years, before deteriorating. Rather than emphasising its monumental supremacy, it thus presents a process, opening onto an uncertain future.

A commemoration of 'today's tomorrow',[53] for one day. Under the glass ceiling of the Palacio de Cristal, in Madrid, the specific position of the sun, changing each day over the course of the exhibition, is recorded by the orientation of panels of coloured glass, projected onto the ground (*Solar Flux Recording*, 2017). Or it could be for one night; the night of 29 December 2013 in the former Locker Plant in Marfa.[54] Train tracks run right through this small Texan town (2,000 inhabitants), not far from the Mexican border. The trains no longer stop there, but pass through: you can hear the blaring of the sirens, the sound of the engine, and the rhythm of the wheels on the rails, in a procession that seems to go on for ever. Marfa's beating heart is on edge waiting for this whistling, puffing breath, which goes through the town, churns up the air for a long while and then disappears. Barba makes use of the passing trains.[55] At night, stage lighting placed outside the Locker Plant projects a very clear circle of light onto its façade, and shines through the bay windows to illuminate some of the inside of the former cold-storage room. For several minutes, the circle

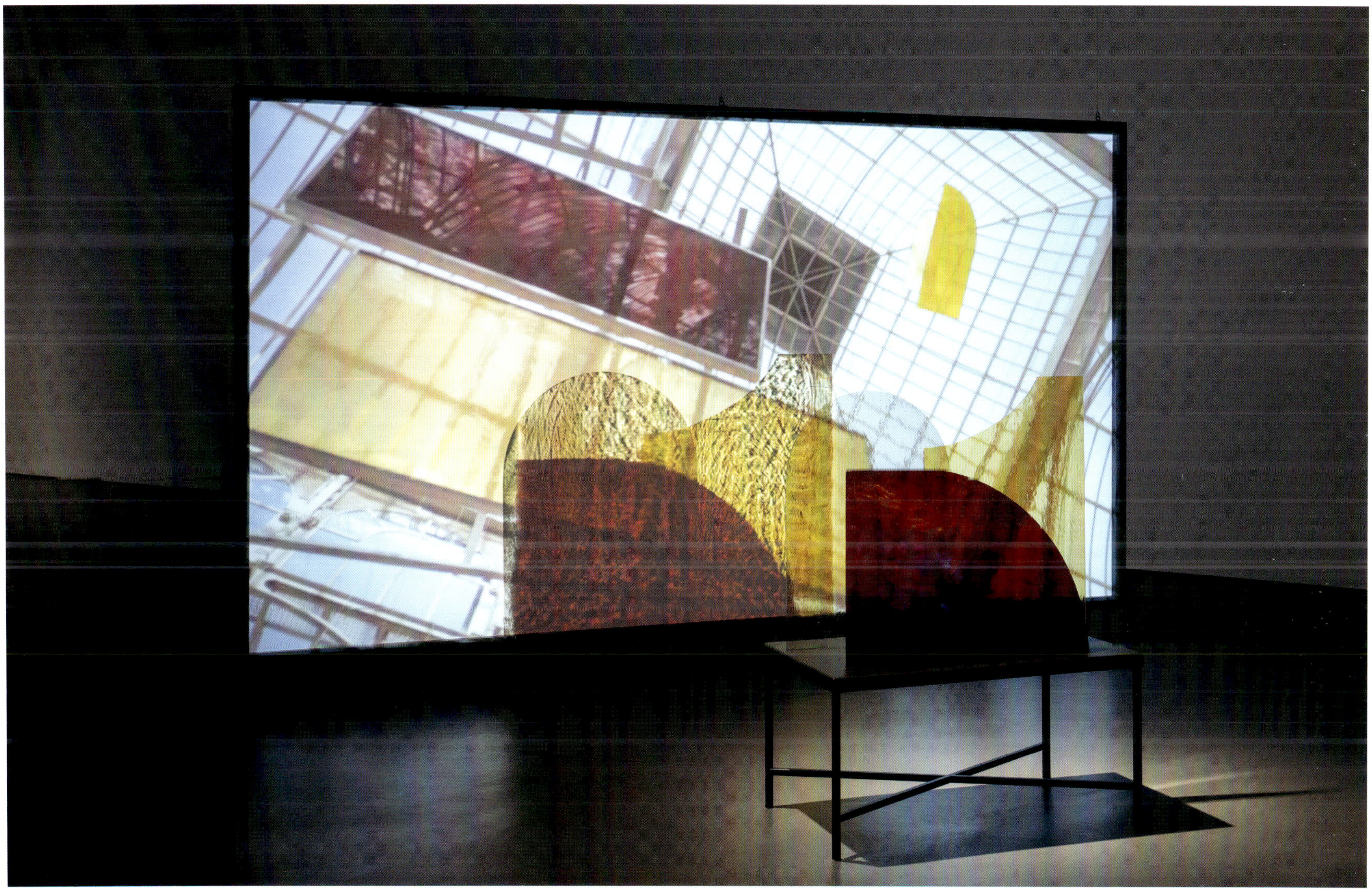

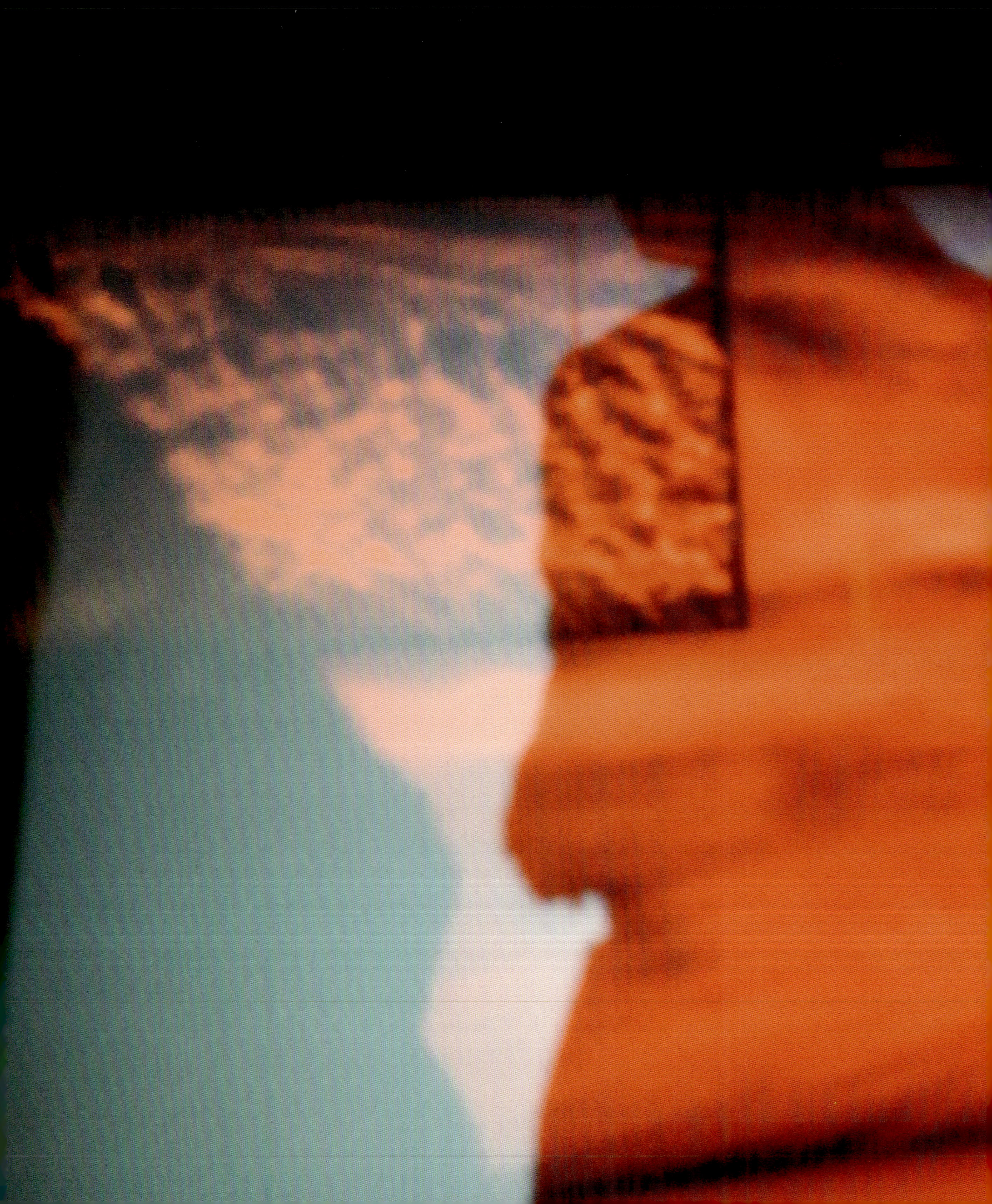

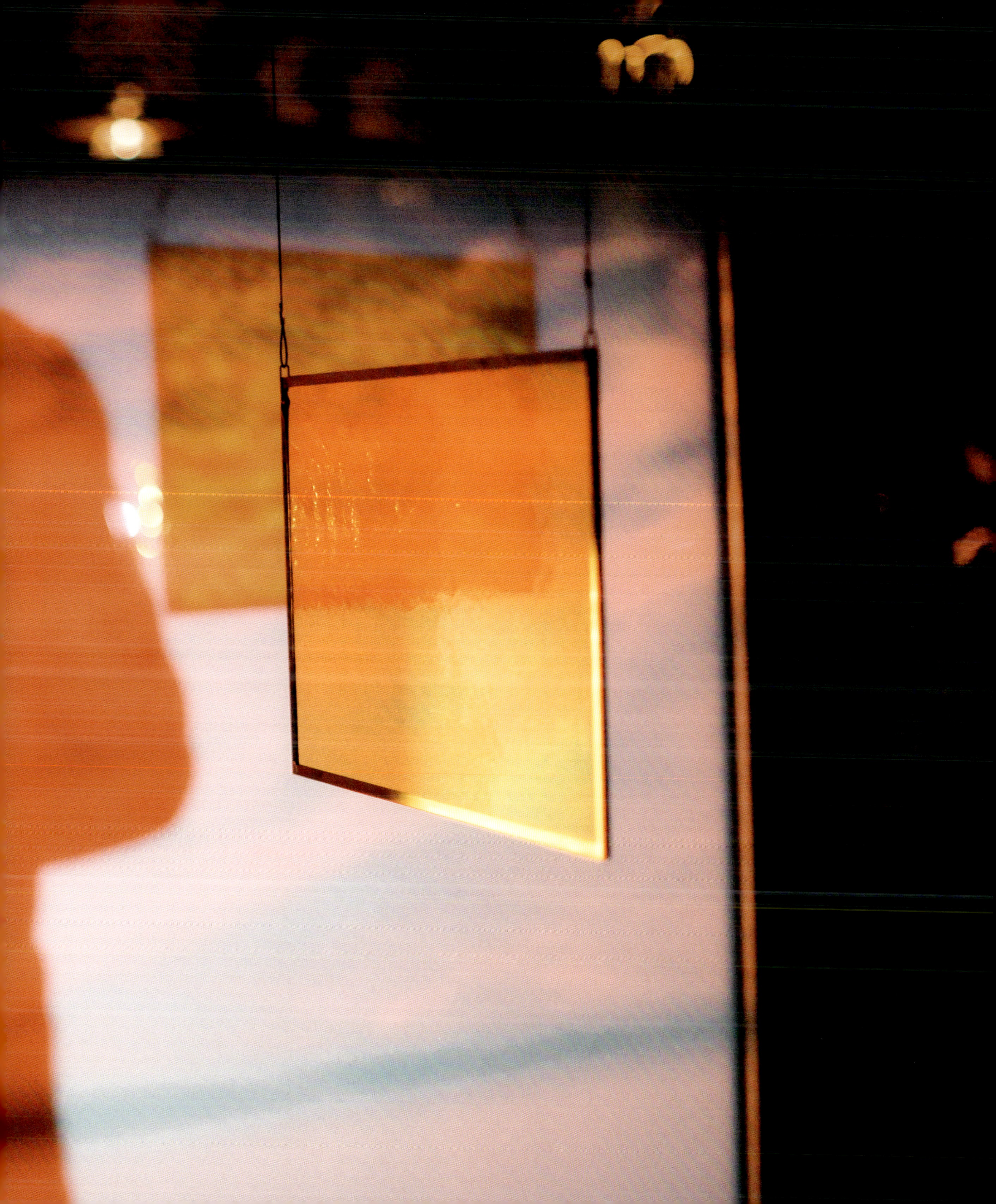

previous pages,
IN A PERPETUAL NOW OF INSTANTANEOUS VISIBILITY, 2019
PERFORMANCE, 16MM PROJECTORS, GLASS FILTERS, 35MM PROJECTOR, SCREENS, DRUMS, CELLO.

PERFORMANCE VIEW WITH CHAD TAYLOR AT PARK AVENUE ARMORY, NEW YORK, 2019.

right,
WIREPIECE, 2022
MODIFIED 16MM PROJECTOR, SNARE DRUM STRING, PLINTH

INSTALLATION VIEW AT TATE MODERN, LONDON, 2023

of light changes as the train passes, and varies in brightness with the wheels of the carriages. Through a microphone device fixed to the rails, Barba's installation converts the sound of the passing train into impulses that determine the amount of light coming from the projector. The shutter speed is greater when the train is closer, slower when the train is approaching or leaving. Until full light is restored. In this way, the abstract film that is projected reflects the 'play' of the wheels on the rails, like a bow pressed against strings. But this can be done the other way round. At the Atelier Calder in Saché, for example, and at the CCC OD in Tours, a drum string, stretched between the ceiling and the floor, is 'played' by a strip of film stock, looped through a prepared projector. Whenever there is friction between the two, the drum string vibrates and makes a sound (*Wirepiece*, 2022).

'I like to bring the sound source into the performance as a visual presence, but also acoustically.'[56] Barba pays particular attention not just to music and ambient sounds, but also to instruments, and to the real or dreamed sounds that they make. This is true no matter what hardware is used to create such an instrument – a train, a projector, murmurs of voices, etc. Take, for example, *Color Clocks*, objects made of metal and Plexiglas, looking like bollards, lightboxes or metronomes. Inside the transparent case of each of these objects, a strip of 35mm film travels in a loop, at its own rhythm, moved by a clockwork mechanism measuring only what is essential: the time of the loop, the distance covered by the film, those things that give it the status of 'sculpture'. The coloured film strips are each imprinted with individual letters, spelling out the words Yellow, Red and Blue, respectively – the three primary colours. The narrative, if such exists, describes their departure from synchronised, unilinear time. As with Félix González-Torres's *Untitled (Perfect Lovers)* (1991),[57] each timeline generously gives the sound of its name to its colour.

The clocks were part of an installation organised over two evenings in the Pompidou Centre, in which Barba combined two performances: *Voice Engine* (2021–23) and *Hear, There, Where the Echoes Are* (2016–23). A choir,[58] arranged in an ellipse, is singing. Each singer, with their hand gestures, takes part in a shared, collegiate conducting of the score in front of them. There is no hierarchy among them, just as there is no hierarchy among the revolving screens with their projected coloured shapes, among the sculptures on the ground or the fixed screens, showing the passing silhouettes of both the singers and the audience. The musical notation, therefore, is not a set of directions given, but rather another type of printed filmic performance. Bursts of projected light sweep over the instruments, the people, the surroundings. The voices cease. Chad Taylor starts drumming. Barba is holding a cello. A horizontal strip of film moves over its strings, activated by a projector on the floor. She 'plays' the instrument on the film strip propelled by the projector motor, and just touching the strings of the cello. This tension not only, therefore, produces sound, but also dramatizes the act of listening: listening to the orchestra of times, a composition by Rosa Barba.

TRANSLATED FROM FRENCH BY SARAH KANE

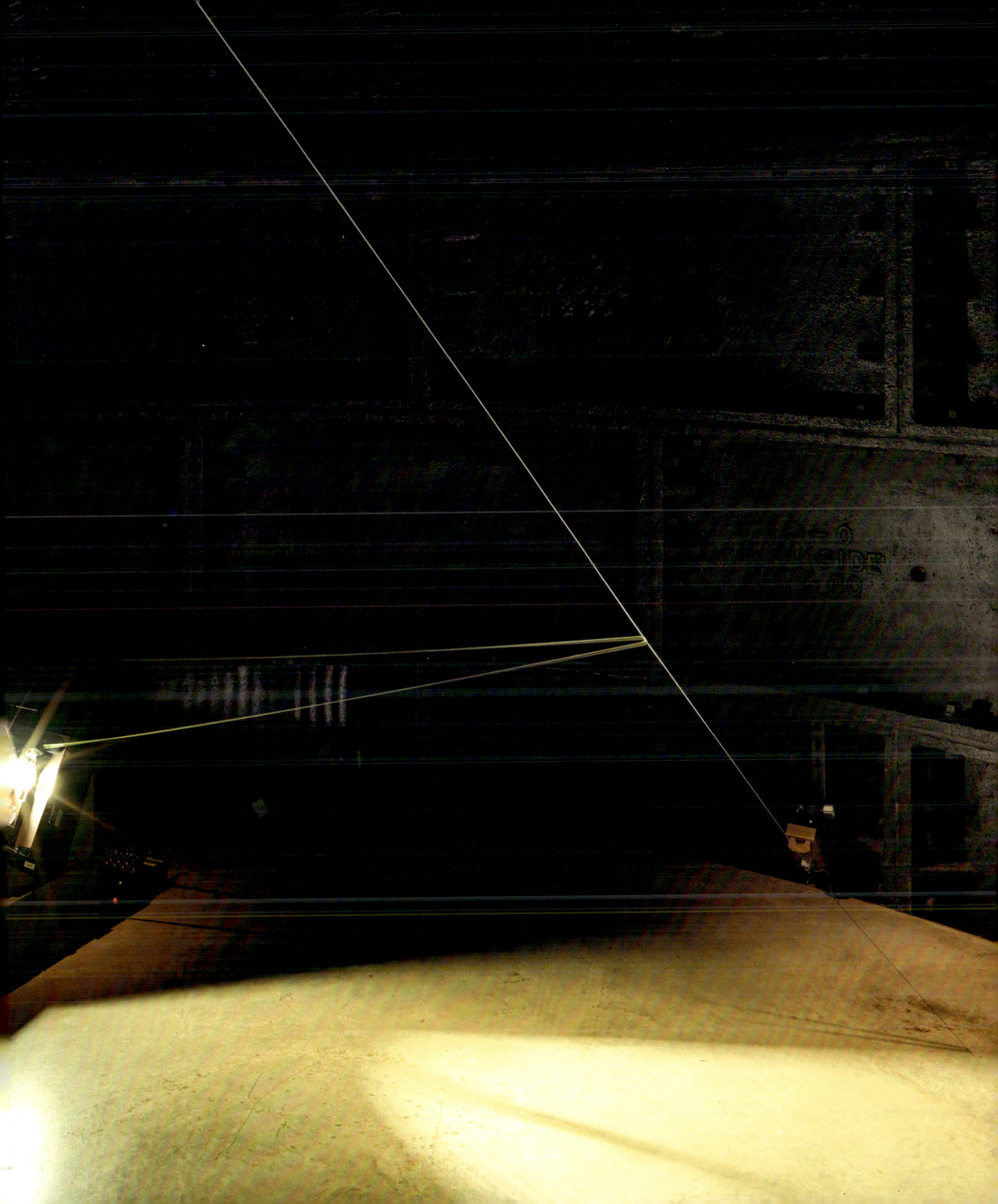

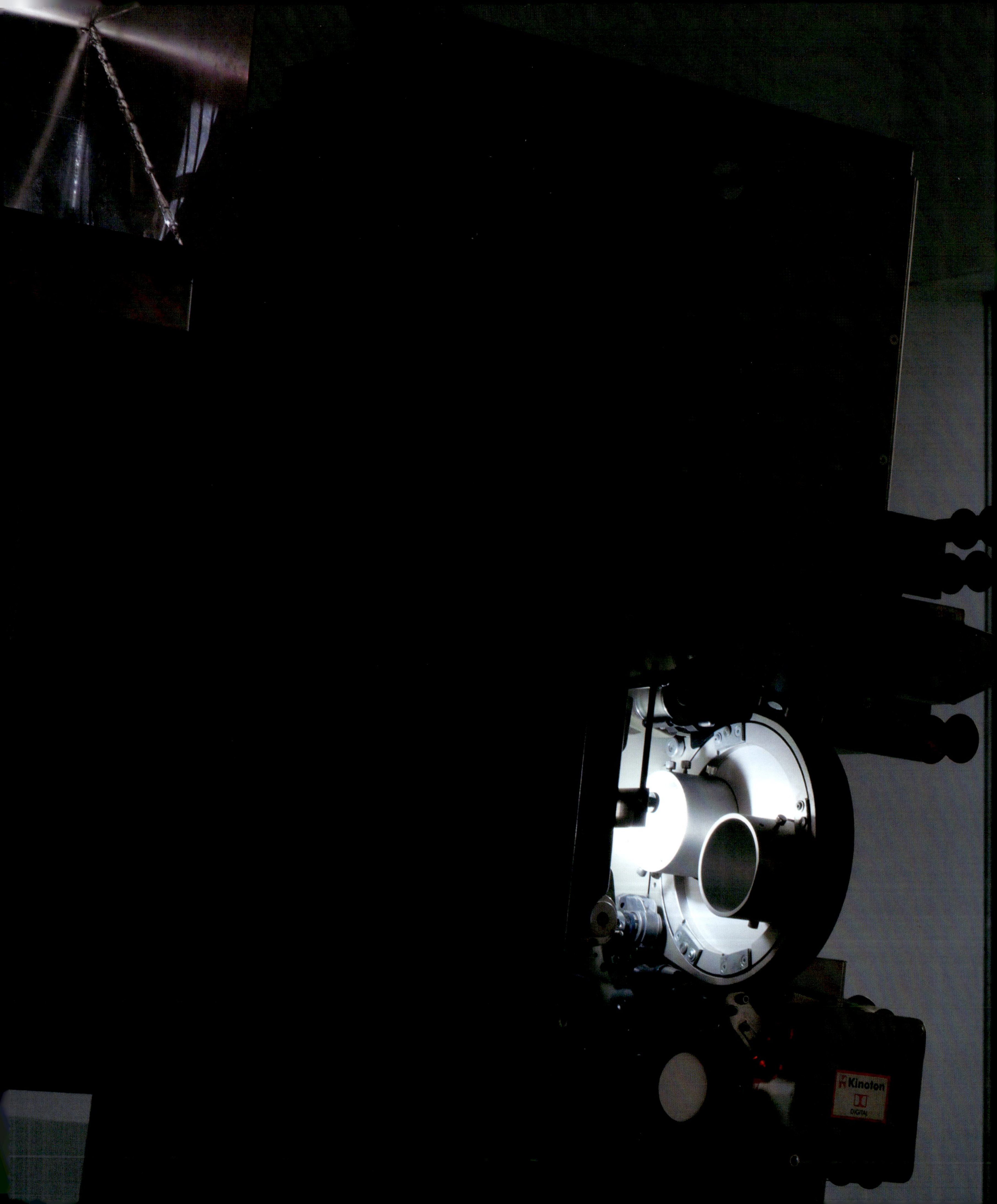
Kinoton

Rosa Barba's Nocturnal Light

Julie Ault

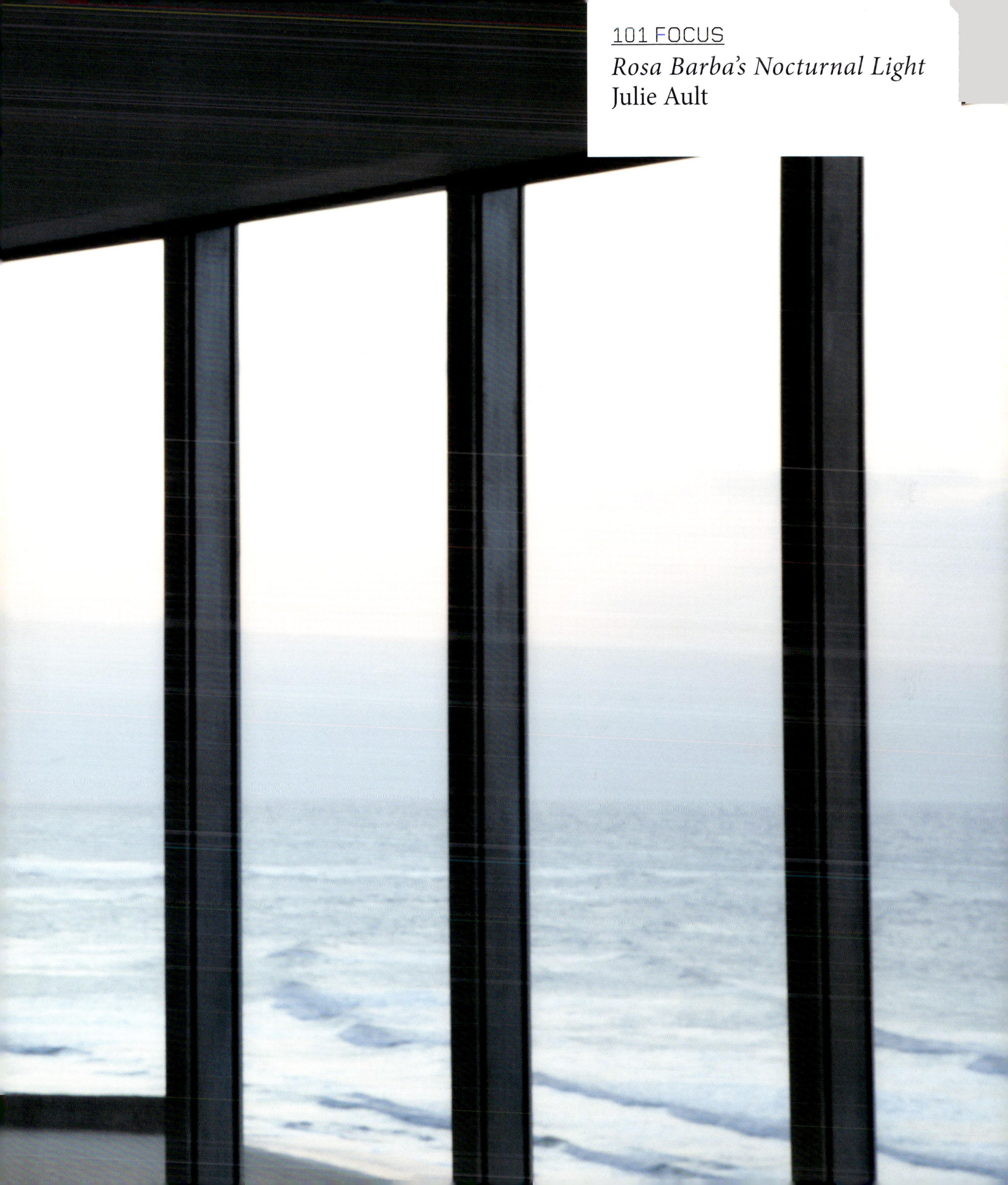

opposite and previous pages,
WHITE MUSEUM (MARGATE),
2010–13
70MM FILM, PROJECTOR

INSTALLATION VIEW AT TURNER
CONTEMPORARY, MARGATE,
ENGLAND, 2013

I also never see my work as a finalized result but rather as ongoing experimentation and thinking.[1]

– Rosa Barba

The primary components of Rosa Barba's White Museum series have remained the same since its 2010 genesis: a projector, a film, a landscape, a building and the diurnal/ nocturnal cycle that makes the filmic sculpture visible. The specifics of the twelve variants to date have been contingent on the location and environment where Barba has elected to actuate the work. Apart from the concept of projecting looped film from a building interior to produce a cinematic light beam directed outside, every aspect of the filmic installation is variable, from the projector and lens specifications and setup, to the character of the light emitted via the film, to the duration of the materialization, to the beam throw distance and direction, to the scale of the rectilinear projection, to the terrain surface that serves as screen for the illumination. Barba determines the particulars from her inquiry into and understanding of the larger site – the materiality of the built environment and natural surround, and intangibles including undercurrents, rumours, legends and chronicles of place.

According to Barba, light is the most vital element for cinema. Attracted to white because it embodies all colours, she uses transparent leader film in some instances and films white light for others. Sometimes she draws onto the leader frames 'to make a kind of notation so the light has a rhythmical staccato', or flicker. Barba observes, 'It is the light itself that has volume, rather than the imprint of the film.' The differences between the celluloid she employs for the series are subtle, intended to 'gradate the light and add or withhold information'.[2]

Barba projects the film, absent of any discernible image, from a building aperture to create a cone of light and a resultant square or rectangular shape when the airy light beam arrives at a tangible surface. 'Usually there is a story in the landscape that I want to capture, but which is not really visible.'[3] Witnesses to the action watch the relatively vacant notional film while simultaneously looking at the real-time illuminated arena. The cinematic rippling light and the emblazoned vista inscribe one another to form a seamless superimposition. The flickering light and an on-the-verge sense of image open an indefinable psychological space that is transportive. Each cycle of the fixed-frame illumination is 'creating an unrepeatable film'.[4]

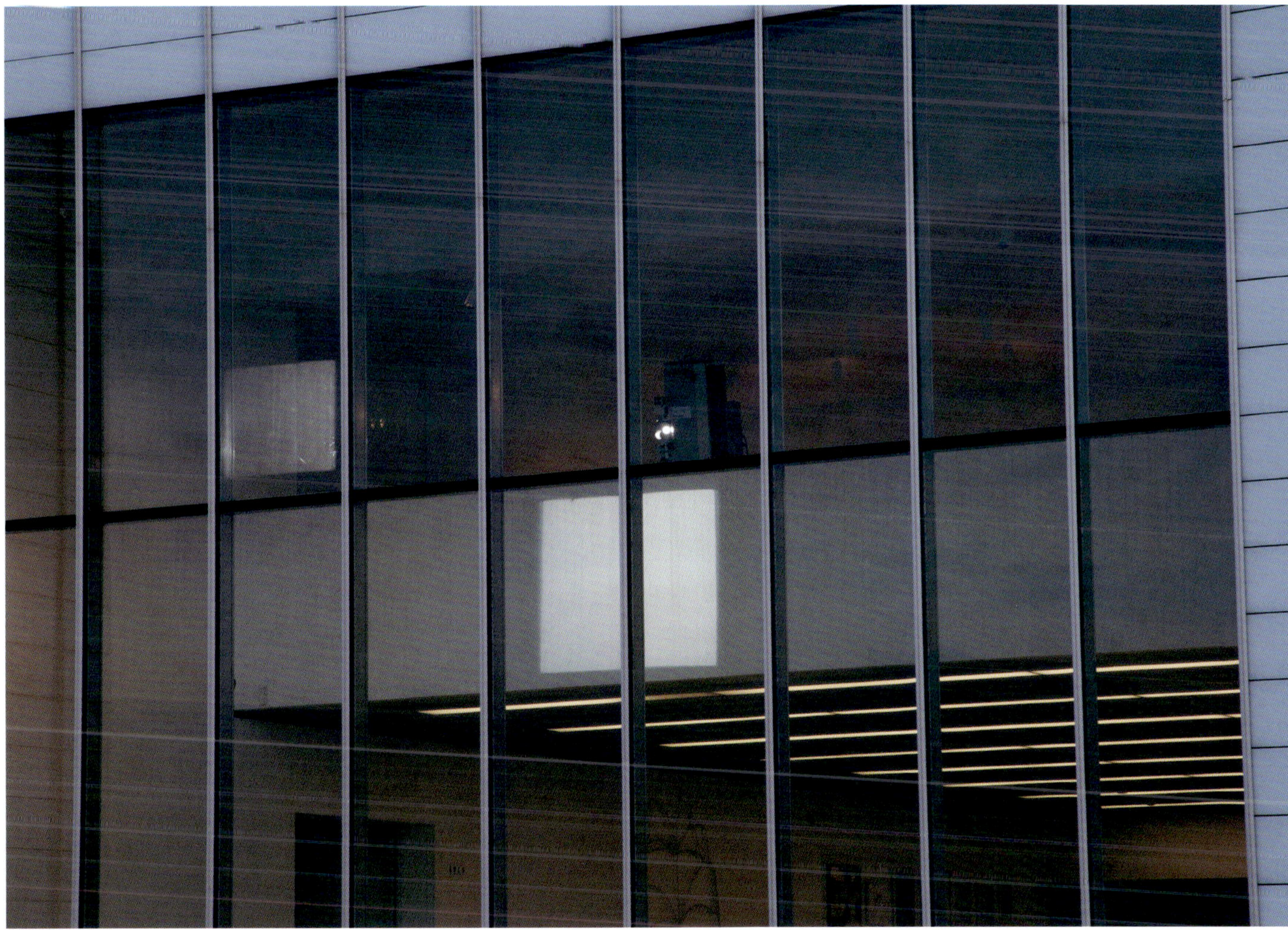

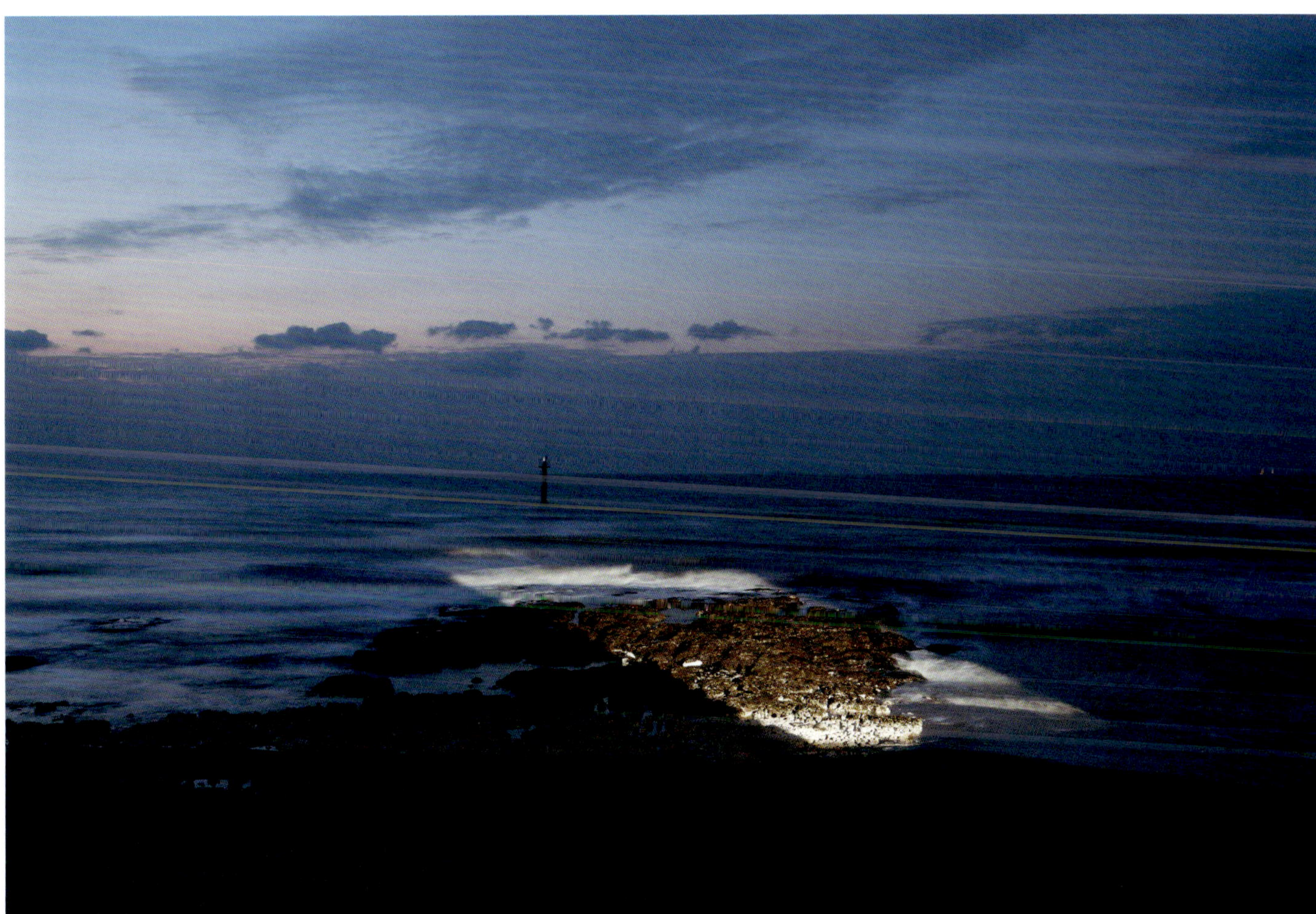

WHITE MUSEUM (WIELS, BRUSSELS), 2010–13
70MM WHITE FILM, PROJECTOR

INSTALLATION VIEW AT WIELS, BRUSSELS, 2013

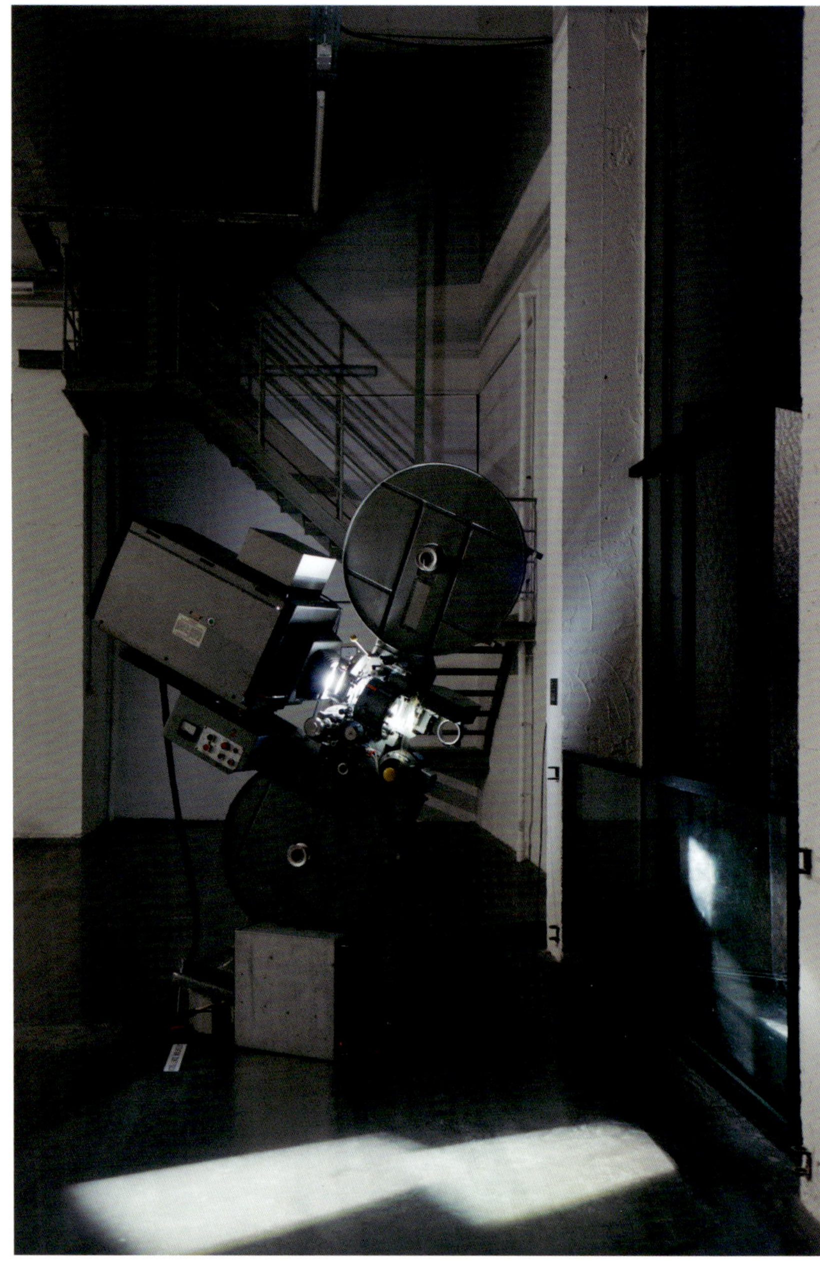

A white cinematic projection is the omission of image. This omission, which allegedly leaves out any narrative, in fact does the opposite. By omitting the … one that comes from the projector, the framed white light creates the opportunity for other narratives to emerge.[5]

Barba is partial to bringing works in various media together and choreographing the exhibition arrangement with the rhythm of moving works guiding viewers through the space. While White Museum is usually part of a larger presentation, here, I primarily focus on a few of the series' iterations to chart her method and thinking.

Barba's interest in the factual and the fictive, the manifest and the incorporeal traces of use on land and locale invites us to delve into personal and collective imagination and the strata of narratives linked to the places she chooses to activate her cinematic light.

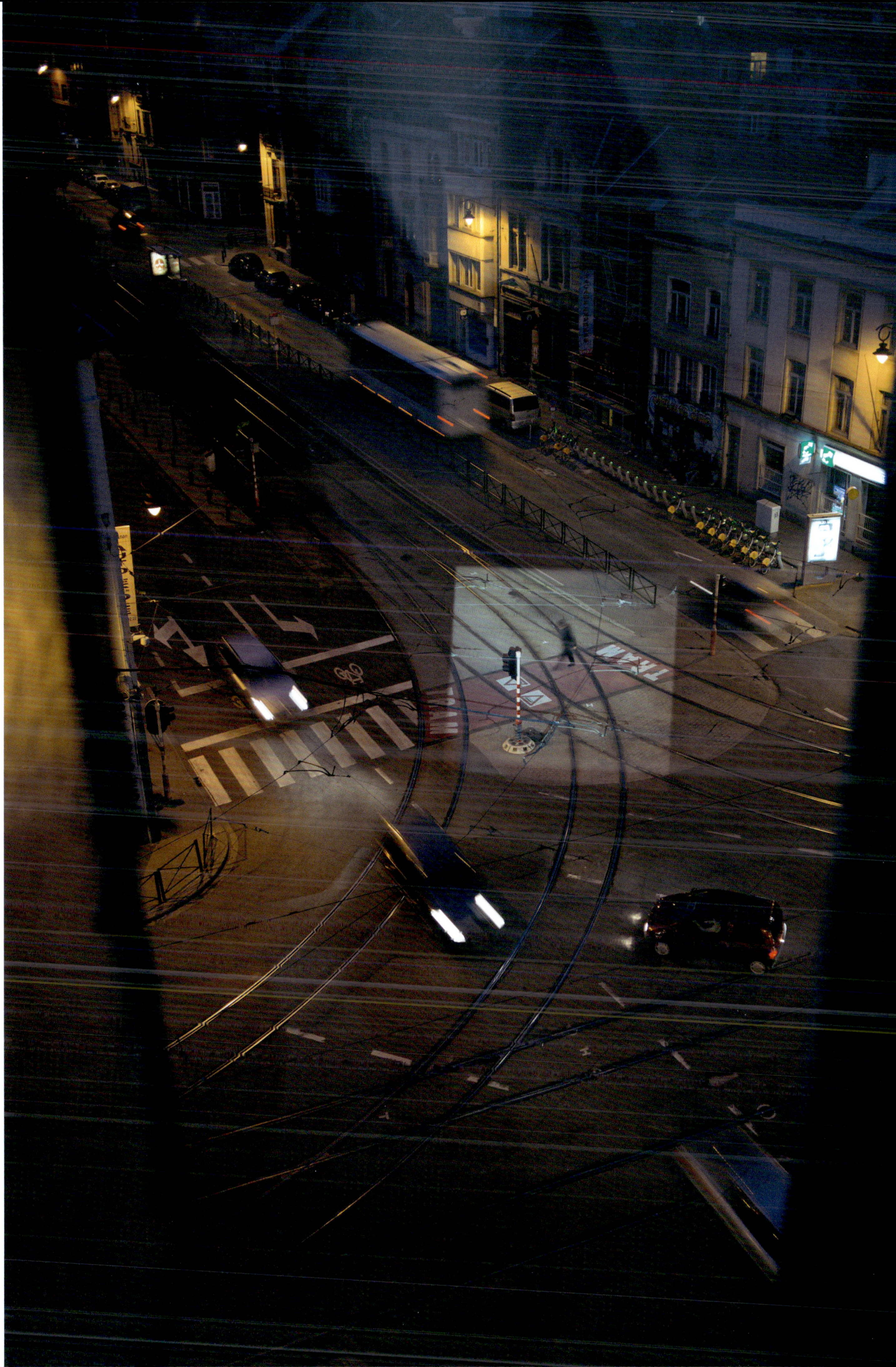

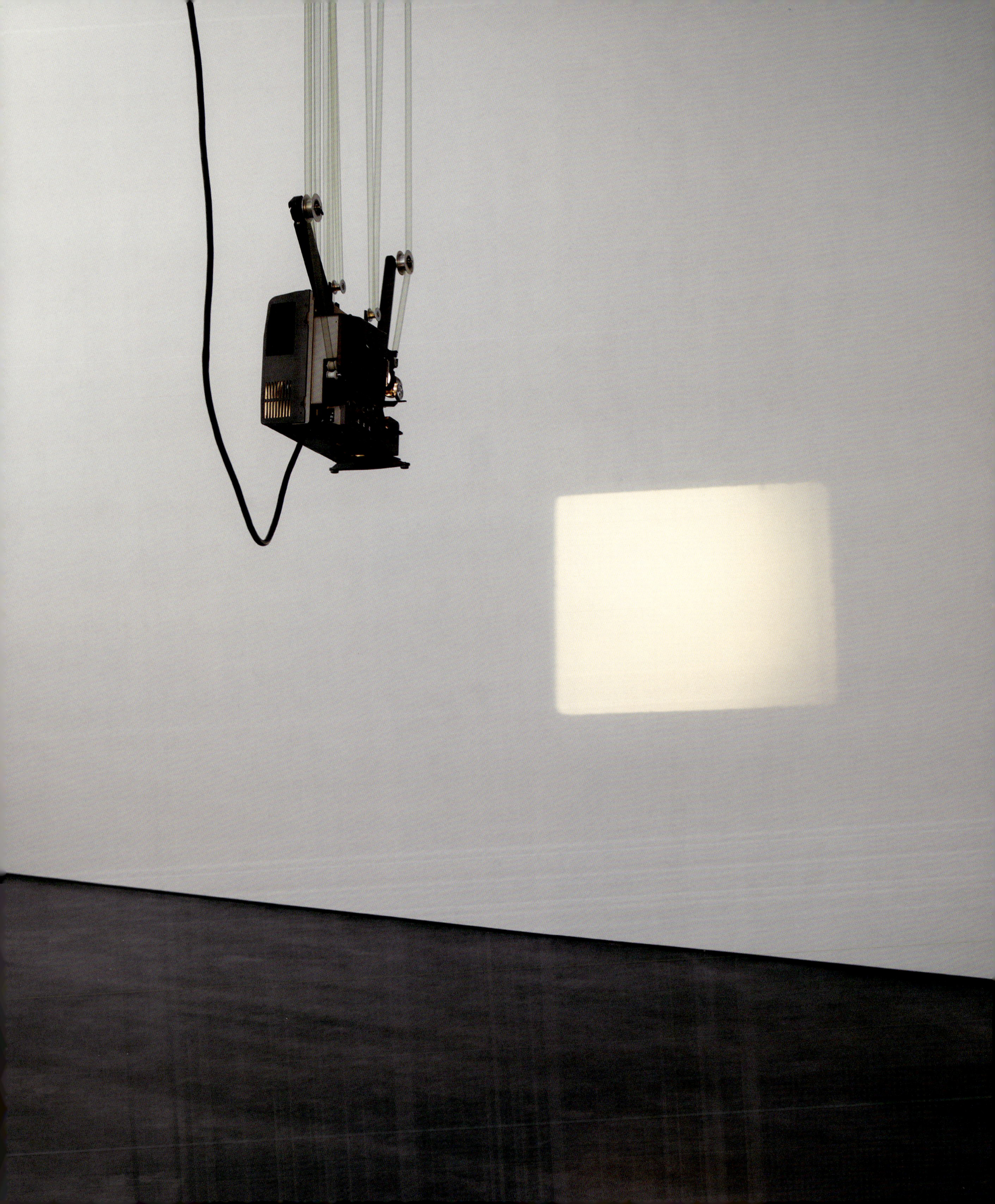

STATING THE REAL SUBLIME, 2009
16MM FILM, MODIFIED PROJECTOR

INSTALLATION VIEW AT WIELS, BRUSSELS, 2013

During a site visit for her solo exhibition at the Centre International d'Art et du Paysage de l'Île de Vassivière designed by architects Aldo Rossi and Xavier Fabre, Barba imagined the small-scale window set high at the far end of the building becoming a projection booth facing outside, thereby 'transforming the museum into a giant projector'.[6] She later learned that Rossi conceived the 40 x 30 cm window looking out onto the encircling lake as a perfect framing, conjuring a landscape painting.

The formerly agrarian Limousin region of France was refashioned between 1946 and 1950 with the construction of the massive hydroelectric Electricité de France dam to generate power for the larger territory. The built environment was decimated, and the Maulde basin flooded to manufacture a reservoir, causing a deluge that fatally engulfed several villages. An eyewitness report from the time identified enormous repercussions on the region: 'Deserted hamlets line the small winding roads of the area which must be submerged … everything was demolished, stone by stone. At the sight of this ghost village, your heart sinks: you would think that the war had passed through there.'[7] The flooding produced a large lake nestled in the Millevaches Regional Natural Park, which is protected for wildlife. Parts of the shoreline were developed for leisure tourism, boating and outdoor sports.

What had previously been a peak in the surrounding plateau became an island in the new artificial lake. Since 1991, that island has been home to the Centre, which encompasses an open-air Sculpture Wood (sculpture park), a lighthouse-like tower, and a voluminous building that, according to Fabre, suggests 'an aqueduct that appears to have fallen into ruins'. He adds, 'It is not a museum; it is a place where art is produced'[8] – an ideal match for Barba and her attentive view to geologic time, natural artifacts, vestiges of human activity, and what they reveal and conceal.

Barba typically speaks with people from the area where she conceives a work to learn about the location and gain insight into its fugitive histories. Visiting Vassivière, she inquired if anyone had resisted the massive dispossession. 'I was told about a man who refused to leave' and still resided in the only surviving house, which before 1950 had been on high ground, a relic of the displaced terrain. Barba notes, 'The transformation – the dam and the lake and everything – were designed around his home.' She went by his house, which is very close to the river on the other side of the island, and thought, 'He had a perfect view of the piece I wanted

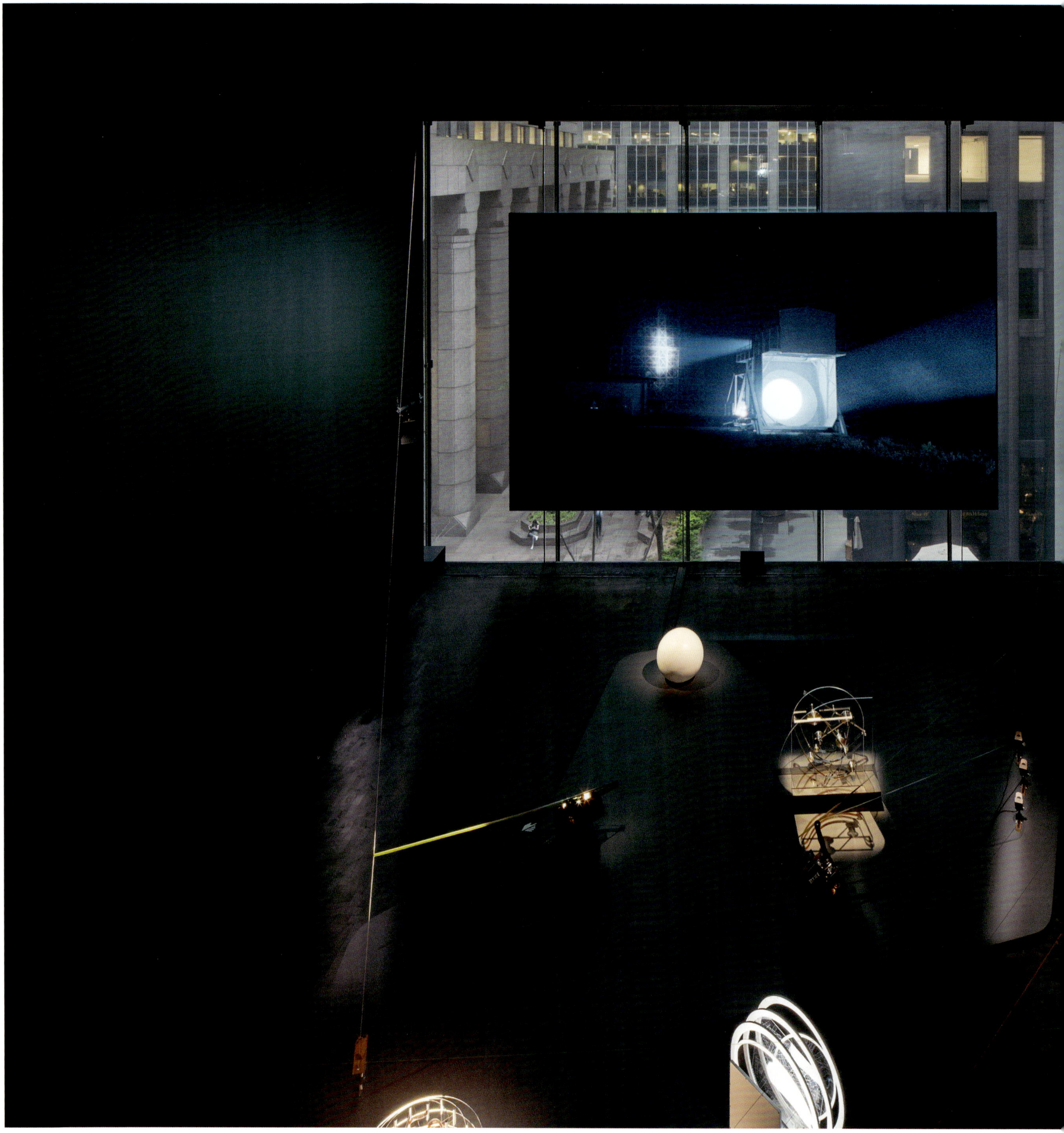

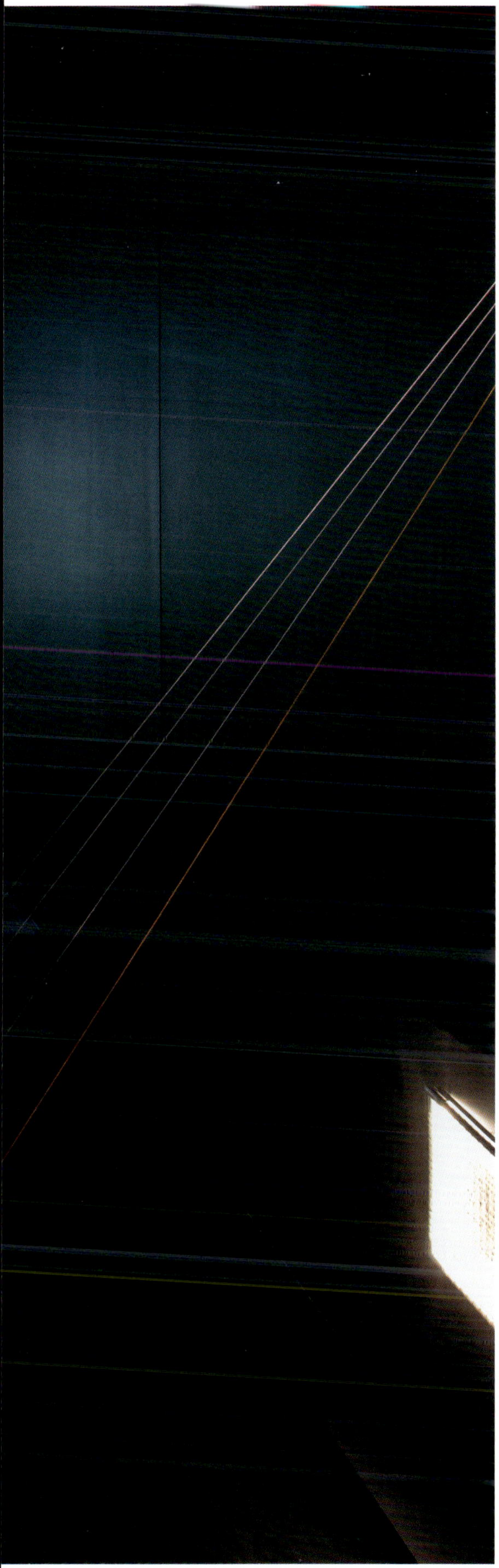

from the back,
CONDUCTOR, 2014
SILICONE MEMBRANE, SPEAKER, SOUND
Ø 60 CM

CHARGE, 2025
35MM FILM, COLOUR, SOUND
25 MIN. 33 SEC.

WIREPIECE, 2022
16MM FILM PROJECTOR, 16MM FILM, LENS, DRUM STRING, BRIDGE SADDLE PIECE, PICKUP MICHROPHONE, PRE-AMP, PLINTH

AS FIXED IN FLUX, 2025
STEEL, ALUMINIUM, GLASS, MOTORS, 35MM FILM
115 X 108 X 39 CM

SENSIBLE SUNS, 2025
ACRYLIC GLASS, POLARIZATION FILMS, STEEL, ALUMINIUM, MOTORS AND LED LIGHT
90 X 68 X 45 CM

WIREPIECE, DOUBLE STOPS, 2025
16MM PROJECTOR, 16MM FILM, LENS, DRUM STRINGS, BRIDGE SADDLE PIECES, PICKUP MICHROPHONES, PRE-AMPS, PLINTH

COMPOSITION IN FIELD, 2022
35MM FILM, KINETIC ALUMINIUM FRAME, MOTORS, PLEXIGLAS AND LED LIGHTS
91 X 120 X 9 CM

INSTALLATION VIEW AT THE MUSEUM OF MODERN ART, NEW YORK, 2025

to project out.' Visitors to the island are required to leave at sundown, but 'the work is only fully visible at night, so I thought he was the only one who would see it.' There is no way of knowing whether the enduring elderly inhabitant noticed, watched, or turned a blind eye to the beacon that Barba dispatched his way nightly. Regardless, 'His presence was important for the conception of the work. I always had him in mind as a viewing point and put my whole imagination into this person that I didn't know. If he hadn't been there, the work may not have become what it is.'[9]

Barba began her exhibition, *Is it a two-dimensional analogy or a metaphor?* in the lighthouse, where she installed a sizeable transparent cylinder with an industrial ventilator inside, high up near the skylight.[10] From the 35mm projector on the floor, blank film with ambient optical sound cycled the vertical distance and projected onto the tower interior. *One Way Out* (2010) was devised for the lighthouse, which Barba regards as the 'subconscious machine' of the Centre's entire edifice.[11] The tower was designed to shed light on the sculpture woodland below. She used it as a loudspeaker to disseminate the film's soundtrack outside. 'On entering the exhibit, the visitor is unaware they are penetrating a space that forms the inside of a huge projector . . . a complex machine.'[12]

Moving through the adjacent viaduct-like gallery building that the artist populated with several works, at its furthermost end, one entered the small theatre, where she positioned *White Museum*.[13] With its back facing the viewer, the 70mm projector was pushed up against the rear wall, casting the cinematic light outwards, and parenthesizing the compound structure with illumination. Barba recalls, 'The projection was running day and night and became a sound piece. When you went through the exhibition to the very end of the building where the projector was leaning out of the window, you would only then see the sculpture.'[14] The projector's sonic stutter heard inside leads to the cinematic flickering outside, which was linked to another 'soundtrack', to which Barba refers as 'underwater'. She abstracted voices and conversations that she recorded through compression, to which she 'added base frequencies to activate the membrane of the water surface. The "speeches" were unrecognizable, but you could understand from the rhythm that there were vocal sounds.'[15] Diffuse traces emerge from the lake, conjuring the obliterated village long since under water.

The sound waves that Barba broadcast from the lighthouse tower radiated outdoors to the far end of the gallery building, linking the structures and their surroundings with a sonic arc. She notes that while she did not 'literally project light from end-to-end, it felt like the light projection as well was channelled through to the small theatre, where it then projected out of the window'.[16] When daylight fades and turns to night, the light beam and its target become more and more visible, foregrounding perception and stimulating focus. 'The darkened void of the outside environment becomes an infinite "dark box", cut through by the shaft of white light.'[17]

Each new experience adds a new possibility for approaching the space beyond cinema that is created by projecting onto the outside from within these edifices.[18]

Barba regards her cinematic light aimed into the open-air darkness as like shining a lamp into a cave or crevice – as a form of archeology. 'The idea of the archive always comes back in my work because I also understand many things as archives – for example, the landscape.'[19] Insight rising from her exploration of a local situation often moves Barba to orchestrate another White Museum.[20]

Wiels Contemporary Art Centre occupies an exceptional modernist industrial building in Brussels, completed in 1931 and named after its architect, Adrien Blomme. The Blomme was the flagship brewhouse of the Wielemans-Ceuppens Breweries. Ceasing production in 1988, the epochal building was subsequently given protected status and procured by the city for repurposing. Wiels opened in 2007.

In 2013, Barba oriented her light beam from a third-storey window in Wiels' façade to a busy intersection below, creating an incorporeal boundary animated by vehicles and pedestrians moving through the scene. 'Siting the projection amid traffic and city lights was a compelling disruption, adding another time-language layer to the work. Pedestrians and cars passing only realized that they were in a film frame when they were coming into it.'[21] The light acts as an optical portal, heightening the perception of exposure and concealment. Looking up, one sees the beam extend from a machine in a window of a building – a searchlight, surveillance camera, or coded signal? Is one being targeted, monitored, or appealed to? Crossing the threshold into an area ambiguously illuminated from above is double-edged.

For a related work the same year, Barba developed the performative event Perpetual Response to Sound and Light during a residency in the remote desert town of Marfa, Texas. The Chianti Foundation manages the programme and provides a former locker plant used for refrigerated

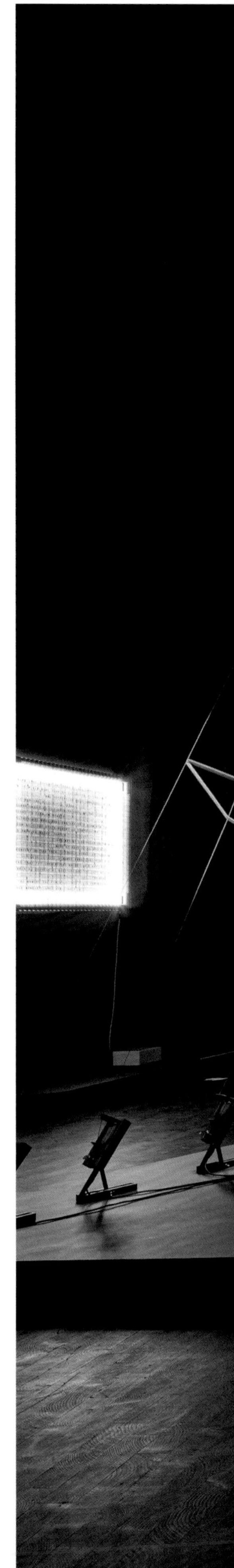

from left,
COMPOSITION IN FIELD, 2022
35MM FILM, KINETIC ALUMINIUM FRAME, MOTORS, PLEXIGLAS AND LED LIGHTS
91 X 120 X 9 CM

WIREPIECE, DOUBLE STOPS, 2025
16MM PROJECTOR, 16MM FILM, LENS, DRUM STRINGS, BRIDGE SADDLE PIECES, PICKUP MICHROPHONES, PREAMPS, PLINTH

STATING THE REAL SUBLIME, 2009
16MM, MODIFIED PROJECTOR

AS FIXED IN FLUX, 2025
STEEL, ALUMINIUM, GLASS, MOTORS, 35MM FILM
115 X 108 X 39 CM

SENSIBLE SUNS, 2025
ACRYLIC GLASS, POLARIZATION FILMS, STEEL, ALUMINIUM, MOTORS AND LED LIGHT
90 X 68 X 45 CM

WIREPIECE, TRIPLE STOPS, 2025
16MM PROJECTOR, 16MM FILM, LENS, DRUM STRING, BRIDGE SADDLE PIECE, PICKUP MICROPHONE, PRE-AMP, AND PLINTH

OFF SPLINTERED TIME, 2021
GLASS, MOTORS, LED LIGHT, 35MM FILM
80 X 80 X 70 CM

WIREPIECE, 2022
16MM FILM PROJECTOR, 16MM FILM, LENS, DRUM STRING, BRIDGE SADDLE PIECE, PICKUP MICHROPHONE, PRE-AMP, PLINT

CONDUCTOR, 2014
SILICONE MEMBRANE, SPEAKER, SOUND
Ø 60 CM

CHARGE, 2025
35MM FILM, COLOUR, SOUND
25 MIN. 33 SEC.

INSTALLATION VIEW AT THE MUSEUM OF MODERN ART, NEW YORK, 2025

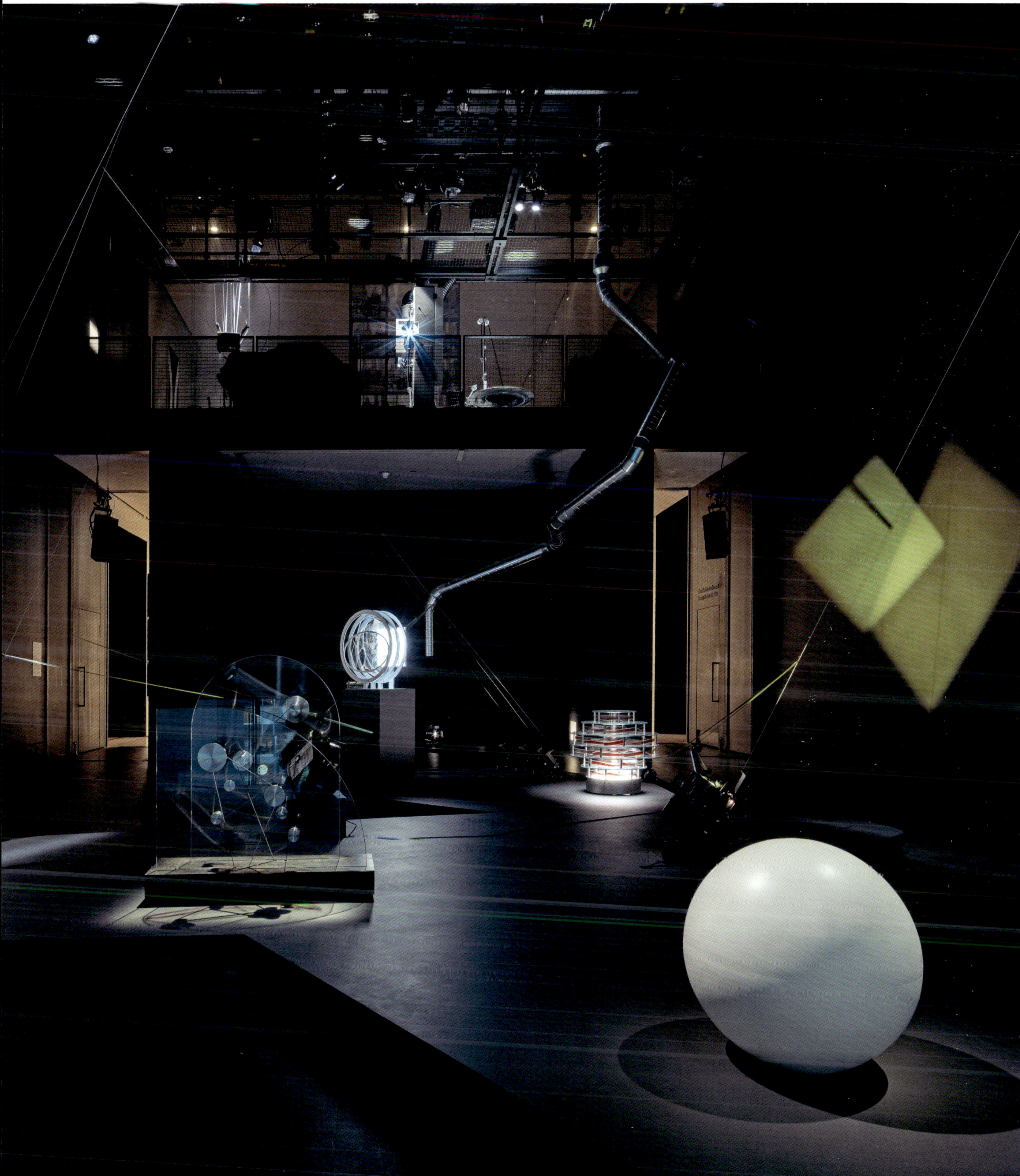

from left,
CHARGE, 2025
35MM FILM, COLOUR, SOUND
25 MIN. 33 SEC.

CONDUCTOR, 2014
SILICONE MEMBRANE,
SPEAKER, SOUND
Ø 60 CM

WIREPIECE, 2022
16MM FILM PROJECTOR, 16MM FILM, LENS, DRUM STRING, BRIDGE SADDLE PIECE, PICKUP MICROPHONE, PRE-AMP, PLINTH

OFF SPLINTERED TIME, 2021
GLASS, MOTORS, LED LIGHT, 35MM FILM
80 X 80 X 70 CM

AS FIXED IN FLUX, 2025
STEEL, ALUMINIUM, GLASS, MOTORS, 35MM FILM
115 X 108 X 39 CM

WIREPIECE, DOUBLE STOPS, 2025
16MM PROJECTOR, 16MM FILM, LENS, DRUM STRINGS, BRIDGE SADDLE PIECES, PICKUP MICROPHONES, PRE-AMPS, PLINTH

INSTALLATION VIEW AT THE MUSEUM OF MODERN ART, NEW YORK, 2025

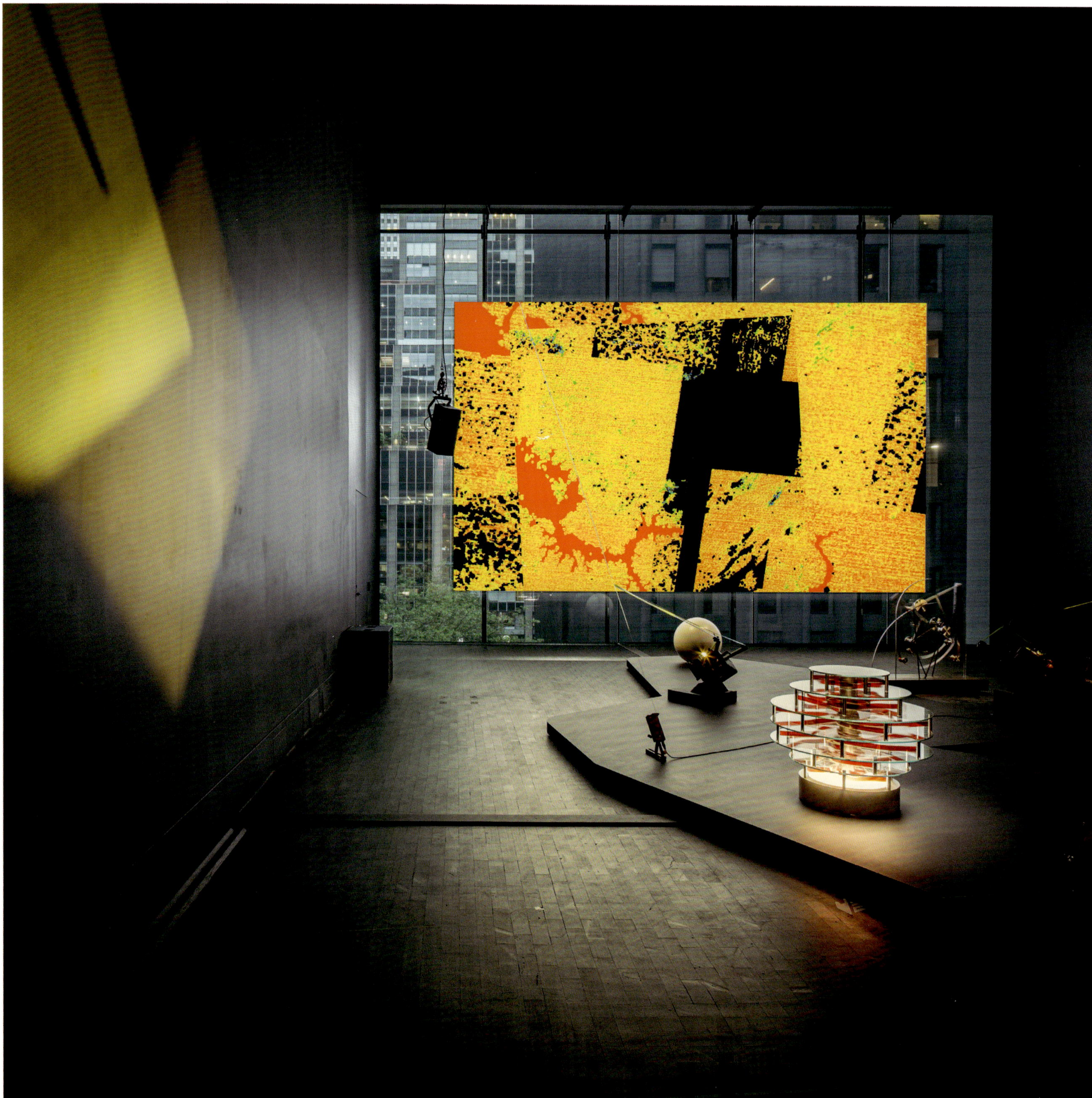

storage in the heart of downtown as studio space. The one-storey storefront faces the train tracks that run through town, and could easily pass for a train station. Barba was struck by the dramatic sensory incidents she experienced whenever a train approached: 'The ground would start to vibrate as much as ten minutes before its arrival, and then the sound would gradually get more intense.'[22]

Barba situated a high-intensity searchlight between the Locker Plant and the tracks, oriented to face the building, and positioned sound detectors under the tracks. 'The trains transport sensitive materials, they follow a secret schedule, and that raised the question of how I could plan the performance. In the end, I decided to make the uncertainty part of the concept. The event would last three or four hours, and during that time only one train might pass, or three or five trains might pass.'[23] For several nights, Barba directed the concentrated beam to form an illuminated circle covering half of the façade, thereby illuminating the interior through the large picture window. She attuned the glaring white light to pulse in time to the rhythmic sound of each passing train. 'Once the train was close, the lamp would pump light into the building, and for a few seconds the building would become a light sculpture.'[24] The shapeshifting interior light surged and softened in a staccato manner, calling to mind the visual flares and shadows cast about by bombs exploding.

Spotlighting the night has many purposes. Spot- and sky-lighting have applications in landscape architecture, to highlight attractions and signal festivity, to publicize premieres and gala events, and to survey parking lots and commercial depots for intruders. Sonic and radar-controlled searchlights were developed for military use to track bomber strikes. By reflecting searchlight beams off the bottom of clouds, army personnel produce 'artificial moonlight' to illuminate dangerous terrain. Spotlights pinpoint enemy forces and dazzle or temporarily blind adversaries.

The subject of immigration and the national borders of the United States and Mexico are embedded in Texas, a territory that was previously part of Mexico. Marfa is a cultural and political oasis in the present-day ultraconservative state, but it is only sixty miles from the border. Searchlights are a common tool used by border patrol, law enforcement and Homeland Security to detect transgressors and locate missing persons and fugitives.

For those invited to attend Barba's performance, Perpetual Response was clearly part of her artistic research. For others, the ambiguous purpose of the searchlight near the train tracks made for a puzzling, provocative and possibly alarming situation, depending on one's circumstances.

Describing one of the ways in which she relates White Museum to architecture, Barba explains, 'How I choose the lens that I use and the size of the image that hits the crossroads or landscape or sea is in dialogue with the building itself. I play with corresponding to the building with the light and the angle, thinking of the whole image and extending the architecture with the light. I go out and see the image from different perspectives, becoming the architect of the extension of the building.'[25]

WHITE MUSEUM (HIRSCH OBSERVATORY), 2010–15
70MM FILM, PROJECTOR

INSTALLATION VIEW AT HIRSCH OBSERVATORY, RENSSELAER POLYTECHNIC INSTITUTE, TROY, NEW YORK, 2015

The artist remade White Museum again in 2013, in the seaside town of Margate in the United Kingdom. The Turner Contemporary, designed by David Chipperfield Architects, is built on the site where a guesthouse frequented by J.M.W. Turner – often called 'the painter of light' – once stood. Barba notes that Turner, 'working very strongly with all the possibility of light, is for me so close to film'.[26] The modern concrete and glass structure is composed of six interlinked rectangular blocks, and looks somewhat industrial, with a shed roofline. The building is known for its exquisite use of daylight: 'the way it washes in through the clerestory windows and rooflights, and the tricks it plays on the building's glass rainscreen façade'.[27]

Large horizontal swarths of the sea-facing side of the building are windowpane, their expanse achieved with multiple vertical panes set on end. 'Placing the projector facing out on the sea was responding to the long horizontal window of the architecture. I situated the projector in the centre of this window, and the projection was vertical, corresponding to the frame of the building."[28] Barba recounts, 'Each night, the white film framed a new image, as the "screen" of the sea and the seabed altered with the shifting of the tides.'[29] 'The alternation from low tide to high tide waves as an additional layer was important to me.'[30] The cycle of daylight turning to dusk to nightfall to darkness to dawn and atmospheric transformations from weather and climate conditions combine and register in the infinite range of light apparitions cast on the water, some of which are clarifying and many of which are breathtakingly delicate. 'The river was constantly changing; it was frozen, it was white from snow, different colours – change happens with what comes into the projection."[31]

Turner's vision is believed to have deteriorated later in his life, perhaps accounting for his increasingly glowing and blurred paintings. Although Barba did not plan to echo his condition, 'there were these kinds of Turner-like paintings appearing every night in the sea, in the place where he was once trying to focus and refocus'.[32] The manipulation and emanation of light that Turner's painting embodied is echoed in Chipperfield's skillful handling of daylight and in the subtle illuminations that Barba's White Museum emitted from its windows.

In 2015, the Experimental Media and Performing Arts Center (EMPAC) in Troy, New York, commissioned Barba to conceptualize two projects for their towering building façade and the nearby Hirsch Observatory. The Hirsch Observatory sits atop the level roof of the Jonsson-Rowland Science Center at the Rensselaer Polytechnic Institute. Completed in

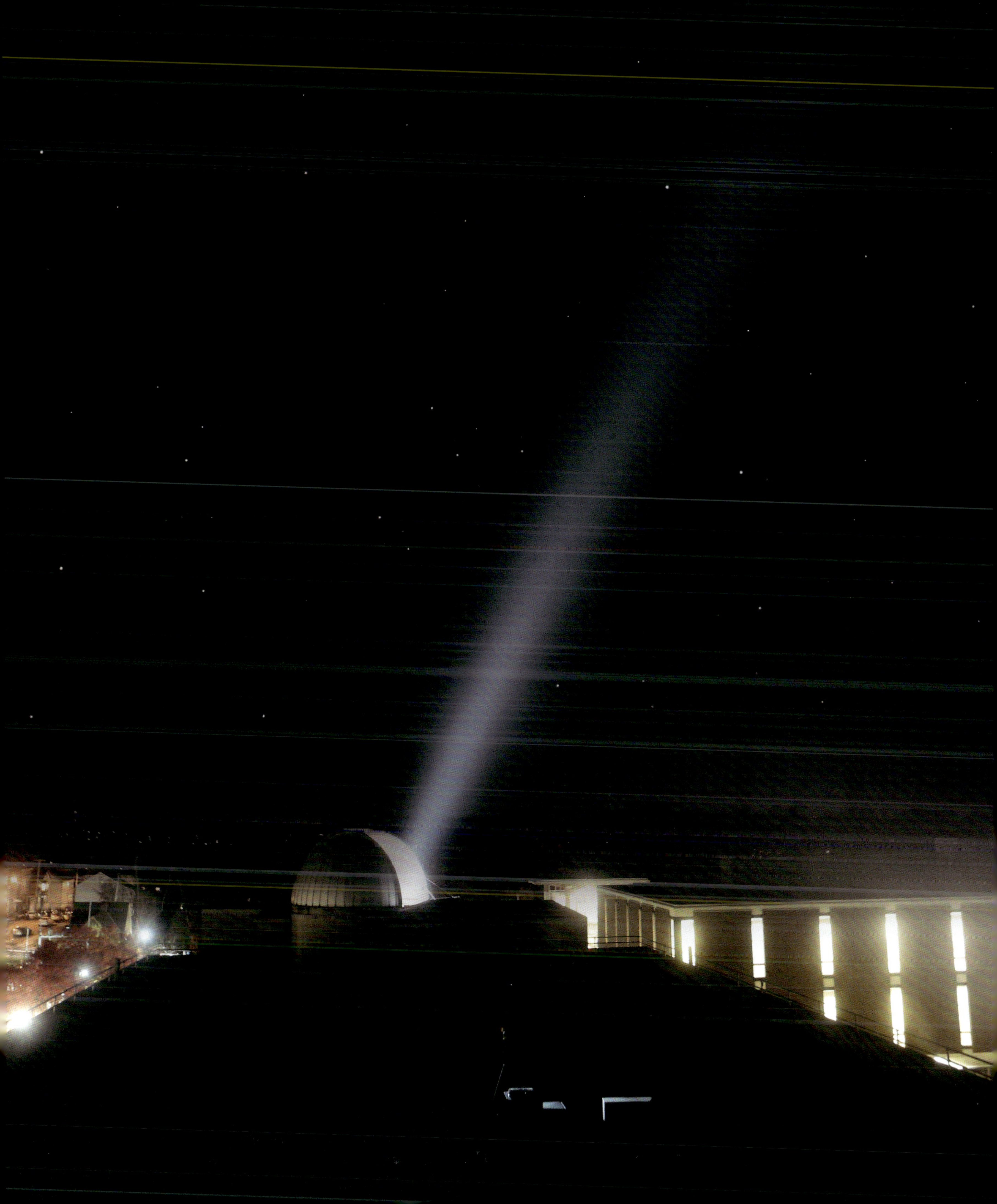

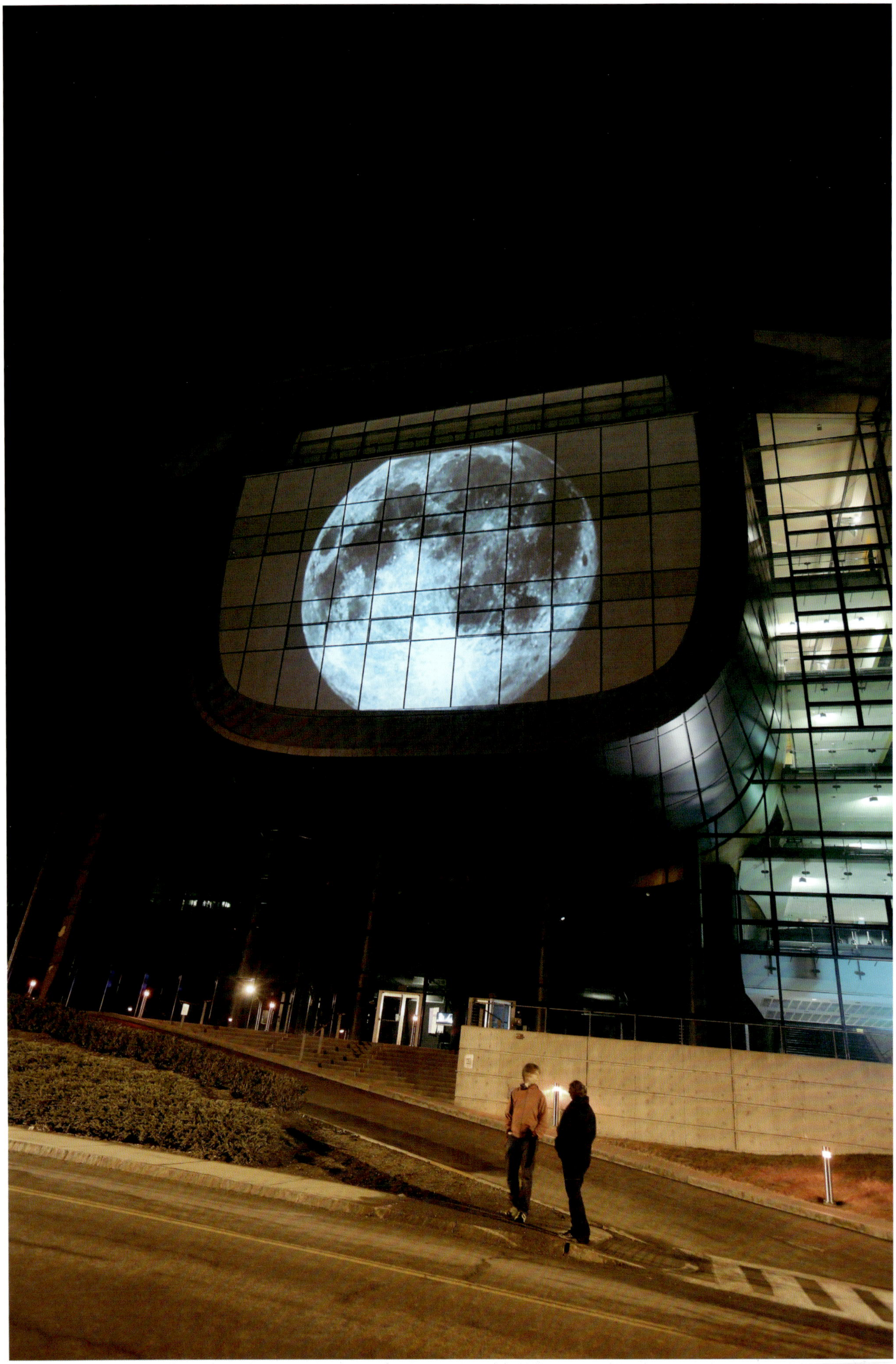

THE COLOR OUT OF SPACE,
2015
HD VIDEO, COLOUR, SOUND
36 MIN.

INSTALLATION VIEW AT HIRSCH OBSERVATORY, RENSSELAER POLYTECHNIC INSTITUTE, TROY, NEW YORK, 2015

1942, the observatory is a research site for the exploration of the universe. Its dome originally housed a twelve-inch equatorial reflector telescope that was designed and fabricated at the institute by its instrument maker, Otto Rasmussen. In the 1960s, a sixteen-inch Boller and Chivens Cassegrain telescope was installed.

The situation foregrounded probing the affinity between astronomy and cinema that Barba had long perceived. She regards both fields as speculative operations primarily based on air, light and distance. Collaborating with physics and astronomy professor and Hirsch Observatory director Heidi Jo Newberg, she enlisted students Nicholas Palmieri and Jake Weiss to shoot long exposures of stars and objects in Earth's solar system from the Observatory. She combined the images with NASA footage of celestial movements for her film, The Color Out of Space, which she projected on EMPAC's glass front, thereby converting the building into a screen – what the curator of time-based visual art for the Rensselaer and EMPAC, Victoria Brooks has called, 'a site-specific cinema for watching the stars beneath the stars'.[33]

An astronomical understanding of light is key to White Museum, which Barba reactivated for the Hirsch Observatory. White Museum embodies omission – filmic white light, void of image – and emission – the luminous emanation, which in this case she directed towards the sky. Astronomers employ the telescope to scrutinize the night sky and decipher light collected from celestial objects. Barba transposed the action, dispensing light to travel skyward. Brooks, recounts, 'In the dry cold of spring in upstate New York, the image bounced upward. Its imprint remained elusive, supported only by a haze of suspended water particles. Each a tiny point of reflection, they collectively formed a pulsing cone of dense light aimed into the sky.'[34]

Barba's research at Troy led her to the Harvard Astronomical Observatory, where, between 1903 and 1921, the American astronomer Henrietta Swan Leavitt worked as a 'human calculator', researching the properties of stars. By studying the colour and luminosity of pulsating stars in relation to Earth, Leavitt discovered a rule for measuring distances in the universe. Her finding led Edwin Hubbard, among others, to the development of an accurate understanding of the scale of the universe. Drawn by the Pulse (2018) is a silent 35mm film sculpture based on the flickering of variable stars and on the images of the photographic plates that Leavitt studied and brought forth her breakthrough. It honours the astronomer, who would have been awarded the Nobel Prize, but died before it was possible. 'Through Leavitt's "Flicker", we come to understand that the universe is much larger than we believed.'[35]

Barba is currently mapping out a new iteration of White Museum for the Centre Pompidou in Paris, which as of the summer of 2025 is closed

DRAWN BY THE PULSE, 2018
35MM FILM SCULPTURE,
SILENT
3 MIN. 8 SEC.

INSTALLATION VIEW AT
KUNSTHALLE BREMEN, 2018

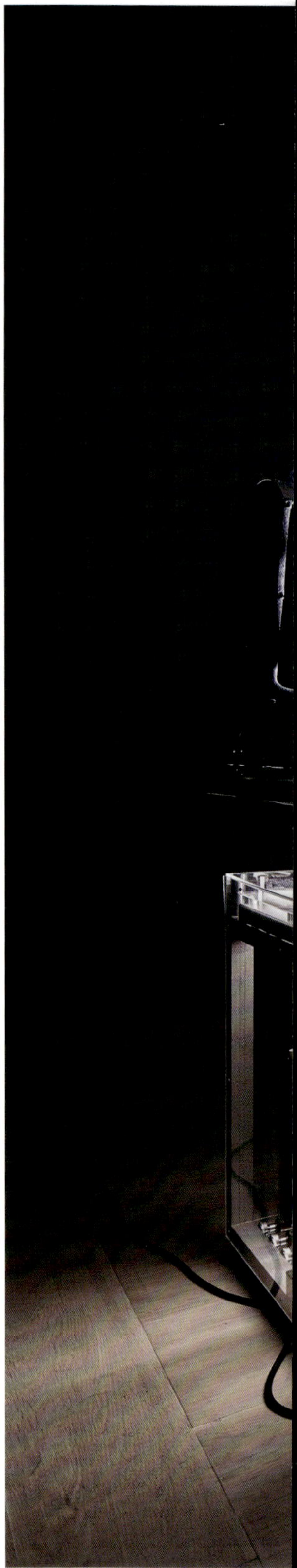

for several years of renovation. The massive glass and metal building designed by Renzo Piano and Richard Rogers is known for its visible infrastructure of colour-coded systems that distribute water, power, airflow and visitor transit situated on the building's exterior. Displaying the operational facilities and equipment resonates with Barba's practice of incorporating filmic equipment and materials into her works. 'From the beginning, I didn't want to put the projector outside the screening room, but rather inside, so it became part of the stage where the viewers do not sit and look at the screens but walk through. Then I just got more and more into the projectors as objects.'[36]

Periodic cleaning of the building's pipe systems involves running powerful air pressure throughout the apparatus. Barba inserts microphones in the conduits to record the activity to produce a layer – along with ambient sound – of the 'optical soundtrack of the film, tracing another volume of the architecture'.[37] The audio will also pass through specially designed metal piping that echoes the cylindrical shape of the 'caterpillar' that encloses the multilevel escalator. Barba plans to situate the projector near the endpoint of one of the enormous, tiered glass tubes that climb the Pompidou's exterior. While technically inside, for all intents and purposes the transparent tubular perimeter is outside. Barba parasites the equipment that composes the filmic sculpture onto the shuttered museum exterior.

Barba's multiform practice revolves around the mechanics and spatial modalities of cinema; film and all it entails are both her method and thematic realm. Intent on generating an experiential language liberated from the conventions of filmmaking and its presentation, she sounds out the practice of light and space. She has termed her endeavour 'the anarchic organization of cinematic spaces', in which 'each project produces its own theater, to unpredictable affect'.[38] The ephemeral and emblematic White Museum series attests to Rosa Barba's unbound vision – channelling light to materialize presence, vitalize evanescent histories, and recast experiences of place and space.

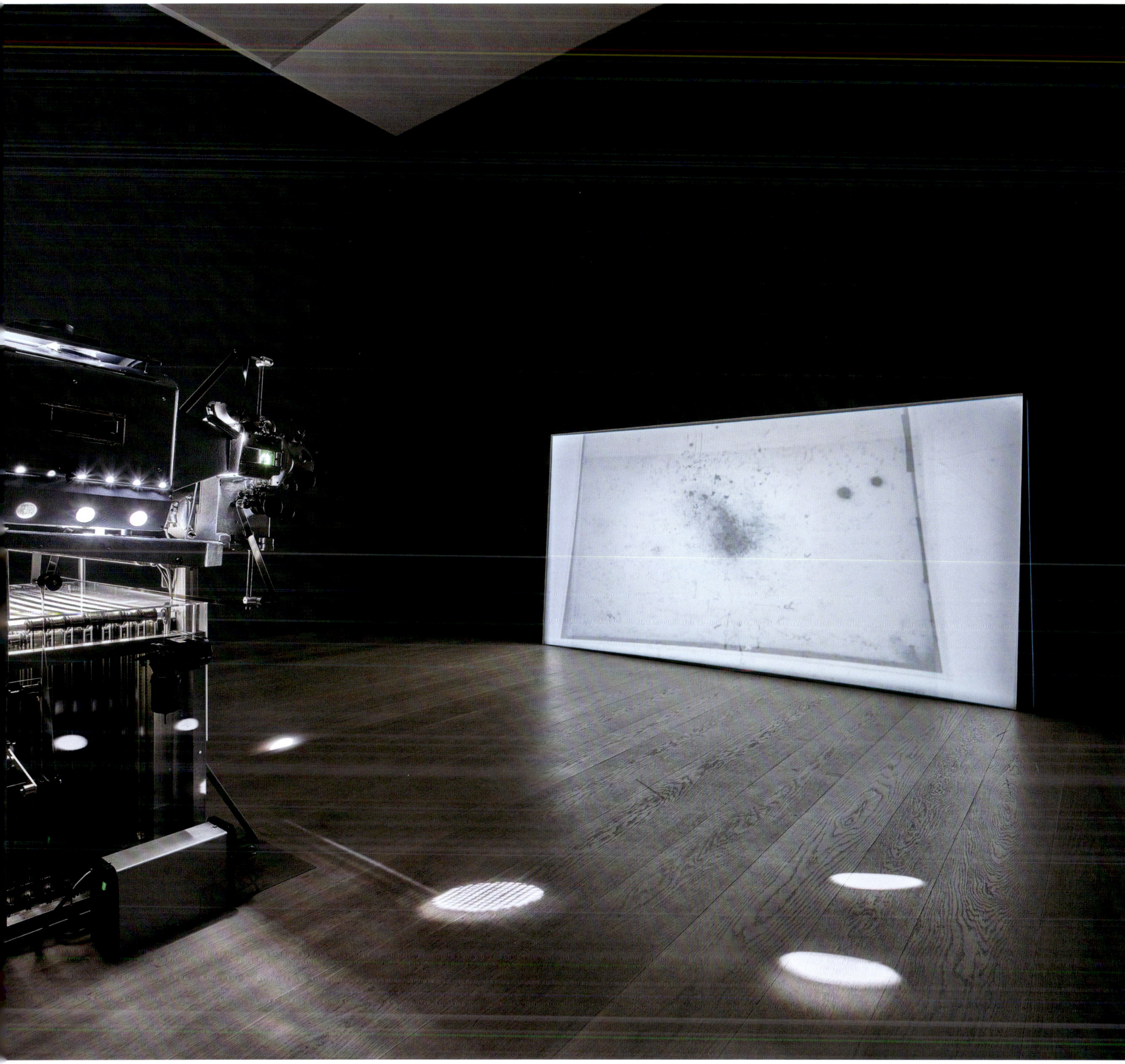

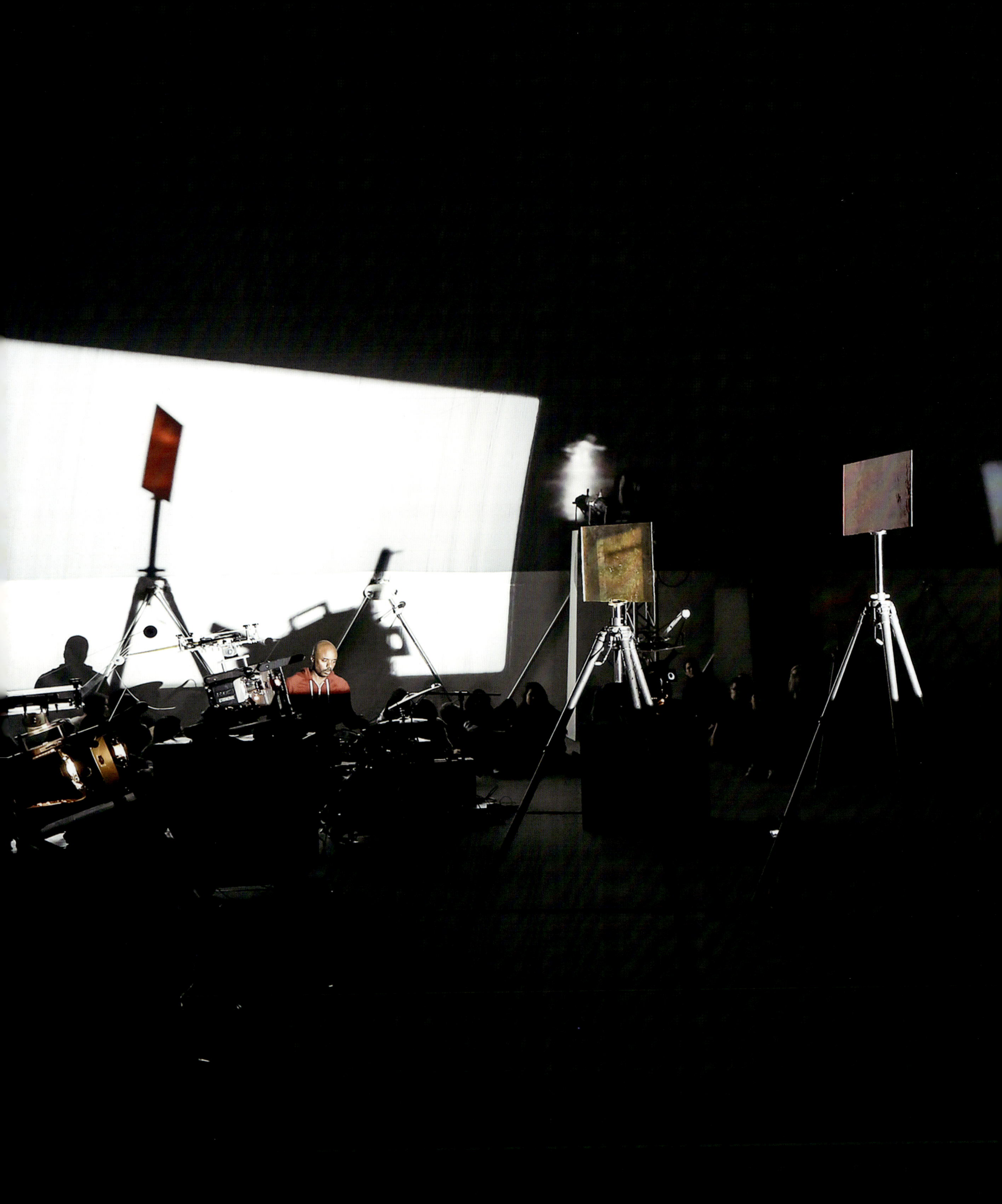

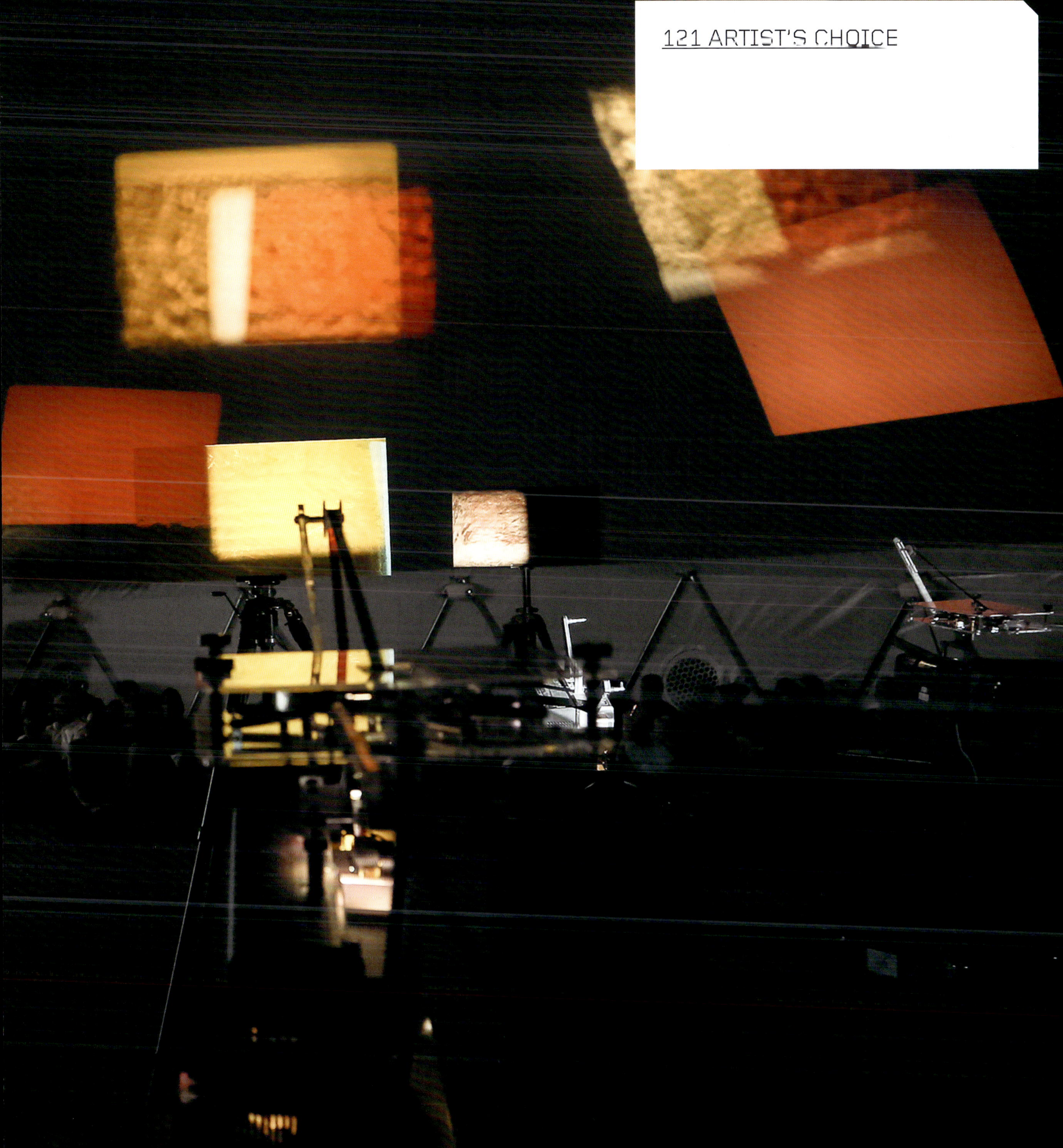

Robert Creeley
The Revelation, 1953

I thought that if I were broken enough
I would see the light
like at the end of a small tube, but approachable.

I thought chickens laid eggs
for a purpose.

For the reason expected, a form occured more
blatant and impossible

to stop me.

Robert Creeley
There Is, 1964

There is
as we go we
see there
is a hairy
hole there is
a darkness expanded
by
there is a
sense of some
imminence immanence
there is
a subject placed
by the verb a
conjunction coordinate
lines
a graph of indeterminate
feelings there is
sorry for itself
lonely generally
unhappy in its
circumstances.

right,
WHITE MUSEUM (HIRSCH OBSERVATORY), 2010–15
70MM FILM, PROJECTOR

INSTALLATION VIEW AT HIRSCH OBSERVATORY, RENSSELAER POLYTECHNIC INSTITUTE, TROY, MICHIGAN, 2015

previous pages,
WHITE MUSEUM – LIVE (MOMA PS1), 2016
DRUMS, PROJECTORS, GLASS PANELS, SCREENS

INSTALLATION VIEW AT MOMA PS1, NEW YORK, 2016

next pages,
WHITE MUSEUM (SÃO PAULO), 2010–16
70MM FILM, PROJECTOR

INSTALLATION VIEW AT SÃO PAULO BIENNIAL, 2016

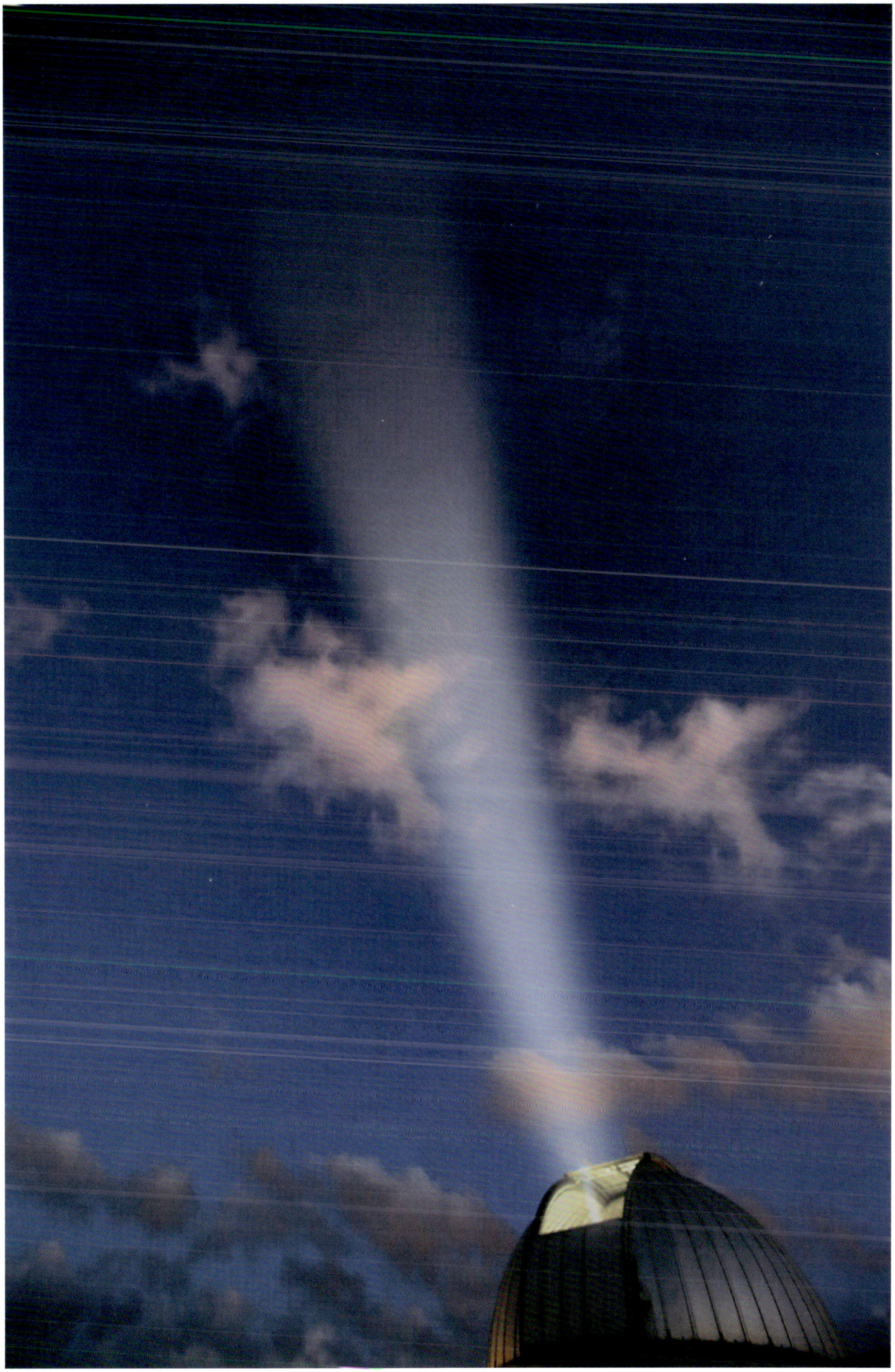

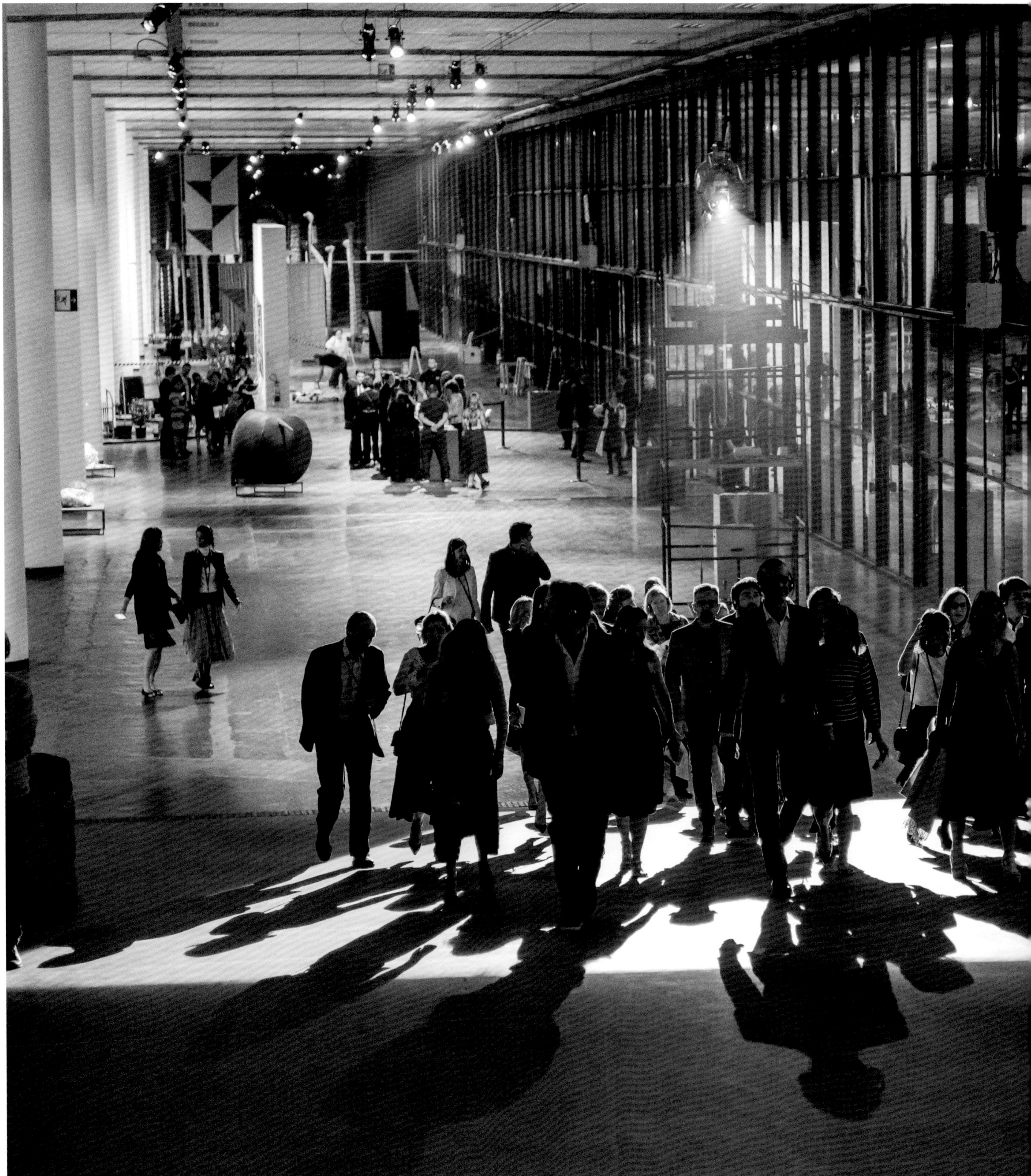

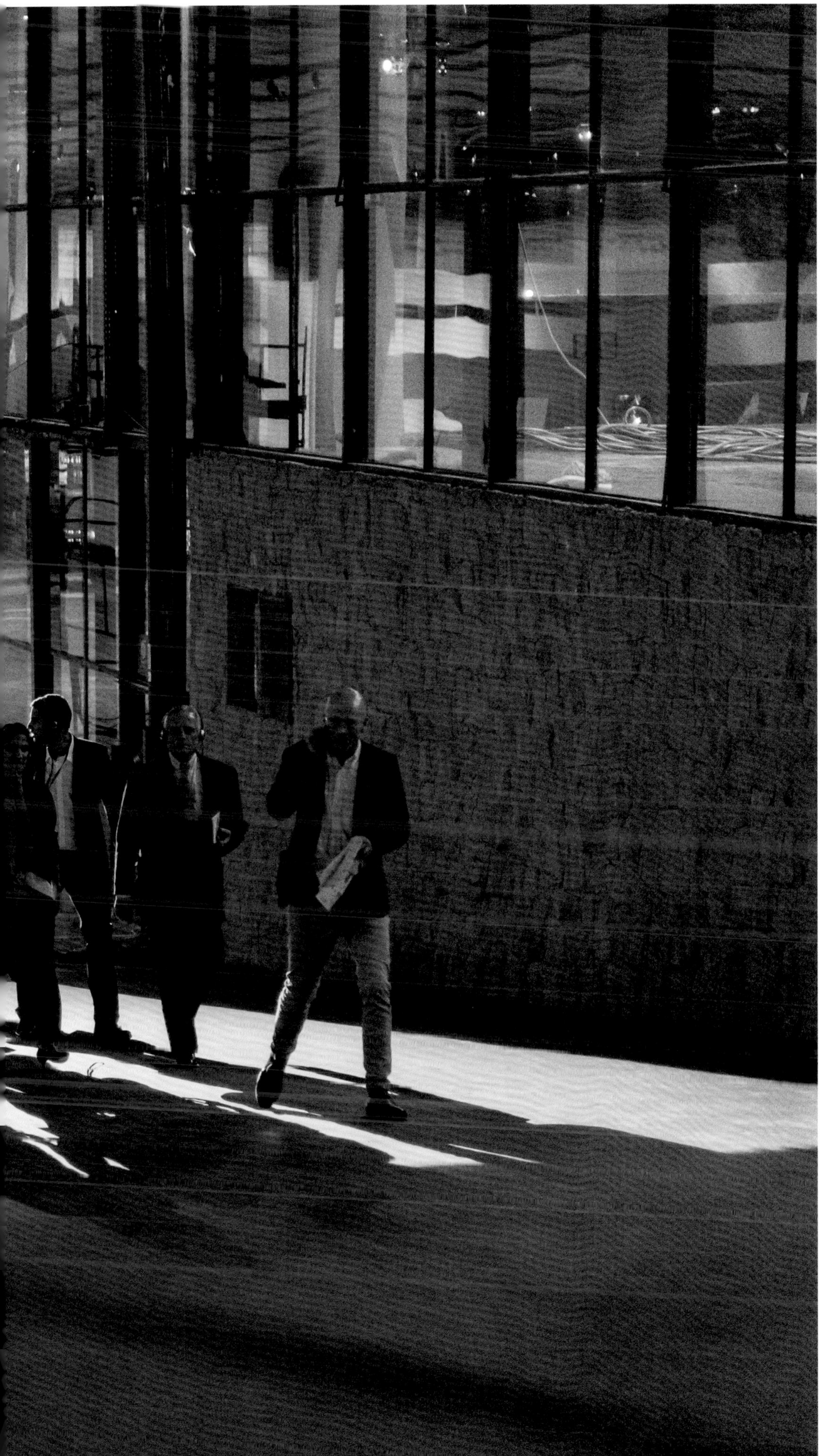

John Temple

Meditation on a Landscape, 1965

As I watch night approaches

The merciless incline east
on 66 into the canyon as in
my life the merciless or
those to whom I would not look
for mercy given that situation have always
inclined east
only in
the sense that world
must turn east if
the sun set
in the west and they have no sense
of movement in their deadly hearts
[...]

Charles Olson

Poem 143: The Festival Aspect, 1965

The world
has become divided
from the Universe. Put the three Towns
together

The individual
has become divided
from the Absolute, it is the times promised
by the poets. Theys hall drop delta
and lingam, all forms
of symbol
and mystery. As well as all
naturalism. And literalness. The truth

is fingers holding it all up
underneath, the Lotus
is a cusp, and its stalk
holds up it all.
It isn't even a burning point, it is a bow
of fingers shooting
a single arrow. The three Towns
are to be destroyed, as well as
that they are to be made known,
that they are to be known,
that there is no three Towns
now, that without three Towns
there is no Society, there is no
know
Absolute : we shall stand on our heads and hands
truly, kicking
all false form off
the surface
of the still, or active,
water-surface. There is no image
which is a revlection. Or a condition. There is solely
the Lotus
upside down. When the World is on again
with the Universal the Flower
will grow down, the Sun
will be samped
on the leather
like a growing
Coin, the earth
will be the light, the air and the dust
of the air will be the perfume
of sense, the gloire
will have returned
of the body seen
against the window. The flesh
will glow.
The three Towns
will have become populated
again. In the first Town
somebody will have addressed
themselves
to someone else. There will be no need
of explicit. In the second Town
the earth
will have replaced
the sun. In the third Town the man
shall have arisen, he shall have concluded
any use of reason, the Dialogue
will have re-begun. The earth
shall have preceded love. The sun
shall have given back its deadly
rays, there shall be no longer any
need to be careful. The third Town
shall have revealed
itself.
[...]
March 29th 1965. (The feet of Maximus in the air.)

PILLAGE OF THE SEA, 2021
FABRIC-CAST SANDBAGS
650 X 200 X 171 CM

PERMANENT INSTALLATION AT
THE 7TH BEAUFORT TRIENNIAL,
OSTEND, BELGIUM, 2021

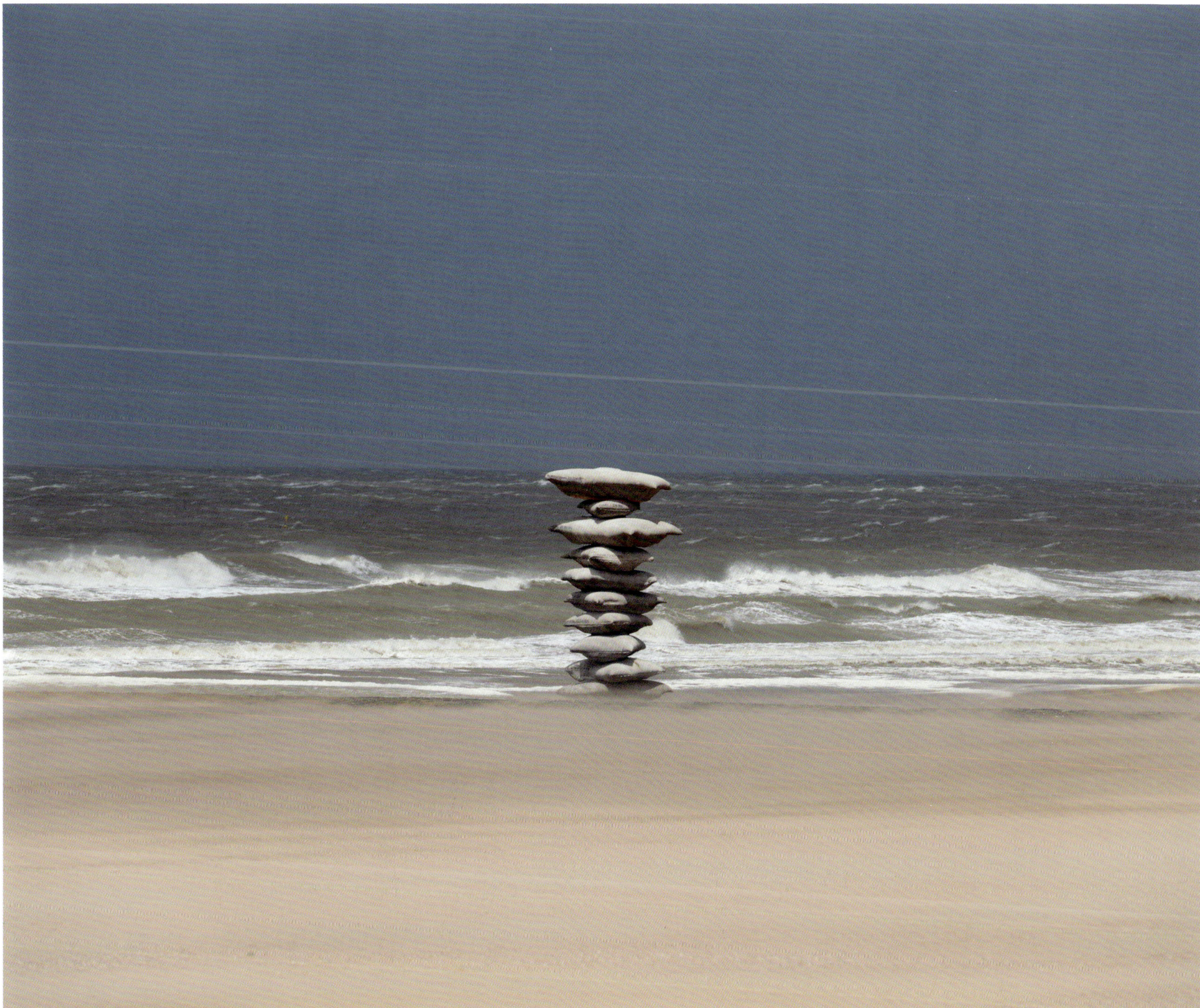

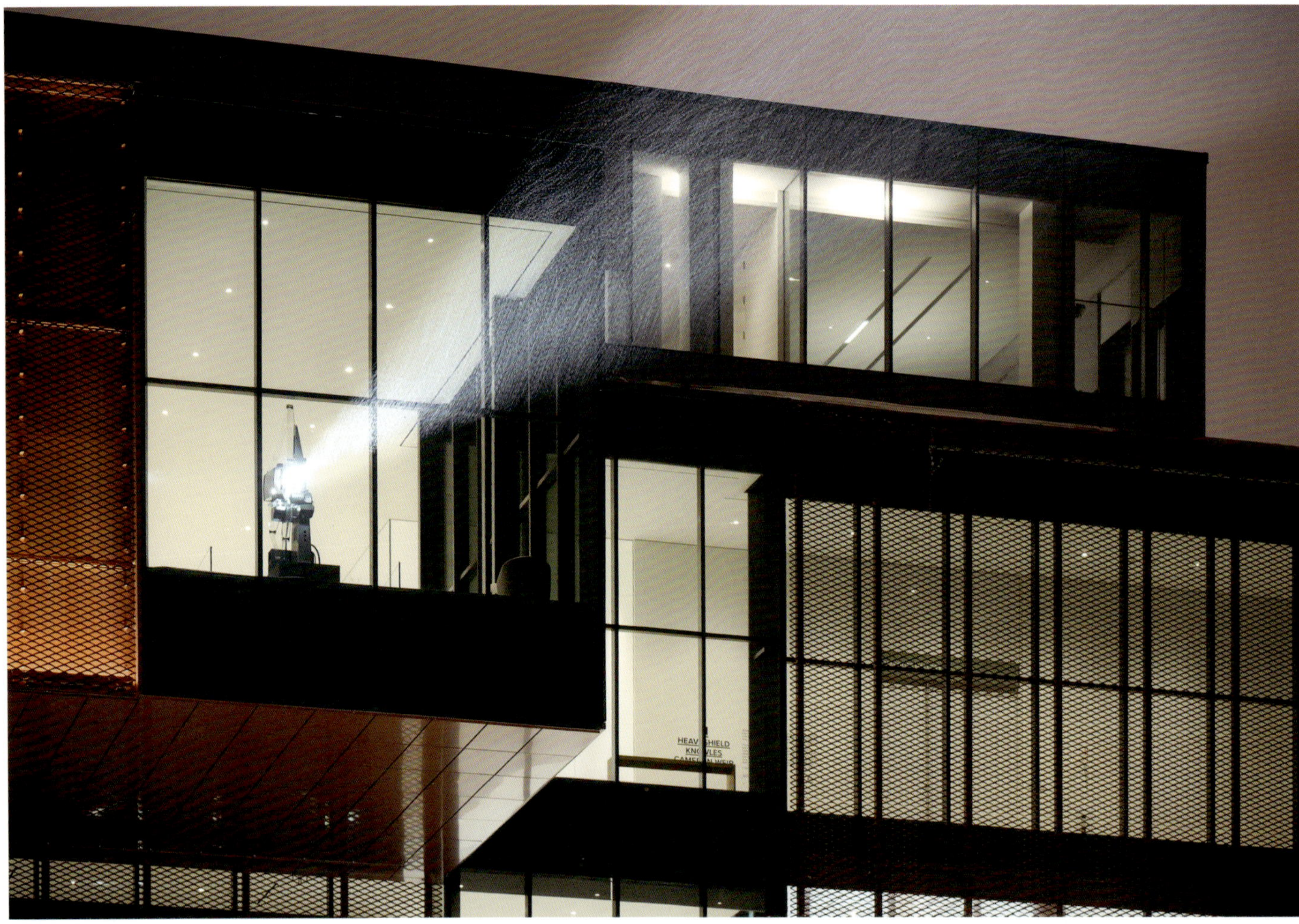

WHITE MUSEUM (SOUTH SASKATCHEWAN RIVER), 2010–18
70MM WHITE FILM, PROJECTOR

INSTALLATION VIEW AT REMAI MODERN, SASKATOON, SASKATCHEWAN, 2018

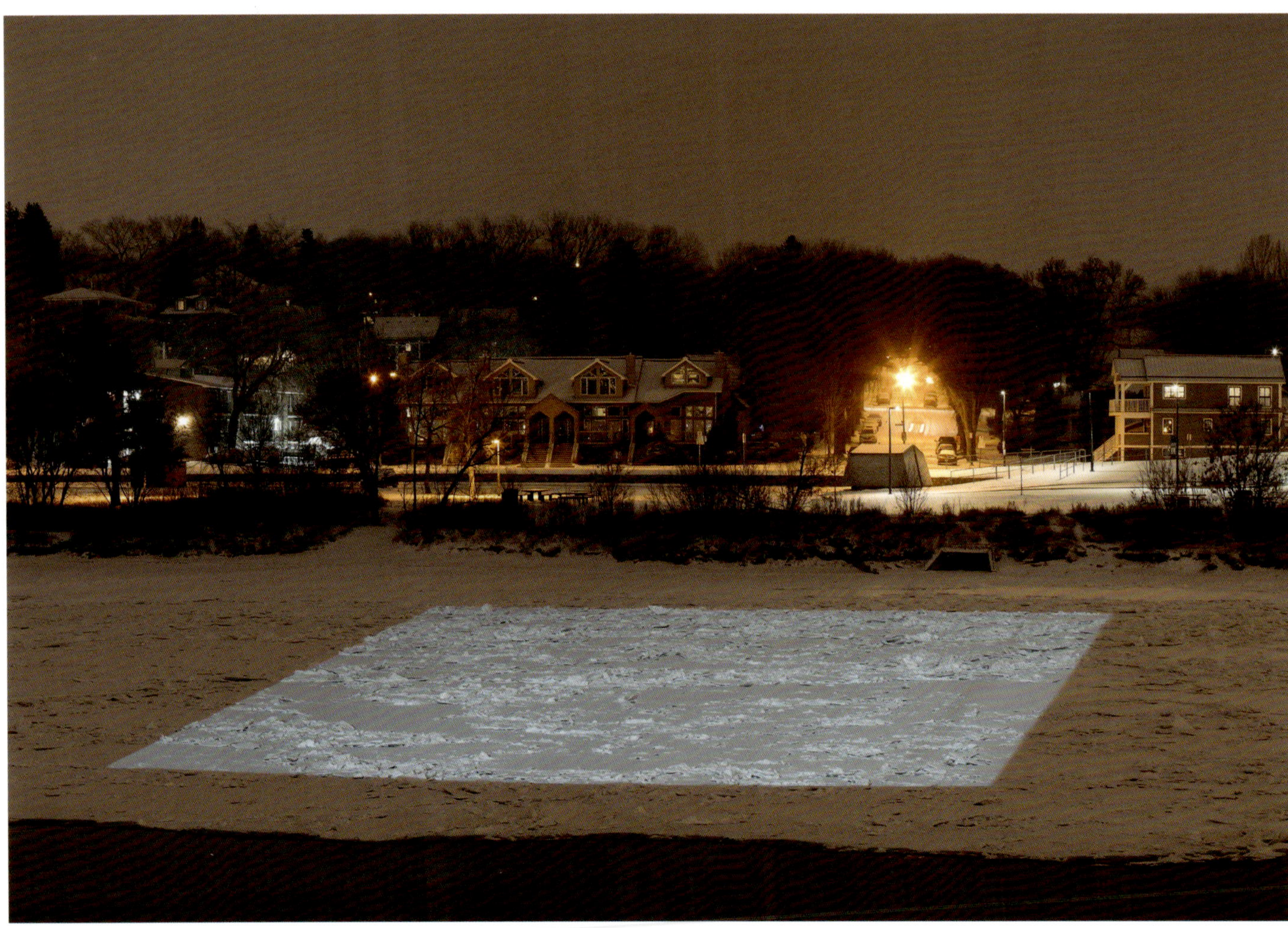

Robert Duncan

Chords, 1965

For the Thing we call Moon contains
" May mountains, many cities, many houses."
And Nature, our Mother,
hides us, even from ourselves, there ;
showing only in changes of the Moon. Time
"a serpent having heads growing from him
a bull and a lion,
the face of a god-man in the middle,
and he has also wings, and is calld
ageless, Xronos, father of the ages,
and Herakles";
[…]

Befor Time's altars, our Mother-Nature
lighting the stars in order,   setting
Her night-light   in the window the Egg will be .
The breath of the stars,   moving before the stars,
breath of great Nature,   our own,   Logos
that is all   milk and light .
These things reborn within Zeus, happening anew.

"A dazzeling light .. aither .. Eros .. Night"
where we are.
The first being Fairyland, the Shining Land.

Susan Howe

Untitled (from Tom Tit Tot), 2013

a mere nitwit, who wasted precious parchment
WOODSLIPPERCOUNTERCLATTER
WOODSLIPPERCOUNTERCLATTER

n certain Shrouds
ne and were gone. He lean
though to meditate on wo

Secret Paintin

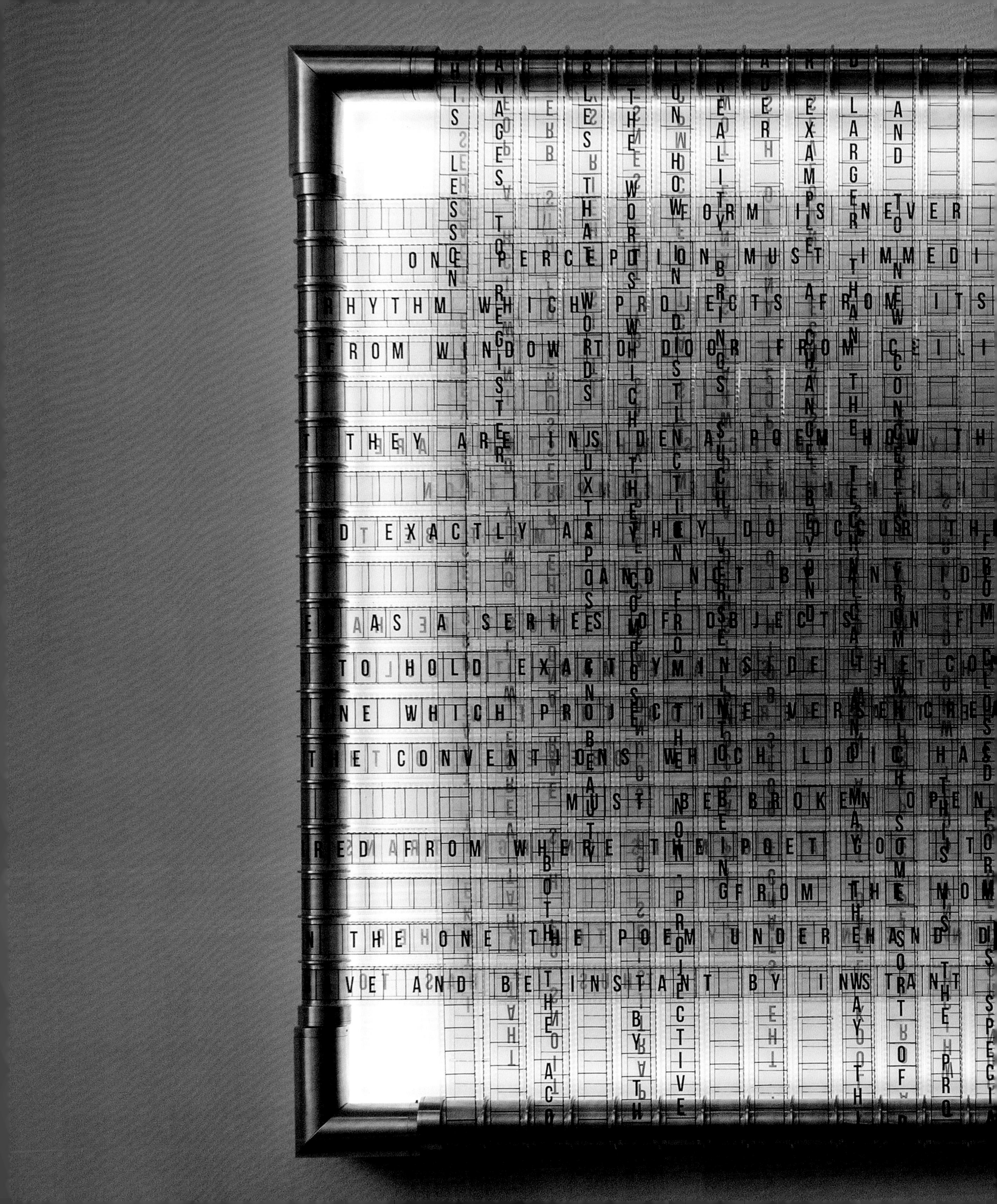

FORM IS NEVER
ONE PERCEPTION MUST
RHYTHM WHICH PROJECTS FROM ITS
FROM WINDOW TO DOOR FROM
THEY ARE IN A POEM HOW
EXACTLY AS THEY DO OCCUR
AND NOT BY ANY
AS A SERIES OF OBJECTS IN
TO HOLD EXACTLY INSIDE THE
WHICH PROJECTIVE VERSE
THE CONVENTIONS WHICH LOGIC HAS
MUST BE BROKEN OPEN
FROM WHERE THE POET GOT
FROM THE
THE ONE THE POEM UNDER HAND
AND BE INSTANT BY INSTANT

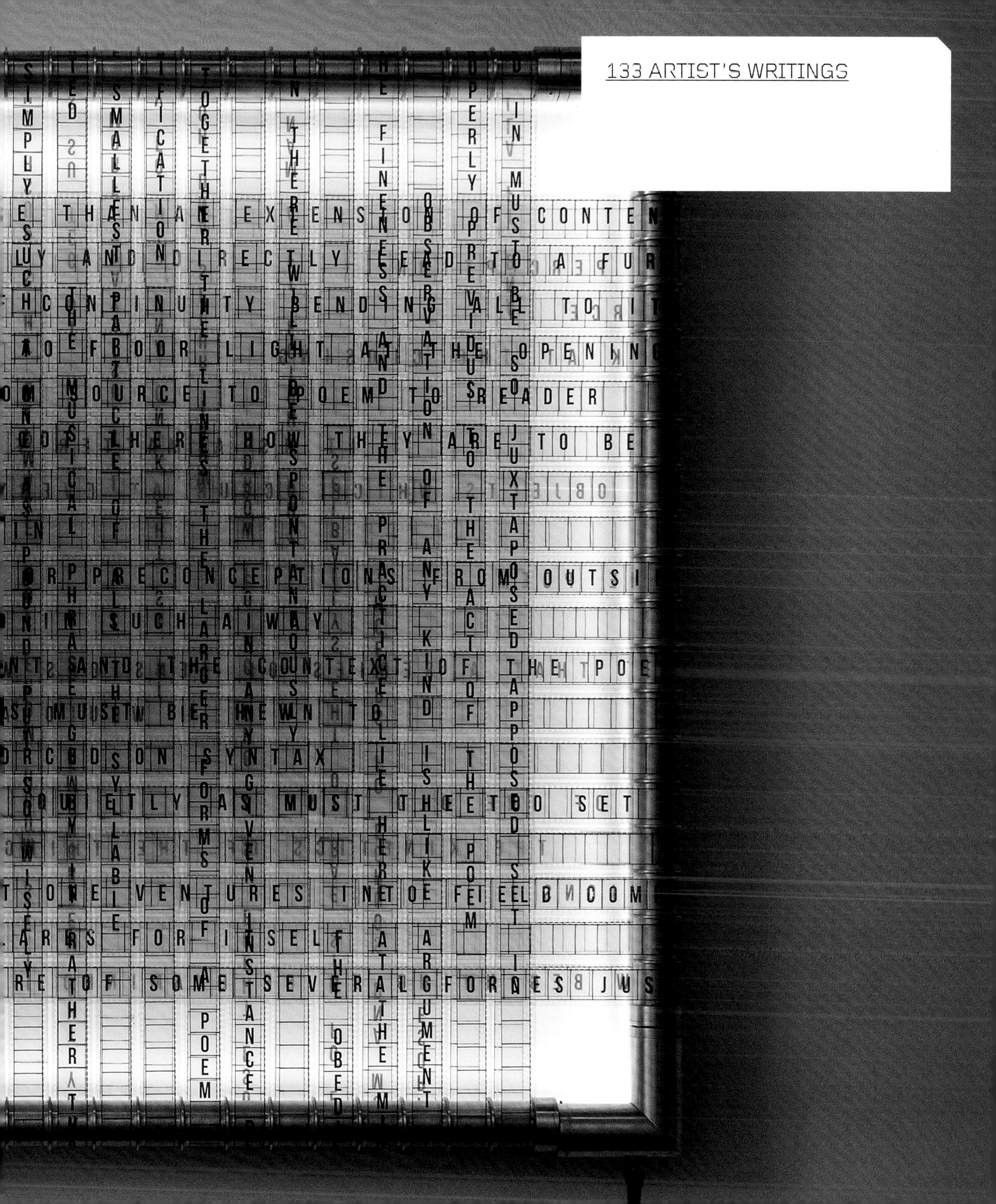

Inventory of Cinematic Spaces: A Fictional Library (excerpt), 2022

previous pages,
COMPOSITION IN FIELD, 2022
35MM FILM, STAINLESS STEEL, ALUMINIUM, MOTOR, PLEXIGLASS, LED LIGHTS
91 X 120 X 9 CM

In my artistic practice, I am looking specifically for incalculable investigations. I am trying to find that space that is not waiting for me – that does not expect my arrival. I also have no intention of making myself comfortable in that space; I would instead like to reach and touch it temporarily, in order to open up other dimensions of thinking and experiencing.

Resisting our present condition in the form of analogue art practices doesn't necessarily imply a nostalgic longing for a pre-mediatic past. For me, it is rather about investing in the pre-existing forms of cinema as instruments and using certain methods to achieve new forms. The collectivity and the fragmentation of material will follow.

Film scholar Mary Ann Doane, in her writings on the subjects of technology, indexicality and contingency, suggests the possibility of artistic production with aims of recording not an indifferent field of information but rather a 'rupture in the fabric of existence' through a mode of registering without consciousness of registration. The emergence of photographic and phonographic technologies in the nineteenth century seemed to make possible what had previously been beyond the grasp of presentation – the inscription of contingency. Anything and everything in the order of materiality could be photographed, filmed or recorded, particularly the unexpected, the rupture in the fabric of existence.

The Inscription of Contingency: Only Visible between the Frames

Landscape: 'Between the process of creation effected by what we call nature and that effected by fiction, a passageway is hollowed out, one that is also a landscape.'

According to philosopher Susan Langer, 'It is, in fact, when the first semblance of organic form is achieved that a work of art exhibits its general symbolic possibilities, like a statement imperfectly made or even merely indicated, but understandable in its general intent.'

Drawing with my camera around and within an object is the act of reaching that organic form through duration and imperfection.

It is a kind of anti-algorithmic filmmaking, which includes absurdity and uncanniness, exposure through the light hitting the material, movement, processing and presentation.

Fact and Fiction in the Public

The key to Michael Warner's definition of a public is the idea of reflexiveness.
–Granville Ganter, review of Publics and Counterpublics by Michael Warner, *St John's University Humanities Review*, no. 1, March 2003

An important methodology for me when working with this public – which can also be a memory of a public, which I like to introduce through work in archives – is the inclusion of language that enters from a participating group and introduces a movement of thought, thus providing a 'real' movement into the image.

Words and themes can modulate a word so that it means something else when it reaches another method. The fiction in my work for me comes from this kind of modulation of text. Flicker here means the becoming legible of the illegibility of the text.

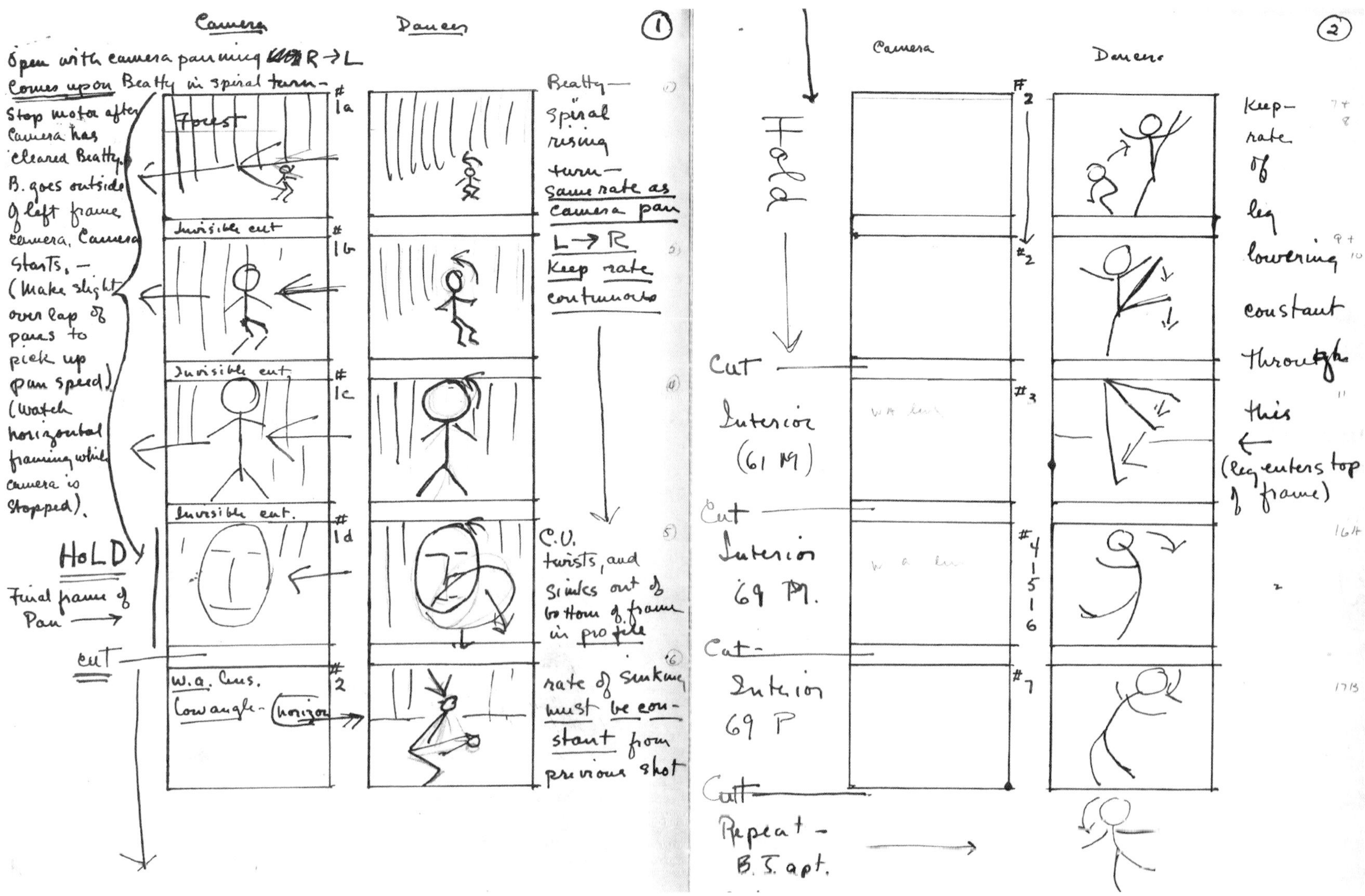

MAYA DEREN
SHOOTING DIAGRAMS FOR CHOREOGRAPHY FOR THE CAMERA, N.D.

Reproduced in VèVè A. Clark, Millicent Hodson and Catarina Neiman, The Legend of Maya Deren: A Documentary Biography and Collected Works, vol. 1, part 2, Chambers (1942–47) (New York, 1988), pp. 269–71.

A core that immediately deteriorates.

I introduce other possibilities into the text, or the people I include in my films introduce wishes or visions for a subject that is not real. These act as instruments to push the idea further. These wishes are anchored in real statements of people or from literature; for example, in *From Source to Poem*, the idea of the Library of Babel correlates with the Library of Congress.

In Jorge Luis Borges's *The Library of Babel*, each book contains the bare necessities for human survival. The narrator notes that the library must contain all useful information, including predictions of the future, biographies of every person, and translations of all books in all languages:

I have just written the word 'infinite.' I have not included that adjective out of mere rhetorical habit; I hereby state that it is not illogical to think that the world is infinite. Those who believe it to have limits hypothesize that in some remote place or places the corridors and staircases and hexagons may, inconceivably end – which is absurd. And yet those who picture the world as unlimited forget that the number of possible books is not. I will be bold enough to suggest this solution to the ancient problem: If an eternal traveller should journey in any direction, he would find after untold centuries that the same volumes are repeated in the same disorder – which, repeated, becomes order: the Order. My solitude is cheered by that elegant hope.[2]

The Library of Congress in Culpeper is mandated to archive all Western cultural output. Both the idea and the attempt create a public in this sense. These are ongoing spaces of encounter, which are also represented in the idea of the Fictional Library.

My work *Outwardly from Earth's Center* (2007) centres on Gotska Sandön, an island in Sweden that is moving by a metre every year. I constructed a narrative about how to tie the island to the sea; the act of anchoring the island suddenly turned the object into an idea. In the film, I start with a specific subject and open up possibilities from that. It ends with an aerial shot and a possible solution.

opposite,
FROM SOURCE TO POEM, 2016
35MM FILM, COLOUR, OPTICAL SOUND
12 MIN

below,
FOOTNOTE (...THE EARTH WILL HAVE MOVED...), 2015
70MM FILM, STAINLESS STEEL, LED, MOTOR
82 X 9 X 10 CM

INSTALLATION VIEW AT ARTON FOUNDATION, WARSAW, 2015

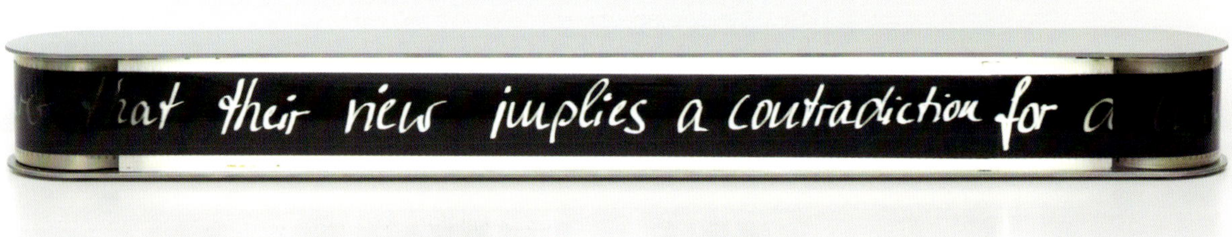

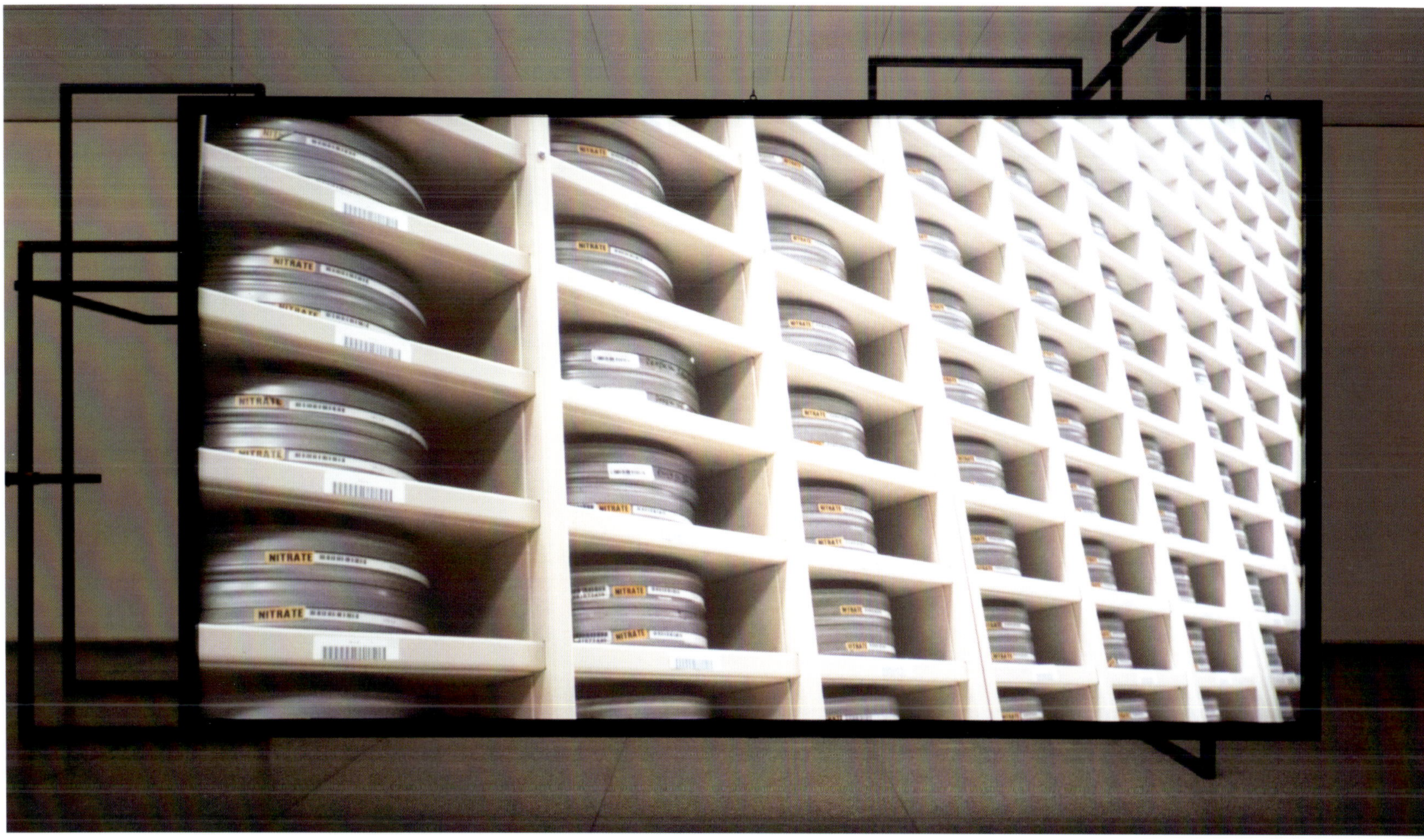

The work speculates on the notion of the document that results in a sculpture – as a side effect of society. There is a temporal element to a document or history that we can observe or enter, and in my films historical data is often transposed into a subjective voiceover. When I say 'history is like a sculpture', I mean the underlying spatial and temporal lines of the poetics of distance. It's a balancing act in an unstable surrounding.

Non-actors as Documents

Freedom is based in the political as a communal act, according to Hannah Arendt. Cristina Sánchez Muñoz explains:

In those situations that Arendt described as 'dark times', that is, times 'in which the public realm has been obscured and the world become so dubious that people have ceased to ask any more of politics than that it show due consideration for their vital interests', the only solution is to resort to the exercise of participative citizen action and to shared public discourse. In acting and deliberating together with others, we establish important connections that do not rely on the agreement achieved, but rather on the feeling of jointly supporting the world we share, the public space in which we express ourselves and show ourselves to others.[3]

Community

... seemingly abandoned communities occupied by the proposition of a central threat of disaster wherein both those depicted and the disasters that threaten them might equally

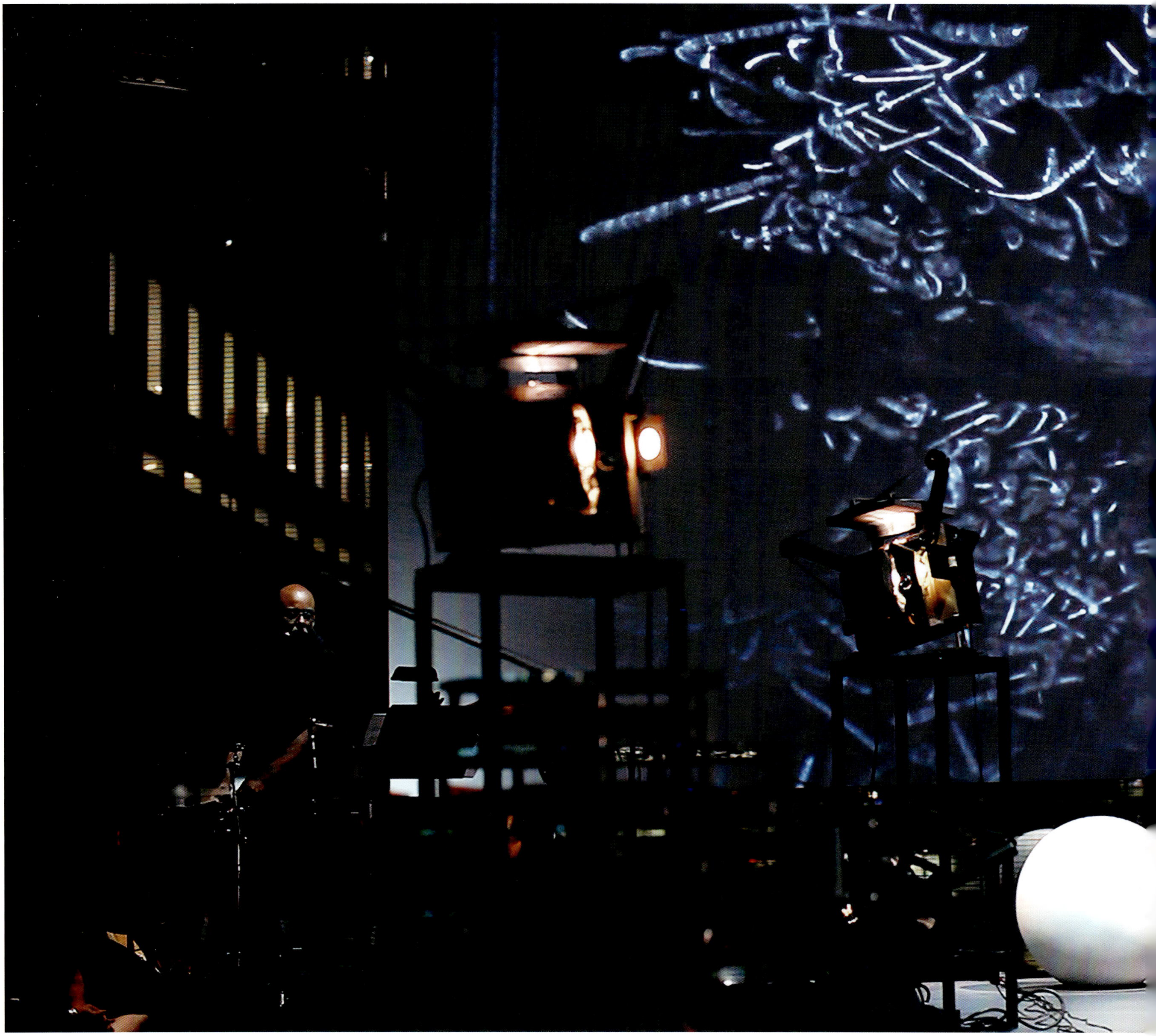

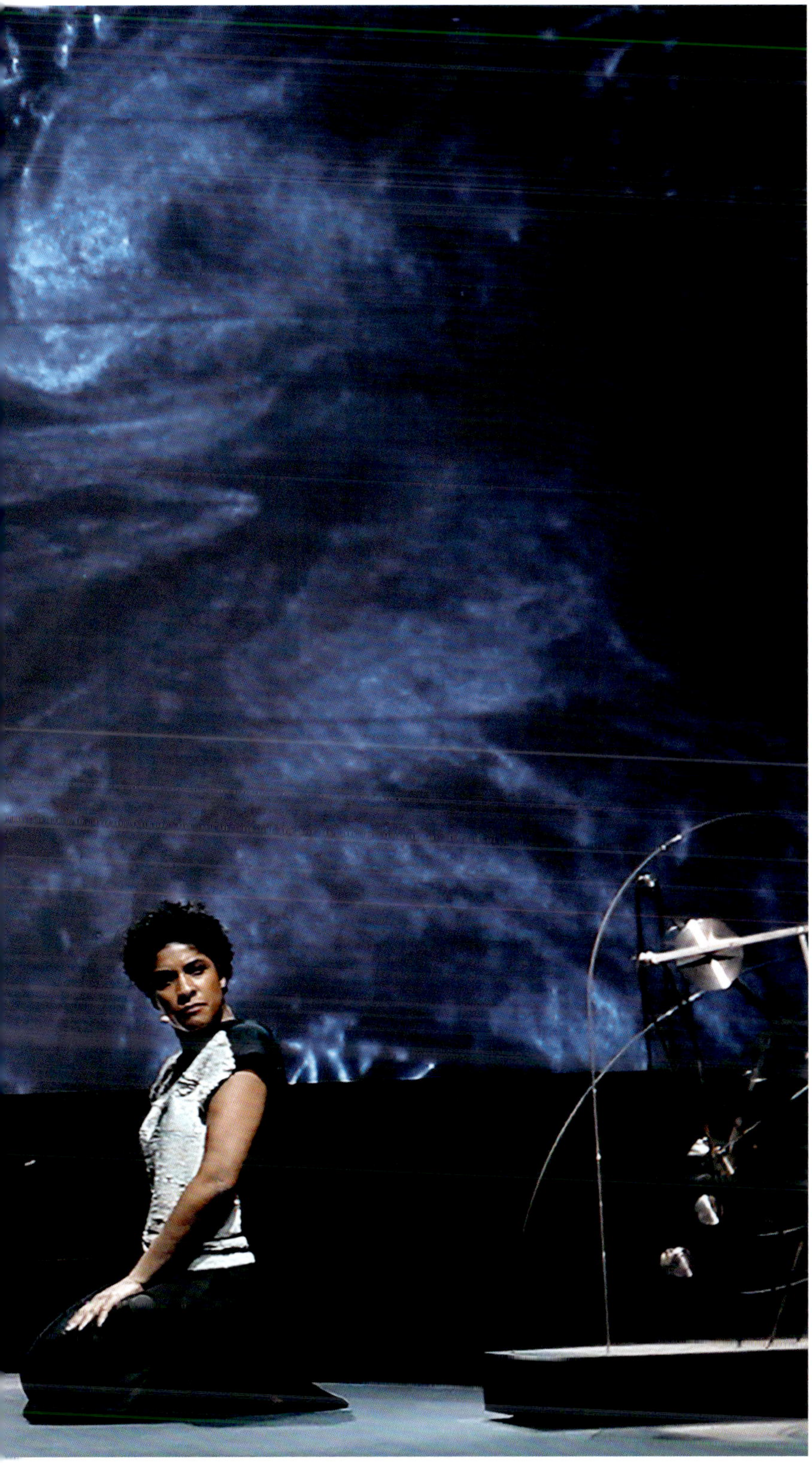

THE OCEAN OF ONE'S PAUSE, 2025
PERFORMANCE
THE MUSEUM OF MODERN ART, NEW YORK, 2025

Music arranged and performed by Rosa Barba (cello), Alicia Hall Moran (vocals), and Chad Taylor (percussion). Audio engineering by Sascha von Oertzen

be read as actual and fictional – to the extent that whether they are one or the other becomes not irrelevant, but an ambiguity that is the very means by which the works themselves function, conceptually.[4]

– Ian White, in *Rosa Barba: White Is an Image*, 2011

This articulation of publicness, and the idea of a participative action to shape discourse, has great resonance for contemporary art practice. In the production of art, as in the production of political discourse, or art as political discourse, there are varying degrees of how participation is defined. Participation ranges from the large-scale choreographies of artists like Tino Sehgal to the theoretical propositions of participation such as creating conditions in which subjects – citizens like Valeria, Dino and Claudio in *Panzano* or the diverse group of local people, workers, and artists who constitute the community depicted in my film *Subconscious Society* (2014) – can define their own roles through both individual and collective actions.

Structuralism has long been accused of supressing the subject. In the above quote, Deleuze asserts that structuralism did not supress the subject but rather broke it up and redistributed it across the system. I would like in the course of my discussion to connect to this view and to expand it.

One way we analyse things is in terms of their structural relationships. However, there is a sense that these relationships are fixed, without any change. I would argue that there is in fact a change. However, who carries out the change is never explained in the classic understanding of structuralism. In Deleuze's rethinking of it, things structure themselves by rubbing or shaking against each other, creating some kind of friction and life by themselves – completely unguided. That's how structure seems to evolve: through internal or relational interaction, but not one led by anyone or anything. This leaves me with the questions: Do we have any role in this change? Do we initiate this change, or are we just simply determined by the structures? And a further question, for me, is: Do structures in rubbing against each other produce their own movement and change? Or is change authored by a particular person? Their choice and their decision?

For me, a machine performs activity: you can see how one thing leads to another, and everything can be examined. When I invent a new machine, it involves playing with these elements. I discover another aspect of cinematic expression by separating off an element, or inventing an element that hadn't been there before. It is this positive act of introducing the element of play that goes against the conventional notions of cinematic production. I question the regularity and closure of the world of production by introducing play: anything can happen there. Play, here, does not indicate a game with rules but rather functions in a more philosophical sense, suggesting a ludic mentality and quality.

I continued to produce film-based works, new technologies developed, and with them a continual intensification. The environment became ever more cinematic, with each new technology leaving less and less room for people to construct the world around them for themselves. Eventually, there were no gaps left, with everything set and seen for us. People were being given the tools and technology to create more images more easily, but paradoxically, the options or possibilities were being limited. The experience of different possible options, of spaces of ambiguity, was taken away from the perceiver, resulting in a closing down of cognitive possibilities and desires.

My response was to intensify my strategies of fragmentation, by dismantling the status quo of cinema, and to focus on certain possibilities that arose from playing around with its components: turning them inside out, upending and involuting them, and redistributing them until they opened up new, anarchic spaces.

I conceive of the concept of 'anarchic' as being key here. It is a way of halting the development of cinema as merely an extension of our current visual-data overload and opening it up to an alternative direction, one that can take an investigative course and that can be in dialogue. 'Anarchic' is used in this context not to signify 'chaotic' but rather to point toward anarchism as a foundation of political and artistic thinking that is distinctly optimistic and egalitarian. Moreover, anarchism is a living, evolving tradition that emphasises the power of the collective rather than individual action. A cinematic experience in anarchic space doesn't follow a precise order; rather, it is created through specific situations, arrangements and methodologies.

I believe that disrupting the status quo of cinema opens up new cognitive spaces that give access to new thinking and experiencing. Why is that significant to do? What is to be gained from such an experiment? The importance of this action is that it breaks with the perceptual habits of the status quo and makes us think in different directions. Thus, this anarchic dimension offers a new foundation for thinking and acting by destabilising the old hierarchy of the components of cinema and freeing them up from their original uses and letting them interact in new and unforeseen ways.

Another important dimension of my work in this context is that of staging and performance, revolving around the question of how a performative setting can be created where fact and fiction can be intertwined. I interrogate the industry of cinema with respect to various forms of staging, such as gesture, genre, information and documentation, taking them out of their conventional contexts and reshaping and representing them anew. In this way, I experiment with and expand time-based forms into sculptural objects or speculations, that is, into spaces that are self-organized; it is an ever-changing, ever-evolving, shifting process. The aim of this process is to create a new form of auditorium, one that allows for an expansion of our thinking. Such an auditorium is not fixed; each project produces its own theatre, to unpredictable effect. This space, however, is not intended to be a 'hall' in the traditional sense of a cinema auditorium, but rather it is an arrangement of the faculties, which hold different 'sensoriums.' Here, the transmitter and receiver are fluent in both directions.

These different approaches to – and forms of – space are therefore at the core of my research, which takes a conceptual approach that regards cinema in an architectural sense but also as a tool. Here, the environment, the screen, and the projection can be combined or pushed forward to create another spatiotemporal dimension that is concurrent with and beyond the context of interior or exterior space. Uncertainty and speculation exist within this expanded space.

My research therefore represents four different modes of enquiry into how this 'space beyond' can be reached or achieved, with each of these four modes creating different anarchic organisations of cinematic spaces.

INSIDE THE OUTSET: EVOKING A SPACE OF PASSAGE, 2021
16MM FILM TRANSFERRED TO DIGITAL AND 8K FILM, SOUND, 31 MIN. 15 SEC.

INSTALLATION VIEW AT THE BUFFER ZONE, DERYNEIA, CYPRUS, 2021

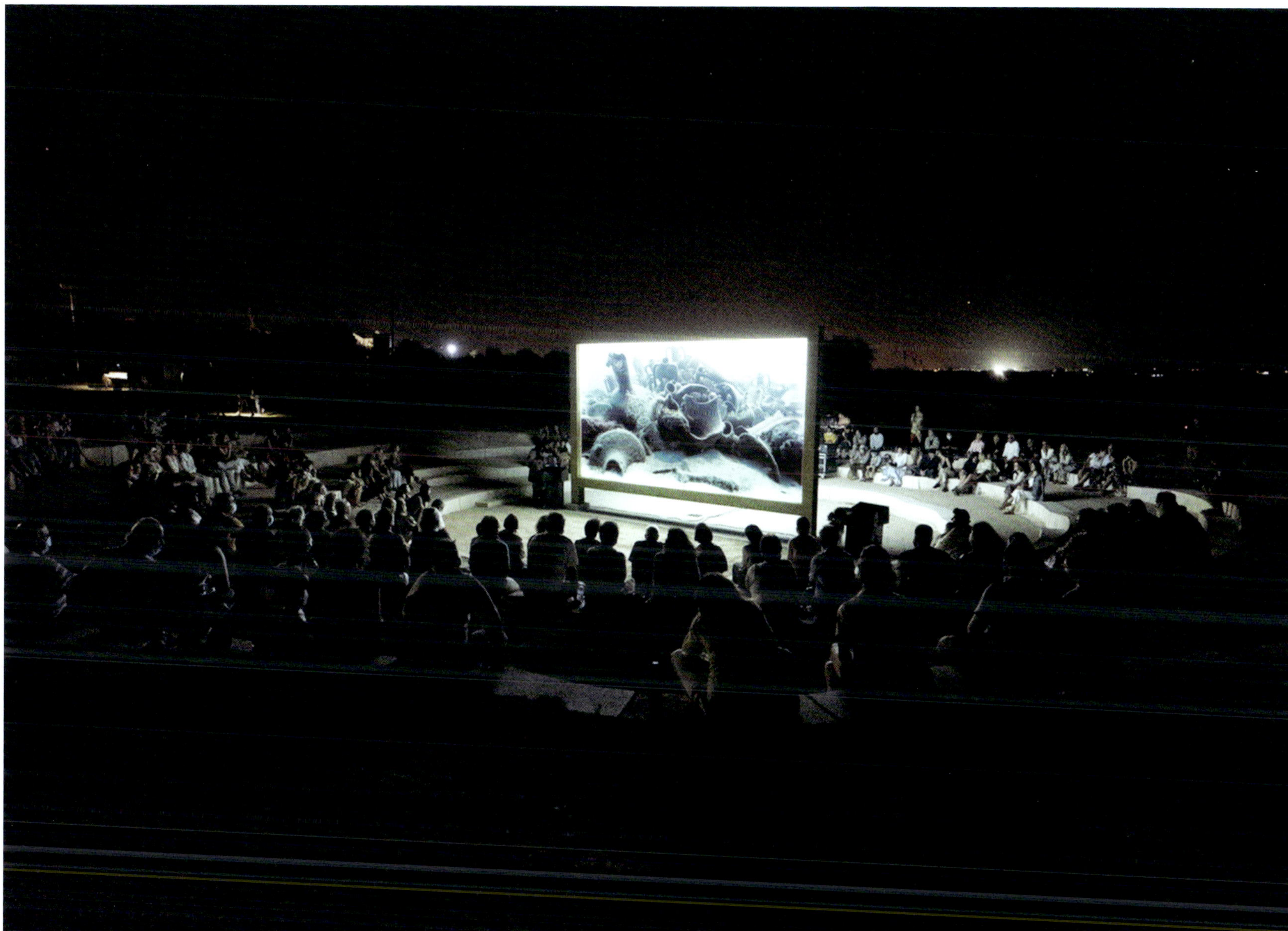

NOTES

SURVEY PAGES 051–071

1 *Here Is Information. Mobilise. Selected Writings by Ian White*, ed. Mike Sperlinger (London: Lux, 2016), 51.
2 These colonial foodstuffs were products of slavery in the West Indies, particularly Saint-Domingue (Haiti), one of the oldest French colonies.
3 Rosa Barba's *Printed Cinema* is a series of artist's books, published and distributed in connection with various solo shows, from 2004 to the present day.
4 Barba has explained that she had already begun to work as an artist when these tours took place, but she took a break to film *Panzano* in Tuscany. Recorded interview with the author, 6 April 2024.
5 Barba, ibid.
6 I have written two texts for Barba: 'Looking for Rosa Barba' (in *White is an Image*, Ostfildern, Germany: Hatje Cantz, 2013) and 'Yes, These Bleak Shores' (in *From Source to Poem*, Ostfildern, Germany: Hatje Cantz, 2017, with Pirelli HangarBicocca, Milan and Malmö Konsthall, Sweden).
7 Gloria Sutton, 'The Principle of Self Organisation in the Work of Rosa Barba', *Rosa Barba: The Color Out of Space* (Cambridge, MA: MIT List Center for Visual Arts, 2016), 72.
8 Giuliana Bruno, 'Site-seeing: Architecture and the Moving Image', *Wide Angle*, 19.4 (1997), 8–24, https://eurofilmnyu.wordpress.com/wp-content/uploads/2014/01/bruno-site-seeing.pdf.
9 Some will be reminded of Lázló Moholy-Nagy's *Light-Space Modulator* (also known as *Light Prop for an Electric Stage*). See Giuliana Bruno, 'Landscapes of Material Projection', *Rosa Barba: From Source to Poem*, op. cit., 19.
10 For more on this, see *Ciné-dispositifs: spectacles, cinéma, télévision, littérature*, ed. François Albera and Maria Tortajada, Geneva: L'Age d'Homme, 2011.
11 See https://www.cnrtl.fr/definition/projection.
12 Ian White, 'An Idea in Three Dimensions', *Rosa Barba: White Is an Image* (Ostfildern, Germany: Hatje Cantz, 2011), 97.
13 Janet Bennett, *Vibrant Matter. A Political Ecology of Things* (Durham and London: Duke University Press 2010), 6.
14 This distinction echoes the differing positions of, respectively, Henri Bergson and Gilles Deleuze. In Bergson's view, movement in the cinema takes place not in the image but in the projector, whereas for Deleuze, the image is movement. See Caroline Chik, 'L'image-mouvement', *L'image paradoxale* (Villeneuve d'Ascq, France: Presses universitaires du Septentrion, 2011), https://books.openedition.org/septentrion/46742?lang=fr.
15 Rosa Barba, *On the Anarchic Organization of Cinematic Spaces: Evoking Spaces beyond Cinema* (Ostfildern, Germany: Hatje Cantz, 2021), 7.
16 Donna Haraway, *Staying with the Trouble: Making Kin in the Chthulucene* (Durham: Duke University Press, 2016). This term has three sources: a small Californian spider, Pimoa cthulhu, whose name Haraway combines with the Greek term *chthonos*, which refers to chthonic forces and creatures. 'Cene' also comes from the Greek: kainos refers to a present timeframe, which Haraway describes as 'thick' – made up of layers, strata that enrich each other, like compost.
17 'The words used to describe a field of activity perhaps have never been less stable than those applied to people making moving images which are not commodifiable feature films. Perhaps this is not incidental. Instability is not commercial ... The artist working with moving images defines a position within, against or circumnavigating the particular economic structures of distribution, exhibition, production, often as the form and content of their work.' Ian White 'The Projected Object', *Here Is Information*, op. cit., 57.
18 'The camera as drawing instrument', Rosa Barba, *On the Anarchic Organization of Cinematic Spaces: Evoking Spaces beyond Cinema*, op. cit. (chapter 2).
19 A minority viewpoint, according to Deleuze.
20 Bernadette Bensaude-Vincent, *Temps-Paysage* (Paris: éditions du Pommier, 2020), 13 (from which I have borrowed many ideas).
21 A polychrony is 'a polyphony of plural temporalities', according to Bensaude-Vincent, ibid.
22 Barbara Adam, 'The Timescapes Challenge: Engagement with the Invisible Temporal', *Researching Lives through Time: Time, Generation and Life Stories*, ed. Rosalind Edwards, Timescapes archives #1, URL: https://timescapes-archive.leeds.ac.uk/wp-content/uploads/sites/47/2020/07/WP1-Researching-Lives-Through-Time-June-2008.pdf
23 *A Curated Conference: On the Future of Collective Strength within an Archive* (Madrid: Museo Reina Sofia, 2010).
24 Barba mentions, for example, 'Sky Hopinka's video meditation on time or Sandra Mujinga's hologram imagination of darkness, both on view at MoMA over the last two years'. 'Rosa Barba's Cinema of Transformation', *MoMA Magazine*, 26 June 2024.
25 'One of the most practically applicable models for exploring how modern representation – be it linguistic or visual – functions is one that takes into consideration the system's dual dimensions: a dimension of "transitivity" or enunciative transparency, in which each representation represents something, and a dimension of reflexivity or enunciative opacity, in which each representation presents itself as representing something.' Louis Marin, 'Paolo Uccello au Chiostro Verde de Santa Maria Novella à Florence', in *Opacité de la peinture. Essai sur la représentation au Quattrocento* (Paris: Usher, 1989), 73. (English translation of this quote is by Michael C. Behrent, from https://booksandideas.net/The-Meaning-of-Representation#nb6/).
26 This phrase is shown on the screen.
27 Barba notes that 'the white frames act like punctuation marks in my editing'. Mirjam Varadinis and Solveig Ovstebo in conversation with Rosa Barba, *Time as Perspective* (Ostfildern, Germany: Hatje Cantz, 2013), 12.
28 'One of my very first solo exhibitions took place in Lima in 2002, joined with a film festival in which I participated and a workshop I gave. After that I went hiking by myself into the Andes. That's when I really thought I would be going to make a film there. It took twenty years. But so much of my work is connected to that experience – whether *The Long Road*, inspired by Inca drawings, our shifting understanding of time, how we don't understand certain signs any more or how we communicate over distinct time zones.' (Barba, interview with the author, op. cit.).
29 Since 2010, the *White Museum* series has been reconfigured, each time in a very different locale: in the landscape of the Centre International d'Art et du Paysage on the island of Vassivière (France), 2010; on an airport runway in Cork (Ireland) 2010–11; on the seashore (Turner Contemporary, Margate, UK), 2013; at the crossroads by the Wiels Contemporary Art Centre (Brussels), 2010–13; on one of the former industrial quaysides on the Hudson River, New York (Pier 54), 2010–14; on the façade of the Hirsch Observatory (Rensselaer Polytechnic Institute, Troy, New York); in São Paulo (32nd Bienal de São Paulo); at the Villa Medici French Academy (Rome), 2010–17; and on the South Saskatchewan river (Canada), 2018
30 When Barba was invited to show at EMPAC, she proposed a collaborative series related to the Hirsch Observatory; the end result was *The Color Out of Space*, 2015, presented at EMPAC, Troy, USA.
31 Isabelle Stengers, *Au temps des catastrophes. Résister à la barbarie qui vient* (Paris: La Découverte, 2009), 14.
32 According to the anthropologist Charles Goodwin, this 'professional vision' involves 'coding; highlighting; producing and articulating material representations'. Goodwin, *American Anthropologist*, September 1994, new series, vol. 96, no. 3, 606ff.
33 Gilles Deleuze, 'Causes et raisons des îles désertes', *L'île déserte et autres textes* (1953–1974) (Paris: Minuit, 2002), 12.
34 Ibid.
35 In Italy, on the initiative of the psychiatrist Franco Basaglia, Law 180, of 1978, stipulated the closure of all the country's psychiatric hospitals, regarded as spaces of lawlessness and social deprivation.
36 Idem re: 'semiotic chaos', https://www.artforum.com/features/ed-halter-on-leslie-thorntons-peggy-and-fred-in-hell-200857/.
37 Ibid.
38 Jane Bennett, op. cit., vii.
39 Lynne Cooke, 'Suspended Stories: Rosa Barba's Strategic Narrativity', *Rosa Barba: White Is an Image*, op. cit., 177.
40 Jane Bennett, op. cit., xvii.
41 *Subconscious Society* was first presented in two parts, screened simultaneously: one in Margate, in the South of the United Kingdom, and the other in Manchester, in the North. The two parts were then brought together at Anthology Film Archives, New York, presented as a 'live' version filmed again by the artist. This latter happening was presented at Pirelli HangarBicocca, Milan.
42 Tom Gunning, 'Le Cinéma d'attraction: le film des premiers temps, son spectateur, et l'avant-garde', Trad.fr *1895 Revue de l'association française de recherches sur le cinéma*, 50/2006, https://doi.org/10.4000/1895.1242.
43 Ian White, *Rosa Barba: White Is an Image*, op. cit.
44 Friedrich Kittler, *Literature, Media, Information Systems (Critical Voices)* (Amsterdam: OPA, 1997), 130.
45 Friedrich Kittler, *Discourse Networks 1800/1900* (Stanford: Stanford University Press, 1990), 124.
46 Rosa Barba, *On the Anarchic Organization of Cinematic Spaces: Evoking Spaces beyond Cinema*, op. cit., 89.
47 Friedrich Kittler, *Literature, Media, Information Systems*, ed. John Johnston (Amsterdam: OPA, 1997), 130–46.
48 Franz Kafka, *In der Strafkolonie, 1914–19, Die Erzählungen und andere ausgewählte Prosa* (Berlin: Fischer Taschenbuch, 2001).
49 Not just in the deserts of the United States, but also in the Algerian Sahara, which suffered a similar fate between 1960 and 1966, when France tested seventeen nuclear bombs over an area of around 100,000 km.
50 Kafka, op. cit. (*The Officer*): 'It's not calligraphy for school children. One has to read it a long time. You too will finally understand it clearly.'
51 Kafka, *Die Erzählungen*, op. cit., 170.
52 Since the inaugural screening, the open-air site has been made available to

the town of Deryneia and to any filmmaker, video maker or artist, to launch a multifaceted dialogue between the audiences or just as a place to meet in the middle of nature.

53 *Bensaude*, op. cit., 112.

54 A cold-storage building, bought up in 1979 by the Chinati Foundation established by the artist Donald Judd.

55 'What got me into art school in Cologne was a photographic work while taking the train from Munich to Rome, a journey I had gone through with my family every year. But while in Munich, I had met this woman, Martina, an animation film maker from Prague amongst a whole group of exiles, who had asked me if I "would take an old woman with you", "—sure, the train leaves at 7 am". We traveled together, Martina was the subject of my photographic work.' Interview with Rosa Barba, op. cit.

56 Ibid.

57 Gloria Sutton, op. cit.,1.

58 Two wall clocks are synchronised to the same time at the beginning of each of their public appearances. Although they are the exact same make, model, material, powered by the same kind of battery, they will fall out of sync and one of them will stop before the other.

59 The voices of Eric D. Clark, Alex Aikiu, Florent Baffi, Soa Bernad, Sara Brunel and Rita Filipe Christiane Prince.

SURVEY: PAGES 073–099

1 Rosa Barba, 'Introduction', in *On the Anarchic Organization of Cinematic Spaces: Evoking Spaces beyond Cinema*, op. cit., 8.

2 Ibid, 8.

3 Ibid, 9.

4 Joanne Moore, 'Introduction', *Inside the Freud Museums: History, Memory and Site Responsive Art* (London: B Tauris, 2017), 16

5 Mies van der Rohe quoted in Jean Louis Cohen, *Mies van der Rohe* (Abingdon: Taylor and Francis, 1995).

6 Rosa Barba, 'Collective Performance as Embarkation: Activating the Subconscious', in *On the Anarchic Organization of Cinematic Spaces: Evoking Spaces beyond Cinema,* op. cit., 116.

7 Jason Farago, 'Rosa Barba examines the everyday chaos of Sao Paulo's giant earthworm highway', *The Guardian*, 20 September 2016, available at https://www.theguardian.com/artanddesign/2016/sep/20/rosa-barba-sao-paulo-biennial-disseminate-and-hold-film.

8 Rosa Barba, 'Introduction', in *On the Anarchic Organization of Cinematic Spaces: Evoking Spaces beyond Cinema,* op. cit., 8.

9 Rosa Barba, 'Collective Performance as Embarkation: Activating the Subconscious', in *On the Anarchic Organization of Cinematic Spaces: Evoking Spaces beyond Cinema,* op. cit., 106–07.

10 *Inside the Outset: Evoking a Space of Passage* has another component, a film by Barba that was screened at the opening of the open air-cinema in September 2021.

11 Rosa Barba, 'Materiality and the Machine: Looping and Fragmenting to Create a New Auditorium', in *On the Anarchic Organization of Cinematic Spaces: Evoking Spaces beyond Cinema,* op. cit., 142

FOCUS: PAGES 101–119

1 Rosa Barba in conversation with Tommaso Isabella, *Mousse Magazine*, (5 October 2017).

2 Rosa Barba, conversation with the author, 12 September 2024.

3 Rosa Barba, quoted in Andrew Maerkle, 'Rosa Barba: Pt. I, Double Whistler', *ART iT*, (7 July 2020), https://www.art-it.asia/en/top_e/admin_ed_feature_e/210169/.

4 Victoria Brooks, 'In the Imaginary Spaces', in *The Color Out of Space*, ed. Henriette Huldisch, Karen Kelly and Barbara Schroeder (Cambridge: MIT List Visual Arts Center/New York: Dancing Foxes Press, 2017), 11.

5 Rosa Barba, *On the Anarchic Organization of Cinematic Spaces* (Ostfildern, Germany: Hatje Cantz, 2021), 21.

6 Barba, conversation with the author, 12 September 2024.

7 André-Robert Soulier and Claude Lacan, quoted in 'Jean Péchalat, ou la mémoire engloutie de Vassivière', *Le Populaire*, 7 February 2012. https://www.lepopulaire.fr/beaumont-du-lac-87120/loisirs/jean-pechalat-ou-la-memoire-engloutie-de-vassiviere_1211071/.

8 Xavier Fabre in 'Vassivière art center – an iconic architecture', Vidéoguide Nouvelle-Aquitaine, 17 July 2019, https://www.youtube.com/watch?v=69BYT3f9GEk.

9 All Barba quotes in this paragraph, conversation with the author, 12 and 29 September 2024.

10 Barba notes: 'Raimundas Malašauskas wrote a text as though he had a conversation with the man, but I never knew if it took place or if it was fiction.' Francesco Manacorda and Raimundas Malašauskas, 'Rosa Barba's Unfilmed Films', in *Rosa Barba: White Is an Image*, ed. Chiara Parisi and Andrea Viliani (Osfildern, Germany: Hatje Cantz, 2011), 97–131. The long-term resident, Jean Péchalat, was eight-seven years old when Barba's exhibition was on view. See 'Jean Péchalat, ou la mémoire engloutie de Vassivière' for his narration of living in the area before and after the construction of the dam, and of the Centre

11 The title is Barba's alteration of 'It is a two dimensional analogy or metaphor—A is Z'. Robert Smithson, 'A Provisional Theory of Nonsites', https://holtsmithsonfoundation.org/provisional-theory-nonsites.

12 Barba, conversation with the author, 29 September 2024.

13 Chiara Parisi and Andrea Viliani (the exhibition curators), website announcement, Centre International d'Art et du Paysage de l'île de Vassivière, https://ciapiledevassiviere.com/item/56.

14 See the exhibition catalogue *Rosa Barba: White Is an Image* for documentation of the whole exhibition.

15 Barba, conversation with the author, 29 September 2024.

16 Ibid.

17 Ibid.

18 Barba, *On the Anarchic Organization*, 53.

19 Barba, quoted in Andrew Maerkle, 'Rosa Barba: Pt. I. Double Whistler', *ART iT* (27 July 2020), https://www.art-it.asia/en/top_e/admin_ed_feature_e/210218/.

20 Barba, quoted in Maerkle, 'Rosa Barba: Pt. II', https://www.art-it.asia/en/top_e/admin_ed_feature_e/210218/.

21 Barba dates each iteration with its realized date coupled with 2010 to reference the inceptive work.

22 Barba, conversation with the author, 29 September 2024.

23 Barba, quoted in Andrew Maerkle, 'Rosa Barba: Pt. II'.

24 Ibid.

25 Ibid.

26 Barba, conversation with the author, 29 September 2024.

27 Rosa Barba, quoted in 'Philosophical Inquiry Session – Carl Andre, Rosa Barba, and JMW Turner', Turner Contemporary, https://www.youtube.com/watch?v=oZSsTpAh75Y. *White Museum* was part of the exhibition 'Rosa Barba: Subject to Constant Change', which included numerous works by Barba, who also selected drawings by Turner for the presentation, 'Turner's Perspective: Selected by Rosa Barba'. The drawings chart the science of perspective, which Turner made as visual aids for lectures he delivered as Professor of Perspective at the Royal Academy in the early 1800s. Barba noted in the exhibition wall text, 'Turner's diagrams and perspective drawings echo my thoughts about orchestrated and fragmented choreographies in spaces and how this experience can be approached from different perspectives.'

28 Christine Murray, 'Turner Contemporary, Margate, by David Chipperfield Architects', *Architects' Journal* (28 April 2011), https://www.architectsjournal.co.uk/archive/turner-contemporary-margate-by-david-chipperfield-architects.

29 Barba, conversation with the author, 29 September 2024.

30 Rosa Barba, *On the Anarchic Organization*, 56.

31 Barba, conversation with the author, 29 September 2024.

32 Ibid.

33 Ibid.

34 Brooks, 'In the Imaginary Spaces', 20. See her essay for a detailed narration of Barba's two-part commission, including the soundtrack that accompanied *The Color Out of Space*. 'The Colour Out of Space' is the title of a short horror story by H. P. Lovecraft.

35 Brooks, 'In the Imaginary Spaces', 10.

36 Barba, quoted in Andrew Maerkle, 'Rosa Barba: Pt. I'.

37 Barba, *On the Anarchic Organization*, 6.

38 Barba, conversation with the author, 29 September 2024.

39 Barba, *On the Anarchic Organization*, 10.

ARTIST'S WRITINGS: PAGES 133–143

1 Granville Ganter, review of 'Publics and Counterpublics by Michael Warner', *St. John's University Humanities Review*, no. 1, March 2003.

2 Cristina Sánchez Muñoz, 'Political Responsibility in the Construction of the Public Realm: Reflections Based on Hannah Arendt', *HannahArendt.net - Journal for Political Thinking* 1, no. 5 (November 2009): http://www.hannaharendt.net/index.php/han/article/view/148/262. See also Hannah Arendt, 'Freedom and Politics: A Lecture', *Chicago Review*, vol. 14, no. 1 (1960).

3 Jorge Luis Borges, 'The Library of Babel', in *Collected Fictions*, trans. Andrew Hurley (New York: Penguin, 1998).

4 Ian White, *Rosa Barba: White Is an Image,* op. cit.

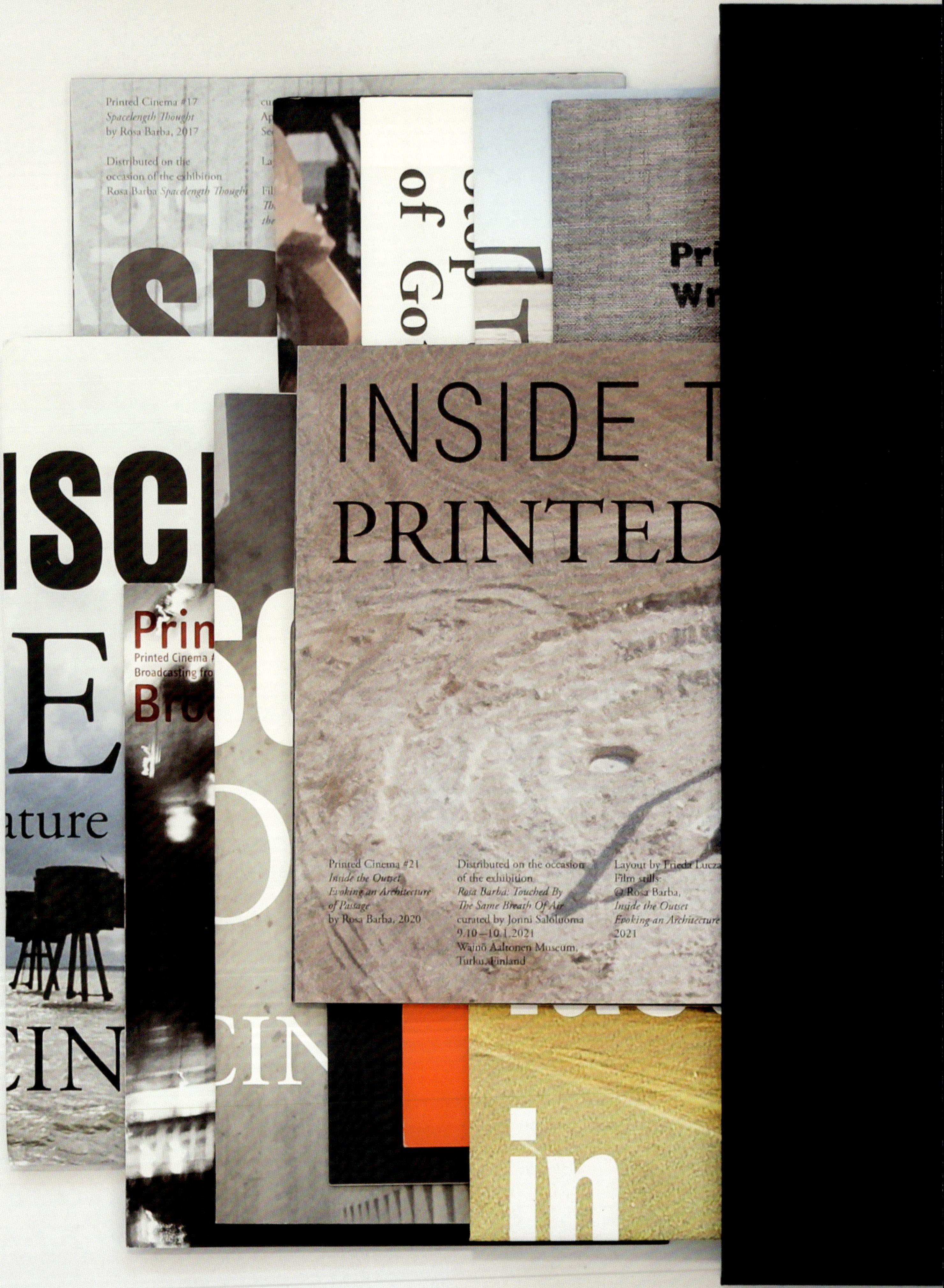
Printed Cinema #17
Spacelength Thought
by Rosa Barba, 2017
Distributed on the
occasion of the exhibition
Rosa Barba Spacelength Thought
INSIDE T
PRINTED
Printed Cinema #21
Inside the Outset
Evoking an Architecture
of Passage
by Rosa Barba, 2020
Distributed on the occasion
of the exhibition
Rosa Barba: Touched By
The Same Breath Of Air
curated by Jonni Saloluoma
9.10–10.1.2021
Wäinö Aaltonen Museum,
Turku, Finland
Film stills:
© Rosa Barba,
Inside the Outset
2021
in

145 CHRONOLGY

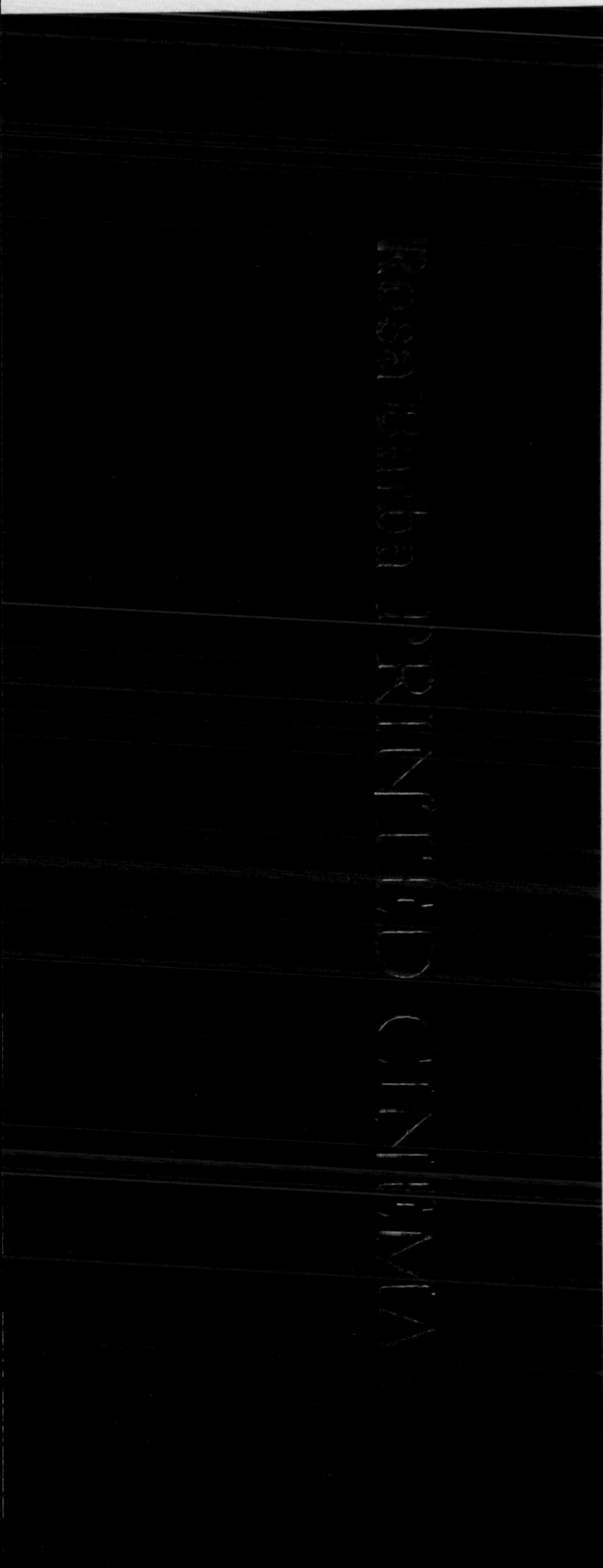

CHRONOLOGY: Rosa Barba, born 1972 in Agrigento, Italy. Lives and works in Berlin.

SELECTED EXHIBITIONS AND PROJECTS
1993–2003

SELECTED ARTICLES AND INTERVIEWS
1999–2003

1993–1995
Theatre and Film studies in Erlangen, Germany

1995–2000
Attends Kunsthochschule für Medien, Cologne

1999
'Copy and Paste',
KUNSTRAUM INNSBRUCK, Austria (group)

'Masterclass',
MONTEVIDEO, Amsterdam (group)

2000
MOLTKEREI WERKSTATT, Cologne (solo)

'Rosa Barba: Navigator im Licht-Raum-Modulator',
ARTOTHEK, Cologne (solo)

'Media Model',
MUESCARNOK/KUNSTHALLE, Budapest (group)

'Wie man sieht',
MUSEUM LUDWIG, Cologne (group)

2001
'Rosa Barba: Navigator',
ANCIENT GALLERY, Cinematexas, Austin (solo)

'Rosa Barba: Flightmachine',
KUNSTVEREIN MEDIENTURM, Graz, Austria (solo)

'Rosa Barba: Counter-Motion',
C3-GALLERY, Budapest (solo)

'See You Hear',
AKADEMIE DER KÜNSTE, Berlin (group)

'KölnQuartett',
KUNSTRAUM FUHRWERKSWAAGE, Cologne (group)

Receives the Music Video Prize at the International Short Film Festival Oberhausen, Germany

Receives the Hermann-Claasen Förderpreis, Cologne

2002
'Rosa Barba',
SALA DE ARTE CONTEMPORANÉO, Lima (solo)

'Rosa Barba: Pirate Spaces',
C/O PETER GORSCHLÜTER, MEYER RIEGGER, Karlsruhe (solo)

'Vision',
MUESCARNOK/KUNSTHALLE, Budapest (group)

2002
Erdmann, Petra, 'Zu den Bildwelten der Medienkünstlerin Rosa Barba', Springerin, no. 2

2003
'Rosa Barba',
KUNSTSTIFTUNG BADEN-WÜRTTEMBERG, Stuttgart (solo)

'Rosa Barba: Compilation1' (with Jeanne Faust and Jennifer Nelson),
KUNSTHALLE DÜSSELDORF (solo)

'Streams of Encounter',
MUSEUM OF FINE ARTS, Taipei (group)

Receives the Uriot Award, Rijksakademie, Amsterdam

2003
Lorch, Catrin, 'Düsseldorf: Compilation I in der Kunsthalle', Kunst Bulletin, March

Michely, Viola, 'Compilation I', Kunstforum International, no. 164, May

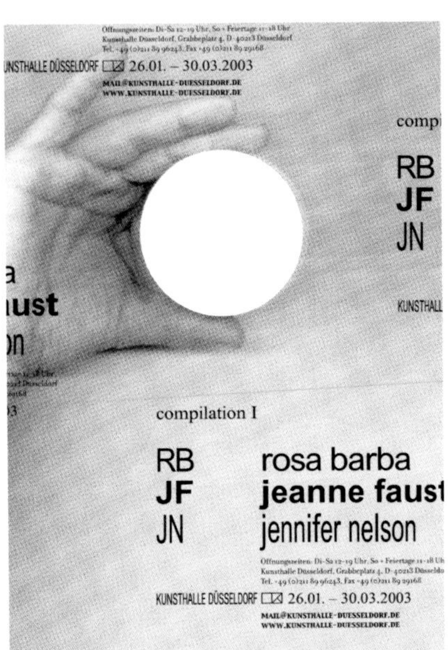

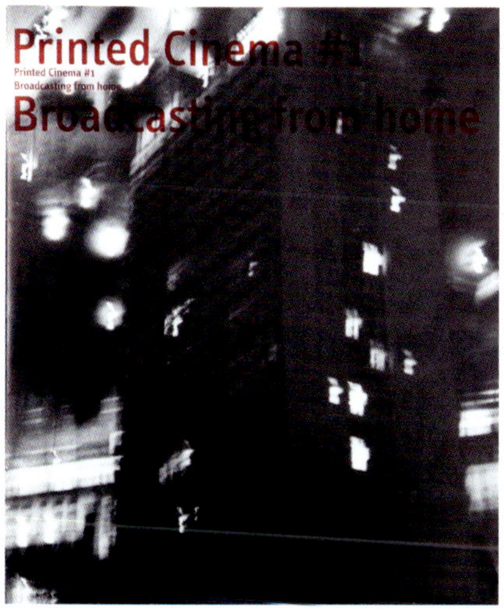

Printed Cinema #4
Who can tell if I am inventing?

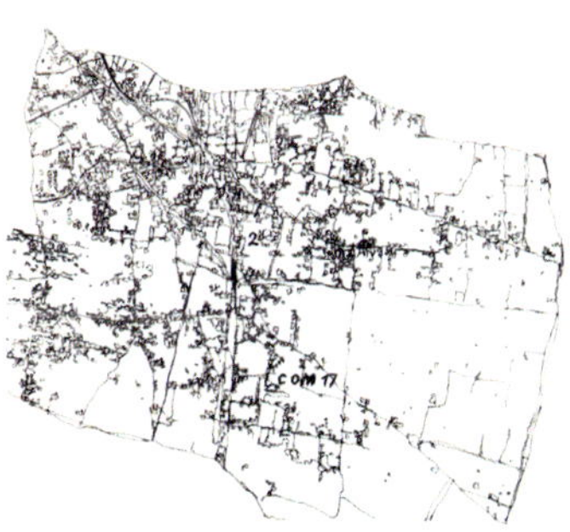

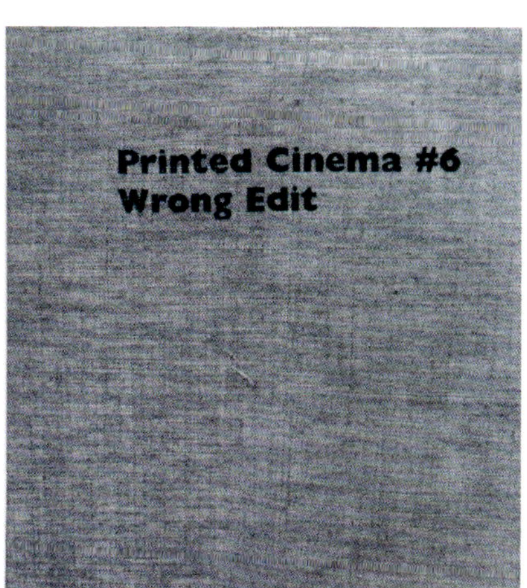

SELECTED EXHIBITIONS AND PROJECTS
2004–07

2004
'Rosa Barba: Buckle and Jitter',
ARGOS, Brussels (solo)

'A Molecular History of Everything',
CENTER FOR CONTEMPORARY ART, Melbourne (group)

'Doku/Fiction',
KUNSTHALLE DÜSSELDORF (group)

'Pole Position',
MANNHEIMER KUNSTVEREIN (group)

'The Ex',
PALAIS DES BEAUX-ARTS, Brussels (group)

4th TRANSMEDIALE, Berlin (group)

'Travelling Without Moving',
W139, Amsterdam (group)

'Born To Be A "Star"',
KÜNSTLERHAUS, Vienna (group)

2005
'Rosa Barba',
TRANSMISSION GALLERY, Glasgow (solo)

'Rosa Barba: You Cannot Remain Indifferent',
KASSELER KUNSTVEREIN, Fridericianum, Kassel, Germany (solo)

'Rosa Barba: A Tangible Accomplishment',
GALLERY VERA GLIEM, Cologne (solo)

'Gravity in Art',
DE APPEL ARTS CENTRE, Amsterdam (group)

2nd SENEF FILM FESTIVAL, Seoul (group)

'Horror, Science Fiction and Porn',
ART GALLERY OF YORK UNIVERSITY, Toronto (group)

2006
'Rosa Barba',
BALTIC ART CENTER, Visby, Sweden (solo)

'Rosa Barba: Who Can Tell If I Am Inventing?',
BADISCHER KUNSTVEREIN, Karlsruhe (solo)

'Rosa Barba: It's Gonna Happen' (with David Maljkovic),
CROY NIELSEN, Berlin (solo)

'Rosa Barba: Printed Cinema',
SCHAUFENSTER IM MUSEUM AM OSTWALL, Dortmund (solo)

'Last Lives in the Universe',
SMART PROJECT SPACE, Amsterdam (group)

'Revisie',
CENTRAAL MUSEUM, Utrecht (group)

'No Picture',
SWISS INSTITUTE, New York (group)

Receives the Artist Book Award from the Ontario Association of Art Galleries, Toronto

2007
'Rosa Barba: They Shine',
STEDELIJK MUSEUM BUREAU, Amsterdam (solo)

SELECTED ARTICLES AND INTERVIEWS
2004–07

2004
Heingartner, Douglas, 'Rosa Barba at Argos Brussels', Frieze, no. 84, June

2006
Alemani, Cecilia, 'It's Gonna Happen', Artforum, March

2007
Sartori, Chiara, 'Interview with Rosa Barba', Arte e Critica, no. 52, September–November

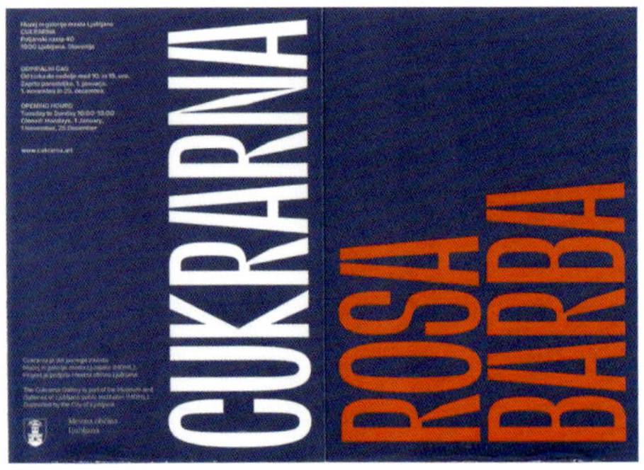

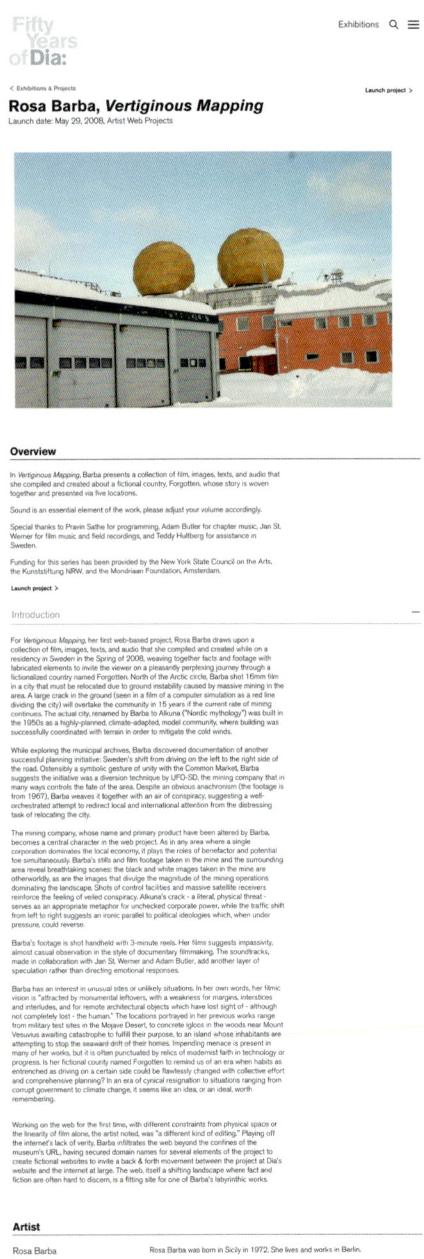

Fifty Years of Dia:

Exhibitions

< Exhibitions & Projects

Launch project >

Rosa Barba, *Vertiginous Mapping*

Launch date: May 29, 2008, Artist Web Projects

Overview

In *Vertiginous Mapping*, Barba presents a collection of film, images, texts, and audio that she compiled and created about a fictional country, Forgotten, whose story is woven together and presented via five locations.

Sound is an essential element of the work, please adjust your volume accordingly.

Special thanks to Pravin Sathe for programming, Adam Butler for chapter music, Jan St. Werner for film music and field recordings, and Teddy Hultberg for assistance in Sweden.

Funding for this series has been provided by the New York State Council on the Arts, the Kunststiftung NRW, and the Mondriaan Foundation, Amsterdam.

Launch project >

Introduction

For *Vertiginous Mapping*, her first web-based project, Rosa Barba draws upon a collection of film, images, texts, and audio that she compiled and created while on a residency in Sweden in the Spring of 2008, weaving together facts and footage with fabricated elements to invite the viewer on a pleasantly perplexing journey through a fictionalized country named Forgotten. North of the Arctic circle, Barba shot 16mm film in a city that must be relocated due to ground instability caused by massive mining in the area. A large crack in the ground (seen in a film of a computer simulation as a red line dividing the city) will overtake the community in 15 years if the current rate of mining continues. The actual city, renamed by Barba to Alkuna ("Nordic mythology") was built in the 1950s as a highly-planned, climate-adapted, model community, where building was successfully coordinated with terrain in order to mitigate the cold winds.

While exploring the municipal archives, Barba discovered documentation of another successful planning initiative: Sweden's shift from driving on the left to the right side of the road. Ostensibly a symbolic gesture of unity with the Common Market, Barba suggests the initiative was a diversion technique by UFO-SD, the mining company that in many ways controls the fate of the area. Despite an obvious anachronism (the footage is from 1967), Barba weaves it together with an air of conspiracy, suggesting a well-orchestrated attempt to redirect local and international attention from the distressing task of relocating the city.

The mining company, whose name and primary product have been altered by Barba, becomes a central character in the web project. As in any area where a single corporation dominates the local economy, it plays the roles of benefactor and potential foe simultaneously. Barba's stills and film footage taken in the mine and the surrounding area reveal breathtaking scenes: the black and white images taken in the mine are otherworldly, as are the images that divulge the magnitude of the mining operations dominating the landscape. Shots of control facilities and massive satellite receivers reinforce the feeling of veiled conspiracy. Alkuna's crack - a literal, physical threat - serves as an appropriate metaphor for unchecked corporate power, while the traffic shift from left to right suggests an ironic parallel to political ideologies which, when under pressure, could reverse.

Barba's footage is shot handheld with 3-minute reels. Her films suggests impassivity, almost casual observation in the style of documentary filmmaking. The soundtracks, made in collaboration with Jan St. Werner and Adam Butler, add another layer of speculation rather than directing emotional responses.

Barba has an interest in unusual sites or unlikely situations. In her own words, her filmic vision is "attracted by monumental leftovers, with a weakness for margins, interstices and interludes, and for remote architectural objects which have lost sight of - although not completely lost - the human." The locations portrayed in her previous works range from military test sites in the Mojave Desert, to concrete igloos in the woods near Mount Vesuvius awaiting catastrophe to fulfill their purpose, to an island whose inhabitants are attempting to stop the seaward drift of their homes. Impending menace is present in many of her works, but it is often punctuated by relics of modernist faith in technology or progress. Is her fictional county named Forgotten to remind us of an era when habits as entrenched as driving on a certain side could be flawlessly changed with collective effort and comprehensive planning? In an era of cynical resignation to situations ranging from corrupt government to climate change, it seems like an idea, or an ideal, worth remembering.

Working on the web for the first time, with different constraints from physical space or the linearity of film alone, the artist noted, was "a different kind of editing." Playing off the internet's lack of verity, Barba infiltrates the web beyond the confines of the museum's URL, having secured domain names for several elements of the project to create fictional websites to invite a back & forth movement between the project at Dia's website and the internet at large. The web, itself a shifting landscape where fact and fiction are often hard to discern, is a fitting site for one of Barba's labyrinthic works.

Artist

Rosa Barba

Rosa Barba was born in Sicily in 1972. She lives and works in Berlin.

View profile >

SELECTED EXHIBITIONS AND PROJECTS
2007–09

2007 (cont.)
'HAP-Grieshaber-Preis',
DEUTSCHER KÜNSTLERBUND, Berlin (solo)

'With a Hidden Noise',
KUNSTVEREIN MEDIENTURM, Graz, Austria (solo)

'Western Round Table',
KOJE MEDIENTURM, Museumsquartier, Vienna (solo)

'Slovenian Pavilion',
52nd VENICE BIENNALE (group)

1st THESSALONIKI BIENNALE OF CONTEMPORARY ART (group)

12th BIENNIAL OF MOVING IMAGES, Geneva (group)

5th LOOP FESTIVAL, Barcelona (group)

Receives the Prix du Centre pour l'Image Contemporaine, Geneva

2008
'Rosa Barba: Outwardly from Earth's Center',
CARLIER | GEBAUER, Berlin (solo)

VILLA ROMANA, Florence (solo)

'Rosa Barba: Handed Over' (with David Maljkovic),
PROJECT ART CENTER, Dublin, toured to ANNET GELINK GALLERY, Amsterdam (solo)

'Rosa Barba: Esbama',
ÉCOLE DES BEAUX-ARTS, Montpellier (solo)

'Rosa Barba: Outwardly from Earth's Center',
BILDMUSEET UMEÅ, Sweden (solo)

'Rosa Barba: Western Round Table',
GALLERY PATRICIA DORFMANN, Paris (solo)

2nd TURIN TRIENNALE (group)

'Video Report Italia 2006–07',
GALLERIA COMUNALE D'ARTE CONTEMPORANEA, Monfalcone, Italy (group)

'Degrees of Remove: Landscape and Affect',
SCULPTURE CENTER, Long Island City, and ANTHOLOGY FILM ARCHIVE, New York (group)

'Italics: Italian Art Between Tradition and Revolution 1968-2008',
PINAULT FOUNDATION, Venice, toured to MUSEUM OF CONTEMPORARY ART, Chicago (group)

'Map-Navigating the Present',
BILDMUSEET, Umea, Sweden (group)

'Visible Cinema',
CENTER OF CONTEMPORARY ARTS, Glasgow (group)

'Abstracts of Syn',
AR/GE KUNST, Bozen, Italy (group)

2009
'Rosa Barba: Western Round Table',
CARLIER | GEBAUER, Berlin (solo)

'Rosa Barba: Stating the Real Sublime',
GIÓ MARCONI, Milan (solo)

53rd VENICE BIENNALE (group)

SELECTED ARTICLES AND INTERVIEWS
2007–09

2007 (cont.)
Egger, Christian, 'Rosa Barba', Spike, no. 13, Autumn

2008
White, Ian, 'Rosa Barba', Camera Austria, no. 101

Van der Vlist, Eline, 'Rosa Barba at Stedelijk Museum Bureau, Amsterdam', Modern Painters, June

Scharrer, Eva, 'Rooms Look Back', Artforum, November

Birnbaum, Daniel, 'Best of 2008', Artforum, December

Tenconi, Roberta, 'Introducing Rosa Barba', Mousse, no. 16, December

2009
Rech, Claudia, 'Rosa Barba', Zoe Magazine, no. 24

Uran, Pelin, 'Interview with Rosa Barba', Archive Journal

Valentini, Veronica, 'The Future Lasts One Day', Flash Art, no. 266, May–June

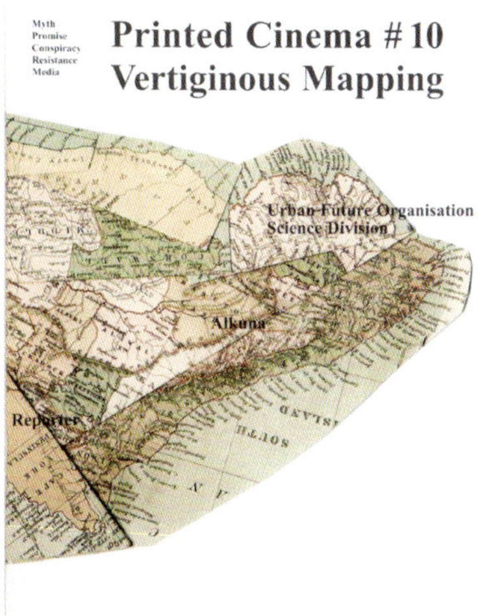

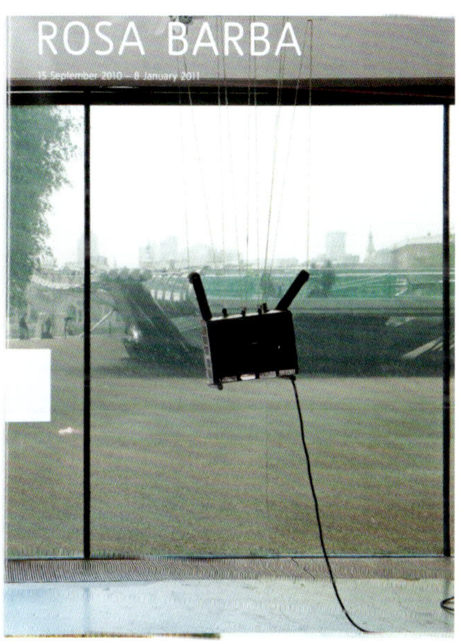

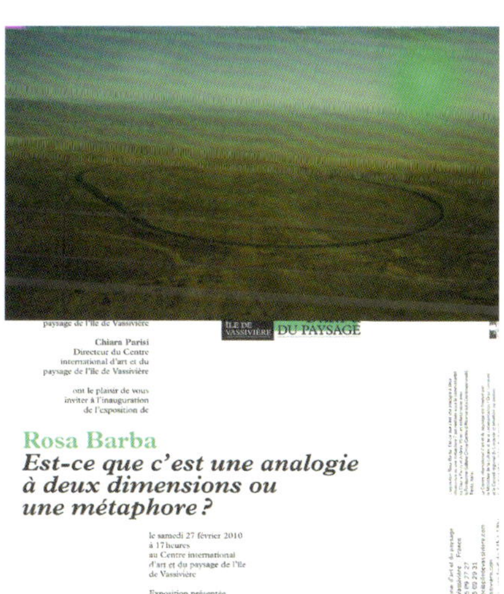

SELECTED EXHIBITIONS AND PROJECTS
2009–10

2009 (cont.)
'And Then Nothing Turned Itself Inside Out',
KUNSTHALLE EXNERGASSE AT WUK, Vienna (group)

'Passaggi in Sicilia',
FONDAZIONE SAMBUCA, Palermo (group)

5th GÖTEBORG BIENNIAL (group)

'Life Forms',
BONNIERS KONSTHALL, Stockholm (group)

'Just in the Dark',
MERCATI DI TRAIANO, Museo dei Fori Imperiali, Rome (group)

23rd IMAGES FESTIVAL, Toronto (group)

'Drifting Histories',
HESSEL MUSEUM AT CENTER FOR CURATORIAL STUDIES BARD COLLEGE, New York (group)

2010
'Rosa Barba',
TATE MODERN, London (solo)

'Rosa Barba: Is it a two-dimensional analogy or a metaphor?',
CENTRE INTERNATIONAL D'ART ET DU PAYSAGE DE L'ÎLE DE VASSIVIÈRE, France (solo)

'Rosa Barba',
CENTER OF CONTEMPORARY ARTS, Tel Aviv (solo)

'Rosa Barba: On the Future of Collective Strength within an Archive'
MUSEO NACIONAL CENTRO DE ARTE REINA SOFÍA, Madrid (solo)

'SI',
MAGASIN, Grenoble, France (group)

'Premio Italia',
MUSEO NAZIONALE DELLE ARTI DEL XXI SECOLO (MAXXI), Rome (group)

'Faux Amis: vidéothèque éphémère',
JEU DE PAUME, Paris (group)

'H-Box',
LABORATORIO DE ARTE ALAMEDA, Mexico City, toured to FONDAZIONE BEYELER, Basel; FONDATION D'ENTREPRISE HERMÈS, Paris; NEW MUSEUM OF CONTEMPORARY ART, New York; MUSEE D'ART MODERNE GRAND-DUC JEAN (MUDAM), Luxembourg (group)

'21/21: 21 Artists for the 21st Century',
FONDAZIONE SANDRETTO RE REBAUDENGO, Turin (group)

'And nothing turned itself inside out',
GALERIA MIROSLAV KRALJEVIC, Zagreb (group)

'A Generation',
PETAH-TIKVA MUSEUM OF ART, Israel (group)

4th ŁÓDŹ BIENNALE (group)

'Nam June Paik Award',
MUSEUM KUNSTPALAST, Düsseldorf (group)

7th LIVERPOOL BIENNALE (group)

Receives the Nam June Paik Award, Museum Kunstpalast, Düsseldorf

Receives the Award of the Kulturni Centar, Belgrade

SELECTED ARTICLES AND INTERVIEWS
2009–10

2009 (cont.)
Ceresoli, Jacqueline, 'Rosa Barba: Gió Marconi, Milano', Flash Art Italia, no. 278, October–November

Gandini, Manuela, 'Rosa Barba nel deserto delle atomiche', La Stampa, 26 October

Cotter, Holland, 'Ecstatic Resistance', The New York Times, 17 December

2010
Comer, Stuart, 'The Best Motion Pictures and Moving Images 2009', Frieze, no. 128, January–February

Lequeux, Emanuelle, 'Rosa Barba enchante l'Île de Vassivière', Beaux Arts, no. 318, February

Alemani, Cecilia, 'Rosa Barba interviewed by Cecilia Alemani', Klat, Spring

Weil, Benjamin, 'Rosa Barba: Le corps des images', Art Press, no. 367, May

Muñoz-Alonso, Lorena, 'Rosa Barba: A Curated Conference', Frieze, no. 130, May–June

Borthwick, Ben, and Melissa Gronlund, 'Rosa Barba: Changing Cinema', Afterall, November

Cooke, Lynne, 'Best of 2010', Artforum, December

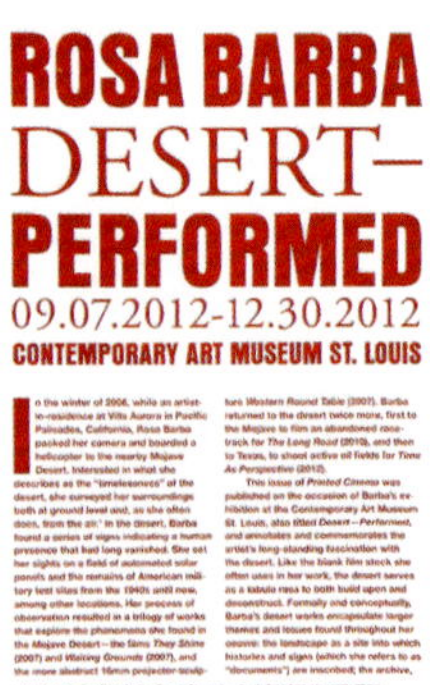

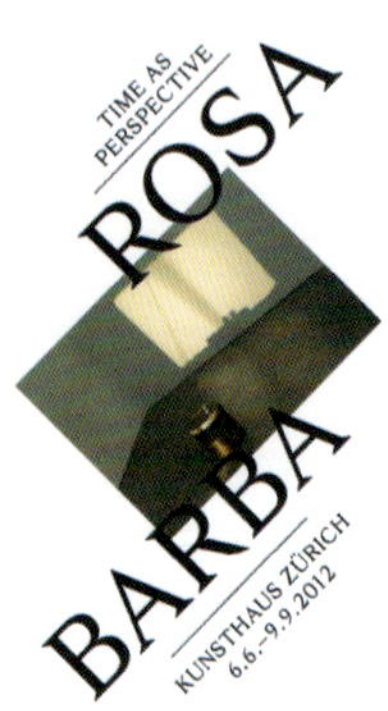

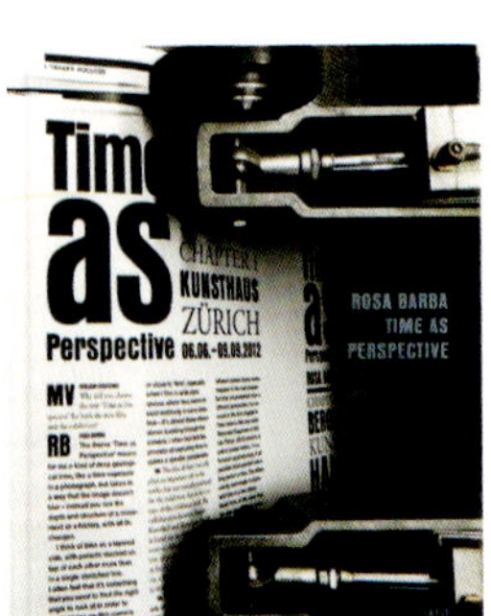

SELECTED EXHIBITIONS AND PROJECTS
2011–12

2011

'Rosa Barba: Stage Archive',
FONDAZIONE GALLERIA CIVICA and MUSEO D'ARTE MODERNA E CONTEMPORANEA (MART) DI TRENTO E ROVERETO, Italy (solo)

'Rosa Barba',
CARLIER | GEBAUER, Berlin (solo)

'Rosa Barba',
KUNSTVEREIN BRAUNSCHWEIG, Germany (solo)

'Rosa Barba: Somnium, XL',
LOBBY NEW ORLEANS GEBOUW, INTERNATIONAL FILM FESTIVAL ROTTERDAM (solo)

'Rosa Barba/David Maljkovic',
LA PEDRERA, Barcelona (solo)

'Never Odd or Even',
GRIMMUSEUM, Berlin (group)

'Øvstebø videocriação',
CENTRO MUNICIPAL DE ARTE HÉLIO OITICICA, Rio de Janeiro (group)

'Les Marques Aveugles',
CENTRE D'ART CONTEMPORAIN, Genève (group)

'Surviving the Future',
MURMANSK ART MUSEUM, Russia (group)

'El Mapa: Cartografías críticas',
MUSEO DE ARTE MODERNO MEDELLIN (MAMM), Colombia (group)

'Staging Documentary',
LOTHRINGER 13, Munich (group)

'Magical Consciousness',
ARNOLFINI ART CENTRE, Bristol (group)

'Terminal Convention',
CORK AIRPORT, Ireland (group)

2012

'Rosa Barba: Time as Perspective',
KUNSTHAUS ZÜRICH (solo)

'Rosa Barba: Back Door Exposure',
JEU DE PAUME, Paris (solo)

'Rosa Barba: A Private Tableaux and Printed Cinema',
MARFA BOOK CO, Texas (solo)

'Rosa Barba: Desert—Performed',
MUSEUM OF CONTEMPORARY ART, St. Louis (solo)

'Rosa Barba: The Move',
ARTER, Istanbul (solo)

'Rosa Barba: October Salon',
KULTURNI CENTER, Belgrade (solo)

'Telling everything, not knowing how: After the Death of Felix Gonzalez-Torres',
CENTRO DE ARTE DOS DE MAYO (CA2M), Madrid (group)

'Man in the Holocene',
MIT LIST VISUAL ARTS CENTER, Cambridge, Massachusetts (group)

'Field Experiences',
CENTRE INTERNATIONAL D'ART & DU PAYSAGE DE VASSIVÈRE, France (group)

SELECTED ARTICLES AND INTERVIEWS
2011–12

2011

Kitamura, Katie, and Mike Sperlinger, 'The Best Motion Pictures and Moving Images of 2010', Frieze Critic's Guide, January

Robecchi, Michele, 'Rosa Barba: La storia è una scultura', Kunst Bulletin, January–February

Bell, Kirsty, 'Suspended Animation', Frieze, no. 139, May

Masoero, Ada, 'Girotondo intorno all'archivio di Rosa', Il Sole 24 Ore, 24 July

Stoeber, Michael, 'Rosa Barba – Braunschweig', Kunstforum International, July–August

Sassone, Gabriele Francesco, 'Rosa Barba: Stage Archive', Camera Austria, no. 115, September

Casadio, Mariuccia, 'Light Shaped', Vogue Italia, September

Sassone, Gabriele Francesco: 'Esegesi della Luce', Flash Art Italia no. 296, October

Miro, Neus, 'Rosa Barba: Leer imágenes', Exit Express, October–November

Lequeux, Emanuelle, 'Vassivière l'art a trouvé son ile', Beaux Arts, no. 239, November

Buhr, Elke, 'Bücher des Monats: Rosa Barba: White is an Image', Monopol M, December

2012

Barry, Robert, 'Les Marques Aveugles,' Frieze, no. 144, January

Buhr, Elke, 'Relikte der Analogtechnik', Monopol M, February

Colard, Jean-Max, 'Rosa Barba, le film d'Ariane', Les Inrockuptibles, June

Steiner, Urs, 'Rosa Barba im Kunsthaus Zürich', Neue Zürcher Zeitung, June

Gat, Orit, 'Dirty Projector: Rosa Barba's filmic sculptures', Modern Painters, June

Grzonka, Patricia, 'Weißes Licht erhellt die Nacht', Kunst Bulletin, August

Campanini, Cristiana, 'Rosa Barba: Scolpire il Cinema', Arte, September

Marchand, Antoine, 'Rosa Barba: Universal Cinema', Zérodeux, Autumn

SELECTED EXHIBITIONS AND PROJECTS
2012–14

SELECTED ARTICLES AND INTERVIEWS
2012–14

2012 (cont.)
'A Trip to the Moon: Before and After Film',
BONNIERS KONSTHALL, Stockholm (group)

'Made in Germany 2',
SPRENGEL MUSEUM, Hannover (group)

'Never Odd or Even',
MUSEUM FOR CONTEMPORARY ART, Roskilde, Denmark (group)

'Unfinished Journeys',
MUSEUM OF CONTEMPORARY ART, Oslo (group)

Receives the ACACIA Award, Museo del Novecento, Milan

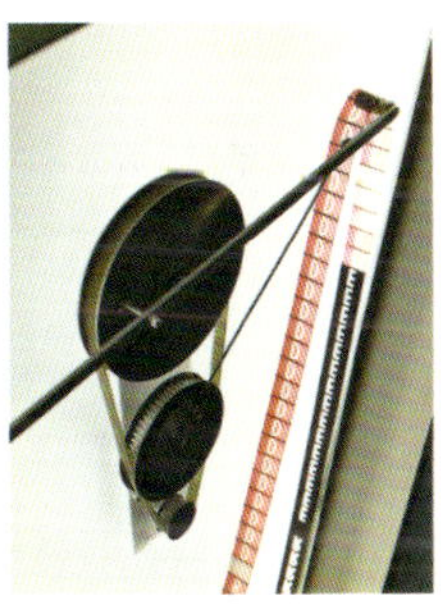

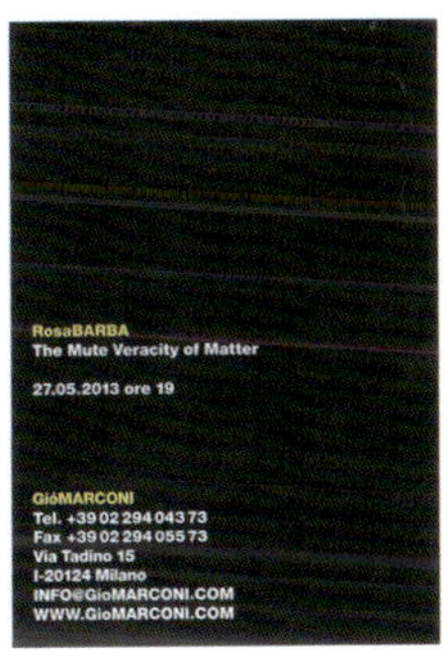

2013
'Rosa Barba: A Home For a Unique Individual',
MUSEO DE ARTE CONTEMPORANEO DE CASTILLA Y LEÓN (MUSAC), Spain (solo)

'Rosa Barba: Subject to Constant Change',
CORNERHOUSE, Manchester, and TURNER CONTEMPORARY, Margate, England (solo)

'Rosa Barba: Time as Perspective',
BERGEN KUNSTHALL, Norway (solo)

'Rosa Barba: The Mute Veracity of Matter',
GIÓ MARCONI, Milan (solo)

PERFORMA 13, New York

'Des Mondes Possibles (Possible Worlds)',
FONDS RÉGIONAL D'ART CONTEMPORAIN (FRAC) FRANCHE-COMTÉ, Besançon, France (group)

'Nur hier. Sammlung zeitgenössischer Kunst der Bundesrepublik Deutschland: Ankäufe von 2007 bis 2011',
KUNST- UND AUSSTELLUNGSHALLE DER BUNDESREPUBLIK DEUTSCHLAND, Bonn (group)

'Film as Sculpture, WIELS, Centre d'Art Contemporain, Brussels
Langages: Entre le dire et le faire',
FONDATION CALOUSTE GULBENKIAN, Paris (group)

2013
Espejo, Bea, 'Rosa Barba, El arte es un lugar che ofrece soluciones utópicas', El Mundo, 18 January

Clark Robert, 'Rosa Barba: Subject to Contstant Change Manchester', The Guardian, 26 January

McCartney, Nicola, 'Raw Materials: Turner selected by Rosa Barba', Apollo, February

Hazelton, Claire: 'Spring Exhibitions at Turner Contemporary, Margate', Aesthetica Magazine, February

Lang, Martin, 'Review: Carl Andre/Rosa Barba', AN Magazine, March

Dickinson, Bob, 'Rosa Barba: Subject to Constant Change', Art Monthly, April

Khanna, Shama, 'Rosa Barba: Subject to Constant Change, Cornerhouse, Manchester', Art Review, May

Sherlock, Amy, 'Cornerhouse, Manchester & Turner Contmporary, Margate', Frieze, no. 155, May

Martin, Alberto, 'Rosa Barba: Un lugar para un único individuo', El País, 11 May

Vishmidt, Marina, 'A Rapid Inventory of the Universe', Texte Zur Kunst, June

Estremo, Vincenzo, 'The Random Image in Rosa Barba's Cinematography', Arte e Critica, June

Huldisch, Henriette, 'Unmoored Future', Artforum, September

De Brugerolle, Marie, 'Film as Sculpture', Zéro Deux, no. 67, Autumn

De Wachter, Ellen Mara, 'Michelangelo Antonioni/Film as Sculpture, Bozar/Wiels', Frieze, no. 158, October

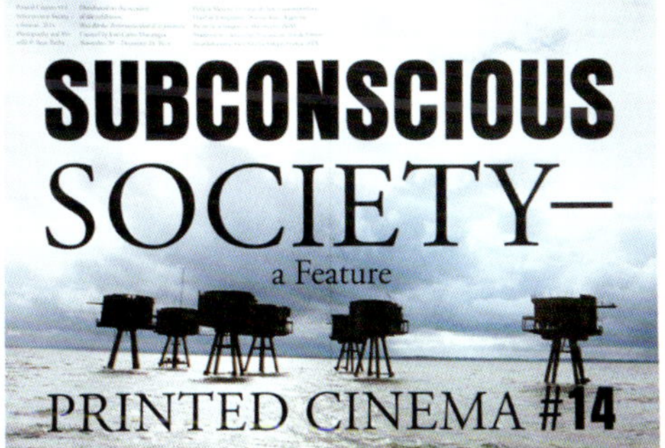

2014
'Rosa Barba: Performativity of Presence',
CENTRE OF CONTEMPORARY ART HOTEL DE INMIGRANTES, Buenos Aires (solo)

'Rosa Barba: A Fictional Library–Live',
CENTER OF CONTEMPORARY ART, Vilnius (solo)

'Rosa Barba: The Mute Veracity of Matter II',
MUSEO NAZIONALE DELLE ARTI DEL XXI SECOLO (MAXXI), Rome (solo)

'Rosa Barba: New Works',
ARTPACE, San Antonio, Texas (solo)

'Playtime, Cornerhouse, Manchester',
PIER 54, HIGH LINE, New York (group)

2014
Thaddeus-Johns, Josie, 'Studio Visit Rosa Barba', Sleek, no. 39

Adams, Rachel, 'Rosa Barba: New Works', Arts and Culture Texas, 14 May

Rees, Lucy, '19th Sydney Biennale: "You Imagine What You Desire"', Flash Art, no. 296, May–June

Wartenberg, Thomas, 'Philosophy Now Reflections on the Death of Celluloid', Philosophy Now, May–June

Borcherdt, Gesine, 'Die Poesie des ratternden Projektors', Art, July

Leitner, David, '"Dying of the Light" at MASS MoCA', Filmmaker Magazine, August

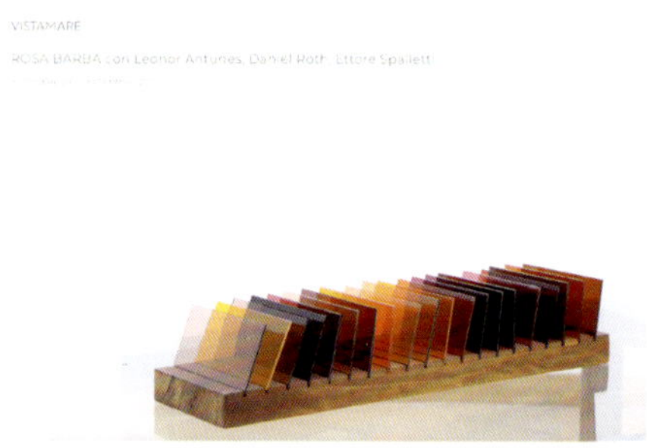

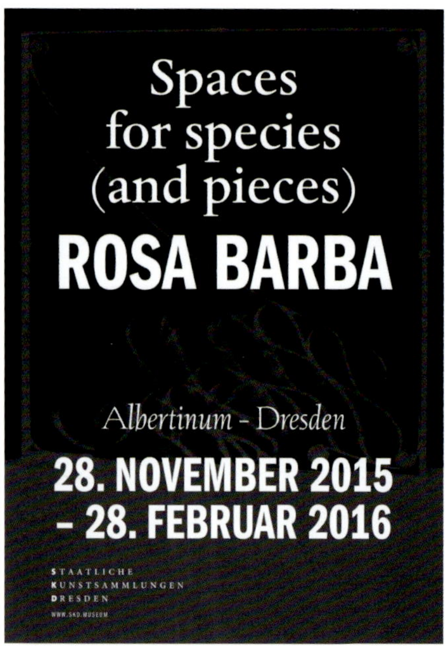

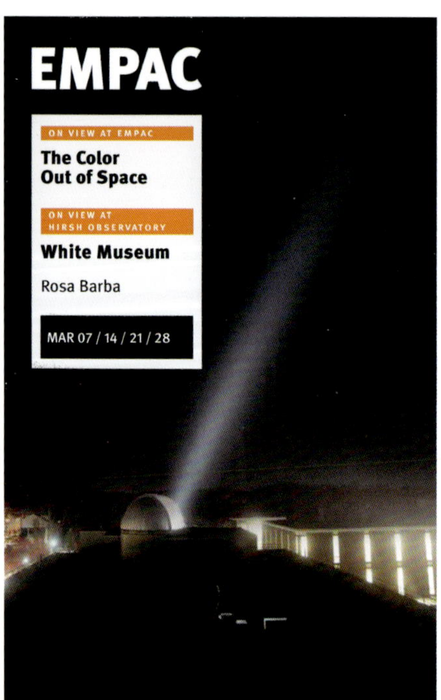

SELECTED EXHIBITIONS AND PROJECTS
2014-16

2014 (cont.)
Islands Off the Shore of Asia,
PARA SITE, SPRING, Hong Kong (group)

INTERNATIONAL TRIENNIAL OF NEW MEDIA ART 2014, Beijing (group)

8th BERLIN BIENNALE (group)

'Le musée imaginaire d'Henri Langlois',
LA CINÉMATHÈQUE FRANÇAISE, Paris (group)

'Words as Door: in Language, Art, Film',
KÜNSTLERHAUS – HALLE FÜR KUNST & MEDIEN, Graz (group)

19th BIENNALE OF SYDNEY (group)

1st INTERNATIONAL BIENNIAL OF CONTEMPORARY ART OF CARTAGENA DE INDIAS, Colombia (group)

'The Dying of the Light: Film as Medium and Metaphor,'
MASS MoCA, North Adams, Massachusetts (group)

'Rosa Barba with Leonor Antunes, Daniel Roth, Ettore Spalletti',
VISTAMARE, Pescara, Italy (group)

2015
'Rosa Barba: Spaces for Species (and Pieces)',
ALBERTINUM, Dresden (solo)

'Rosa Barba: The Color Out of Space',
EXPERIMENTAL MEDIA AND PERFORMING ARTS CENTER (EMPAC) RENSSELAER POLYTECHNIC INSTITUTE, Troy, New York, toured to MIT LIST VISUAL ARTS CENTER, Cambridge, Massachusetts (solo)

'Rosa Barba: Inside a Magnified Picture',
MEYER RIEGGER, Berlin (solo)

'Rosa Barba: Verdingte Wahrscheinlichkeit' (with Ingrid Wiener),
GALERIE CHARIM, Vienna (solo)

'Plagiarizing the Future',
HANGAR – CENTRO DE INVESTIGAÇÃO ARTISTICA, Lisbon (group)

'Sequential Strings',
TIMISOARA ART MUSEUM, Romania (group)

'A Space Is A Space Is A Space',
DEUTSCHES ARCHITEKTUR ZENTRUM, Berlin (group)

56th VENICE BIENNALE (group)

'The Coming Museum',
FUNDAÇÃO EUGÉNIO DE ALMEIDA, Évora, Portugal (group)

'Landschaft in Bewegung: Filmische Ausblicke auf ein unbestimmtes Morgen',
KUNSTHAUS GRAZ (group)

Receives the 46th Prix International d'Art Contemporain, Fondation Prince Pierre de Monaco

2016
'Rosa Barba: The Color Out of Space',
NEUER BERLINER KUNSTVEREIN (NBK), Berlin (solo)

'Rosa Barba: From Source to Poem',
CAPC MUSÉE D'ART CONTEMPORAIN DE BORDEAUX (solo)

'Rosa Barba: Blind Volumes',
SCHIRN KUNSTHALLE, Frankfurt (solo)

SELECTED ARTICLES AND INTERVIEWS
2014-16

2014 (cont.)
Schmidt, Sabine Maria, 'Rosa Barba – A Fictional Library – Live', Springerin, no. 14, Fall

Watts, Jonathan P, 'Into the Light', Tate ETC, no. 32, Autumn

2015
Budzynski, Scott, 'Remembering the Future in Subconscious Society: A Conversation with Rosa Barba'; Michele Robecchi, 'Rosa Barba: Metaphors for History, Time and Society'; Artpulse, no. 22

Jonas, Joan, and Rosa Barba, 'Artists in Conversation', Bomb, no. 131, Spring

Mania, Astrid, 'Geld ist ein Chamäleon', Süddeutsche Zeitung, 2–3 May

Di Drusco, Fabia, 'Aqua di Parma presenta a Palazzo Cusani "I'll be there forever"', L'Uomo Vogue, no 461, May–June

Smee, Sebastian, 'Using dated technology, Rosa Barba evokes the sublime', Boston Globe, 29 October

Hindahl, Philipp, 'Museum mit Meerblic'; Elke Buhr, 'Rosa Barba in Dresden: Auferstanden aus den Katakomben', Monopol M, November

Smee, Sebastian, 'The Ticket: Art', Boston Globe, 14 November

2016
Young, Gillian, 'Rosa Barba: MIT List Visual Arts Center', Art in America, February

Woeller, Marcus, 'Wie sollte man bewegte Bilder ins Museum hängen?' Die Welt, 19 February

De La Villa, Rocio, 'Nuevos y viejos formatos de notación: Rosa Barba Thoughts of Sorts', El Cultural, 11–18 March

SELECTED EXHIBITIONS AND PROJECTS
2016-17

2016 (cont.)
'Rosa Barba: Thoughts of Sorts',
PARRA & ROMERO, Madrid (solo)

'Rosa Barba, White Museum – Live, Sunday Sessions',
MoMA PS1, Long Island City, New York (solo)

'The Artist's Museum',
INSTITUTE OF CONTEMPORARY ART (ICA) Boston (group)

16th QUADRIENNALE D'ARTE, Rome (group)

'Ernst Ludwig Kirchner: Hieroglyphen',
HAMBURGER BAHNHOF MUSEUM FÜR GEGENWART, Berlin (group)

'Celluloid: Rosa Barba - Tacita Dean - João Maria Gusmão & Pedro Paiva - Luis Recoder & Sandra Gibson',
EYE FILMMUSEUM, Amsterdam (group)

32nd BIENAL DE SÃO PAULO (group)

'Sublime',
CENTRE POMPIDOU, Metz (group)

'Fertile Lands',
FONDATION D'ENTREPRISE RICARD, Paris (group)

Receives the Experimental Film Award, 24th Curtas Vila do Conde International Film Festival, Portugal

Receives the No Violence Award, 54th Ann Arbor Film Festival, Michigan

2017
'Rosa Barba: Solar Flux Recordings',
PALACIO DE CRISTAL, MUSEO NACIONAL CENTRO DE ARTE REINA SOFÍA, Madrid (solo)

'Rosa Barba: From Source to Poem to Rhythm to Reader',
PIRELLI HANGARBICOCCA, Milan (solo)

'Rosa Barba: Spacelength Thought',
SECESSION, Vienna (solo)

'Rosa Barba: Elements of Conduct',
MALMÖ KONSTHALL, Sweden (solo)

'Da Io a Noi: la città senza confini,
PALAZZO DEL QUIRINALE, Rome (group)

'Never Ending Stories: Der Loop in Kunst, Film, Architektur, Musik, Literatur und Kulturgeschichte',
KUNSTMUSEUM WOLFSBURG, Germany (group)

TRIGON 67, Graz (group)

7th BIENNALE FÜR AKTUELLE FOTOGRAFIE, Mannheim (group)

'Sculpture on Screen: The Very Impress of the Object',
CALOUSTE GULBENKIAN MUSEUM, Lisbon (group)

'Toujours: El museo como testigo',
MUSEO AMPARO, Peubla, Mexico (group)

'Collecting Europe',
VICTORIA & ALBERT MUSEUM, London (group)

'The String Traveller',
STEDELIJK MUSEUM VOOR ACTUELE KUNST (SMAK), Gent (group)

SELECTED ARTICLES AND INTERVIEWS
2016-17

2016 (cont.)
Farago, Jason, 'Rosa Barba examines the everyday chaos of São Paulo's "giant earthworm" highway', The Guardian, 20 September

Marti, Silas, 'Cinema Concreto, Artista Rosa Barba investiga as memórias do Minhocão em filme na Bienal', Folha de São Paulo, November

2017
Gregori, Daniela, 'Film und Skulptur, Medium und Material,' Ray Filmmagazin, April

Möller, Sabrina, 'Science-Fiction und Loops als zeitneutraler Sprachraum: Interview with Rosa Barba', Kunstmagazin Parnass, 26 April

Scheyerer, Nicole, 'Summ summ im Schatten der Containerkräne', Stadtzeitung Wien, 3 May

Espejo, Bea, 'Rosa Barba: El paisaje es como una página enblanco', El País, 15 May

Isabella, Tommaso, 'From Source to Poem to Rhythm to Reader: Conversation with Rosa Barba', Mousse Magazine, no. 59, Summer

Balsom, Erika, 'Historical Projections: Erika Balsom on the art of Rosa Barba', Artforum, September

Baldacci, Cristina, 'Re-enactment e altre storie: Dall'archivio alla contro-narrazione per immagini nell'arte contemporanea', Engramma, no. 150, October

Borja Villel, Manuel, 'Best of 2017', Artforum, December

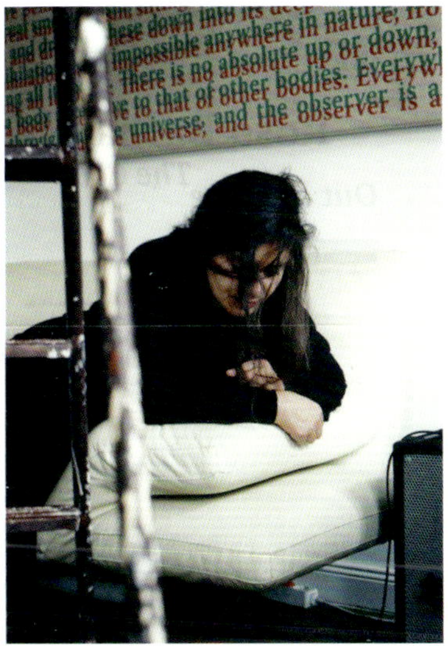

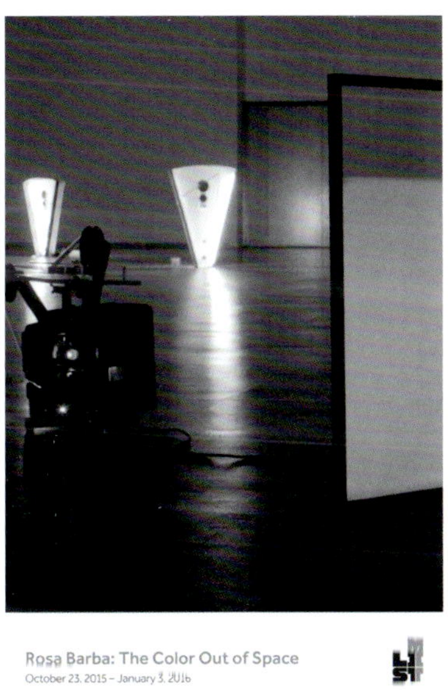

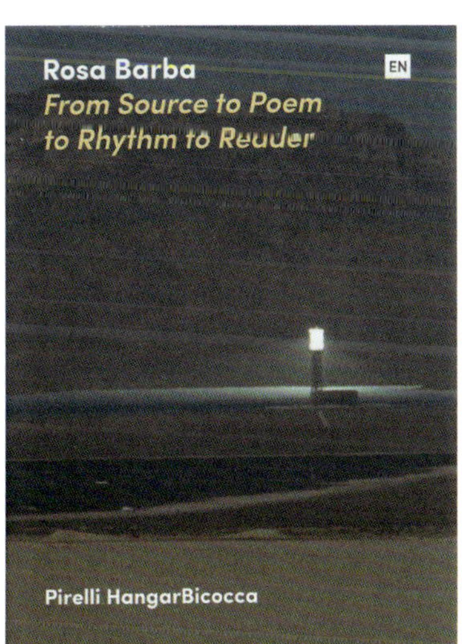

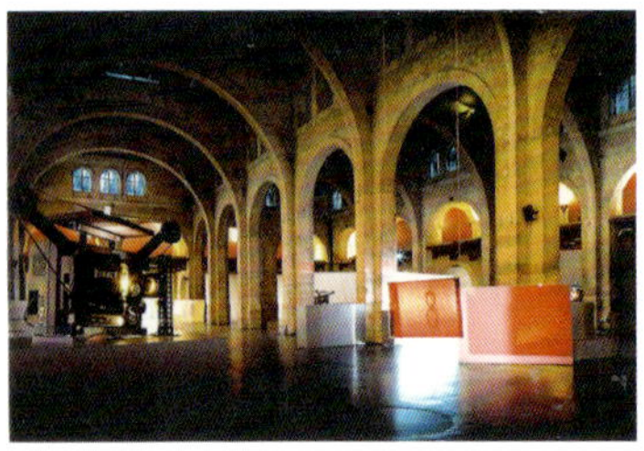

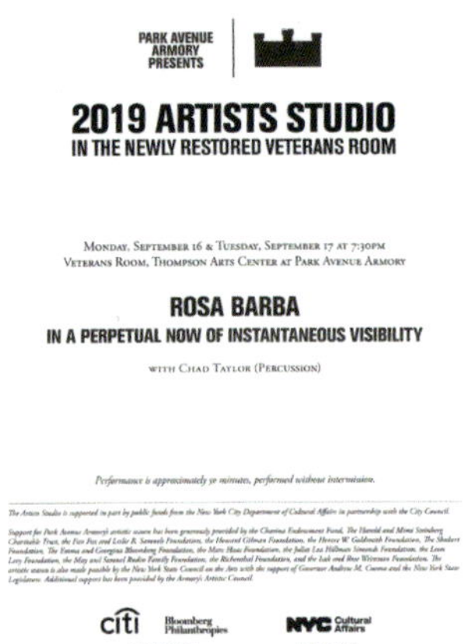

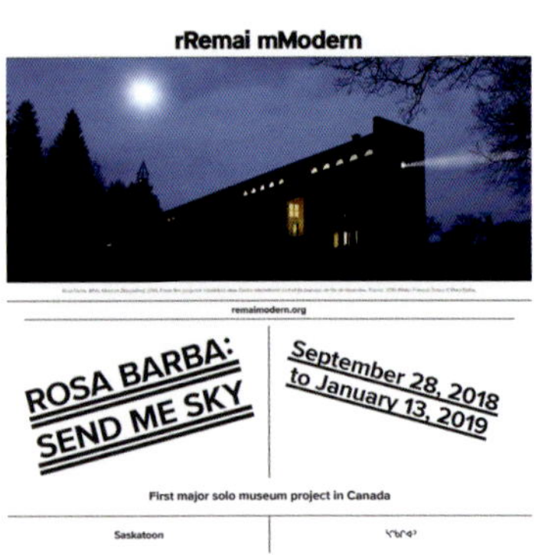

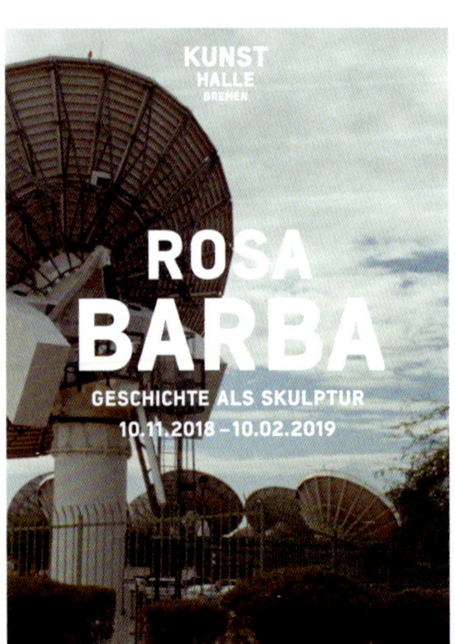

SELECTED EXHIBITIONS AND PROJECTS
2018-20

2018

'Rosa Barba: On the Anarchic Organisation of Cinematic Spaces – Evoking Spaces Beyond Cinema',
GALLERY KHM1 AT MALMÖ ART ACADEMY, Sweden (solo)

'Rosa Barba: Geschichte als Skulptur/History as a Sculpture',
KUNSTHALLE BREMEN (solo)

'Rosa Barba: Send Me Sky',
REMAI MODERN, Saskatoon, California (solo)

'Rosa Barba: Pensiero Spaziolungo',
VISTAMARESTUDIO, Milan (solo)

'Rosa Barba: Drawn by the Pulse',
TABAKALERA, San Sebastián (solo)

'Rosa Barba: Between Objects in the Waking World',
VOID CONTEMPORARY ART CENTRE, Derry, Northern Ireland (solo)

18th TRANSMEDIALE, Berlin (group)

'The Moon',
LOUISIANA MUSEUM OF MODERN ART, Humlebæk, Denmark (group)

'Crossroad',
SAN FRANCISCO MUSEUM OF MODERN ART (group)

'A Visibility Matrix',
DOUGLAS HYDE GALLERY, Dublin (group)

'Walk-in Cinema',
SALT BEYOĞLU, Istanbul (group)

'Un Campo Oscuro',
CENTRO JOSÉ GUERRERO, Granada, Spain (group)

'Artists' Film International',
WHITECHAPEL GALLERY, London (group)

2019

'Rosa Barba: The Hidden Conference',
ARTER, Istanbul (solo)

'Rosa Barba',
CENTER FOR CONTEMPORARY ART KITAKYUSHU, Japan (solo)

'Rosa Barba: Artist's Studio',
ARMORY PARK AVENUE, New York (solo)

4th SETOUCHI TRIENNALE, Japan (group)

'La Source',
FONDATION CARMIGNAC, PORQUEROLLES, France (group)

'Fly me to the Moon',
KUNSTHALLE ZÜRICH (group)

'Anarchive',
GALERIE FÜR ZEITGENÖSSISCHE KUNST, Leipzig (group)

2020

'Rosa Barba, Touched by the Same Breath of Air',
WÄINÖ AALTONEN MUSEUM OF ART, Turku, Finland (solo)

'Rosa Barba: Turn and Wind',
PARRA & ROMERO, Madrid (solo)

'Not I (Throwing Voices)',
LOS ANGELES COUNTY MUSEUM OF ART (group)

SELECTED ARTICLES AND INTERVIEWS
2018-20

2018

Sarasola, Ainhoa, 'Argi dirdirek sortutakoak', Berria, 23 June

Díaz, Alejandro Alons, 'Rosa Barba's Poetry of Science, Ghosts and Machines', Frieze, no. 297, September

Balsom, Erika, 'Rosa Barba: Send Me Sky', Artforum, September

Wischnewski, Manuel, 'Rosa Barba: In Limbo', Eikon, no. 104, November

2019

Enright, Robert, 'Tracing Meaning From Scratch', Bordercrossings, no. 149, March

Buoso, Sara, 'A Material Discursivity of Light, An Investigation in Light of Rosa Barba's Pratice', The International Journal of Arts Theory and History, January

2020

Genç, Kaya, 'Rosa Barba Reveals the Secret Lives of Artworks', Art in America, January

Berger, Hugo, 'Rosa Barba', The Light Observer, January

'News: Rosa Barba wins $50,000 Calder Prize', Artforum, February

Stolz, Georg, 'Rosa Barba: Turn and Wind', Art Review, April

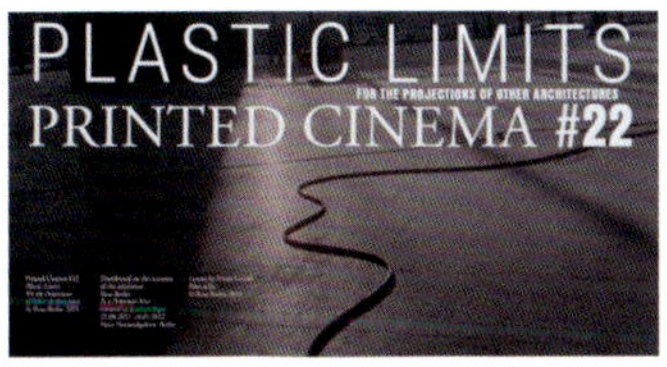

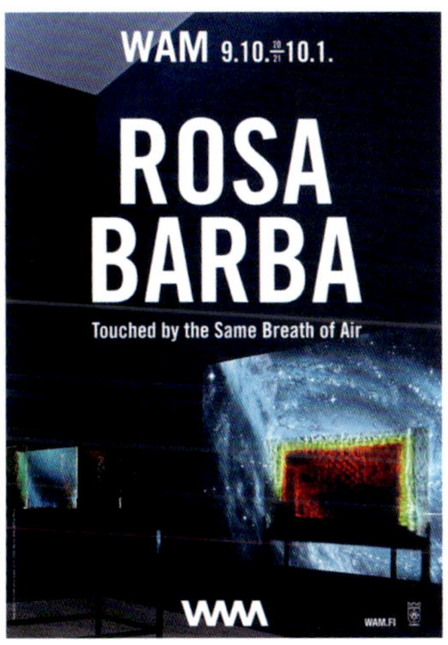

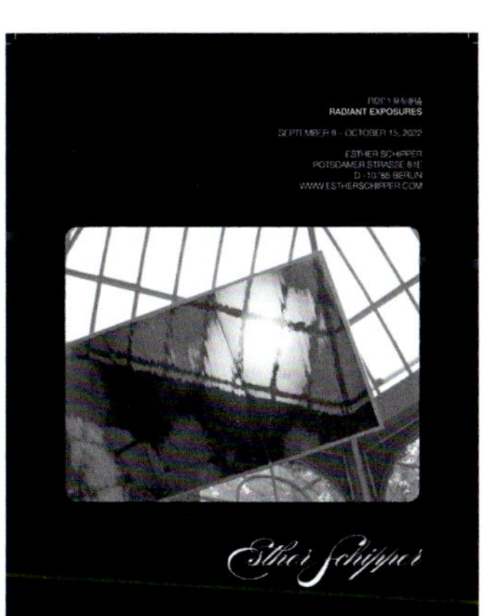

SELECTED EXHIBITIONS AND PROJECTS
2020-22

2020 (cont.)
'Push the Limits',
FONDAZIONE MERZ, Turin (group)

7th YOKOHAMA TRIENNALE (group)

'Time Machine: Cinematic Temporalities',
PALAZZO DEL GOVERNATORE, Parma (group)

'Unfolding Questions, Codes, and Contours',
TROMSO KUNSTFORENING, Norway (group)

Receives the Calder Prize, Calder Foundation, New York

2021
'Rosa Barba: In a Perpetual Now',
NEUE NATIONALGALERIE, Berlin (solo)

'Rosa Barba: Inside the Outset',
CYPRUS BUFFER ZONE (permanent open-air cinema sculpture)

'Rosa Barba: Pillage of the Sea',
7th BEAUFORT TRIENNIAL, Belgium (permanent sea sculpture)

'Nothingtoseeness: Void/White/Silence',
AKADEMIE DER KÜNSTE, Berlin (group)

4th BIENNIAL IN TIMISOARA, Romania (group)

Receives the Best Experimental Short Film Award, South Film and Arts Academy, Rancagua, Chile

2022
'Rosa Barba: Weavers,
CENTRE DE CRÉATION CONTEMPORAINE OLIVIER DEBRÉ (CCCOD), Tours, France (solo)

'Rosa Barba: Art Club #36',
VILLA MEDICI, Rome (solo)

'Rosa Barba: Durch die Etagen',
EDITION BLOCK, Berlin (solo)

'Rosa Barba',
LUHRING AUGUSTINE, New York (solo)

'Rosa Barba',
CUKRARNA, Ljubljana (solo)

'Rosa Barba: Radiant Exposures',
ESTHER SCHIPPER, Berlin (solo)

SELECTED ARTICLES AND INTERVIEWS
2020-22

2020 (cont.)
Montes, Javier, 'Back to the Future', Texte zur Kunst, June

Maerkle, Andrew, 'Rosa Barba: Double Whistler PT1-3', ART iT Asia, July

Teixeira Pinto, Ana, 'Rosa Barba', Artforum, July–August

Hickley, Catherine, 'Berlin's Neue Nationalgalerie to open after six-year renovation with Calder exhibition' The Art Newspaper, October

Turna, Taner, 'Behind the Wall: Rosa Barba', Based Istanbul, no. 38, Winter

2021
Buhr, Elke, 'Neue Nationalgalerie Berlin: Abstraktion und Modernismus laden stilvoll zur Party', Monopol M, April

Timm, Tobias,'Ein unvershämter Bau', Die Zeit, 13 May

Rieger, Birgit, 'Rosa, Mies und Alexander', Der Tagesspiegel, 29 May

'Alexander Calder + Rosa Barba', Art, June

Petretto, Francesca, 'Il film-architettura di Rosa Barba che riguarda Mies', Il Giornale delle Mostre, July

Kuiper, Stefan, 'Die Kunstwerk op het strand zal langzaam in zee verdwijnen – met opzet', De Volksrant, 15 July

Rabottini , Alessandro, 'Perpetual Interference: Rosa Barba', Mousse, no. 90, July

McHugh, Camila, 'Rosa Barba's The Perpetual Now at Neue Nationalgalerie, Berlin', Flash Art, no. 335, July–September

Nedo, Kito, 'Großes Kino', ART, August

Hauenstein, Hanno, 'Rosa Barba', Berliner Zeitung, 20 August

Schütze, Christopher F, 'A Museum Refit Turns Back the clock to 1968', The New York Times, 23 August

Camblin, Victoria, 'In a Perpetual Now: Rosa Barba at the Neue Nationalgalerie', 032c, August

Parkes, Isabel, 'Rosa Barba's Lyrical and Political Exercise in Imagination'; 'Exhibition Review: Top five shows to see in Europe', Frieze, no. 220, October

2022
Geene, Stephan, '2dimension und Repetition Stephan Geene Über Rosa Barba in Neuen National Galerie, Berlin', Texte Zur Kunst, March

Nicodemus, Katja, 'Rosa Barba: Wie macht sie das?', Die Zeit, 2 May

McElheny, Josiah, 'Rosa Barba at Luhring Augustine', Artforum, September

Watligton, Emily, 'Mesmerizing Machinery: Rosa Barba at Esther Schipper' Art In America, October

SELECTED EXHIBITIONS AND PROJECTS
2022-25

SELECTED ARTICLES AND INTERVIEWS
2022-25

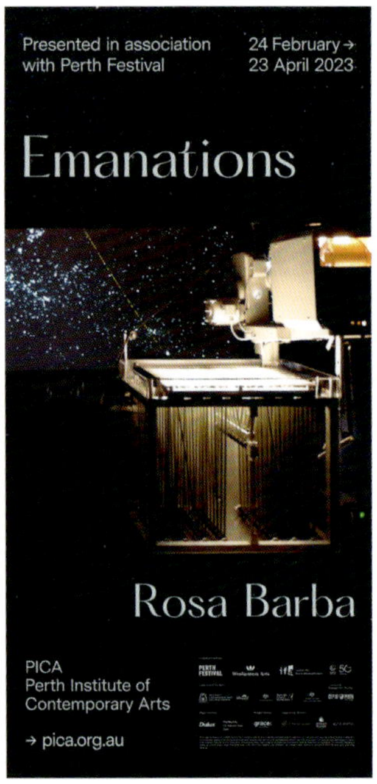

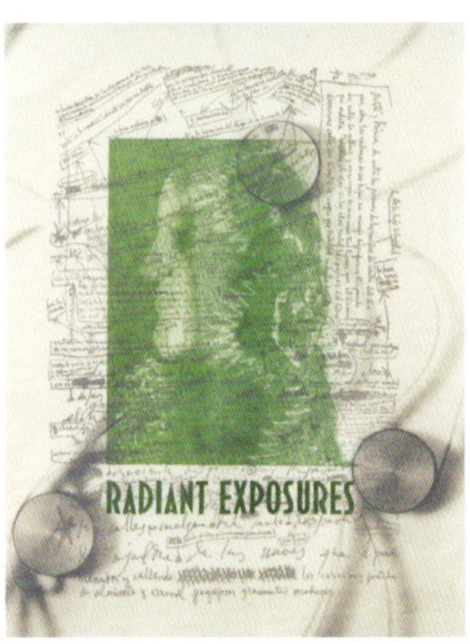

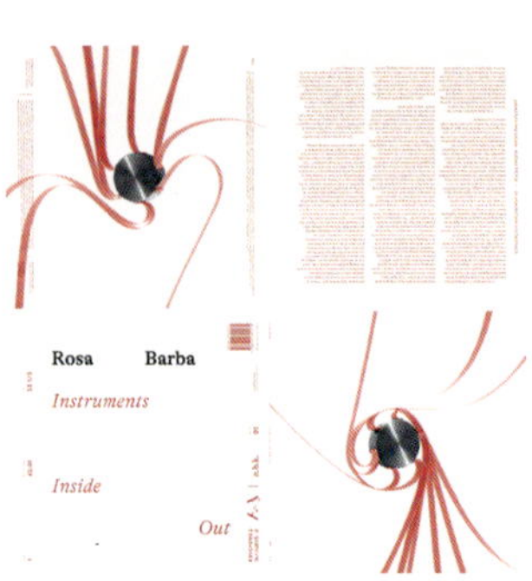

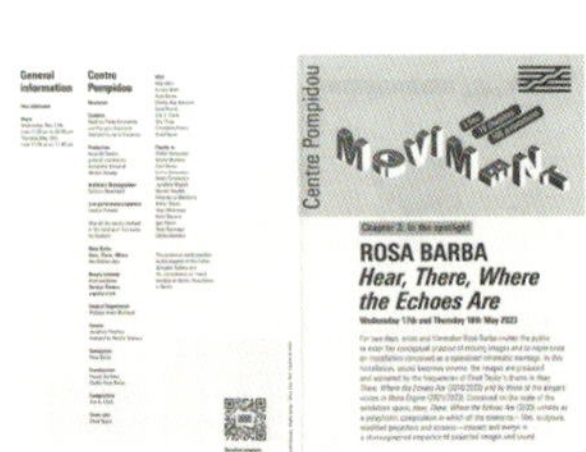

2022 (cont.)
'Il Video Rende Felici: Video Arte in Italia',
PALAZZO DELLE ESPOSIZIONI, Rome (group)

'Opera Opera: Allegro ma non troppo',
PALAIS POPULAIRE BY DEUTSCHE BANK, Berlin (group)

'Farbe als Programm',
BUNDESKUNSTHALLE, Bonn (group)

'At Dawn',
JULIA STOSCHEK FOUNDATION, Berlin (group)

'What a Wonderful World',
MUSEO DELLE ARTI DEL XXI SECOLO (MAXXI), Rome (group)

2023
'Rosa Barba: The Hidden Conference',
TATE MODERN, London (solo)

'Rosa Barba: Emanations',
PERTH INSTITUTE OF CONTEMPORARY ARTS (PICA), Australia (solo)

'Rosa Barba: Hear, There, Where the Echoes Are',
CENTRE POMPIDOU, Paris (solo)

'Rosa Barba: Beginning What and Ending Away',
ESTHER SCHIPPER, Seoul (solo)

'The King Is Dead, Long Live the Queen',
MUSEUM FRIEDER BURDA, Baden Baden, Germany (group)

2023
Butler, Andrew, 'Rosa Barba's Emanations', The Saturday Paper, 1 April

Walsh, Maria, 'On Camera: Rosa Barba interviewed by Maria Walsh', Art Monthly, no. 465, April

Nicodemus, Katja, 'Wie macht sie das?', Die Zeit, 15 May

Borcherdt, Gesine, 'Nichts von dieser Welt', Welt am Sonntag, 15 August

2024
'Rosa Barba: Evoking a Space Beyond the Cinema',
MUSEO ARTE LIMA (MALI) (solo)

'Rosa Barba: The Color Out of Space,
TECHNISCHE UNIVERSITAT (TU) DRESDEN, Germany (solo)

'After Images',
STOSCHEK FOUNDATION, Berlin (group)

1st MALTA BIENNALE, La Valletta (group)

2024
Fangacio Arakaki, Juan Carlos, 'El celuloide no ha muerto, y esta exposición de Rosa Barba en el MALI lo demuestra', El Comercio, 21 February

Ault, Julie, 'Rosa Barba on Conducting Sunlight and Unbodied Performance', Ocula, 14 August

2025
'Rosa Barba: The Ocean of One's Pause',
THE MUSEUM OF MODERN ART, New York (solo)

'Rosa Barba',
MUSEO NAZIONALE DELLE ARTI DEL XXI SECOLO (MAXXI), Rome (solo)

'Rosa Barba',
MUZEJ SUVREMENE UMJETNOSTI, Zagreb (solo)

'Rosa Barba: Charge',
TIMES SQUARE, New York (solo)

'Rosa Barba: Poised Compression',
CORBETT VS. DEMPSEY, Chicago (solo)

'Rosa Barba: Under the Canopy',
MUSEUM DER BILDENDED KÜNSTE (MDBK), Leipzig (solo)

'Copystes',
CENTRE POMPIDOU, Metz (group)

Receives the 2026 Zurich Art Prize, Haus der Konstructiv, Zurich

2025
'Rosa Barba Lights Up MoMA With Her Love of Cinema', The New York Times, 27 April

Price, Yasmina, 'Rosa Barba's Vision of Cinematic Anarchy, Frieze, no. 251, May

Berndt, Lisa-Marie, 'Besuch bei Künstlerin Rosa Barba: Alles in Bewegung', Monopol M, May

Wellington, Emily, 'In the Show of the Summer, Rosa Barba Remakes the World', ARTNews, June

Pietropaolo, Francesca, 'Conversation with Rosa Barba', The Brooklyn Railway, June

Trinks, Stefan, 'Künsterlin Rosa Barba im New Yorker MoMA: Die Landschaft erinnert sich an euch', Frankfurter Allgemeine, 13 June

Carollo, Elisa, 'Rosa Barba Reimagines Cinematic Space With Light, Sound and Time at MoMA', Observer, 13 June

SELECTED SCREENINGS FILM FESTIVALS AND PERFORMANCES

1998
27th INTERNATIONAL FILM FESTIVAL, Rotterdam

2000
'Live performances with Microstoria (selection)', SOUNDS LIKE FILM, Kölnischer Kunstverein, Cologne

29th INTERNATIONAL FILM FESTIVAL, Rotterdam

2002
'Rosa Barba', CIRKO-GEJZÍR, Budapest

2004
'2004 Club Transmediale', BEURSSHOWBURG, Brussels

2008
'Handed Over' (with David Maljkovic), FRASCATI THEATER, Amsterdam

2009
'To Retrieve New Places', BONNIERS KONSTHALL, Stockholm,

2010
'Maps for the 21st Century', DIGITAL-LIFE-DESIGN CONFERENCE, Munich

2011
'Moves # 22: Rosa Barba', IMAGE MOVEMENT, Berlin

'Séance # 3 Rosa Barba', FONDS D'ART CONTEMPORAIN (FRAC) FRANCHE-COMTÉ, BESANÇON

40th INTERNATIONAL FILM FESTIVAL ROTTERDAM

2013
FILMFORUM, Gorizia, Italy

2015
'The Color Out of Space', EXPERIMENTAL MEDIA AND PERFORMING ARTS CENTER (EMPAC), Troy, New York

'An Exhibition of a Film', CENTRE POMPIDOU, Paris;

2016
EDINBURGH INTERNATIONAL FILM FESTIVAL

2017
'10th Imagine Science Film Festival', WHITNEY MUSEUM OF AMERICAN ART, New York

45th INTERNATIONAL FILM FESTIVAL ROTTERDAM

2018
46th INTERNATIONAL FILM FESTIVAL ROTTERDAM

2019
'Artists Studio: Rosa Barba', PARK AVENUE ARMORY, New York

'In a Perpetual Now of Instantaneous Visibility' (with Chad Taylor), RAYO FESTIVAL, Madrid

'Desert Encrypts Vol. II' (with Chad Taylor), CHINATI FOUNDATION, Marfa, Texas

2020
48th INTERNATIONAL FILM FESTIVAL ROTTERDAM

2021
'Rosa Barba: Voice Engine', 49th INTERNATIONAL FILM FESTIVAL, Rotterdam, toured to CALLIES, Berlin

2022
'Artist's Films: Rosa Barba', INSTITUTE OF CONTEMPORARY ARTS, London

2023
'By Night with a Torch', THE LOUVRE, Paris

2024
'Rosa Barba: Voice Engine and Hear, There, Where the Echoes Are', MUSEUM BOIJMANS VAN BEUNINGEN, Rotterdam

2025
'Uncertainty: CERN Art and Science Summit', ORGANISATION EUROPÉENNE POUR LA RECHERCHE NUCLÉAIRE (CERN), Geneva

SELECTED BIBLIOGRAPHY

MONOGRAPHS AND ARTIST'S BOOKS

Barba, Rosa, Ulrike Groos (ed.), Carlos Garza, Peter Gorschlüter, Iris Kadel, Olaf Karnik, Micah Magee, José-Carlos Mariátegui, Ralph McKay, Nils Röller, Laetitia Sander, Klaus Sander and Siegfried Zielinski, Rosa Barba: off sites/sets, Kunsthalle Düsseldorf, and Walther König, Cologne, 2003

Barba, Rosa, and Sara Tucker, Rosa Barba: Vertiginous Mapping, Dia Art Foundation, New York, 2008

Barba, Rosa, Chiara Parisi, Andrea Viliani (eds), Lynne Cooke, Élisabeth Lebovici, Raimundas Malašauskas, Francesco Manacorda, Nataša Petrešin-Bachelez and Ian White, Rosa Barba: White Is an Image, Hatje Cantz, Ostfildern, Germany, 2011

Barba, Rosa, and Filipa Oliveira, Rosa Barba: Back Door Exposure, Satellite 5, Jeu de Paume, Paris, 2012

Barba, Rosa, Gil Leung, Hilke Wagner, Kirsty Bell and Sergio Edelsztein, Rosa Barba in Conversation, Mousse Publishing, Milan, 2012

Barba, Rosa, Mirjam Varadinis, Solveig Øvstebø (eds), Laurie Anderson, Harun Farocki, Giovanni P. Ricciardi and Ingrid Wiener, Rosa Barba: Time as Perspective, Kunsthaus Zurich and Hatje Cantz, Ostfildern, Germany, 2013

Barba, Rosa, and Esther Schlicht, Rosa Barba: Blind Volumes, Schirn Kunsthalle Frankfurt, 2016

Barba, Rosa, Henriette Huldisch, Karen Kelly, Barbara Schroeder (eds), Victoria Brooks, Henriette Huldisch and Gloria Sutton, Rosa Barba: The Color Out of Space, MIT List Visual Arts Center/Dancing Foxes Press, New York, 2016

Barba, Rosa, Manuel Borja-Villel, Giuliana Bruno, Joan Jonas, Élisabeth Lebovici and Roberta Tenconi, Rosa Barba: From Source to Poem, Pirelli HangarBicocca, Milan, and Hatje Cantz, Ostfildern, Germany, 2017

Barba, Rosa, and Marjorie Micucci, Lecture #4: Rosa Barba – Coro Spezzato: The Future Lasts One Day – Fosse d'Orchestre – Conductor, Fonds Régional d'Art Contemporain Franche-Comté, Besançon, France, 2017

Barba, Rosa, and María Inés Rodríguez, Rosa Barba: De la source au poème, CAPC Musée d'Art Contemporain de Bordeaux, 2017

Barba, Rosa, On the Anarchic Organization of Cinematic Spaces – Evoking Spaces beyond Cinema, Hatje Cantz, Berlin, 2022

Barba, Rosa, Instruments Inside Out, Walther König, Cologne, 2023

Barba, Rosa, Stuart Comer, Shanay Jhaveri, Élisabeth Lebovici, Julie Ault and Michele Robecchi (ed.), Rosa Barba, Phaidon, London, 2026

SELECTED PUBLIC COLLECTIONS

CALOUSTE GULBENKIAN MUSEUM, Lisbon

CAPC MUSÉE D'ART CONTEMPORAIN DE BORDEAUX

CENTRE NATIONAL DES ARTS PLASTIQUES, Paris

CENTRE POMPIDOU, Paris

FONDO REGIONALE D'ARTE CONTEMPORANEA (FRAC) PIEMONTE, Vercelli, Italy

FONDS MUNICIPAL D'ART CONTEMPORAIN (FMAC), Geneva

FONDS RÉGIONAL D'ART CONTEMPORAIN (FRAC) CHAMPAGNE-ARDENNE, Reims

FONDS RÉGIONAL D'ART CONTEMPORAIN (FRAC) FRANCHE-COMTÉ, Besançon

FUNDACIÓN TANTICA, Buenos Aires

GALLERIA CIVICA D'ARTE MODERNA E CONTEMPORANEA, Turin

HAMBURGER KUNSTHALLE, Hamburg

KUNSTHALLE BREMEN

KUNSTHAUS ZÜRICH

LENBACHHAUS, Munich

LOUISIANA MUSEUM OF MODERN ART, Humlebæk, Denmark

MIT LIST VISUAL ARTS CENTER, Cambridge, Massachusetts

MUSEO DE ARTE CONTEMPORANÉO, Castilla y Léon, Spain

MUSEO DE ARTE DE LIMA, Peru

MUSEO DELLE ARTI DEL XXI SECOLO (MAXXI), Rome

MUSEO DI ARTE MODERNA E CONTEMPORANEA DI TRENTO E ROVERETO (MART), Italy

MUSEO DEL NOVECENTO, Milan

MUSEO NACIONAL CENTRO DE ARTE REINA SOFÍA, Madrid

MUSEU D'ART CONTEMPORANI DE BARCELONA

THE MUSEUM OF MODERN ART, New York

NEUER BERLINER KUNSTVEREIN, Berlin

NOMAS FOUNDATION, ROME

PACE FOUNDATION, San Antonio, Texas

PHILADELPHIA MUSEUM OF ART

SAMMLUNG ZEITGENÖSSISCHER KUNST DER BUNDESREPUBLIK DEUTSCHLAND, Berlin

SAN FRANCISCO MUSEUM OF MODERN ART

SHARJAH ART FOUNDATION, United Arab Emirates

STAATLICHE MUSEEN BERLIN, HAMBURGER BAHNHOF

STAATLICHE MUSEEN BERLIN, NEUE NATIONALGALERIE

TATE MODERN, London

VEHBI KOC FONDATION, Istanbul

WÄINÖ AALTONEN MUSEUM OF ART, Turku, Finland

WALKER ART CENTER, Minneapolis

ILLUSTRATED WORKS

ABOVE THE PLATE AND RECEIVER, 2016, pages 54-55

AGGREGATE STATES OF MATTERS, 2019, pages 25, 26, 27

A HOME FOR A UNIQUE INDIVIDUAL, 2013, pages 12, 13

A PRIVATE TABLEAUX, 2010, pages 66, 67

AS FIXED IN FLUX, 2025, pages 2, 108, 111, 112

BACKGROUND, FROM LEFT, OFF SPLINTERED TIME, 2021, page 84

BLIND VOLUMES, 2016, pages 54-55, 56, 57, 81

BOUNDARIES OF CONSUMPTION, 2012, pages 12, 38–39

CHARGE, 2025, pages 2, 7, 46, 47, 48, 49, 84, 108, 111, 112

COLOR CLOCKS: VERTICALS LEAN OCCASIONALLY CONSISTENTLY AWAY FROM VIEWPOINTS, 2012, page 91

THE COLOR OUT OF SPACE, 2015, page 116

COLOR STUDIES, 2013, pages 34–35, 37, 91

COMPOSITION IN FIELD, 2022, pages 109, 110, 132–133

CONDUCTOR, 2014, pages 2, 37, 54–55, 56, 108, 111, 112

DISSEMINATE AND HOLD, 2016, page 65

DRAWN BY THE PULSE, 2018, page 119

THE EMPIRICAL EFFECT, 2010, pages 13, 14

ENIGMATIC WHISPER, 2017, page 90

ENIGMATIC WHISTLER, 2009, page 23

FOOTNOTE (...THE EARTH WILL HAVE MOVED...), 2015, page 136

FROM SOURCE TO POEM, 2016, pages 12, 13, 15, 34–35, 37, 62, 63, 81, 137

HEAR, THERE, WHERE THE ECHOES ARE, 2016–21, pages 12, 34–35, 36, 56, 57

THE HIDDEN CONFERENCE: ABOUT THE DISCONTINUOUS HISTORY OF THINGS WE SEE AND DON'T SEE, 2010, pages 72, 89

THE HIDDEN CONFERENCE: ABOUT THE SHELF AND MANTEL, 2015, pages 28–29, 73

THE HIDDEN CONFERENCE: A FRACTURED PLAY, 2011, pages 60, 61, 73, 89

I MADE A CIRCUIT AND THEN A SECOND CIRCUIT, 2010, page 52

IN A PERPETUAL NOW OF INSTANTANEOUS VISIBILITY, 2019, pages 96–97

THE INDIFFERENT BACK OF A VIEW RATHER THAN ITS FACE, 2009, page 88

INSIDE THE OUTSET: EVOKING A SPACE OF PASSAGE, 2021, pages 44, 45, 50–51, 141

THE LONG POEM MANIPULATES SPATIAL ORGANIZATIONS, 2014, pages 34–35

THE LONG ROAD, 2010, pages 18, 20–21, 23

THE OCEAN OF ONE'S PAUSE, 2025, pages 138-139

OFF SPLINTERED TIME, 2021, pages 3, 53, 111, 112

ONE WAY OUT, 2009, pages 53, 85

OUTWARDLY FROM EARTH'S CENTER, 2007, pages 40–41, 42, 43, 87

PANZANO, 2000, page 9

PERPETUAL RESPONSE TO SOUND AND LIGHT (AT THE LOCKER PLANT), 2013, page 11

PILLAGE OF THE SEA, 2021 , page 127

PLASTIC LIMITS – FOR THE PROJECTION OF OTHER ARCHITECTURES, 2021, page 58

RADIANT EXPOSURES – FACTS RUN ON LIGHT BEAMS THESE DAYS, 2022, page 94

SENSIBLE SUNS, 2025, pages 53, 84, 108, 111

SOLAR FLUX RECORDINGS, 2017, pages 32, 33, 95

SPACELENGTH THOUGHT, 2012, pages 8, 53, 85

STATING THE REAL SUBLIME, 2009, pages 23, 53, 79, 91, 106, 111

SUBCONSCIOUS SOCIETY, A FEATURE, 2014, pages 71, 78–79

THEY SHINE, 2007, page 19

THIS SPACE POPULATED BY INFINITE COLORS, 2021, page 36

TIME AS PERSPECTIVE, 2012, pages 89, 91, 92–93

UNA CONFERENCIA COMISARIADA: SOBRE EL FUTURO DE LA FUERZA COLECTIVA DENTRO DEL ARCHIVO, 2010, pages 30, 31

UNCERTAIN THEME – AND THEREFORE ABSTRACT, 2021, pages 36, 76, 77

VOICE ENGINE, 2021–23, pages 74, 75

WAITING GROUNDS, 2007, page 22

WEAVERS, 2021, page 78

WESTERN ROUND TABLE, 2007, pages 16–17

WHITE MUSEUM (HIRSCH OBSERVATORY), 2010–15, pages 115, 123

WHITE MUSEUM – LIVE (MOMA PS1), 2016, pages 120–121

WHITE MUSEUM (MARGATE), 2010–13, pages 100–101, 103

WHITE MUSEUM (SÃO PAULO), 2010–16, PAGES 124–125

WHITE MUSEUM (SOUTH SASKATCHEWAN RIVER), 2010–18, page 128

WHITE MUSEUM (VASSIVIÈRE), 2010, pages 82, 83

WHITE MUSEUM (WIELS, BRUSSELS), 2010–13, pages 104, 105

WIREPIECE, 2022, pages 2, 53, 78, 85, 99, 108, 111, 112

WIREPIECE, DOUBLE STOPS, 2025, pages 2, 7, 85, 108, 111, 112

WIREPIECE, TRIPLE STOPS, 2025, pages 85, 111

COMPARATIVE IMAGES

CARL ANDRE
MAGNESIUM CROPPER PLAIN, 1969, pages 30, 31

DARA BIRNBAUM
TECHNOLOGY/ TRANSFORMATION: WONDERWOMAN, 1978–79, page 31

MARIA BLANCHARD
MUJER CON GUITARRA, 1917, page 30

LOUISE BOURGEOIS
SPIDER, 1994, page 30

ROBERT BREER
RECREATION, 1956–57, page 31

GUY DEBORD
SUR LE PASSAGE DE QUELQUES PERSONNES À TRAVERS UNE ASSEZ COURTE UNITÉ DE TEMPS, 1959, page 30

MAYA DEREN
SHOOTING DIAGRAMS FOR CHOREOGRAPHY FOR THE CAMERA, N.D., page 135

MARCEL DUCHAMP
LA MARIÉE MISE À NU PAR SES CÉLIBATAIRES MÊME (BOÎTE VERTE), 1934, page 30

VALIE EXPORT
SYNTAGMA, 1983, page 30

SKY HOPINKA
FAINTING SPELLS, 2018, page 19

JOAN JONAS
WIND, 1968, page 94

JOAN JONAS
VERTICAL ROLL, 1972, page 31

DAVID LAMELAS
TO POUR MILK INTO A GLASS, 1972, page 31

ZOE LEONARD
100 NORTH NEVILL STREET, 2013, page 12

GEORGE MACIUNAS
ARTYPE, 1966, page 31

SANDRA MUJINGA
FLO, 2019, page 24

YOKO ONO
EYE BLINK, 1966 page 31

EWA PARTUM
EXCERPT FROM ACTIVE POETRY, POEM BY EWA, 1971–73, page 31

LILIANA PORTER
FOR YOU, 1999, page 31

MARTHA ROSLER
SEMIOTICS OF THE KITCHEN, 1975, page 31

PAUL SIETSEMA
FIGURE 3, 2008, page 31

LESLIE THORNTON
PEGGY & FRED IN HELL, 1985, page 86

PHAIDON PRESS LTD.
2 COOPERAGE YARD
LONDON E15 2QR

PHAIDON PRESS INC.
111 BROADWAY
NEW YORK, NY 10006

PHAIDON SARL
55, RUE TRAVERSIÈRE
75012 PARIS

PHAIDON.COM

First published 2026

ISBN:
978-1-83866-885-3
Signed edition:
978-1-83729-240-0

A CIP catalogue record of this book is available from the British Library and the Library of Congress.

Commissioning Editor
Michele Robecchi

Production Controller
Andie Trainer

Design
Melanie Mues, Mues Design, London

Layout
Cantina, London

Printed in China

PUBLISHER'S ACKNOWLEDGEMENTS

Special thanks to Franck Bordese and Suin Kwon at Rosa Barba Studio, Berlin; Esther Schipper and Manuel Miseur at Esther Schipper, Berlin, Paris and Seoul; Benedetta Spalletti and Azzurra Ricci at Vistamare, Milan and Pescara, Italy; Caitlin Arnell Argles, Clive Burrough, James Brown, Adela Cory, Gary Hayes, Sky Hopinka, Susan Howe, Joan Jonas, Melissa Larner, Zoe Leonard, Violeta Mitrova, João Mota, Sandra Mujinga, Camilla Pagliano, Phoebe Stephenson, Skyla Rickard, Tracey Smith, Hans Stofregen, Leslie Thornton, Elaine Ward, Jonathan Whale.

We would also like to thank the following institutions: Solomon R. Guggenheim Museum, New York/the Photography Council; The Museum of Modern Art, New York/Fund for the Twenty-First Century; Museu d'Art Contemporani de Barcelona; Museo Nacional Centro de Arte Reina Sofía, Madrid; The Chinati Foundation Marfa, Texas.

Photographers: Arnas Anskaitis, Filippo Armellin, Rosa Barba, Bernd Borchardt Amélie Boulin, Blaine Campbell, CHROMA, Filip Claessens, Joaquín Cortés/Román Lores, Da Ping Luo, Jonathan Dorado, Fred Dott, François Doury, Jenny Ekholm, Peio Erroteta, Peter Harris, Mizuki Kin, Lily Lyons, Marcus Meyer, Norbert Miguletz, Fredrik Nilsen, Agostino Osio, Martin Parsekian, Arthur Pequin, Jeff Preiss, Kris Qua, Andrea Rossetti, Reece Straw, Marios Stylianou, Helene Toresdotter, Saskia Uppenkamp, Julien Vassallo.

ARTIST'S ACKNOWLEDGEMENTS

My warmest thank yous to Michele Robecchi, Julie Ault, Stuart Comer, Élisabeth Lebovici, Shanay Jhavery and Susan Howe for their writing and editing.

Continued thanks to Esther Schipper, Florian Woijnar and their gallery team for their ongoing support, as well as to Benedetta Spalletti and Lodovica Busiri Vici and their team at Vistamare.

Franck Bordese and Suin Kwon and everyone at the studio.

Collaborators, performers and scientists.

Assunta Gaziano, and in memory of Alfonso Barba, for their passion.

Uma, Jan St. Werner, Chad Taylor, Alicia Hall Moran and Ellison Renee Glenn for the music.

To the people who made the exhibitions illustrated in this book happen: Lynne Cooke, Rob Weiner, Roberta Tenconi, Vicente Todolí, the late Achim Borchardt-Hume, Frances Morris, Corinne Diserens, Mats Stjernstedt, Chiara Parisi, Andrea Viliani, Hilke Wagner, Mirjam Varadinis, Jason Moran, Vic Brooks, Christoph Grunenberg, Eefke Kleimann, Ben Borthwick, Manolo Borja-Villel, Joachim Jäger, Jonathan Pouthier, Philippe-Alain Michaud, Andre Zivanari, Kate Scherer, Jesse Gold, Esther Schlicht, Max Hollein, Lorenzo Fusi, Jochen Volz, Andrea Lissoni, Carly Whitefield, Valentine Umansky, Nobuo Nakamuro, Sandra Guimarães, Ayako Yamada and the late Okwui Enwezor.

Merten Houfek, Hendrik John, Robert Haag, Maya Shopova, Ruben Woodin Dechamps, Henrietta Swan Leavitt, Errico Scott, Mary Lynch-Lloyd, Ibrahim Thiaw, Igor Panek, Adela Yawitz, Manuel Miseur, Azzurra Ricci, Camilla Pagliano, Joan Jonas, Jarrett Gregory, Georgia Horn, Josiah McElheny, Zoe Leonard, Peaches, John Corbett/Corbett vs. Dempsey, Sarat Maharaj, Gertrud Sandqvist, Gee Wesley, Andec, Cinegrell, Fotokem, Kodak and Cinelab for the film and space love.

Thank you to Andie Trainer, Gary Hayes, James Brown and everyone at Phaidon who dedicated time and expertise to make this book.

And appreciation for my friends, family, supporters, peers and poets.

CONTEMPORARY ARTISTS:

Contemporary Artists is a series of authoritative and extensively illustrated studies of today's most important artists. Each title offers a comprehensive survey of an individual artist's work and a range of art writing contributed by an international spectrum of authors, all leading figures in their fields, from art history and criticism to philosophy, cultural theory and fiction. Each study provides incisive analysis and multiple perspectives on contemporary art and its inspiration. These are essential source books for everyone concerned with art today.

MARINA ABRAMOVIĆ KLAUS BIESENBACH, KRISTINE STILES, CHRISSIE ILES VITO ACCONCI FRAZER WARD, MARK C. TAYLOR, JENNIFER BLOOMER AI WEIWEI HANS ULRICH OBRIST, KAREN SMITH, BERNARD FIBICHER DOUG AITKEN DANIEL BIRNBAUM, AMANDA SHARP, JÖRG HEISER PAWEŁ ALTHAMER ADAM SZYMCZYK, ROMAN KURZMEYER, SUZANNE COTTER FRANCIS ALŸS CUAUHTÉMOC MEDINA, RUSSELL FERGUSON, JEAN FISHER, MICHAEL TAUSSIG ROSA BARBA STUART COMER, SHANAY JHAVERI, ÉLISABETH LEBOVICI, JULIE AULT UTA BARTH PAMELA M. LEE, MATTHEW HIGGS, JEREMY GILBERT-ROLFE CHRISTIAN BOLTANSKI DIDIER SEMIN, TAMAR GARB, DONALD KUSPIT MONICA BONVICINI ALEXANDER ALBERRO, JANET KRAYNAK, JULIANE REBENTISCH LOUISE BOURGEOIS PAULO HERKENHOFF (WITH THYRZA GOODEVE), ROBERT STORR, ALLAN SCHWARTZMAN MARK BRADFORD ANITA HILL, SEBASTIAN SMEE, CONNIE BUTLER CECILY BROWN COURTNEY J. MARTIN, JASON ROSENFELD, FRANCINE PROSE CAI GUO-QIANG DANA FRIIS-HANSEN, OCTAVIO ZAYA, TAKASHI SERIZAWA JORDAN CASTEEL LEGACY RUSSELL, ASMA NAEEM, KATHERINE BRINSON MAURIZIO CATTELAN NANCY SPECTOR, FRANCESCO BONAMI, BARBARA VANDERLINDEN, MASSIMILIANO GIONI VIJA CELMINS ROBERT GOBER, LANE RELYEA, BRIONY FER NIGEL COOKE DARIAN LEADER, TONY GODFREY, MARIE DARRIEUSSECQ RICHARD DEACON PIER LUIGI TAZZI, JON THOMPSON, PETER SCHJELDAHL, PENELOPE CURTIS TACITA DEAN JEAN-CHRISTOPHE ROYOUX, MARINA WARNER, GERMAINE GREER MARK DION LISA GRAZIOSE CORRIN, MIWON KWON, NORMAN BRYSON PETER DOIG ADRIAN SEARLE, KITTY SCOTT, CATHERINE GRENIER STAN DOUGLAS SCOTT WATSON, DIANA THATER, CAROL J. CLOVER MARLENE DUMAS DOMINIC VAN DEN BOOGERD, BARBARA BLOOM, MARIUCCIA CASADIO, ILARIA BONACOSSA JIMMIE DURHAM LAURA MULVEY, DIRK SNAUWAERT, MARK ALICE DURANT, KATE NESIN OLAFUR ELIASSON MADELEINE GRYNSZTEJN, DANIEL BIRNBAUM, MICHAEL SPEAKS ELMGREEN & DRAGSET LINDA YABLONSKY, MARTIN HERBERT, CONNIE BUTLER, JASON SCHMIDT CERITH WYN EVANS HANS ULRICH OBRIST, NANCY SPECTOR, DANIEL BIRNBAUM PETER FISCHLI AND DAVID WEISS ROBERT FLECK, BEATE SÖNTGEN, ARTHUR C. DANTO TOM FRIEDMAN DENNIS COOPER, BRUCE HAINLEY, ADRIAN SEARLE THEASTER GATES CAROL BECKER, LISA YUN LEE, ACHIM BORCHARDT-HUME ISA GENZKEN ALEX FARQUHARSON, DIEDRICH DIEDERICHSEN, SABINE BREITWIESER ANTONY GORMLEY ERNST GOMBRICH, JOHN HUTCHINSON, LELA B. NJATIN, W. J. T. MITCHELL DAN GRAHAM BIRGIT PELZER, MARK FRANCIS, BEATRIZ COLOMINA PAUL GRAHAM ANDREW WILSON, GILLIAN WEARING, CAROL SQUIERS SHILPA GUPTA ALEXANDRA MUNROE, NAV HAQ, ELVIRA DYANGANI OSE HANS HAACKE WALTER GRASSKAMP, MOLLY NESBIT, JON BIRD MONA HATOUM GUY BRETT, MICHAEL ARCHER, CATHERINE DE ZEGHER, NANCY SPECTOR SHARON HAYES JULIA BRYAN-WILSON, JEANNINE TANG, LANKA TATTERSALL THOMAS HIRSCHHORN BENJAMIN H. D. BUCHLOH, ALISON M. GINGERAS, CARLOS BASUALDO JIM HODGES JANE M SAKS, ROBERT HOBBS, JULIE AULT /JENNY HOLZER DAVID JOSELIT, JOAN SIMON, RENATA SALECL RONI HORN LOUISE NERI, LYNNE COOKE, THIERRY DE DUVE CAMERON JAMIE PHILIPPE VERGNE, RALPH RUGOFF, ELENA FILIPOVIC CHRIS JOHANSON CORRINA PEIPON, BOB NICKAS, JULIE DEAMER RASHID JOHNSON CLAUDIA RANKINE, SAMPADA ARANKE, AKILI TOMMASINO ILYA KABAKOV BORIS GROYS, DAVID A. ROSS, IWONA BLAZWICK ALEX KATZ ROBERT STORR, CARTER RATCLIFF, IWONA BLAZWICK, BARRY SCHWABSKY ON KAWARA 'TRIBUTE', JONATHAN WATKINS, RENÉ DENIZOT MIKE KELLEY ISABELLE GRAW, JOHN C. WELCHMAN, ANTHONY VIDLER MARY KELLY MARGARET IVERSEN, DOUGLAS CRIMP, HOMI K. BHABHA WILLIAM KENTRIDGE CAROLYN CHRISTOV-BAKARGIEV, DAN CAMERON, J. M. COETZEE JANNIS KOUNELLIS 'TRIBUTE', PHILIP LARRATT-SMITH, RUDI FUCHS YAYOI KUSAMA AKIRA TATEHATA, LAURA HOPTMAN, UDO KULTERMANN, CHATERINE TAFT CHRISTIAN MARCLAY JENNIFER GONZALEZ, KIM GORDON, MATTHEW HIGGS KERRY JAMES MARSHALL CHARLES GAINES, GREG TATE, LAURENCE RASSEL PAUL McCARTHY KRISTINE STILES, RALPH RUGOFF, MASSIMILIANO GIONI, ROBERT STORR CILDO MEIRELES PAULO HERKENHOFF, GERARDO MOSQUERA, DAN CAMERON WILLIAM MONK ISABELLE GRAW, TERRY R. MYERS, ÀNGELS MIRALDA WANGECHI MUTU ADRIENNE EDWARDS, COURTNEY J. MARTIN, KELLIE JONES, CHIKA OKEKE-AGULU YOKO ONO LAURIE ANDERSON, ERIKO OSAKA, THIERRY RASPAIL LUCY ORTA ROBERTO PINTO, NICOLAS BOURRIAUD, MAIA DAMIANOVIC JEAN-MICHEL OTHONIEL GAY GASSMANN, CATHERINE GRENIER, ROBERT STORR TREVOR PAGLEN LAUREN CORNELL, JULIA BRYAN-WILSON, OMAR KHOLEIF JORGE PARDO CHRISTINE VÉGH, LANE RELYEA, CHRIS KRAUS NICOLAS PARTY STÉPHANE AQUIN, STEFAN BANZ, ALI SUBOTNICK, MELISSA HYDE ADAM PENDLETON ALEC MAPES-FRANCES, ADRIENNE EDWARDS, ANDRÉA PICARD RAYMOND PETTIBON DENNIS COOPER, ROBERT STORR, ULRICH LOOCK RICHARD PRINCE ROSETTA BROOKS, JEFF RIAN, LUC SANTE NEO RAUCH INGRID MÖSSINGER, RALPH KEUNING, DAVID SALLE LILI REYNAUD-DEWAR ÉLISABETH LEBOVICI, DIEDRICH DIEDERICHSEN, MONIKA SZEWCZYK PIPILOTTI RIST HANS ULRICH OBRIST, PEGGY PHELAN, ELIZABETH BRONFEN UGO RONDINONE LAURA HOPTMAN, ERIK VERHAGEN, NICHOLAS BAUME, JASON SCHMIDT DAAN ROOSEGAARDE NICO DASWANI, FUMIO NANJO, CAROL BECKER STERLING RUBY KATE FOWLE, FRANKLIN SIRMANS, JESSICA MORGAN ANRI SALA HANS ULRICH OBRIST, MARK GODFREY, LIAM GILLICK DORIS SALCEDO NANCY PRINCENTHAL, CARLOS BASUALDO, ANDREAS HUYSSEN WILHELM SASNAL ANDRZEJ PRZYWARA, DOMINIC EICHLER, JÖRG HEISER THOMAS SCHÜTTE JULIAN HEYNEN, JAMES LINGWOOD, ANGELA VETTESE DANA SCHUTZ HAMZA WALKER, DAN NADEL, LYNNE TILLMAN /STEPHEN SHORE MICHAEL FRIED, CHRISTY LANGE, JOEL STERNFELD ROMAN SIGNER PAULA VAN DEN BOSCH, GERHARD MACK, JEREMY MILLAR LORNA SIMPSON KELLIE JONES, THELMA GOLDEN, CHRISSIE ILES, NAOMI BECKWITH NANCY SPERO JON BIRD, JO ANNA ISAAK, SYLVÈRE LOTRINGER SIMON STARLING FRANCESCO MANACORDA, DIETER ROELSTRAETE, JANET HARBORD FRANK STELLA ANDRIANNA CAMPBELL, KATE NESIN, LUCAS BLALOCK, TERRY RICHARDSON JESSICA STOCKHOLDER BARRY SCHWABSKY, LYNNE TILLMAN, LYNNE COOKE, GERMANO CELANT TAVARES STRACHAN MICHELE ROBECCHI, GAVIN DELAHUNTY, EMMA DABIRI, JASON SCHMIDT SARAH SZE OKWUI ENWEZOR, BENJAMIN H. D. BUCHLOH, LAURA HOPTMAN WOLFGANG TILLMANS PETER HALLEY, JAN VERWOERT, MIDORI MATSUI, JOHANNA BURTON LUC TUYMANS ULRICH LOOCK, JUAN VICENTE ALIAGA, NANCY SPECTOR, HANS RUDOLF REUST BERNAR VENET FLORENCE DERIEUX, BARRY SCHWABSKY, CLAIRE LILLEY ADRIÁN VILLAR-ROJAS HANS ULRICH OBRIST, CAROLYN CHRISTOV-BAKARGIEV, EUNGIE JOO JEFF WALL THIERRY DE DUVE, ARIELLE PÉLENC, BORIS GROYS, JEAN-FRANÇOIS CHEVRIER, MARK LEWIS GILLIAN WEARING RUSSELL FERGUSON, DONNA DE SALVO, JOHN SLYCE LAWRENCE WEINER BENJAMIN H. D. BUCHLOH, ALEXANDER ALBERRO AND ALICE ZIMMERMAN, DAVID BATCHELOR FRANZ WEST ROBERT FLECK, BICE CURIGER, NEAL BENEZRA JONAS WOOD MARK GROTJAHN, HELEN MOLESWORTH, IAN ALTEVEER YIN XIUZHEN HOU HANRU, WU HUNG, STEPHANIE ROSENTHAL LISA YUSKAVAGE ARIEL LEVY, BARRY SCHWABSKY, LENA DUNHAM ZHANG HUAN ROSELEE GOLDBERG, YILMAZ DZIEWOR, ROBERT STORR